AF737853

FREE HANDS AND MINDS

Peter Brett (1918–1975), Alice Erh-Soon Tay (1934–2004) and Geoffrey Sawer (1910–1996) are key, yet largely overlooked, members of Australia's first community of legal scholars. This book is a critical study of how their ideas and endeavours contributed to Australia's discipline of law and the first Australian legal theories. It examines how three marginal figures – a Jewish man (Brett), a Chinese woman (Tay), and a war orphan (Sawer) – rose to prominence during a transformative period for Australian legal education and scholarship.

Drawing on in-depth interviews with former colleagues and students, extensive archival research, and an appraisal of their contributions to scholarship and teaching, this book explores the three professors' international networks and broader social and historical milieux. Their pivotal leadership roles in law departments at the University of Melbourne, University of Sydney, and the Australian National University are also critically assessed.

Ranging from local experiences and the concerns of a nascent Australian legal academy to the complex transnational phenomena of legal scholarship and theory, Free Hands and Minds makes a compelling case for contextualising law and legal culture within society. At a time of renewed crisis in legal education and research in the common law world, it also offers a vivid, nuanced and critical account of the enduring liberal foundations of Australia's discipline of law.

Free Hands and Minds

Pioneering Australian Legal Scholars

Susan Bartie

•HART•
OXFORD • LONDON • NEW YORK • NEW DELHI • SYDNEY

HART PUBLISHING

Bloomsbury Publishing Plc

Kemp House, Chawley Park, Cumnor Hill, Oxford, OX2 9PH, UK

HART PUBLISHING, the Hart/Stag logo, BLOOMSBURY and the Diana logo are trademarks of Bloomsbury Publishing Plc

First published in Great Britain 2019

Copyright © Susan Bartie, 2019

Susan Bartie has asserted her right under the Copyright, Designs and Patents Act 1988 to be identified as Author of this work.

All rights reserved. No part of this publication may be reproduced or transmitted in any form or by any means, electronic or mechanical, including photocopying, recording, or any information storage or retrieval system, without prior permission in writing from the publishers.

While every care has been taken to ensure the accuracy of this work, no responsibility for loss or damage occasioned to any person acting or refraining from action as a result of any statement in it can be accepted by the authors, editors or publishers.

All UK Government legislation and other public sector information used in the work is Crown Copyright ©. All House of Lords and House of Commons information used in the work is Parliamentary Copyright ©. This information is reused under the terms of the Open Government Licence v3.0 (http://www.nationalarchives.gov.uk/doc/open-government-licence/version/3) except where otherwise stated.

All Eur-lex material used in the work is © European Union, http://eur-lex.europa.eu/, 1998–2019.

A catalogue record for this book is available from the British Library.

Library of Congress Cataloging-in-Publication data

Names: Bartie, Susan, author.

Title: Free hands and minds : pioneering Australian legal scholars / Susan Bartie.

Description: Chicago : Hart Publishing, 2019. | Includes bibliographical references and index.

Identifiers: LCCN 2019021095 (print) | LCCN 2019021907 (ebook) | ISBN 9781509922628 (EPub) | ISBN 9781509922611 (hardback : alk. paper)

Subjects: LCSH: Law teachers—Australia—Biography. | Lawyers—Australia—Biography.

Classification: LCC KU105 (ebook) | LCC KU105 .B37 2019 (print) | DDC 340.092/294—dc23

LC record available at https://lccn.loc.gov/2019021095

ISBN: HB: 978-1-50992-261-1
ePDF: 978-1-50992-263-5
ePub: 978-1-50992-262-8

Typeset by Compuscript Ltd, Shannon
Printed and bound in Great Britain by CPI Group (UK) Ltd, Croydon CR0 4YY

FSC www.fsc.org MIX Paper from responsible sources FSC® C013604

To find out more about our authors and books visit www.hartpublishing.co.uk. Here you will find extracts, author information, details of forthcoming events and the option to sign up for our newsletters.

To pioneering legal scholars, past, present and future

FOREWORD

Dr Susan Bartie has rescued the memories of three significant members of the Australian legal academy: Peter Brett, Alice Erh-Soon Tay and Geoffrey Sawer. She has done this in order to explore her proposition that members of the academic community in Australia, as elsewhere, have played an important role in the development of the country's legal rules and culture.

Self-evidently, in a federal country like Australia, lawyers, and especially judges, play a significant role in public life. Sometimes, as in deciding key questions on the location and contents of political power, they directly influence the course of political events. But even in the determination of the myriad of smaller and less controversial questions, their work affects the lives of fellow citizens in ways that other professions cannot match. Courts, after all, are the 'third branch of government'. They are made up of lawyers, influenced by the advocacy of other lawyers, all of whom are taught their skills by still other lawyers. Potentially, law is a cloistered and closed world. But what influence within this world do the law teachers really exert? By taking these three leaders, the author has sought to answer these questions. And to challenge a common assumption that the role of law teachers is negligible, even paltry.

Selecting law teachers in order to trace the influence of their minds and values, as revealed in scholarship and instruction, is becoming more important today than it was, even in the recent past. A surprisingly gripping story has recently explored the lives and influence of two law teachers, deriving from the unlikely shared experience at the law school in Lemberg, later Lwów in Poland, later still and now Lviv in Estonia. Professor Philippe Sands has traced the international crimes of genocide and crimes against humanity to these two students and scholars originally from that seemingly insignificant place: Rafael Lemkin and (Sir) Hersch Lauterpacht, respectively. Sands's powerful book is *East West Street*.[1] Anyone in doubt about the potential of brilliant lawyers and law teachers to influence the shape of the law and the directions of human history should read the story told by Sands.

Dr Bartie has not attempted the same exercise in her book. Her objective is at once more modest and more broadly focused. By telling the stories of her chosen three Australian legal academics – one, Brett, a Jewish migrant who changed his

[1] P Sands, *East West Street: On the Origins of Genocide and Crimes Against Humanity* (London, Weidenfeld and Nicolson, 2016).

name (né Bretzfelder); another, Tay, a Chinese woman, feisty and combative, who came to Australia amidst scandal from Singapore; and the third, a war orphan, Sawer – the author seeks to generalise about the impact on the contents of law of important legal scholars. Specifically, their impact beyond their classrooms and even beyond their universities. In short, their impact on the content and power balances of the disciplines that they studied and taught. It is an idea with a broader focus than that which Philippe Sands has adopted. But its purpose is to uncover the clues about the wider effects that law teachers in modern Australian universities may have had on their pupils, their discipline and their society.

There are several reasons why a book like this would not, and could not, have been published about Australia even a couple of decades ago, and certainly not when the three scholars concerned were busy at their work in the legal institutions they made their homes. A reflection on these considerations is essential in approaching the originality and novelty of Dr Bartie's objective.

- When each of the three scholars was at their prime, Australia was already formally an independent nation. Yet, generally speaking, its lawyers, with few exceptions, regarded themselves as members of a branch office of the worldwide English-speaking community of law centred on London. For most of the lives of each of the three subjects of this book Australia's final court of appeal, in most matters, was the Privy Council in London. It was not the High Court of Australia. Its judges treated decisions of the English House of Lords as binding, although it had never been part of the Australian judicial hierarchy. The Australian Constitution was regarded as an imperial statute, binding in Australia for that reason. Case and text books on the shelves of judges and lawyers were mostly from England. That was where the spirit and the letter of our law were to be found by judges, scholars and law students.
- The years of the labours of the three were still the era of the common law. The mighty engine of legislation had not yet swamped the reasoning of judges in providing the bedrock of Australian law. To this extent, law was to be derived from an analysis of the ideas and values of judges, most of them English. Few Australian lawyers questioned this reality. Virtually none criticised it or found it odd.
- Amongst Australian judges of the time, one was particularly influential because of his powers of analysis and lengthy years of service: Sir Owen Dixon, High Court Justice and later Chief Justice. He propounded emphatically a traditional English positivism. The law, he declared, would have lost its meaning if it did not pre-exist the judicial decisions that revealed its content. 'Strict and complete legalism' was the rule.[2] The speculations and hypotheses of academics were

[2] O Dixon, 'Concerning Judicial Method' in SHZ Woinarski (ed), *Jesting Pilate* (Melbourne, Law Book Co, 1965) 155; RP Austin, 'Academics, Practitioners and Judges' (2004) 26 *Sydney Law Review* 463.

basically unimportant. They were rarely referred to by judges such as Dixon. The priestly cast of the judiciary had the only sure key that would unlock the certainties of law. The job of academics was basically to analyse and expound judicial reasoning. Criticism was not encouraged.

- For the first half of the twentieth century there were very few full-time academics teaching law in Australia. In effect, we followed the English tradition of the Inns. Busy barristers at the fag end of working day (or some early in the morning) would rush from their chambers to teach their docile students from ancient cyclostyled notes.
- Well into the last decades of the twentieth century, the intellectual ethos of Australian universities was uniformly and decidedly modest. Substantially, this was because of an inherited English tradition of good manners, understatement and personal reserve. Advancing one's academic career by publicity and public criticism of received wisdom was generally frowned upon at that time. Very few Australian legal academics then (and not a few now) felt that it was any part of their duty to speak out about the law, beyond the classroom – to engage ordinary citizens about the law's content, to question long-held views about the law governing Indigenes, women, non-White Australians and gay people in the law. This was not perceived as the role of the lawyer in Australia. Hence, it was not part of the role of the legal academic.

Dr Bartie is at pains to explain why she chose her three protagonists and how she justifies thereby excluding others. Of course, any short list would be contestable. But, in truth, it was not really so difficult to identify the intellectual leaders. Although some others could have been added, the three selected are sufficient to respond to the central task that Dr Bartie has set for herself. For those who suggest that others might have been added, the answer comes back that most of the others set themselves extremely modest goals for their scholarship and teaching. They disdained big challenges.

I did not know Peter Brett. At the time that he was in his last years of teaching criminal law theory at the Melbourne Law School, I was commencing practice at the Bar in Sydney. His retirement and death coincided with my first appointment as a judge and as Chairman of the Australian Law Reform Commission (1975). I was not the beneficiary of the book he wrote with Professor Louis Waller: *Cases and Materials in Criminal Law.*[3] In my day at the Sydney Law School, we were taught criminal law by reference to the English textbooks of Rupert Cross and PA Jones.[4] No Australian cases or statutes intruded into those English texts. Little wonder that Brett and Waller were angry and were determined to change this blind submission to English judgments. As change it did.

[3] P Brett and PL Waller, *Cases and Materials in Criminal Law* (Sydney, Butterworths, 1962).

[4] R Cross and PA Jones, *An Introduction to Criminal Law*, 3rd edn (London, Butterworth & Co, 1953); R Cross and PA Jones, *Cases on Criminal Law*, 2nd edn (London, Butterworth & Co, 1953).

I did know Alice Tay. Indeed, with Eugene Kamenka, she assessed the thesis I wrote for my Sydney LLM in 1966. It was on Karl Marx's thesis on the 'withering away' of the state on the attainment of communism. She gave me top marks. Despite this somewhat esoteric introduction, we later became firm friends. She was bossy and pushy. But she was also principled and grand. I loved the way she stood up for women and people of different races. Advocates of her ilk were rare indeed amongst the legal academy in those days. Alice Tay made a big impact on her chosen country. She challenged the legal formalists until some of them, at least, began to listen to her views.

Geoffrey Sawer I also knew. When I was offered appointment as inaugural Chairman of the Australian Law Reform Commission, one or two professors urged me to defer to the claims of Geoffrey Sawer. He himself, I think, considered that the post might come his way for his skills as a 'constitutionalist'.[5] Chief Justice Sir Anthony Mason says that Professor Sawer was not a positivist. He was a qualified realist, willing to acknowledge the influence of values on judicial (especially constitutional) decisions. But he was a minimalist. If institutional law reform were to take off in Australia, it needed publicity and advocacy. When that faded, so did the formula for success.[6] Later, Professor Sawer told me many times of how he supported my efforts to put law reform on the front page. He acknowledged that doing this was beyond his skills – but skills he had in challenging the law and its institutions in Australia. However, he did this from the vantage point of a greatly respected scholar who spoke the language of those who still wielded the law's power in Australia.

Legal academics, including the three singled out for special attention in Dr Bartie's book, are not the only causative agents explaining the important changes that have happened in recent decades. Still, they have played an important role. Dr Bartie is to be thanked and congratulated for elaborating their impact. And the ultimate lesson to be found in her analysis is that law teaching and scholarship in Australia constitute an important and influential part of the inescapable dynamic of the law. The dividends and intellectual rewards paid to law teachers come decades after their classroom encounters. They come when ideas, planted in the minds of law students, by words and writings, find their way into the expositions and applications of law and justice that eventually help shape the societies in which we live.

The Hon Michael Kirby AC CMG*
January 2019

[5] AF Mason, 'Geoffrey Sawer: The Priceless Professor', *Canberra Times*, 21 December 1990. See chapter one, n 23.

[6] MD Kirby, 'The Decline and Fall of Australia's Law Reform Institutions – and the Prospects for Revival' (2017) 91 *Australian Law Journal* 841.

* Justice of the High Court of Australia (1996–2009); President of the Court of Appeal of New South Wales (1984–96); and Chairman of the Australian Law Reform Commission (1975–84).

ACKNOWLEDGEMENTS

Throughout this project I have been supported and encouraged by many kind and clever lawyers, judges, librarians, historians and scholars.

The 33 interview participants showed great generosity in granting interviews, reviewing and commenting on transcripts and draft chapters, and providing me with hospitality during interstate visits: Margaret Allars SC; James Allsop (Chief Justice of the Federal Court of Australia); John Atkin; Professor Lauchlan Chipman; Christopher Birch SC; Jonathan Brett; Robin Brett QC; Sir Ross Cranston (Judge, High Court of England, Queens Bench Division); Professor James Crawford (Judge of the International Court of Justice); Gareth Evans AC QC; Professor Richard Fox; David Henshall; Professor Mary Hiscock; Michael Kirby AC CMG; Martin Krygier; Emeritus Fellow Ian Leader-Elliot; Professor Geoffrey Lindell; Dennis Mahoney AO QC; Sir Anthony Mason; Professor Gabriel Moens; Professor Ron McCallum AO; Allan Myers AO QC; Professor Dennis Pearce; Hamish Redd; Professor Wojciech Sadurski; John Taylor; Pat Urban; Professor Louis Waller; Julie Ward (Justice of the Court of Appeal of NSW); Professor Jeremy Webber; Roger Wilkins AO; Associate Professor Klaus Ziegert.[1] I would particularly like to thank Professor Waller, who kindly agreed to two interviews (each of which occupied several hours) and provided two photographs of Peter Brett that are now found in the pages of this book. Jonathan Brett kindly supplied the photograph of his father which appears on the front cover. I am delighted that The Hon Michael Kirby agreed to write the Foreword to this work and very generously completed the task within a very short time.

Numerous librarians and archivists have helped me in many different ways. In Melbourne, Katie Wood, of the University of Melbourne Archives, and John Waugh, author of the definitive institutional history of Melbourne Law School, provided invaluable guidance on navigating the law school's archives. Carole Hinchcliff, Law Librarian at the University of Melbourne, provided numerous suggestions and leads and, of her own volition, contacted Peter Lindeman from Fairfax for further photographs of Brett. Thanks to them, this book includes photos of Brett in action during the Tait case.

In Sydney, Julia Horne, the University of Sydney's historian, met with me and helpfully discussed her experience of interviewing Alice Erh-Soon Tay. I am also indebted to Tim Robinson, Manager of the University of Sydney Archives, and

[1] One interviewee wished to remain anonymous; I refer to them as 'Participant A'.

his colleague, archivist Nyree Morrison. Mr Robinson searched a number of the closed files for matters that could be relevant to my project and, with the consent of Professor Ron McCallum, facilitated access to critical documents. Tay's nephew, Professor Peter Kwan, provided valuable information about Tay's personal papers. I am grateful to Greg Weight for allowing me to reproduce his portrait of Tay, which is displayed prominently in this book.

In Canberra, Margaret Avard, Jane Beattie and Greg Bell of the Noel Butlin Archive Centre at the Australian National University, as well as various librarians and archivists at the National Library of Australia (NLA), provided me with numerous materials and sourced some of the photographs of Geoffrey Sawer included in this book. I am extremely grateful to Sawer's daughter, Elizabeth Penhallurick, for granting permission to access crucial files, Sawer's diaries and unpublished biography, and for me to use several photos of her father in this book.

In the United States, Lesley Schoenfeld, Public Services and Visual Collections Coordinator of the Historical and Special Collection of the Harvard Law School Library, scanned and sent very useful documents relating to Brett's time at Harvard. Dr Gail Hupper, historian and former Assistant Dean of the Graduate Programme at Harvard Law School, provided a thoughtful account of the SJD at Harvard, based on her considerable research into the topic. In England, Reader Maksymilian Del Mar of Queen Mary University of London very generously located and sent copies of correspondence between Tay and Neil MacCormick. Martin Maw, archivist at Oxford University Press, located and made available several documents concerning Sawer's book, *Law in Society*, which Caisen Mirassou kindly photographed and sent to me.

In my home town, Deborah Bowring, formerly of the University of Tasmania Law Library, provided assistance throughout this project and responded to a range of questions about research techniques and sourcing literature. I am especially grateful to Professor Margaret Otlowski, former Dean of Law at the University of Tasmania, for helping me to arrange my teaching commitments in a way that allowed for the timely completion of this project. I am also appreciative of all the staff and postgraduate students of the Faculty of Law at the University of Tasmania for providing such a collegial and supportive environment for this work, including Bruce Newey who provided much needed advice on matters of style and assembly. I would also like to thank Michael Stokes for allowing me to attend his thought-provoking and lively Jurisprudence classes and for discussing various theories with me, particularly in relation to HLA Hart.

This project began as a PhD dissertation which was examined by Emeritus Professors David Sugarman and William Twining. That pioneering scholars of their ilk – who had for many years inspired my work – agreed to take on this task was humbling. This book would not exist were it not for their ongoing encouragement, friendship and advice.

My dissertation was supervised by Professor Ngaire Naffine and Dr John Gava of the University of Adelaide. I owe both of them a great debt for their careful review of chapters and for making me believe that this project and my ideas were worthwhile. Early in the project Ngaire instilled in me a conviction that this work should have a strong feminist dimension. It is thanks to her, along with invitations, discussions and guidance from Professors Fiona Cownie, Ulrike Schultz and Margaret Thornton that I was encouraged to write about and consider the issue of gender in life history in some depth.

I am also very grateful for the support of Professors Wilfrid Press and Mark Lunney, who gave advice and direction from the inception of this project and provided much needed feedback on my book proposal. Historian Dr Tanya Josev provided some excellent comments on the first chapter on Brett. Friends of many years, Dr Christine Beuermann and Meredith Hagger, endured – and sometimes even encouraged – lengthy discussions about Brett, Tay and Sawer and Australian law schools.

I am also very grateful for several scholarships which have allowed me to concentrate on the project and travel to conduct interviews, review archives and attend conferences: a DR Stranks Travel Fellowship; a Kercher Legal History Scholarship, funded by historian Bruce Kercher; a University of Adelaide faculty grant; and two living allowance scholarships (a University of Adelaide Divisional scholarship, and a Zelling Gray scholarship, funded by The Hon Tom Gray).

At Hart Publishing, I would like to thank Kate Whetter, Sinead Moloney, Ceri Warner and Rosamund Jubber, whose timely advice and guidance have made the final assembly of the manuscript for this book easy. I also thank Bill Asquith for his initial interest in this book and for facilitating reviews.

During the final stages of the book, friend and historian Jacqueline Fox edited the manuscript with great care and intelligence, and in the process helped me clarify my ideas and my writing. For the dissertation, professional editor Rosemary Peers performed a sterling edit of my thesis.

Finally, I would like to thank my husband, David, our Cairn Terrier, Jock, and our Irish donkeys, Walt and Ernie, for their companionship and for providing very welcome distractions. One of them also kindly proof read several draft chapters.

TABLE OF CONTENTS

1

Introduction

This book reveals the distinctive ideas and endeavours which accompanied the birth and early growth of Australia's modern legal academy. Through a series of life histories, it illuminates the serious intellectual and enterprising attempts made to shape the discipline of law and its contribution to Australian society. This is a study of three key – yet largely overlooked – figures: Peter Brett (1918–1975), Professor of Jurisprudence at the University of Melbourne; Alice Erh-Soon Tay (1934–2004), Professor of Jurisprudence at the University of Sydney; and Geoffrey Sawer (1910–1996), Head of the Department of Law in the Research School of Social Sciences (RSSS) at the Australian National University (ANU).

All three professors were part of the first community of legal scholars who established the enduring liberal-progressive foundations of Australia's discipline of law.[1] This book is a vivid, nuanced and contextual account of those foundations. By undertaking this study, I set out to challenge the persistent myth that members of this community are unimportant to understandings of Australian law, legal culture and society, and unremarkable when compared with leading scholars in other common law nations.

Drawing on in-depth interviews with former colleagues, family members and students, extensive archival research, and an appraisal of their contributions to scholarship[2] and teaching, I explore the three professors' international networks and broader social and historical milieux. I also identify some of the central qualities of the first Australian legal theories and explain how Australian scholars engaged with English, American and other foreign ideas. Ranging from local experiences and the concerns of a nascent Australian legal academy, to the complex transnational phenomena of legal scholarship and theory, I make a case for contextualising law and legal culture within society. Further, my exploration of how Australian scholars adopted and adapted US theory also lends weight to recent revisionist accounts of American jurisprudence.

[1] The expression 'first community' is used here to mean the growing number of full-time legal academics employed from the 1950s to replace the part-time practitioner-teachers who had previously taught a large proportion of the law school curriculum. This expression was first used in: S Bartie, 'A Full Day's Work: A Study of Australia's First Legal Scholarly Community' (2010) 29 *University of Queensland Law Review* 67. See also S Bartie, 'Towards a History of Law as an Academic Discipline' (2014) 38 *Melbourne University Law Review* 444, 449–50.

[2] I read and analysed all the published scholarship, as well as unpublished manuscripts, of Brett, Tay and Sawer. A full list is set out at the end of this book.

This is a study of intellectuals rather than abstract ideas. I examine not only the contributions made by Brett, Tay and Sawer to scholarship, but also their contributions to institution building, administration, law making, public debate and advocacy. I explain their efforts to shape the professional identity of lawyers and to counter attempts to treat law as separate from politics. For example, focusing on the Department of Jurisprudence at the University of Sydney and the Department of Law within the RSSS at ANU, allows me to critically examine how Tay and Sawer ran two novel institutions that had the potential to radically change the discipline's identity and culture. I scrutinise their decisions to capitalise on some opportunities while rejecting others, and consider how the discipline might have changed had they managed their departments differently.

This book also counters fatalist accounts of the legal academy by telling the personal stories of three unlikely marginal figures: a Jewish man (Brett); a Chinese woman (Tay); and a war orphan (Sawer). All three rose to prominence within the academy and overcame various obstacles and opposition to create novel roles for themselves and their successors. By choosing one woman and two men as my subjects, I also very consciously explore the role of women within the academy.

In essence, my goal for this study is to make a strong contribution to understandings of a critical phase in the history of the common law and legal education. I hope to provide an important foundation for new lines of inquiry and exploration that will provoke novel ways of thinking about Australia's legal academy and law schools. I therefore dedicate this book to current and future generations of pioneering Australian legal scholars, in the hope that it will be read by those scholars as well as by foreign observers, and also those interested more generally in Australia's intellectual history, the history of Australian universities, jurisprudential movements and legal education.

History and Legal Education

The motivation for this study was my strong curiosity about earlier generations of Australian legal scholars and by my suspicion that existing accounts did not sufficiently examine their activities. In other portrayals, this generation of scholars has either been subsumed under vague labels, such as 'narrow positivists',[3]

[3] See, eg, J Gava, 'Introductory Essay' (1988–89) 5 *Australian Journal of Law and Society* 1, 3; N James, 'Power-Knowledge in Australian Legal Education: Corporatism's Reign' (2004) 26 *Sydney Law Review* 587, 596; M Thornton, 'The Dissolution of the Social in the Legal Academy' (2006) 25 *Australian Feminist Law Journal* 3, 15; F Carrigan, 'They Make a Desert and Call It Peace' (2014) 23 *Legal Education Review* 313, 315–16, citing M Thornton, 'Portia Lost in the Groves of Academe Wondering What to Do about Legal Education' (1991) 34 *Australian Universities' Review* 26, 26; D Pearce, E Campbell and D Harding, *Australian Law Schools: A Discipline Assessment for the Commonwealth Tertiary Education Commission* (Canberra, Australian Government Publishing Service, 1987) [1.20] ('*Pearce Report*'). A similar point is made, and the same authorities cited, in Bartie, 'Towards a History' (n 1).

or swept up within larger social phenomena, such as 'modernisation'.[4] Conventional wisdom holds that early Australian scholars were narrow, conservative and doctrinal in orientation, that they primarily served the interests of the profession, and that there was no distinctively Australian jurisprudence or legal theory to speak of.[5]

Almost from the time of their inception in the 1960s and 1970s, the more radical law schools – those offering alternative visions – came under attack, from both outside and within. The ongoing impact of this friction has been significant and negative, both in terms of stifling the diversity of legal education, and stunting or, even more disturbingly, cutting short individual careers. To provoke change, it seemed necessary for subsequent generations of legal scholars to condemn or ignore earlier generations.

While we might sympathise with the objectives underpinning these critiques of the old order, we can lament the ways that the history of legal education is being enlisted. Many historians would object to any strategic use of history. However, my objections to the accounts that have been made of Australian legal scholars are of a different kind: I argue that that they create caricatures, straw men (they do not mention many women), that present as slogans or propaganda rather than lessons. As a result, we learn nothing. The purpose of this work is not to glorify this early generation of legal scholars, but to provide a balanced and probing account of their contributions to the legal academy.

Even in the United States, historians continue to provide new explanations for the origins and growth of modern university legal education which challenge conventional wisdom. For example, during the conception of this project David Rabban made some important and startling discoveries about a founding period of American legal education. These discoveries demonstrate the dangers of making assumptions about who, or what, is important in legal education. He notes that biographers of one of his subjects, Henry Adams, have attached little importance to the seven years Adams spent as an academic at Harvard.[6] By contrast, Rabban argues, this period is crucial to any explanation of the field of American legal history and that 'Adams and his students virtually created the field and provided a model for subsequent legal historians in England as well as in their own country'.[7] Given the attention that American legal scholars have received, it is both startling and telling that such new and important insights could be revealed by approaching these scholars through the lens of legal education; by seeking to understand scholars based on their placement in law schools at a particular moment, rather

[4] eg, J Lancaster, *The Modernisation of Legal Education: A Critique of the Martin, Bowen and Pearce Reports* (Sydney, Centre for Legal Education, 1993).

[5] M Chesterman and D Weisbrot, 'Legal Scholarship in Australia' (1987) 50 *Modern Law Review* 709, 724.

[6] DM Rabban, *Law's History* (Cambridge, Cambridge University Press, 2013) 153.

[7] ibid.

than by the way their work was subsequently remembered and incorporated into works of legal scholarship. Rabban's work makes a compelling case for testing conventional wisdom about the history of law schools and the discipline of law through open-minded exploration.

Several fundamental lessons emerge from histories of university legal education which are crucial to the health of the discipline. Most obviously, they demonstrate that in the past universities, law professors and law schools have fulfilled roles and engaged in activities that are very different from those pursued today.[8] Acknowledging these alternatives may prompt current legal scholars to question whether their priorities and activities are in fact central to universities, and to reject the sense that the current arrangements accord with a natural order. Sometimes, histories of both law schools and universities are presented in a linear fashion to suggest that both grew in maturity over the course of the twentieth century. As Hannah Forsyth explains in her history of the modern university, for Australian universities this maturity is demonstrated by the post-1950s emphasis on, and eventual commodification of, research.[9] This research emphasis initially did not gain much traction in the field of law. Yet, by the end of the twentieth century, the rise in the number of PhDs in law, increased pressures for legal scholars to seek research funding, and a growing emphasis on publication of monographs and articles rather than textbooks, confirm the penetration of these broader university trends. In linear histories, these changes are presented as evidence of the growing sophistication of the discipline. The earlier central emphasis on teaching is treated as misguided and a product of narrow thinking that reflected the supposed early doctrinal and positivist emphasis. In other words, it is symptomatic of an outmoded belief that law ought to be studied as an autonomous discipline. This linear history approach reinforces the idea that law schools should reject earlier traditions and practices on the basis that they are misguided (and therefore irrelevant), and instead place primary emphasis on research over scholarship and teaching. Standing in opposition to these ideas, this study suggests that earlier debates and thinking about the role of universities, law schools and law professors remain relevant to the current – and ostensibly more mature – age.

Many criticisms could be levelled at previous (and present) generations of Australian legal scholars, but the use of linear histories to dismiss the efforts of their predecessors limits the range of alternatives that might be considered by current professors and managers. In the process, it provides greater force to the status quo. Better understandings of the efforts and endeavours of our predecessors – examining their ambitions and priorities – provides material which may be used to challenge dominant narratives and values, and encourages legal academics to develop an appreciation of a broader range of activities, perhaps with

[8] For a similar argument on the value of history, see M MacMillan, *History's People* (London, Profile Books Ltd, 2017) xv–xvi.

[9] H Forsyth, *A History of the Modern Australian University* (Sydney, NewSouth, 2014).

the ultimate goal of liberating law schools and universities from current ways of thinking about their role in society. As the father of English legal history opined over a century ago, this approach has the potential to 'free [current and future legal scholars] from superstitions and teach them that they have free hands'.[10] As I have argued elsewhere, the underlying assumption behind writing the life history of a legal scholar

> is that how a scholar balanced their personal desire to succeed, along with their learning and their own altruistic notions of the discipline's best interests, mattered to the future of law schools. This in turn suggests that a current legal scholar's current daily musing on such things also matters to the future of law school.[11]

Histories of Christopher Columbus Langdell, for example, not only bring to light the strategic motivations behind his appeals to 'science', but also the absence of any empirical basis for his claims that his approach to legal education would reform the profession.[12] They demonstrate how a very intelligent lawyer may advance fundamentally flawed ideas that have an enormous impact on the nature and advancement of law. They also illustrate the importance of caution and humility in the running of law schools and in the exercise of academic leadership. In a similar vein, institutional accounts of law schools, such as those led by Robert Stevens and Brian Tamanaha, show that law professors are mere mortals: they can be seduced by the prospect of elevated status and financial gain to lead law schools in ways that are largely self-serving.[13] Rather than reach for a utopia, history encourages a frank appraisal of circumstances and possibilities, and an awareness that bright legal academics may advance both worthwhile and fundamentally flawed agendas, sometimes simultaneously.

This book, therefore, is a call to develop greater curiosity and to better understand the past decades of Australian university legal education in order to think with greater ingenuity, optimism and depth about the opportunities and problems of the present.

The university's prioritisation of attracting research funding over other pursuits, and the growth in size of the student body, as well as the number of law schools,

[10] FW Maitland to AV Dicey (c July 1896), in CHS Fifoot and PNR Zutshi (eds), *The Letters of Frederic William Maitland*, 2 vols (Cambridge and London, Seldon Society, 1995) 11. In more recent times, Robert Gordon, citing Maitland, has approved of this use of history: see RW Gordon, 'The Past as Authority and as Social Critic: Stabilizing and Destabilizing Functions of History in Legal Argument' in TJ McDonald (ed), *The Historic Turn in the Human Sciences* (University of Michigan Press, 1996) 359; David Sugarman, 'Robert W Gordon in Conversation with David Sugarman' (October 2018) 1(3) *Law and History Review: The Docket*, www.lawandhistoryreview.org/article/robert-w-gordon-in-conversation-with-david-sugarman/.

[11] S Bartie, 'Histories of Legal Scholars – The Power of Possibility' (2014) 34 *Legal Studies* 305, 319.

[12] The best account of Langdell's methods is BA Kimball, *The Inception of Modern Professional Education – CC Langdell, 1826–1906* (Chapel Hill, University of North Carolina Press, 2009).

[13] R Stevens, *Law School: Legal Education in America from the 1850s to the 1980s* (Chapel Hill, University of North Carolina Press, 1983); B Tamanaha, *Failing Law Schools* (Chicago, University of Chicago Press, 2012). See also Bartie (n 11) 309.

raises critical questions about the role of law schools and legal academics that ought to attract the attention of the discipline's brightest minds. Each year thousands of young, and not so young, Australian and international students invest considerable sums of money and time, along with their hopes, into Australian law schools. Dramatic changes in the nature of lawyering affect our graduates' prospects of employment and the role that they, and the law more generally, will play in society. All these forces require changes to existing law school models, which should be driven by intelligent, pioneering and creative legal scholars.[14] It is a desire to search for leaders within the academy and seek out an intellectual and, perhaps also, a moral core (or cores) for the discipline that drives this exercise in introspection.[15] A discipline that has little history or tradition and no real understanding of its identity or where it came from is vulnerable to external policies that fail to thoughtfully respond to the needs of society. It is at greater risk of losing its sense of self.[16]

Brett, Tay and Sawer

Rather than provide a survey of groups within the legal academy to add to the broad generalisations and vague labels, I have limited my study to three scholars in order to closely investigate the whole of their careers and thickly describe their principal innovations.[17] This has meant concentrating on their experiences within three institutions. Australia's federal character and the geographical isolation of its major cities mean that experiences vary between different states. In each part, the local conditions are explained.

Peter Brett

Peter Brett began his academic career at the University of Western Australia in 1950 and held the Chair of Jurisprudence at the University of Melbourne from 1964 to 1975. Born Isidore Peter Bretzfelder to Jewish parents in England, Brett

[14] For some vivid accounts of the changes and their potential implications, see R Susskind and D Susskind, *How Technology will Transform the Work of the Professions* (Oxford, Oxford University Press, 2015); R Susskind, *Tomorrow's Lawyers: An Introduction to your Future*, 2nd edn (Oxford, Oxford University Press, 2017); M Kowalski, *Avoiding Extinction: Reimagining Legal Services for the 21st Century* (Bloomington, IN, iUniverse, 2012). For an Australian example, see V Waye, M Verreynne and J Knowler, 'Innovation in the Australian Legal Profession' (2018) 25 *International Journal of the Legal Profession* 213.

[15] Some of my motivations are explained further in Bartie (n 11).

[16] ibid.

[17] C Geertz, 'Thick Description: Toward an Interpretive Theory of Culture' in C Geertz, *The Interpretation of Cultures* (New York, Basic Books, 1973) 3, 6–10.

began practising law at the age of 16, studied law part-time, worked at the Treasury Solicitor's Office, and served in the British Army during the Second World War. Despite his considerable achievements and his contributions to the Australian legal academy, Brett is not well known and very little has been written about him.[18]

Brett's commitment to reforming Australian legal culture bordered on obsession. He was a man of boundless energy, great industry and frank speech, who believed that complacency and elitism within the legal profession were creating terrible injustices within Australian society. He believed that his role as a legal scholar at the University of Melbourne gave him the opportunity to lead the reform of both Australia's law and legal profession. This belief led him to make several contributions that are essential to any understanding of the founding of modern Australian university legal education.

Brett's war experience, Jewish identity, employment at the University of Melbourne and studies at Harvard Law School led him to advance an ambitious scholarly agenda to improve the intellectual identity and credentials of Australia's discipline of law. By arranging for him to study at Harvard, the then Dean at Melbourne, Zelman Cowen, helped Brett believe that he could contribute to the leading debates in criminal law theory and adopt an academic agenda that resembled those of the leading jurisprudential thinkers of the common law world. This confidence resulted in a monograph that was the first of its kind in Australia. In this ground-breaking text, Brett suggested a novel solution to the problem of identifying and attributing moral responsibility in criminal law. The work also, by way of example, set forth a new agenda for Australian legal academics that involved updating the foundations of law in accordance with the best of modern learning.

Brett's experience also sheds light on one type of influence that American law schools, in particular Harvard, had on Australian legal scholars. This book reveals that Brett brought to Australia the leading American jurisprudential school of his time, the Legal Process School. He was the only Australian legal scholar to advance a scholarly agenda that rested on the philosophy of science, which sat at the heart of this American school, and who was committed to the idea that for the law to be just, it needed to bridge the gap between science and morality. At Harvard, Brett was one of Henry Hart's most devoted students. Studying his efforts to bring Legal Process ideas to Australian shores and to the criminal law provides an insight into Australian scholars' appetite for American ideas, and sheds new light on how the US SJD (Doctor of Juridical Science) programme

[18] Brett is mentioned briefly in J Waugh, *First Principles – The Melbourne Law School 1857–2007* (Melbourne, Miegunyah Press, 2007); Z Cowen, *A Public Life – The Memoirs of Zelman Cowen* (Melbourne, Miegunyah Press, 2006); R Campbell, *A History of the Melbourne Law School 1857–1973* (Melbourne, University of Melbourne Press, 1977). The following short piece, written soon after Brett's death, is devoted to him: L Waller, 'Peter Brett Remembered' (1975) *Summons* 100.

facilitated the transplantation of American norms to Australian legal education and scholarship. This assessment of Brett's use of US legal theory also lends weight to recent US revisionist histories of the Legal Process School and provides material for new revisions.

Brett's theorising made its way into the classroom in the form of Australia's first full-length criminal textbook on Australian law.[19] Another reason that Brett is such an important figure is the popularity and longevity of this textbook and the problem method it expounded. The work was one of the first Australian textbooks to embody a clear pedagogical theory and concept of law. It raised the standard of textbook writing in Australia, and also provided a means for challenging narrow readings of Dixon's strict legalism. Brett and his co-author, Louis Waller, aimed to do more than educate competent lawyers. Their goal was to change the very culture of Australia's legal profession: to create more liberal, ethically minded and reformist-orientated lawyers. They sought to lift the profession out of the conservative and positivist quagmire in which they believed it was stuck.

Finally, Brett is an important figure because of the way in which he advocated for the rights of those he believed had been wrongly convicted of crimes. His tireless attempts to remedy substantial miscarriages of justice in notorious murder cases (the *Tait*, *Beamish* and *Ratten* cases), as well as his determination to improve the workings of Australian universities, provide us with further insights into what it meant to be a liberal lawyer in an Australian law schools in the 1950s and 1960s. While Brett's efforts were well known at the time, he has played little part in subsequent histories of Australian law schools and universities. In part, this is because many people did not warm to him personally. Brett did not make a good first impression, with many colleagues and acquaintances noting an arrogance and fierceness. With perseverance, some grew to develop a strong sense of admiration, both for his principles and his intellect, which resulted in deep and loyal friendships. Others continued to believe him to be a dogmatic and unsympathetic man. Students either admired or feared him, the latter believing he took pleasure in ridiculing them in class.

In this book, I attempt to challenge the marginalised place that Brett now occupies in the history of Australian legal education. I argue that his endeavours and intellectual agenda provide crucial insights into the motivations of Australian legal academics, the beginning of Australia's legal academy and the modern discipline of law.

Alice Erh-Soon Tay

Born in Singapore to Chinese parents, Alice Erh-Soon Tay began her academic career at the University of Malaya (now the National University of Singapore) in

[19] P Brett and PL Waller, *Cases and Materials in Criminal Law* (Sydney, Butterworths, 1962).

1958. In the 1960s, Tay moved to Australia, where she became a lecturer in the Faculty of Law at ANU. Personal circumstances, rather than career ambitions, had brought Tay to the nation's capital, Canberra. While at the University of Malaya, she had fallen in love with Eugene Kamenka, a married Australian intellectual historian, and to avoid further scandal over this relationship the couple returned to his home country. In Canberra, Tay commenced, while Kamenka completed, a PhD at the ANU Research School of Social Sciences (RSSS). Tay's thesis was an impressive work on the topic of possession; soon afterwards, however, her scholarship moved to a topic that more closely aligned with Kamenka's principal scholarly interests: Marxism. Tay's scholarly stature grew as she travelled with Kamenka to Russia, China and New York and wrote about the role of law within communist societies. She sat firmly within the sociological tradition, and one of her greatest contributions was to devise a set of ideal types that sought to highlight the commonalities between legal systems to allow for stronger comparisons.

Holding a doctorate, travelling overseas to conduct field work, and publishing numerous articles within the sociological tradition made Tay seem more accomplished than most other members of Australia's overwhelmingly male legal academy. These activities, and the networks she established, led to the defining moment of her career: her appointment in 1975 as Challis Professor of Jurisprudence and Head of the Department of Jurisprudence at the University of Sydney. In many ways, it is remarkable that at this early time, when so few women held academic positions or practised as lawyers in Australia, and even fewer were Chinese, Tay should have been elevated to this post. In 1998, towards the end of her career, she was recognised yet again through her appointment as President of the Human Rights and Equal Opportunities Commission. This book considers the role of gender and race in Tay's elevation.

In this book, I argue that Tay's primary contribution to Australia's legal academy was her maintenance, in the face of considerable opposition, of the Department of Jurisprudence at the University of Sydney. Tay cut a new figure for the Australian legal academy, that of an academic entrepreneur, and she funnelled her intellectual convictions into a partly organisational role. She sought to provide a safe haven for jurisprudential scholars, where they would be freed from the increasing external pressures that she believed would fundamentally compromise their ability to advance free and fearless criticism. They were thereby empowered to serve as a counterweight to governmental agendas, prejudices and acts of oppression. Through her networking and entrepreneurial activities, Tay sought to place the Australian discipline of law on the world stage, and she encouraged legal scholars to seek out broader horizons. She reacted against the mediocrity and complacency that she perceived within Australia's legal academy, believing that this not only served as poor opposition to tyrannical aspects of government, but also promoted ideas that would erode existing safeguards in Australia's legal system. She railed against the growing managerialism within universities, the attempts to measure intangible products that promoted competition over collegiality, and the commodification of research.

This part of the book relies heavily on Tay's scholarship, as well as on 18 interviews conducted with her former colleagues, associates and students. In several ways, of the three scholars studied in this book, Tay was the most difficult to depict. This was partly because she was the most divisive figure and remains intensely disliked by some. As explained in this book, by fighting to maintain the existence of a separate Department of Jurisprudence she sustained a divide that had already existed within the Faculty of Law at the University of Sydney for many decades. One obvious way to get a more objective sense of how she treated others, and what her motivations were, would be through an investigation of personal papers, particularly letters. As Twining relayed of his study of American legal realist Karl Llewellyn:

> Rootling through a person's papers, especially those of an untidy magpie, is one of the best ways of getting to know them. I learned more about Karl from this exercise than I did from my direct contact with him in 1957–58, or from interviews, or even from casual reading of his works.[20]

My problem, however, was that, unlike Brett and Sawer, none of Tay's papers have been provided to a public library, and the University of Sydney Archives holds very few documents relating to Tay beyond the law school's minutes of meeting. The existence of such papers might have provided stronger evidence for making an evaluation of Tay's personality and actions.

Interviews form an important component of this part of this book, not only because of the paucity of personal papers, but also because they revealed how important the 'social dimension'[21] is to understanding Tay and her contribution to the academy. Interviews were sought with people who had had substantial dealings with Tay and who either supported or objected to the continuation of the Department of Jurisprudence at the University of Sydney. This therefore helped to fill a large part of the void created by the inability to access personal papers. Shortly before Tay's death, she agreed to an oral history interview with the University of Sydney's historian, Julia Horne. Horne published aspects of that interview in two articles, which are also relied upon in this study.[22] The window into Tay's life has been blurred, but not entirely obscured, by the evidentiary challenges. Perhaps, in time, her papers will be released and more can be added to the insights presented in this book.

[20] W Twining, *Karl Llewellyn and the Realist Movement*, 2nd edn (Cambridge, Cambridge University Press, 2012) 401.

[21] KA Ziegert, 'AEST – An Attempt at Explaining the Phenomenon' in G Doeker-Mach and KA Ziegert (eds), *Alice Erh-Soon Tay – Lawyer Scholar, Civil Servant* (Stuttgart, Franz Steiner Verlag, 2004) 7, 7.

[22] J Horne, 'Alice Erh-Soon Tay, The Making of an Intellectual' in G Doeker-Mach and KA Ziegert, *Alice Erh-Soon Tay – Lawyer, Scholar, Civil Servant* (Stuttgart, Franz Steiner Verlag, 2004) 13; J Horne, 'The Cosmopolitan Life of Alice Erh-Soon Tay' (2010) 21 *Journal of World History* 419.

Geoffrey Sawer

Geoffrey Sawer began his academic career in 1940 at the University of Melbourne. In 1950, he was appointed founding Professor of Law at the newly created RSSS at the recently established ANU in Canberra. Here Sawer developed his most enduring scholarly agenda. He was the first Australian lawyer to hold a full-time research position and the first to be employed to work within a school of social scientists.

Sawer pioneered a distinct brand of constitutionalism.[23] He also advanced significant bodies of scholarship that provided strong foundations for studies in Australian public law and politics. The final part of this book concentrates on the various ways in which Sawer challenged the concept that law was an autonomous entity, including through his leadership of a Department of Law within a School of Social Sciences.[24]

Sawer's most remarkable contributions consisted, first, of the robust case he made against law's autonomy and, second, the solid foundations he laid for Australian constitutional law and scholarship. Through both contributions he sought to treat law as a collection of social facts rather than a body of rules, and he encouraged others to study law alongside other social facts. For Sawer, the discipline of law was not a social science. Yet, he believed that it ought to be a subject of social science; he also believed that lawyers ought to consider ideas from social scientists. The historical work he performed early in his career on Australian law and politics provided irrefutable evidence of the political nature of law and legal reasoning. His books on law and politics, written for a general audience, were designed to educate both the profession and the public on broader thinking about law. Rather than condemning or criticising the conservative and narrow elements of the profession who thought of law in a legalistic and mechanical way, Sawer provided materials and arguments that might persuade them to look afresh at their strongly held beliefs. He therefore sought to improve the intellectual standing of law by drawing on social science methods and learning, while pitching his position in a way that did not alienate the profession and legal academy. He perceived a strong need for change and reform, both in the discipline and the political system, but also saw merit in existing practices.

In this part, I raise the question whether Sawer's appointment to the RSSS constituted a missed opportunity. Of the three scholars studied here, Sawer has received the greatest praise, and he continues to be remembered fondly by many.

[23] Former Chief Justice of the High Court of Australia, Sir Anthony Mason, described Sawer as a 'constitutionalist': see A Mason, 'Geoffrey Sawer: The Priceless Professor', *Canberra Times* 21 December 1990, 7; Interview with Sir Anthony Mason (Sir Anthony Mason's Chambers in Sydney, 9 December 2014).

[24] To date, the most substantial works on Sawer are M Coper, 'Geoffrey Sawer and the Art of the Academic Commentator: A Preliminary Biographical Sketch' (2014) 42 *Federal Law Review* 389; R Cranston, 'Lawyer in the Social Sciences – Geoffrey Sawer' (1980) 11 *Federal Law Review* 263.

Nonetheless, several of his associates remain puzzled that he did so little to build his law department within the RSSS. I outline the many reasons and circumstances that help explain his decision to keep the department small, including the expectations of the broader university and government as well as attitudes of the legal profession. However, I also suggest that his scholarly position, sceptically appraising ambitious sociological theories and taking a measured approach to the potential of social science for law, limited his enthusiasm for increasing the size of the department. Another scholar, sitting more firmly within a sociological tradition, might have fostered a more vibrant and ambitious department that demonstrated the potential for legal research to extend well beyond doctrinal studies and to be led by disciplinary practices from the humanities and social sciences. I also consider, with the benefit of hindsight, what this missed opportunity meant for a discipline that is judged largely by its research outputs, and is increasingly being judged by its ability to compete with other disciplines for research funding.

Why Brett, Tay and Sawer?

My goal in writing this book was to understand how legal scholars who were theoretically inclined and reflective sought to improve the standing and intellectual credentials of Australia's discipline of law during its early modern formation. I therefore needed to find scholars of this ilk. I do not claim that Brett, Tay and Sawer were the most important law professors of the twentieth century, and my curiosity about the discipline extends far beyond these three individuals. I do, however, suggest that these three professors matched the profile of well-known international pioneering legal scholars and that these commonalities speak of their potential to shape the intellectual and cultural underpinnings of Australia's discipline of law.

This matching exercise involves seeing similarities between the efforts of Langdell[25] and the English dons[26] to create an enduring textbook tradition based on a liberal science paradigm, with Brett's creation of the most popular early Australian legal textbook embodying a scientific and philosophical paradigm. It draws parallels between Tay and Sawer's leadership of law departments and attempts by some American Legal Realists to challenge formalist paradigms in legal education by creating interdisciplinary departments.[27] It makes connections

[25] See Kimball (n 12).

[26] D Sugarman, 'Legal Theory, the Common Law Mind and the Making of the Textbook Tradition' in W Twining (ed), *Legal Theory and Common Law* (Oxford, Blackwell, 1986) 26. This tradition is explained further in chapter two.

[27] See JH Schlegel, *American Legal Realism and Empirical Social Science* (Chapel Hill, University of North Carolina Press, 1995).

between the pioneers of all major jurisprudential movements and Brett's argument that the discipline ought to draw from the best of modern learning, Sawer's efforts to demonstrate the value of studying law with politics, and Tay's attempt to foster comparative sociologist analysis in order to break down Australian insularities. Further, Sawer and Brett's efforts to free practitioners from restrictive interpretations of Sir Owen Dixon's strict and complete legalism reveal the desire for cultural change that has been felt by many of the better known American legal theorists.[28]

Brett, Tay and Sawer held crucial leadership positions at a time of transformation within Australian universities and law schools, and there are signs that they moved beyond the noble drudgery associated with creating essential Australian legal materials for students and the profession. This book critically analyses how they responded to the opportunities they were given.

My selection of subjects for this study would always be controversial, and to some it might seem strange. Beyond Julius Stone, Australian legal scholars have not (in keeping with their ahistorical tendencies) identified prominent figures who have shaped the discipline in a similar manner to their international counterparts, such as Langdell or HLA Hart. When speaking of leadership, discussion often moves to Deans. To me, this seems to overlook the reality that while sometimes institutional and intellectual leadership combine, this is not always the case.

It might seem peculiar to group together scholars who studied very different fields: criminal law theory (Brett); comparative law and the sociology of law (Tay); and constitutionalism (Sawer). However, their importance to this study rests with their shared pioneering characteristics rather than the artificial divides created by disciplinary categorisations. Brett, Tay and Sawer are studied through the lens of legal education,[29] rather than their particular scholarly specialty. They were selected through a process of deduction, working through a list of all potential candidates. Other strong contenders included Julius Stone, Zelman Cowen and David Derham, and initially Stone and Derham were included in this project. Stone was, however, removed from this study as his scholarly agenda was formed before his move to Australia and he wrote very little on the importance of legal education and Australian law schools.[30] Moreover, including Stone among the subjects of this book risked confirming, rather than debunking, the common myth that he was the only notable scholar of this period. Some aspects of Stone's legacy are, however, addressed in the chapters on Tay. Derham was respected as a teacher of

[28] Most obviously Langdell (Kimball, n 12) and many others: see, eg, the efforts of Herbert Wechsler explained in A Walker, 'The Anti-Case Method: Herbert Wechsler and the Political History of the Criminal Law Course' (2009) 7 *Ohio State Journal of Criminal Law* 217.

[29] The importance of studying scholars through the lens of legal education is explained in Bartie, 'Towards a History' (n 1).

[30] J Stone, 'The Role of Universities: Views of a Scholar of the Last Century' in H Irving, J Mowbray and K Walton (eds), *Julius Stone, A Study in Influence* (Sydney, Federation Press, 2010).

jurisprudence; however, he was removed from this study as he published very little on the topic and his greatest contribution was to University governance. Cowen was not included because his career, as Dean and Vice Chancellor, was focused on institution building and there are few signs that he was a legal theorist. Other theoretically inclined scholars, such as Norval Morris and John Fleming, moved to the US or UK early in their careers, never to return. Daniel O'Connell was also considered but eventually rejected as he spent the latter years of his career largely at the University of Oxford.

As it turns out, Brett, Tay and Sawer had more in common than simply their roles and potential. All three were imbued with post-war optimism and the liberal spirit. By 'liberal' I mean simply that they were committed to the rule of law, held faith in the common law and the democratic system, and looked to them to provide protections to human rights and help achieve equality. They were not legal liberals in the American sense of this phrase. For example, Owen Fiss[31] (following from Laura Kalman[32]) defines American legal liberals as lawyers who held faith in the US Supreme Court to act in dynamic ways to protect against social injustice, as inspired by the Warren Court in *Brown v Board of Education*.[33] Sir Owen Dixon's presence as Chief Justice no doubt quelled any ambitions Australian legal scholars might have had for Australia's High Court to assume a similar mantle. While they would not have objected to the outcome in *Brown*, Brett, Tay and Sawer disapproved of the Warren Court's instrumental reasoning in the 1950s and 1960s. They believed that Australian courts should robustly develop the common law with an awareness of the broader social context. But they also believed that there remained a strong role for principle and reason. Furthermore, all three rejected the central tenets of Marxism, and rejected it as a source for thinking about Australian law.

Brett, Tay and Sawer viewed social issues through this liberal paradigm. For example, Tay's position on feminism was liberal, as she believed that equality could be achieved through the existing system and a human rights paradigm.[34] Neither Brett nor Sawer wrote on women's rights and feminism. Brett, Tay and Sawer all wrote a small number of pieces on Aboriginal issues from liberal perspectives and Tay, as a part-time commissioner of the Australian Law Reform Commission, participated in inquiries into Aboriginal Customary Law. While never a radical, Tay was deeply dismayed at Australia's treatment of Aboriginal and Torres Strait Islander peoples and believed that wide-ranging political reform was required.

[31] O Fiss, *Pillars of Justice: Lawyers and the Liberal Tradition* (Cambridge, Harvard University Press, 2017) 1–2.

[32] L Kalman, *The Strange Career of Legal Liberalism* (New Haven, Yale University Press, 1996) 4.

[33] 347 US 483 (1954). Fiss identifies the following lawyers as possessing this faith: Thurgood Marshall, William Brennan, John Doar and Burke Marshall.

[34] This is considered further in chapter eleven and in S Bartie, 'Studying Women Legal Scholars: The Challenges of Life History' (2018) 25 *International Journal of the Legal Profession* 279.

All three believed that Parliament held the greatest promise for achieving social reform (as opposed to the courts), and each was involved in lobbying and advising government on social justice issues. To some, these attitudes would peg them as conservatives, but of course this is a relative term and Tay, Brett and Sawer would no doubt have rejected this label. Brett and Sawer, in particular, were dismayed at what they perceived as a deep conservatism throughout Australia's legal profession, as well as Dixon's influence which encouraged practitioners to see the common law as autonomous from other bodies of learning and almost mechanical in its operation. Compared with the practising lawyers of their age, and several of their 1950s and 1960s colleagues, they were progressive liberals. As their brand of liberalism increasingly comes under attack, it is worth considering their reasoning and rationale and its continued presence in the legal academy today.

Feminism and Life History

This book is based on 33 interviews, archival work and an analysis of the scholarship of Brett, Tay and Sawer. Of the 32 interviewees who were willing to be named, 28 were men over the age of 60 and had been judges, senior lawyers and law professors. By contrast, I am a woman, who was then in my late thirties. As a feminist, I wanted to learn more about how my subjects treated women and what role gender played in Tay's rise to prominence.[35] While I felt that the responses of each interview participant to this line of questioning were frank, I cannot be sure that this was the case. Would different responses have been elicited if I were a man? I therefore 'must accept responsibility for [my] share in creating new evidence'.[36] I was concerned that Sawer and Brett showed so little regard for the interests of women and proceeded throughout the academy assuming that it would be dominated by men. Given that much of their careers were devoted to exploring issues of social justice and equality, this struck me as particularly odd. I was not wholly placated by the fact that few other men of their generation had taken up the cause. The fact that both Brett and Sawer seemed to do little to smooth the road for the few women in their classes also bothered me. However, I did not want these matters to overwhelm my project, as my object was to survey the whole of their contributions.

Tay's position on the plight on women within law and legal academy seemed more complex. She was one of the first Australian legal scholars to write on the topic of gender inequality in law and therefore was more enlightened than either Brett or Sawer. On the other hand, she appeared to do relatively little to mentor

[35] I consider that this work contains many of the hallmarks of feminist legal history identified by Ericka Rackley and Rosemary Auchmuty: E Rackley and R Auchmuty, 'Introduction' in *Women's Legal Landmarks* (Oxford, Hart Publishing, 2018) 1, 5.

[36] J Tosh with S Lang, *The Pursuit of History*, 4th edn (Cambridge, Pearson Education, 2006) 318.

or advance the careers of women law graduates – something I found disappointing. Unlike Brett and Sawer, Tay's rise to prominence coincided with a larger number of women students entering law schools, and she taught some very bright women law graduates. While I would have liked Tay to be a strong ambassador for women's rights and to help other women prosper in the legal academy, I am also conscious of the tendency of some feminist writers to create life histories of women that construct the 'lady-teacher as hero'[37] and also to rob them of their context. In the body of this work, I have tried to explain the conflicting strands and noted her views on the law's treatment of women and feminist legal scholarship.

Concluding Remarks

The objective behind this book is not to put the discipline of law back on the course set for it by early scholars. Just as it has been recognised that the natural sciences have not advanced in a coherent or cumulative manner,[38] it would be wrong to suggest that Australia's discipline of law has been systematically built up from the contributions of successive leading scholars. This is not a chronological study of a particular idea or fashion within the discipline across three scholars. Nonetheless, understanding the central initiatives and motivations of some of the discipline's most prominent scholars allows for a more productive and honest examination of the assumptions and ideas that shaped the discipline during its pioneering phases. These assumptions and ideas might serve as more reliable and interesting reference points than the vague portrayals of the discipline previously offered. They might support more robust and critical appraisals of the current generation's contributions and practices.

In short, in this book I do as much as I can within the space afforded to explain how each of the three scholars studied and responded to their intellectual and institutional environments to set the discipline of law in Australia on a strong path. They wrote, taught and engaged in other activities with the infant status of the discipline in mind. While they had considerable freedom to choose the topics that played to their strengths and interests, they did not simply advance the ideas and initiatives that they found the most interesting. This study demonstrates that Australia has had scholars of a similar type and with similar motivations to

[37] M Theobald, 'Teachers, Memory and Oral History' in K Weiler and S Middleton (eds), *Telling Women's Lives – Narrative Inquiries in the History of Women's Education* (Philadelphia, Open University Press, 1999) 9, 17. This tendency is discussed in detail in Bartie (n 34).

[38] TS Kuhn, *The Structure of Scientific Revolutions*, 3rd edn (Chicago, University of Chicago Press, 1996). Legal scholars have similarly recognised that, in the discipline of law, 'the impression is not one of continuity': R Cotterrell, *The Politics of Jurisprudence – A Critical Introduction to Legal Philosophy* (London, Butterworths, 1989) 18.

the English and American legal scholars who have become household names. It demonstrates that some early Australian legal scholars advanced distinctively Australian legal theories. The fact that Brett, Tay and Sawer and their initiatives are not widely known among Australian legal scholars raises interesting questions about both the culture of the discipline, past and present, and the nature of their individual contributions. This book provides part of the basis for meaningful and critical questioning of the discipline.

2

Australian Legal Academics: A Short Intellectual History

Introduction

The first university law school in the Australian colonies was established in Melbourne in 1857, almost a century before Peter Brett, Geoffrey Sawer and Alice Erh-Soon Tay joined Australia's fledgling legal academy.[1] During their first 100 years, Australia's law schools, all located within universities, were small affairs with tiny student numbers and meagre funding. There was no legal academy to speak of, with law schools employing just one or two full-time law professors. To fill out the curriculum, the universities engaged practising lawyers to teach on a part-time basis. The considerable differences between the first 100 years of law schools and the subsequent 50 years might suggest that the two periods could be studied independently of one another. Yet, to ignore the first 100 years would be to overlook the assumptions, practices and ideas that were inherited by subsequent generations and which form the basis of valuable lines of inquiry.

Geoffrey Sawer was one of the few Australian legal academics to begin their academic career under the old order. Taking up a position at the University of Melbourne in 1934, before the significant increase in the number of law schools, law students and legal academics, Sawer rose to prominence as law schools grew and changed significantly. However, he was not the only one touched by the old order. The legal academics who began their careers in the 1950s and 1960s joined law schools with histories forged by law professors of mostly good standing. They also embarked on teaching and research at a time when there were already many Australian judges and lawyers who had experienced a university legal education and therefore held strong views about its role and value. In order to understand Sawer, Brett and Tay it is therefore necessary to understand something of the intellectual and institutional traditions that they inherited.

Several features of the first 100 years of Australian university legal education had the potential to shape the role and standing of law schools throughout the

[1] This is not to suggest that this was the first time that law was formally taught in Australia. Law (or lore) teaching within Aboriginal nations in Australia has a far longer history than the university law teaching studied in this book.

twentieth century. First, it is important to recognise that the ideas of the early professors about how law ought to be taught and studied had very little bearing on the foundation and early progression of law schools. Instead, the impetus for creating and maintaining university legal education came from outside the university – from judges and barristers. In a sense, this meant that the law professors served at the pleasure of the profession. The ideas of the law professors, and the quality of the education they delivered, was marginal to the stronghold law schools became within the university landscape over their first 100 years of operation. This had implications for the status of university legal education.

Second, England's long and seemingly grand tradition of legal thought and law teaching, and its status within Australia, suggested that there was little need or room for Australian models or innovations. There are, however, signs that Australia's law professors pursued some distinctive interests, and devised practices that were novel to those pursued by the English jurists. Despite these differences, it would be an exaggeration to say that the early professors created a robust model (or models) of Australian legal education and scholarship. There is little to suggest that the early law professors provided future generations of Australian legal scholars with a strong template backed by substantial intellectual capital. Instead, from the early period the academy inherited loose preferences for certain conceptions of law. This suggests that subsequent generations had a strong degree of intellectual freedom to devise their own teaching and scholarly practices. If they felt bounded, it was not because their predecessors had established strong disciplinary boundaries.

Writing of settler communities in the common law world, historian Tamson Pietsch argues: 'If we are to understand the intellectual history of the late nineteenth and early twentieth centuries, we need to know a lot more about those who made knowledge, and a lot more about the worlds that made them.'[2] Legal academic Mark Lunney astutely points out that Australian intellectual histories have tended to neglect the contributions of the law and legal institutions.[3] This is regrettable. To date no one has attempted to understand the contribution made by the early law professors to thinking about Australian law and Australian legal thought more generally. Historian Michael Roe's pioneering studies of Jethro Brown, the first law professor at the University of Tasmania (later of the University of Adelaide) are exemplary and engage closely with the ideas of his subject and locate them within the broader context.[4] However, as Roe is largely concerned

[2] T Pietsch, *Empire of Scholars – Universities, Networks and the British Academic World 1850–1939* (Manchester, Manchester University Press, 2015) 4.

[3] M Lunney, *A History of Australian Tort Law 1901–1945: England's Obedient Servant?* (Cambridge, Cambridge University Press, 2018) 30.

[4] M Roe, 'Jethro Brown – The First Teacher of Law and History in the University of Tasmania' (1977) *University of Tasmania Law Review* 210; M Roe, *Nine Australian Progressives: Vitalism in Bourgeois Social Thought 1890–1960* (St Lucia, University of Queensland Press, 1984); M Roe 'William Jethro Brown' (Occasional Paper, Hobart, University of Tasmania, 27 April 1977).

with the broader intellectual milieu, his work does not speak to what other Australian law professors and lawyers of this early period were doing or thinking, or how Brown's thought related to it. In the absence of a thoroughgoing study of the scholarship and teaching practices of the first generation of Australian legal scholars, the conclusions drawn in this chapter about this early intellectual history are, necessarily, tentative.

Law Professors and the Case for University Legal Education

Existing accounts of Australian university legal education suggests that law was simply placed in universities and grew independently from anything the law professors thought or did. To put it another way, the content of the law curriculum, the style of teaching or the quality of Australian legal scholarship did very little to influence decisions about whether law should be taught at university in Australia and whether university studies in law should be a requirement for legal practice.

This is significant because it explains the first important difference between the Australian experience and the two legal traditions that most influenced early Australian legal education: those of England and the United States. Histories of English and American legal education posit that the ideas of law professors, and the role the professors established for themselves, played a significant part in the maintenance and growth of university legal education.[5] This suggests that the ideas of these law professors were significant to any understanding of university legal education and, in the case of the US, the ideas that shaped this relationship helped to elevate the status of law professors and law schools within the profession and society.

Australian universities and law schools are of very recent foundation in comparison to similar institutions globally. The University of Sydney was established in 1850, in the same year that convict transportation to the colony of New South Wales was abolished. It opened its doors just 62 years after the arrival of the First Fleet in 1788, and 27 years after the creation of a Supreme Court that replaced military tribunals. Next was the University of Melbourne in 1852, followed by the University of Adelaide in 1872, and the University of Tasmania in 1891. The University of Sydney began teaching law in 1855, but it did not establish a separate law school until 1890. Melbourne can claim the first proper law school (1857), followed by Adelaide (1883) and Tasmania (1893). After Federation

[5] See BA Kimball, *The Inception of Modern Professional Education – CC Langdell, 1826–1906* (Chapel Hill, University of North Carolina Press, 2009); D Sugarman, 'Legal Theory, the Common Law Mind and the Making of the Textbook Tradition' in W Twining (ed), *Legal Theory and Common Law* (Oxford, Blackwell, 1986) 26.

joined the former colonies together in the new Commonwealth of Australia in 1901, two more universities (with law schools) were established to serve the new Australian states: the University of Queensland began in 1909, with the law school founded in 1936; the University of Western Australia was established in 1913, with the law school opening over a decade later in 1927.

The decision to place law within Australia's first universities is largely in keeping with the reasons for establishing the universities. Put simply, Australian universities were created due to a desire to 'civilise' the colony. Writing of universities in the settler colonies, Pietsch explains that:

> They were not set up by British officials, as in India and later Africa, but rather by self-confident settler elites who saw them as both symbols and disseminators of European civilisation in the colonies. Providing a classical and liberal (and often religious) education, they were designed to cultivate both the morals and minds of the young men who would lead the economically successful colonial societies of the mid-nineteenth century.[6]

While their founders placed an emphasis on civilising and improving the moral credentials of colonial men, Australia's universities did not enlist religion. Instead, in an effort 'to avoid controversy in a colony riven with political and religious dispute',[7] the first three universities were secular, showing 'in part how *avant garde* they were: the idea of the secular university was still novel and somewhat contentious in Britain'.[8]

At both the universities of Melbourne and Sydney, the creation of law teaching and law schools formed part of broader suite of initiatives designed first to civilise Australian society and, second, to ensure the survival and growth of Australia's universities.

Sydney Law School

Linda Martin's investigation into the establishment of law teaching at Sydney Law School remains the most probing study of an Australian law school.[9] As noted earlier, law was first taught at Sydney in 1855, but a law school was not created until 1890. Martin's work investigates the reasons for this delay. She explains it was due to the attitude of judges and barristers, several of whom who were involved in university governance, who believed that the university would best serve the

[6] Pietsch (n 2) 5. See also H Forsyth, *A History of the Modern Australian University* (Sydney, NewSouth, 2014) 10.

[7] S Macintyre and RJW Selleck, *A Short History of the University of Melbourne* (Melbourne, Melbourne University Press, 2003) 7. See also Pietsch (n 2) 21.

[8] Forsyth (n 6) 12.

[9] L Martin, 'From Apprenticeship to Law School: A Social History of Legal Education in Nineteenth Century New South Wales' (1986) 9 *University of New South Wales Law Journal* 111.

profession by providing future barristers with an education in the classics.[10] In the absence of the Inns of Court or an aristocracy, a university degree would help barristers to distinguish themselves from the lower branches and provide grounds for their social as well as professional elevation. A 'vocational' legal education was something that the profession, not the university, would supply in the course of practice. This arrangement, which kept the university out of the profession's 'practical' affairs, meant that barristers and judges would remain the ultimate purveyors of legal knowledge.

This situation changed in the 1880s, following the appointment of William Montagu Manning as Vice Chancellor of the University of Sydney in 1878, and with the growing realisation that the University would continue to struggle unless it attracted greater student numbers.[11] Talk of an amalgamated profession with common standards, and the possibility of state intervention into the profession, also encouraged barristers to look more sympathetically towards establishing a law school as a way to maintain the existing professional hierarchy.[12] As Vice Chancellor, Manning envisaged a role for the University which was very different from that contemplated by the institution's founders. The classical and more liberal studies, which had previously been indispensable to education of a gentleman, were now regarded by Manning as 'better suited to a leisured class than to such a busy working world as ours'.[13] Several barristers objected to Manning's proposal; for example, George Knox argued that 'it was wrong to appeal to the public in this case, when the founders of the colony were not (as in America) puritans in search of utopia, but all Europe's surplussage, out for material gain'.[14] But Manning eventually got his way. In 1890, the law school was established and, despite a bumpy road – Manning at first received no assurance from the profession that the degree would be recognised as qualifying graduates for practice – it has remained a part of the Sydney landscape.

What is particularly important to note from Martin's intellectual history is that the first professor of law at Sydney law school, William Pitt Cobbett, was initially left out of decisions concerning the content of the curriculum, as well the appointment of barristers to his teaching staff. Instead, before his appointment, both matters were settled by the University's Senate, which included several barristers[15] and which took advice from English law professors (Frederick Pollock and John Westlake).[16] The failure to involve the new professor in matters so central to the school suggests that barristers and judges thought of themselves as the ruling class of both professional and academic law, subject (perhaps) only to the English. It also

[10] ibid 118–19.
[11] ibid 131.
[12] ibid 142.
[13] ibid 132.
[14] ibid 133.
[15] ibid 143.
[16] ibid 139.

speaks of the early subordination of law teachers. This impression is enhanced by the University's decision, following pressure from the profession, to move the law school away from the main campus and locate it in the central business district, among law offices.[17] This was done against Cobbett's wishes, who believed the law school's presence on the main university campus would help foster stronger relationships with the other disciplines.[18]

Melbourne Law School

The motivations and interests sitting behind the establishment of Melbourne's Law School have received less scrutiny than those at Sydney. This may be because the explanation is not as controversial, as the movement of professional legal training into the university was largely consensual. The movement occurred at a much earlier time than at Sydney: 'Law appeared as a certificate course of articled clerks in 1858; a Bachelor of Laws was first offered in 1861'.[19] John Waugh, who has written the most substantial institutional history of Melbourne Law School, explains that Redmond Barry's position as both justice of the Supreme Court of Victoria and Chancellor of the University in the 1850s meant that he was able to bring about the reform of admission rules so that they recognised a period of legal study at university.[20] The profession was largely supportive of the move and no one forcefully argued, at least at this early juncture, that professional legal education ought to be left in the hands of the profession or professional bodies. Waugh explains that

> University training … served the profession's own purposes, by taking up the recommendations for systematic legal education circulating in Britain and responding to concerns about the poor quality of Melbourne's gold-era lawyers. The new admission rules were in place before the start of the first term, 1857, and exempted successful students at the university from the Supreme Court's law exams. They created a fundamental difference in law teaching between the universities of Melbourne and Sydney that lasted until the 1890s.[21]

Waugh's commentary implies that the need to maintain, or promote, strong standards was felt with even greater urgency in Melbourne than in Sydney. He explains that throughout the 1850s and 1860s, the

> population had been increasing so rapidly, and the threats to the social order were so patent to old colonists such as …. [the then] chief justice, Sir William à Beckett,

[17] ibid 143; JM Bennett, 'Out of Nothing – Professor Pitt Cobbett 1890–1909' in J Mackinolty and J Mackinolty (eds), *A Century Down Town – Sydney University Law School's First Hundred Years* (Sydney, Sydney University Law School, 1991) 57.
[18] ibid 39.
[19] Macintyre and Selleck (n 7) 4.
[20] J Waugh, *First Principles* (Melbourne, Miegunyah Press, 2007) 7.
[21] ibid 7.

> that legal standards must have seemed to need defending against erosion by a long tail of less able barristers who lacked the skill and professional acculturation of their better-known colleagues (the early lecturers among them).[22]

Those governing the University of Melbourne realised much earlier than their counterparts in Sydney that the University's survival depended on professional degrees in law (and medicine) that would be recognised as requirements for practice.[23] Like Beckett and Barry, William Stawell (who succeeded Beckett as Chief Justice in 1857) was a strong supporter of university legal education.[24] According to Waugh, the requirement in 1872 that all barristers graduate with a full bachelor of laws degree,[25] and the fact that there were no other competing bodies, secured the early success of Melbourne's Law School.[26]

Waugh identifies the Faculty, University Council, University Senate and judges of the Supreme Court as having had some influence on the form of the law degree, with judges holding control over admission to practice since 1852.[27] Nonetheless, the first law teachers at Melbourne appeared to have some autonomy over what was taught; for example, what books and theories were deployed, and methods of instruction. The very first reader, Richard Clarke Sewell, proved to have little talent for teaching and did not last for very long in the role.[28] Sewell's successor, Henry Chapman, was a more successful teacher and his interests were a little broader, though less scholarly, than Sewell's.[29] Despite their autonomy, there is little to suggest that the academic agendas and teaching of either man influenced the profession's receptiveness to university legal education during this early period. What mattered to the leaders of the profession was that the university offered a degree in law and that the existence of the degree meant that more stringent requirements were placed on those wanting to enter practice, especially the barristers. The academic agendas pursued by Sewell and Chapman were largely irrelevant to the support of barristers and judges for university legal education. The fact that their ideas were of relatively little importance suggests that they were subordinated in a similar manner to their Sydney counterparts. The warmer reception in Melbourne to university legal education perhaps made it easier for the early law professors to carve out a stronger role for themselves and the future legal academy and provided them with a clearer sense of direction. However, their legal expertise and teaching abilities were not held in any special reverence and they were cast as 'doers' rather than creators.

The experience at both Sydney and Melbourne suggests that establishing Australian university legal education, at least in the most prominent early law

[22] ibid 18; see also Macintyre and Selleck (n 7) 3.
[23] ibid 7.
[24] Waugh (n 20) 24.
[25] ibid 23.
[26] ibid 24–25.
[27] ibid 85.
[28] ibid 14.
[29] ibid 26.

schools in the two largest cities, had more to do with ensuring the university's survival and notions of elevating the profession than with the quality of the ideas or practices of law professors. This subordinated both the law professors and university legal knowledge to the operational needs of the fledgling institutions and the aspirations of a hierarchical profession.

Tradition and Change – Founding an Australian Intellectual Tradition

English Ties

While the first law professors played little role in the early establishment of law schools – and, in some instances, university boards dictated the subjects first taught – in time, Australia's law professors gained greater control over the way that law was taught and had greater say in the content of the curriculum.[30] Speaking of Melbourne Law School in the 1930s, Macintyre and Selleck note that as 'most of these men [the professors] ran their departments with absolute authority, decision-making at the university level was inseparable from the personalities of those who made them'.[31] The early law professors and readers were learned men, with liberal educations and qualifications from British universities. As Pietsch explains in the context of settler universities, the 'informal connections that underpinned academic appointments were forged by cultures of academic sociability that were not only raced, but gendered and classed as well'.[32] The first Australian legal scholar to be born and educated in a country other than Australia or Britain was Wolfgang Friedmann, appointed as the Professor of Public Law at the University of Melbourne in 1947, leaving three years later in 1950.[33] In 1941, the appointment of Julius Stone, a Jewish man from England, to the chair of jurisprudence and international law brought to the surface a strong strain of anti-Semitism which was seen in not only some of Sydney's leading lawyers,[34] but also the new Dean of the Law School, New Zealander James Williams.[35] None of the early law professors were Aboriginal or Torres Strait Islander people.

[30] There is, however, some evidence of meddling; for example, the University Council at Melbourne rejected Edward Jenks' proposal to remove international law from the curriculum. Waugh (n 20) 52–57.

[31] Macintyre and Selleck (n 7) 91.

[32] Pietsch (n 2) 79.

[33] For an explanation of Friedmann's contribution to Australian legal scholarship, see M Lunney, 'Legal Emigrés and the Development of Australian Tort Law' (2012) 36 *Melbourne University Law Review* 494.

[34] L Starr, *Julius Stone – An Intellectual Life* (Oxford, Oxford University Press, 1992) 59–64.

[35] ibid 65.

The need to build student numbers and attract more funding led to the admission of women to Australian universities taking place earlier than in Britain. Nonetheless, women did not enter Australian universities in significant numbers until the second half of the twentieth century.[36] During the first 100 years of university legal education, no woman was appointed to teach law and there were very few women students. In 1902, Ada Evans became the first woman to graduate from an Australian law school;[37] in 1957, Rosemary Norris was the first woman appointed to a full-time academic position in an Australian law school.[38] Women who attended law school found it to be a largely inhospitable environment.[39] Law schools were most obviously places intended for the male children of Australia's elite, along with a growing body of male students from other class backgrounds.[40]

English political and legal ties, and the University Council's deference to the English law professors, would suggest that Australian university legal education followed English models. This is a matter worthy of further scrutiny. In the context of tort law, Lunney has made a compelling case that, between 1901 and 1945, Australian innovations were masked and have been misunderstood due to a failure to recognise 'that Australian lawyers were part of a wider community that saw British race patriotism as core to its identity'.[41] He explains that, 'Australian lawyers of the period were not interested in setting up their own independent legal rules or system. They saw themselves as part of a wider entity, the British race'.[42] This patriotism, he argues consistently with historical studies beyond law, did not involve a subservience to English law and practices, but rather included a nationalistic urge to improve upon English practices.[43] Australian lawyers innovated and departed from English law and practice in some areas.[44] However, rather than seeing these deviations as points of distinction, they thought of them as improvements on a larger tradition: 'What to a later generation of lawyers and academics might appear as an independent Australian legal development might be seen as a mere gloss on the law of the mother country a half-century before'.[45]

Lunney finds evidence of British race patriotism in the activities and beliefs of several of the early law professors: Sydney law professor and Dean, John

[36] Forsyth (n 6) 10–11; Pietsch (n 2) 5, 28.

[37] B McPaul, 'A Woman Pioneer' (1948) 20 *Australian Law Journal* 1, 1–2. See also H Kerwin and K Rubenstein, 'Law' in *Australian Encyclopaedia of Women and Leadership in Twentieth Century Australia* (Carlton, Victoria, Australian Women's Archive Project, 2014), www.womenaustralia.info/leaders/biogs/WLE0624b.htm.

[38] Waugh (n 20) 164.

[39] Pietsch (n 2) 80–81.

[40] Forsyth (n 6) 14–15. Pietsch explains that educational historians are divided on just how elitist Australian universities were: Pietsch (n 2) 10.

[41] Lunney (n 3) 7–8.

[42] ibid 8–9. See also Pietsch (n 2) 1.

[43] ibid 18.

[44] ibid 279.

[45] ibid 14.

Peden; Dean of Melbourne law school, William Harrison Moore; law professor at Melbourne Law School, Kenneth Bailey; and law professor at the University of Tasmania, and then Adelaide, Jethro Brown.[46] These early law professors were part of the network of academics created between Britain and the settler world. They were educated in England, knew and corresponded with English law professors, and were well apprised of the English ideas. However, they also displayed a strong independent spirit that was based on their desire to do good within their local contexts.

If Lunney's thesis holds true (as seems likely), it suggests that, even if the early professors developed theories of law and models of legal education that were significantly different from the English versions, they would not have presented them as pioneering developments. They would certainly not have presented them as the beginnings of a distinctively Australian tradition of legal education and scholarship. It is therefore necessary to carefully scrutinise the differences between Australian and English practice with these attitudes in mind.

The English Ledge

To understand how Australia's intellectual tradition might have been different from that of England, it is first necessary to provide an outline of the English traditions. In a seminal piece on the classical English jurists of the late nineteenth and early twentieth century, David Sugarman explains how the central normative assumptions and expertise of the early law professors were manifested in the legal textbooks they created. He argues that the foundations of modern English legal education were forged during an exceptional moment in English law; a time when the English forms of action were dismantled and equity and law were fused.[47] The English classical jurists responded by creating textbooks that 'unearthed' and organised the principles within a set of common law categories that they identified: from chaos, they created order. According to the jurists, they 'merely divined and distilled the best practice or principles of the law, especially those enunciated by "the great judges", past and present'.[48] But to others, such as the father of constitutional history, AV Dicey, the textbooks had a revolutionary legislative element.[49] Through the exposition of rules and principles, the classical jurists constructed new codes.

A central component of Sugarman's thesis is that the jurists' cataloguing and organising exercises were completed with an awareness of the interests of the practising profession – as well as the low esteem in which the profession held

[46] Lunney (n 3) 23–26.
[47] Sugarman (n 5) 32–33.
[48] ibid 36.
[49] ibid 32.

academic law. For the enterprise to succeed, the jurists needed to convince both the profession and the universities of the value of university legal education. To achieve this, they needed to embody a 'competency that was both useful to the aristocracy of the profession' and was of '[sufficient] scholarly merit'.[50] As such, the creation of the textbook tradition was as much a product of a 'social contract' as it was an intellectual exercise.[51] Through this exercise, jurists created for themselves what Sugarman describes as a narrow 'ledge' of expertise which set them apart from what would become the more lawyerly tasks of marshalling facts and considering the application of law to those facts.[52] This 'ledge' meant that the jurists did not threaten the status of judges and barristers as the supreme legal knowers.

This ledge consisted almost exclusively of the study of superior court decision-making and in showing the uniformity and consistency within the supreme body of the common law.[53] These concerns led the law professors to believe that statute law was an inferior mode of governance and that its growth ought to be opposed.[54] The ideas of jurists such as Jeremy Bentham, who enthusiastically embraced the growth of statutes, were rejected.[55] Further, they focused largely on private, as opposed to public law: 'According to Dicey's influential denunciation, administrative law was a French aberration that smacked of "collectivism". It was unknown to the common law, and contradictory to the common law'.[56] This had a number of important implications, including that, while the jurists' textbooks provided new expressions of principle and thereby served as code-like authorities, they did not contain any material which might be used to scrutinise the nature of lawyering or the legal profession.[57] The textbook tradition therefore played to the legal elite's interest in maintaining 'the status quo – economic, political, cultural and, above all, professional'.[58] It legitimised and upheld existing frameworks and tended 'to marginalize those forms of legal education and thought which sought to transcend the conception of law as an autonomous body of rules'.[59]

Australian Exceptionalism?

The most obvious difference between the classical English jurists and the early Australian scholars is that the latter did not attempt to create a textbook tradition.

[50] D Sugarman, 'A Special Relationship? American Influences on English Legal Education, c 1870–1965' (2011) 18 *International Journal of the Legal Profession* 7, 10.
[51] Sugarman (n 5) 45.
[52] ibid 33–36.
[53] ibid 34–35.
[54] ibid 34–35.
[55] ibid 35.
[56] Sugarman (n 50) 11.
[57] Sugarman (n 5) 42.
[58] Sugarman (n 50) 13.
[59] Sugarman (n 5) 33.

A tradition of Australian law book writing was not established until the 1960s. The idea of an organic and 'universal' common law[60] encouraged the view that English textbooks would largely be sufficient for Australia's purposes. The fact that legal education was instigated by, and its growth was due largely to the efforts of, barristers and judges meant that the law professors were not pressured to make a case for university legal education through their scholarship in the same way as their English counterparts. As there were so few law Australian professors – and all of them were burdened with heavy teaching commitments as well as responsibilities beyond the university – there was little opportunity to create Australian textbooks. Small student numbers also suggested that textbooks would not be viable. For these reasons, the early Australian law professors depended on English law books, and any ambitions they might have had to assume a expository mantle similar to that of their English counterparts were quelled.

Another difference between the classical English jurists and the early Australian scholars concerns the role of public law. Sugarman suggests that, although the English classical legal scholars were extremely active in assisting Parliament, they were 'in denial about their lawyer-statesman role' and 'strenuously resisted university legal education or indeed any formal instruction in the policy bases of the common law and legislation'.[61] By contrast, the Australian law professors strongly embraced this field of study. At Melbourne, they created a professorship in Public Law,[62] and some of the strongest scholarly contributions made by this early group was in this field. The absence of English books on public law meant that colonial writing on the subject would not challenge the authority of English jurists or their notion of a coherent, unified common law. The decade leading up to the creation of the Commonwealth of Australia gave law professors something concrete and monumental to consider in their studies, and they provided guidance to the founders of the Constitution.[63]

Unlike private law, public law was a field where Australia's law professors, and judges, were compelled to note the novelty of Australian law.[64] At Melbourne Law School, the majority of full-time law professors during the period 1857 to 1950 developed strong reputations as public lawyers. While some, such as William Hearn, were fiercely loyal to Britain's system of law and governance,[65] all were required to contemplate Australia's peculiarities and tailor their prescriptions and commentary to meet their local predicament and challenges. This interest in public law also brought with it an interest in legislation that sat uneasily with the commitments of the English jurists. For example, Wilfrid Prest notes that Hearn

[60] See Lunney (n 3) 2.
[61] Sugarman (n 50) 12.
[62] Waugh (n 20) 111.
[63] See, eg, Roe's explanation of Jethro Brown's contributions: see n 4 above.
[64] Lunney (n 3) 11.
[65] Waugh (n 20) 33.

'was a committed Utilitarian, whose ultimately unsuccessful efforts to codify the laws of Victoria owed a large debt to Jeremy Bentham and Bentham's jurisprudential disciple John Austin'.[66]

Pitt Cobbett, the first professor at Sydney's law school, was also devoted to matters of public and constitutional law, although his central focus was international law where, through the textbook *Leading Cases*, he hoped to make a case that the field did, in fact, reveal a strong body of law.[67] Archibald Hamilton Charteris, appointed the first Challis Professor of International Law and Jurisprudence at Sydney in 1920, enjoyed a considerable reputation in the field of international law, and also considered matters of governance.[68] His colleague John Peden, a technical black letter scholar, also taught in constitutional law.[69] Jethro Brown, first a professor at the University of Tasmania and then Adelaide, was keenly interested in matters of governance.[70]

A further difference between the Australian and English experience, often mentioned in the literature, concerns the extent to which Australian early law professors were attracted to US models and ideas. Commentators suggest that some of the early law professors followed US trends in preference to English traditions. It is important, however, to treat signs of this early enthusiasm for American legal education with some caution and to question whether the adoption of some US ideas actually constituted a departure from aspects of the English model, which was also evolving.

Sugarman has made a strong case that it is wrong to think of the English and US models as offering clear alternatives. He argues that, between 1870 to 1914, an 'atmosphere of friendship' and 'informal community' was created between the elite jurists from both countries.[71] Significantly, a 'mutual respect' existed between the 'four pillars of this brotherhood': American jurists Christopher Columbus Langdell and Oliver Wendell Holmes, and English legal scholars James Bryce and Frederick Pollock.[72] All four shared a commitment to liberal science which was embodied in the textbook tradition.[73] Moreover, some English law professors strongly approved

[66] W Prest, 'Antipodean Blackstone: The *Commentaries* 'Down Under' (2003) 6 *Flinders Journal of Law Reform* 151, 162.

[67] Bennett (n 17) 53. Pitt Cobbett also published books entitled *Peace* (1909) and *War and Neutrality* (1913), along with articles on Australian constitutional law. FC Hutley, 'Cobbett, William Pitt (1853–1919)' in *Australian Dictionary of Biography* (Melbourne, Melbourne University Press, 2012) vol 8, adb.anu.edu.au/biography/cobbett-william-pitt-5699.

[68] T Bavin, *The Jubilee Book of the Law School of the University of Sydney 1890–1940* (Sydney, University of Sydney 1940) 40–41. J Mackinolty, 'Learned Practitioners – Professor John Peden 1910–41' in Mackinolty and Mackinolty (eds), *A Century Down Town – Sydney University Law School's First Hundred Years* (Sydney, Sydney University Law School, 1991) 57, 77.

[69] Mackinolty (n 68).

[70] See n 4 above.

[71] Sugarman (n 50) 9.

[72] ibid 9.

[73] ibid 9–10.

of the challenges made to this orthodoxy by the American sociological jurists and the American legal realists in the early 1900s.[74] These similarities between England and the US, and the English interest in American ideas, suggest that Australian enthusiasms for American legal education were consistent with, rather than divergent from, English attitudes.

The first two Australian law professors to visit US law schools, Brown from Adelaide and Moore from Melbourne, were greatly impressed with the Americans' richly resourced campuses and libraries, as well as the dynamic case and Socratic teaching methods.[75] They envied the seemingly strong relationship between the elite law schools and the profession.[76] These were all qualities that the English discipline lacked. However, reading their assessments in context reveals that their admiration did not constitute an abandonment of the English notion that a gentlemanly education required students to learn something more than how to handle cases.

Brown, for example, critiqued the American law schools for not going far enough in their teaching of history and theory. He said:

> I cannot help feeling that the theoretic subjects deserve more attention than they receive in America … There is a real danger … that the devotion of three years to the exclusively practical side of law may effect an undue separation between general culture and the special subject to which [a law student] is to devote his life.[77]

Brown was clearly influenced by the English paradigm, with its emphasis on culture cultivated through studies of the classics. English luminaries Frederic William Maitland and James Bryce and American judge and scholar Oliver Wendell Holmes were important mentors.[78] Brown was also influenced by German jurists, such as Rudoph Von Jhering, whose scholarship complemented, rather than challenged, the English liberal science tradition.[79] Brown's close association with Maitland (a 'friend' and 'patron' to Brown[80]) and his strong advocacy for history suggests that he was attempting to found an Australian tradition that was, perhaps, richer than the overarching English liberal science paradigm.

Moore, the second Australian law professor to tour the United States, also criticised the Americans for placing too great an emphasis on the study of cases. He argued that the practice 'tends to exaggerate the logical side of the law, to consider it too exclusively on its formal side, to over-emphasise the consistency and harmony of law'.[81] His critique was based more on sociology than the classical thought upon which Brown relied. Moore feared that the emphasis on cases would encourage

[74] ibid 25.
[75] W Harrison Moore, 'Legal Education in the United States' (1913) 13 *Journal of the Society of Comparative Legislation* 207; J Brown, 'The American Law School' (1905) 21 *Law Quarterly Review* 69.
[76] Moore, ibid; Brown, ibid.
[77] Brown (n 75) 77–78.
[78] Roe, 'William Jethro Brown' (n 4) 17.
[79] ibid 17; Sugarman (n 50) 46.
[80] ibid 3.
[81] Moore (n 75) 211.

students to see law as 'less and less an instrument for accomplishing present social ends, and more an institution to the needs of which social ends themselves must be adapted'.[82] This sentiment suggests that he believed Australian students should be taught to think more critically about law, and that to do so they needed to study materials and subjects beyond the law itself.

Moore is one of several early Melbourne law professors to voice support for sociological approaches to law. Kenneth Bailey, appointed Professor of Jurisprudence in 1927 and later Dean and Professor of Public Law, is noted for saying that 'Law was best studied as one of the social sciences against a social science background'.[83] Despite this sentiment, there are few signs that Melbourne's curriculum took on a strong sociological component. The Melbourne professors' interests in public law no doubt enhanced the attraction of sociological jurisprudence and the thinking of the American Legal Jurists, permitting them to acknowledge the creative and progressive element of this aspect of Australian law and that it ought to be studied alongside of politics. However, there is little to suggest that these interests diminished their support of England's legal systems and the prevailing order. Australia's leading jurisprudential scholar before the 1950s, George Paton, displayed a strong curiosity in American Legal Realism but also a healthy scepticism that led him to reject its more radical components: Paton found it useful only insofar as it encouraged recognition of the discretionary elements within judicial decision-making.[84]

Jethro Brown's biographer, Michael Roe, argues that he, too, was heavily influenced by the sociological jurisprudence associated with Roscoe Pound and that, 'if Brown has to bear a label, it must be as a sympathizer with the American realists'.[85] However, American Realism is a broad church, and some of the classical English legal scholars were also attracted to Holmes and Pound's conception of law, so Brown and Moore's preferences do not necessarily indicate that they departed from English moulds. Instead, consistent with Lunney's thesis, the pair appeared to be proposing ways to improve the common law model that England shared with the US and Australia. Nonetheless, the absence of a textbook tradition, the law professors' strong interest in public law, and at times strong support for American Legal Realism, sociological jurisprudence and Maitland's brand of legal history, suggests that the intellectual foundations of Australia's discipline of law differed from those prevailing in England.

Freedom to Innovate

Whether these differences resulted in a distinctive Australian tradition of legal education is complicated by the absence of a strong body of Australian legal

[82] ibid.
[83] Waugh (n 20) 110.
[84] This is considered further in the chapters on Geoffrey Sawer.
[85] Roe, 'William Jethro Brown' (n 4) 15.

scholarship, the small number of full-time legal academics, and sentiments of British race patriotism. What can be said, however, is that the early lone law professors left their successors, the post-1950s generation of Australian legal scholars, with a sense of freedom to innovate that was perhaps greater than their English and American contemporaries enjoyed. The absence of Australian textbooks meant that these subsequent generations were presented with little in the way of a printed record that prescribed how law was to be taught in Australia. The absence also suggested that these law professors had invested less intellectual capital than their English and American counterparts in a particular pedagogy or dominant concept of law. Creating new and different practices and traditions would not require them to abandon or reject the products of their predecessors' substantial intellectual labour.

In other words, the absence of strong local models and traditions meant that Australian law professors did not create the same strictures for the discipline as did the early English law dons or Langdell. By the middle of the twentieth century, the discipline had not become as bounded as either of the foreign law disciplines from which the Australian law professors took inspiration. In theory at least, this meant that as loyalties to empire diminished in the second half of the twentieth century, Australian law schools had the opportunity to develop their curriculum in more egalitarian ways and to expand the scope of disciplinary knowledge so that their graduates had a strong foundation of knowledge from which to question existing professional practices and engage in law reform.

The Status of Academic Law

In the middle decades of the twentieth century, Australian law schools had yet to obtain commanding positions within Australian society or the legal profession. While several of the individual law professors were greatly accomplished and admired by the profession, their personal esteem did not translate to the law schools. In one sense, this is surprising. Leaders of the legal profession generally agreed that strong leadership was needed to reform the profession and elevate it within society.[86] The absence of an Inns of Court, and the difficulties associated with establishing professional societies,[87] placed the university in a strong position to lead and promote greater cooperation, in the place of competition, between Australian lawyers. This encouraged the profession to recognise law degrees as a means to qualify for practice at a much faster pace than in England.[88] In the

[86] See 'First Conference of Australian Legal Societies' (1933) *Australian Law Journal* 14; 'Law Council of Australia – Legal Convention' (1935) 9 ALJ 245; 'An Australian Law Association' (1927) *Australian Law Journal* 184.

[87] R McQueen, 'Together We Fall, Divided We Stand: The Victorian Legal Profession in Crisis 1890–1940' in WW Pue and D Sugarman (eds), *Lawyers and Vampires: Cultural Histories of the Legal Profession* (Oxford, Hart Publishing, 2003) 293.

[88] Sugarman (n 50) 15.

US, similar circumstances helped law schools and law professors make extremely successful cases for university legal education, which, in time, would allow them to occupy exulted positions within the profession and society.[89]

For several reasons Australia's law schools remained of marginal importance during the mid-twentieth century. As we have already seen, the ongoing existence of law schools did not result from a sense that the particular ideas and endeavours of law professors were of great benefit to the legal profession. Instead, it was based on vague notions of what a generic university legal education, similar to that in England, might achieve. The law professors were freed from the pressure of creating an Australian textbook tradition but this also removed an early opportunity for the professors to prove their worth.

The third reason has also already been touched upon. Unlike in the United States, Australia's legal profession was led by an elite class of judges and lawyers. As noted earlier, particularly in relation to Sydney, these leaders were instrumental in establishing the law schools, and an implicit understanding existed that the creation of university law schools would not erode position of the legal elite as possessors of the most authoritative legal knowledge. The inclusion of barristers as part-time teachers within Australia's law schools further entrenched this notion. This hierarchy subordinated the law schools. By contrast, the US legal profession did not possess an upper branch.

Fourth, with the exception of the elite leaders of the profession and part-time practitioner–teachers, practising lawyers paid little attention to university law schools. Writing in the early twentieth century, Jethro Brown explained that the issue was not so much that Australian lawyers were hostile to university legal education; rather, they were apathetic. He considered that the success of US legal education was due, in part, to the strong relationship between law schools and the profession. By contrast, he noted, that in Australia the 'individual lawyers who are interested in the work of legal education are few indeed'.[90] The legal elite's emphasis on classical education and its superiority to legal studies further demoted university legal education. Brown deduced that, although Australian law schools were more practical in nature than the earlier English models, many Australian lawyers retained the English lawyer's prejudice against law schools.

The more significant reason Brown gave for the lack of interest in universities concerned what he described as 'the want of *esprit de corps* in the profession itself'.[91] Writing in 1908, he reasoned that:

> A profession which is divided against itself is not easily persuaded to take a corporate interest in anything. How then could it be expected to take such an interest in the training of those who are ambitious to have a share in its fees and rewards? An interest of this kind, especially if it is to be active and sustained, presupposes the high professional ideals, the jealous and affectionate regard for the dignity and responsibilities of

[89] ibid 16.
[90] WJ Brown, 'Law Schools and the Legal Profession' (1908) 6 *Commonwealth Law Review* 3, 10.
[91] ibid 10.

> one's calling, which can only accompany a highly developed sense of corporate unity. There have been times and places in the world when such a sense has been present among lawyers; but its realisation in Australia is a dream of the future rather than a reality of the present.[92]

There is little to suggest that the profession became more enthusiastic about university legal education during the first half of the twentieth century. In addition to the reasons Brown provides, many practitioners were generally underwhelmed by the quality of the education they had received, while the better students believed that they received greater benefit from activities and subjects outside the discipline of law. While some held the full-time law professors in high regard (including Brown and Moore), the part-time practitioner–teachers were generally considered to deliver dull and unhelpful lectures.[93] Such experiences discouraged the profession from throwing support behind law schools.

A further reason why Australian law schools did not reach exulted positions concerns the poor funding of universities. The early law professors did not have the resources to replicate the grand American law schools and capture the imagination of the profession. Australian universities simply could not afford to employ enough full-time teachers to innovate and create more Australian materials and resources, and the law libraries were largely inadequate for the needs of law students.

During their first 100 years, Australian law schools were of marginal importance to the profession and society. Law professors were not regarded as innovators, and law schools advanced independently of their ideas and endeavours. In short, a distinctive Australian law school model did not emerge. These findings suggest that legal scholars of Brett, Tay and Sawer's generation had a difficult task ahead, if they wished to elevate the discipline, and their ideas, to occupy a more commanding position within the profession. At the same time, this new generation of legal academics possessed greater freedom to innovate than their English and American counterparts. While the early law professors sought to entrench the liberal foundations of the discipline and uphold the common law as the path to individual freedom,[94] their interest in public law provoked new ways of thinking about how law ought to be conceptualised and studied.

A Period of Change: 1950–2000

Law Schools

From the 1950s, Australia's law schools grew: new law schools were established and universities became the dominant providers of legal education.[95] The creation

[92] ibid 10.
[93] Waugh (n 20) 130–31.
[94] Sugarman (n 5) 27.
[95] For an account of this development, see D Weisbrot, *Australian Lawyers* (Melbourne, Longman Cheshire, 1990) ch 5.

of new universities and new law schools, along with lower university entrance cut-off scores and Commonwealth Government funding for tertiary education,[96] led to a dramatic increase in the number of student places and the number of lawyers in Australian society. It has also meant that, in more recent years, many law graduates have sought employment outside traditional practice. Law graduates have become a distinctive and growing body of the Australian labour force, operating in a range of sectors. Not only have these changes brought about a new type of university graduate, but they have also created a new vocation: the professional university law teacher. Since the mid- to late-1950s, a new community of full-time legal academics has emerged, supplementing the handful of existing full-time teachers and replacing many of the practising lawyers who formerly taught at law schools on a part-time basis. This new community represents the birth – or at least the realisation – of modern Australian legal education. However, as with the earlier period, the drive behind the increase in student numbers and the number of law schools had very little to do with the agendas of this new wave of legal academics. Instead, it came from on the government's belief that lawyers were essential to nation building, and that universities would provide the ideal training ground. This impetus speaks of one of the most significant changes to universities and law schools over the second half of the twentieth century: government intervention.[97] It is important to appreciate the political philosophy, increasingly grounded in neo-liberalism, that this intervention has brought to universities[98] – as well as its relatively recent origins.

The birth of modern law schools can be divided into two parts. First, the transformation of the original law schools founded before the Second World War (Melbourne, Sydney, Adelaide, Tasmania, Western Australia and Queensland) from relatively small affairs (a small number of students taught by a small group of teachers) to much larger professionalised bodies. In this early period, we also find the creation of a Chair of Law in a body created as a Research School of Social Sciences (RSSS) at the Australian National University, providing yet another opportunity to change the conceptualisation of the university study of law.

The second phase of the birth of modern law schools saw the creation of new law schools in the 1960s and 1970s, fuelling the further expansion of university legal education. Five new law schools at relatively new universities were created during this time: Monash; the University of New South Wales; Macquarie; the Queensland Institute of Technology (now the Queensland University of Technology); and the New South Wales Institute of Technology (now the

[96] The funding was granted following recommendations made in the following reports: Committee on Australian Universities, Commonwealth of Australia, *Report* (1957) (the *Murray Report*); The Australian Universities Commission's Committee on the Future of Tertiary Education in Australia, Commonwealth of Australia, *Report* (1964) (the *Martin Report*.)

[97] See J Lancaster, *The Modernisation of Legal Education: A Critique of the Martin Bowen and Pearce Reports* (Sydney, Centre for Legal Education, 1993).

[98] M Thornton, *Privatising the Public University: The Case of Law* (Abingdon, Routledge, 2011) xii.

University of Technology, Sydney). A legal studies school was also created at La Trobe University in Melbourne. Despite only being presented with 10–20 years of a so-called 'orthodoxy' in Australian university legal education, many of these new law schools sought to distinguish their approaches from the older schools. Several of the schools were staffed by teachers from the older schools who treated their move as an opportunity for a fresh start. The large pool of funds given to several of these schools, relative to funding at existing institutions, brought with it further opportunities to realise some other ambitions for Australian legal education and, in some instances, to attempt to 'outdo' the existing law schools by attracting staff with the offer of more favourable working conditions.[99] The new law schools also meant that a larger pool of Australians could access legal education, increasing class, gender and ethnic diversity within the student and staff body – although this did not translate seamlessly to diversity within legal practice. Again, it was a period of change and re-creation, bringing with it the opportunity to develop new legal theories and to think again about what and how to write and teach.

This book is located within this second period, and is particularly concerned with the transformation of the old law schools and the creation of the RSSS in the 1950s and 1960s. All of the scholars studied here developed their academic agendas during this period. While Tay's career extended beyond the 1970s, she was based at one of the older law schools that were transformed. This is a study of some of the thought and endeavour that assisted with that transformation. In this book, I consider the intellectual framing and answering of the problems posed by large-scale university legal education. I am attracted to the pioneering spirit of this early generation who were presented with – in a sense – untapped opportunity. For the first time in Australia, legal scholars could devise initiatives that other career legal scholars could implement in a setting where students largely studied law on a full-time basis. They could develop classes and materials and advance scholarship befitting a large and ambitious discipline. To what extent did they capitalise on this opportunity? And to what extent did the profession and government curb their ambitions?[100]

Universities

Australian universities also changed dramatically during the second half of the twentieth century, and those changes are still being felt today. The greatest change

[99] This occurred when a second law school was created in Victoria: see P Yule and F Woodhouse, *Pericleans, Plumbers and Practitioners: The First Fifty Years of the Monash University Law School* (Melbourne, Monash University, 2015).

[100] David Barker provides an account of the various bodies that have sought to regulate law schools as well as the various inquiries and reports on Australian law schools: see D Barker, *A History of Australian Legal Education* (Sydney, Federation Press, 2017) 127–59, 161–70, 184–226.

concerns the role that universities play within Australian society and how they are valued. As noted earlier, during the first 100 years universities were small affairs with low student numbers and few full-time professors. They were valued initially as a means of civilising the colony and, in time, and in order to remain viable, they later took on the role as gatekeeper of professions such as law.[101] As Hannah Forsyth explains, in the decades following the Second World War

> six small state universities, educating less than 0.2 per cent of the nation, became 39 institutions enrolling more than one-quarter of high school graduates, a proportion that continues to increase and shows no sign of plateauing.[102]

It is clear that the changes to universities were not merely a matter of scale.

> A small elite institution is different to the mass system we see today, and represents a whole other philosophy of higher education. Take the idea of research, for instance. Before the Second World War, university academics focused their energy on scholarship (reading, understanding and maintaining 'mastery' of their field) and teaching or examining students. Only rarely – and then only in particular fields – did they conduct research. Later in the 20th century, scholarly leaders began to declare research central to the idea of the university, suggesting it was not a 'real' university without research.[103]

This book provides some insight into how the early and leading law professors anticipated and responded to these changes.

Forsyth warns against the frequent portrayal of academics as 'passive recipients' of governmental and other agendas who are 'acted *on*'.[104] She further argues that 'The great changes to the universities that followed the Second World War were a result of decisions made within institutions to position academia to best advantage. It was a grab for power'.[105] She urges her readers to consider the interests that sat behind the dramatic changes in legal education. With this in mind, this book considers whether Brett, Tay and Sawer served the interests of the law school, the university and the profession, and how well they anticipated and prepared the law school for these dramatic changes.

Conclusion

In one sense the first and second halves of the twentieth century appear to be worlds apart – foreign lands where universities and professors responded to very different priorities, philosophies and ideas. At the same time, law and legal culture have often been characterised as conservative in nature, with lawyers valuing tradition and certainty over radical change. The dual identity of many law

[101] Forsyth (n 6) 13.
[102] ibid 1–2.
[103] ibid 2.
[104] ibid 45.
[105] ibid.

professors – as a teacher and scholar of law and also as a qualified lawyer – points to tensions suggesting that the discipline may have great capacity to hold on to the interests, concerns and values of an earlier age, resisting broader university-wide (and Australia-wide) agendas. Further, the presence of many lawyers and law professors in university governance positions throughout the twentieth century might have also encouraged law professors to believe that they could dictate and control their own destinies to greater extent than their non-law colleagues. Legal academics are, and have always been, the primary conduits of the external agendas imposed on law schools, whether those agendas originate from universities, government or the profession. To understand the discipline and its history, we therefore need to understand how law professors, individually and collectively, navigated tradition and change within both the legal profession and universities. We need to take their ideas and practices seriously, on their own terms and in their own time. With the early intellectual history of the discipline firmly in mind, as well as the more recent changes, this book investigates the endeavours and ideas of three prominent, reflective and theoretically inclined law professors, who advanced their agendas during a transformative period for law schools and universities.

PART A

Peter Brett

3

Brett and the Americanisation of Australian Law Schools

Introduction

> I have not attempted to conceal from my colleagues that I think I learnt more from you than from anyone else who has ever taught me law.[1]

When it comes to American influences on Australian law teaching, emphasis is most often placed on the Case and Socratic methods associated with the initiatives put in place at Harvard by Christopher Columbus Langdell and others. In the 1950s and 1960s, there was much debate about these forms of instruction in Australian law schools and at conferences of the newly formed Australian Law Teachers Association. Most Australian scholars seemed more interested in the elite US system of legal education than in English models.[2] Discussions centred upon the merits of these forms of instruction, as opposed to more traditional didactic methods, and while the Case and Socratic methods were never wholly adopted in any of Australia's law schools, different manifestations of each were trialled by many; in time casebooks became a permanent fixture of the legal textbook market.[3] What has been considered far less is whether the anxieties and fundamental questions that drove US scholars such as Langdell to adopt and promote the Case and Socratic methods were also transferred to Australia. Did Australian legal scholars simply experiment with some of the American teaching methods, or, did they also adopt some of the theoretical innovations that lay behind major US educational reform?

[1] Peter Brett to Henry Hart, 2 May 1961, Henry Melvin Hart Papers, Harvard Law School Library, Historical and Special Collections.

[2] For empirical support for this point see S Bartie, 'A Full Day's Work – A Study of Australia's First Legal Scholarly Community' (2010) 29 *University of Queensland Law Journal* 67. Several other studies have demonstrated the increasing influence of US models over English models in various countries: see, eg, P Lahav, 'American Moment[s]: When, How, and Why Did Israeli Law Faculties Come to Resemble Elite US Law Schools?' (2009) 10 *Theoretical Inquiries in Law* 653; W Pue, 'British Empire Perspectives on the Case Method of Legal Education' in W Pue, *Lawyers' Empire* (Vancouver, UBC Press, 2017) 149; D Sugarman, 'A Special Relationship? American Influences on English Legal Education, c 1870–1965' (2011) 18 *International Journal of the Legal Profession* 7.

[3] See, eg, W Morison, 'Book Review: *Cases on Private International Law* by Morris' (1954) 85 *Sydney Law Review* 285; RW Baker, 'Book Review: *Cases on Constitutional and Administrative Law* by Peter Brett' (1962) 1 *University of Tasmania Law Review* 760.

As the extract of a letter from Peter Brett to Henry Hart which begins this chapter suggests, some American law professors had a considerable influence on members of the Australian legal academy. Brett was one of several Australian scholars to study at elite US law schools in the 1950s and 1960s, thanks largely to the relationship that Zelman Cowen, then Dean of Melbourne Law School, had established with the Dean of Harvard Law School, Erwin Griswold. Brett was different, however, from the other Australian scholars who travelled to the US in that he was the only Australian schooled in the leading US legal theory of the time: the Legal Process School. It is no exaggeration to say that Henry Hart fundamentally shaped the way Brett taught and studied law in Australia. Brett's scholarship and teaching sat firmly within the Legal Process mould.

Brett's admiration for Hart and his commitment to Legal Process ideas meant that of all the Australian scholars of the time he was perhaps in the best position to accomplish what has been identified as one of the central ambitions behind the American doctorate in law, the SJD (Doctor of Juridical Science). The SJD was offered to local and international students at the elite law schools with the aim of spreading legal norms both within and beyond the United States.[4] It contributed to the birth of modern American legal education by encouraging the idea that scholarship was important to law teaching.[5] It appears that Harvard advanced this so-called 'missionary' function of the SJD with particular zeal. Griswold was evangelical about the SJD, and the political environment supported his push to attract more foreign students and influence legal education on a global scale.[6] As Gail Hupper writes:

> The early post-war period witnessed an explosion of interest in international legal studies in US legal education. The reasons were in large part geopolitical, in that they reflected the United States' new role as a world power in a radically changed international order. Old empires were breaking up, and the paradigm that was taking its place was Communism vs The West. Meanwhile, the nuclear threat had raised the stakes of disorder or of letting the other side become too powerful. Part of the response to the new paradigm was to turn to law – as the only acceptable alternative to force, as a way of governing the new international organisations that were being created, as a means to promote economic development, and as an expression of Western ideas of human dignity.[7]

While Australian legal scholar Julius Stone had also completed a SJD at Harvard, his studies were in the 1930s and his major intellectual commitments are associated with a much earlier body of legal thought stemming from the Sociological School and American Legal Realism. As this book makes clear, the idea that Stone

[4] GJ Hupper, 'The Academic Doctorate in Law: A Vehicle for Legal Transplants' (2008) 58 *Journal of Legal Education* 413.

[5] ibid 429.

[6] GJ Hupper, 'Educational Ambivalence: The Rise of a Foreign-Student Doctorate in Law' (2015) 49 *New England Law Review* 319, 397–98.

[7] ibid 396.

was the only scholar in the first community of Australian legal scholars to bring American thinking to the Australian legal academy is a myth which persists in the literature on Australian legal education. Its resilience perhaps stems from the large number of reflections about legal education from Sydney law school alumni.

Brett was not only a model Legal Process student, but was also employed at what was then arguably Australia's most progressive law school. There, he was encouraged by a broad-minded Dean and ambitious colleagues, several of whom believed that, in time and with more resources, Melbourne could rival the leading US law schools.[8] Cowen was a 'great encourager of people'[9] and his leadership has been described as 'outstanding'.[10] Brett was also very well read and an extremely bright man. His experience in the Second World War, as a Jew fighting for England, drove his commitment to improving law in line with morality.

Letters between Griswold and members of the Melbourne Law School in the 1950s and 1960s suggest that Griswold was well aware of Melbourne's potential to lead the discipline in Australia. He hoped that such leadership would encourage the Australian academy to adopt the latest Harvard conceptions of law and legal education. And he was quick to dismiss any suggestion that Australians should look to other models. An article by Griswold, published in the *Western Australian Law Review* in 1953, provides strong evidence of these concerns.[11] Griswold used the article to criticise the state of Australian legal education, and singled out the Department of Law at the Australian National University, run by Geoffrey Sawer. Archival records suggest that Griswold was retaliating against Sawer's earlier published remarks about American Law Schools. Reporting on his tour of American law schools, Sawer had written that he was largely unimpressed by the American models and suggested that Harvard was not the best US law school.[12]

In light of Griswold's aspirations, it is little wonder that he stayed in touch with Brett throughout his career, took note of his scholarship and initiatives, sent him letters of encouragement, and arranged visiting postings for Brett in the US and Canada.[13] While he also corresponded with other Melbourne scholars, Brett represented perhaps Griswold's best chance to embed the central ideas and

[8] See, eg, P Ayres (ed), *David Derham: Talks on Universities, History and the Law* (Melbourne, Oryx Publishing, 2009) 21–43.

[9] Interview with Richard Fox (Law School, Monash University, 23 October 2013).

[10] P Yule and F Woodhouse, *Pericleans, Plumbers and Practitioners: The First Fifty Years of the Monash University Law School* (Melbourne, Monash University, 2015) 5.

[11] EN Griswold, 'Observations on Legal Education in Australia' (1953) 2 *University of Western Australia Law Review* 197.

[12] G Sawer, 'Legal Education in the United States' (1950) 1 *University of Western Australia Annual Law Review* 398.

[13] See, eg, Erwin Griswold to Peter Brett, 18 August 1966, Peter Brett Papers, National Library of Australia Manuscript Collection; Brett to Griswold, 3 March 1967, Peter Brett Papers, National Library of Australia Manuscript Collection.

motivations of Harvard's leading legal theorists within Australian law schools during the formative stages of Australia's legal academy.

In this and the following chapter, I consider whether this attempt to transplant the central ideas underpinning Harvard legal education to Australia was successful. Rather than leaving the reader in suspense, I will state my conclusion here: neither Australian law schools in general, nor the Melbourne law school in particular, went on to become mini Harvard law schools. Both the scholarship and teaching within Australian law schools was, and continues to be, distinctly different from both the US and English traditions. Moreover, Brett largely failed to persuade Australian legal scholars and law students to adopt Legal Process thinking. Despite his lack of success, examining Brett's attempts to bring Legal Process thinking to Australia is both interesting and worthwhile.

First, it helps us understand where the efforts of the elite US scholars to spread their ideas (as documented by US legal scholars and historians such as Hupper) ultimately led. Second, it provides an insight into the way that local and foreign conditions combine to create environments that are open to some ideas but resistant to others. Conditions in Australia, in particular the influence of High Court justice Sir Owen Dixon, meant that the Legal Process School potentially had a greater chance of success in shaping both the discipline and practice of law in Australia than it did in the US. However, because the broader Australian legal academy did not take up the philosophical foundations of the School, it was never embedded within Australian culture.

Third, Brett's experience lends weight to existing revisionist histories of the Legal Process School. Brett was the Professor of Jurisprudence at the University of Melbourne from 1964 until his death in 1975. Throughout this time his primary goal was to reform Australia's legal profession and laws in accordance with the tenets of the Legal Process School and, therefore, he continued with this mission long after Harvard's central proponents had left the academy. Brett's experience can provide new insights into the School and speaks of an international legacy that, until now, has been overlooked. My goal is not to make a case for reinstating the Legal Process School, but, rather, to acknowledge its role in the legal academy and legal education.

Finally, this investigation provides a sharper picture of the central ideas that informed the birth of modern Australian legal education. Unlike the picture in the US, few Australian studies have considered the normative premises that underlie the scholarship and teaching of legal scholars at various points in time. Generalisations have been made and studies of individual scholars have been conducted, but rarely do these studies consider what the whole of a leading scholar's body of work and endeavours says about the role and intellectual foundations of law schools. These chapters suggest that both Brett's work and reactions to it reveal some important insights into the foundation and growth of Australian university legal education. They argue that Dixonian strict legalism shaped the thinking of Australia's legal culture in unexpected ways, and that the idea of 'legal science' did not take hold in Australia's legal academy in the twentieth century.

Brett and the Melbourne Law School

Born in London on 4 September 1918, Brett spent the bulk of his academic career, a total of 20 years from 1955 to 1975, at the University of Melbourne. Securing the position at Melbourne was not easy. He first applied for a position in 1949 while still living in London, but lost out to Norval Morris.[14] Wolfgang Friedmann, the Professor of Public Law at Melbourne, interviewed both Brett and Morris during a trip to London.[15] At the age of 26, Morris was the younger applicant (Brett was then 31), and had only received second class honours to Brett's first. Unlike Brett, however, Morris, had postgraduate qualifications: an LLM from Melbourne and a PhD in law and criminology from the London School of Economics (LSE). Brett had qualified for law through a period of articles, begun at the age of 16, along with part-time legal studies at the University of London, which he completed in 1939 when he was 21. Morris's thesis had been published as a book entitled *The Habitual Criminal*,[16] which earned him the Hutchinson Silver Medal for Social Sciences at the LSE and was regarded highly by leading criminologists.[17] He therefore had a strong publication record, whereas Brett's record was non-existent at that time. Brett's break into Australian academia came a short time later, when he won a position at the University of Western Australia (UWA) as a Senior Lecturer in 1951. However, he had not forgotten about Melbourne. Perth gave him an opportunity to demonstrate his scholarly ability and begin plotting an academic agenda that would eventually take him east.

Moving to Perth with his wife Margaret and their baby son Robin was, by any measure, a considerable undertaking.[18] Margaret was originally from Melbourne but Brett had never been to Australia. Neither of them had inherited, or was supported by, family wealth. Perth in the 1950s was a small country town rather than a city. The culture shock of the move from London to Perth would have been considerable, although Brett's war experience and the dogged determination he displayed throughout his life suggest that he would not have been daunted by the strangeness of the place. Descriptions of him vary from brash and confident to intense and playful. Physically, he was 'short in stature' with 'greying curls and a mobile face, dominated by flashing eyes which were magnified by

[14] JF Foster to the Registrar of the University of Melbourne, 14 December 1949, and accompanying note entitled 'Summary of Applications for the Senior Lectureship in Law', University of Melbourne Registrar's Correspondence, University of Melbourne Archives.

[15] Note entitled 'Senior Lectureship in Law 1950', University of Melbourne Registrar's Correspondence, University of Melbourne Archives.

[16] N Morris, *The Habitual Criminal* (Harvard, Harvard University Press, 1951).

[17] See, eg, JB White, 'Book Review: *The Habitual Criminal* by Norval Morris' (1952) 52 *Columbia Law Review* 435.

[18] Brett was married twice, first to Doris Moses, whom he later divorced, and then to Margaret Stobo, an Australian nurse living in London. They had three sons together and adopted a daughter.

thick spectacles'.[19] Despite his adaptable personality, Brett still aspired to be part of the best Australian law school and live in a more substantial and civilised city. Melbourne, not Perth, fitted the bill.

While at UWA, fieldwork for his Masters thesis took Brett to Melbourne. These dealings gave those at the University of Melbourne an opportunity to learn more about Brett's capabilities, and gave him the chance to assess the faculty. Although UWA awarded the degree, Brett gave his greatest thanks to Norval Morris at Melbourne, with whom 'he had many valuable discussions of problems in the fields of criminology and penology'.[20] Such statements not only suggest that they shared similar interests, but also that there was no lingering bitterness over Morris's earlier appointment. Brett saw Morris as the brilliant criminologist that others later recognised him to be.[21] Writing to Cowen in 1954, Brett referred to the 'previous good relations' he had had with all members of the faculty.[22] These connections no doubt helped him secure a position at the School, as a Senior Lecturer, in 1955.

For 11 of the 20 years Brett spent at Melbourne, Cowen was Dean at the School. While Cowen was not part of Brett's close circle of friends and their intellectual interests did not overlap, correspondence between the two suggests they were generally on friendly terms.[23] Brett's flourishing career at Melbourne demonstrated Cowen's close interest in members of his faculty and the strong opportunities he afforded them to develop their intellectual interests and profile. For example, because of Cowen and the connections he had made as Australian Commonwealth Liaison Officer to the British Colonial Office, after just one year at Melbourne Brett was invited to travel to Borneo to review their land law and draft a land code. While the code was not adopted for political reasons,[24] the high

[19] L Waller, 'Brett, Peter (1918–1975)', *Australian Dictionary of Biography* (Canberra, National Centre of Biography, Australian National University, 1993), adb.anu.edu.au/biography/brett-peter-9577/text16875.

[20] P Brett, *The Penal System of Western Australia, A Critical Study* (Masters Thesis, University of Western Australia, 1953) ii.

[21] He was described as 'the most influential American criminologist of his time'. M Tonry, 'Norval Morris', *Guardian* (online), 9 April 2004, www.theguardian.com/news/2004/apr/09/guardianobituaries.prisonsandprobation.

[22] Peter Brett to Zelman Cowen, 11 December 1954, Law Dean's Correspondence 1953–1961, University of Melbourne Archives.

[23] In his history of the Melbourne Law School, Waugh suggests that in 1961 Brett blamed Cowen for 'failing to deliver promised support for his application' for the Chair of Commercial Law and that Cowen regarded it as 'the only bad *personal* time in my experience in the school'. Waugh explains that Brett took steps to mend the relationship, and it is clear from correspondence that the two remained on friendly terms and Cowen continued to support Brett's promotion: J Waugh, *First Principles – The Melbourne Law School 1857–2007* (Melbourne, Miegunyah Press, 2007) 158; Zelman Cowen to Harold Ford, 1 May 1964, Harold Arthur Ford Papers, University of Melbourne Archives.

[24] Z Cowen, *A Public Life – The Memoirs of Zelman Cowen* (Melbourne, Miegunyah Press, 2006) 201–02; Peter Brett to Zelman Cowen, 13 September 1957, Peter Brett, University of Melbourne Archives.

quality of Brett's work was recognised. Soon after, he was commissioned to draft a land code for the Solomon Islands, which was implemented.[25]

Cowen also took measures to ensure that his colleagues' teaching matched their scholarly interests. Cowen altered teaching arrangements so that Brett and his collaborator, Louis Waller, could teach criminal law in accordance with an ambitious plan the two had cooked up.[26] Cowen also allowed Brett to teach the subjects that held the greatest fascination for him.[27] Brett and Waller's collaboration led to the publication of an innovative criminal law textbook that established the reputations of both authors. And it was with Cowen's support that Brett was appointed to a professorship, the Hearn Professor of Law, in 1963.

Cowen played an important part in Brett's elevation, by giving him the freedom to develop his academic agenda as well as providing opportunities that played to Brett's strengths and interests. Cowen knew that Brett was a very bright man and got the best out of him.[28] Had Brett not travelled to Harvard at Cowen's instigation, had he not been encouraged to develop an innovative criminal law course, and had he not been allowed to work with a person who shared his interests and enthusiasm, it is unlikely that he would have turned as forcefully towards legal theory (a subject in which he had no prior learning) or advanced what might be described as one of the greatest Australian legal teaching initiatives of the twentieth century.[29]

By the beginning of 1956, the Melbourne Law School consisted of three professors, five senior lecturers and a full-time tutor.[30] Brett had chosen well when he sought out Melbourne. In the 1950s the faculty had created what was, on most accounts, Australia's greatest law school.[31] Other law schools did not fare so well. The law schools at UWA and the University of Sydney were both beset with political difficulties and did not possess the strong congenial atmosphere of Melbourne.[32] While Brett remained in contact with Frank Beasley, Dean of the Law School at UWA, there is evidence that Beasley at times made his life difficult and that this treatment was a factor in prompting Brett's move to Melbourne.[33] Similarly, the

[25] Cowen described Brett as 'One of the ablest and most versatile members of the faculty' and said that the work 'was done expertly and imaginatively': Cowen (n 24) 201–02.

[26] Interviews with Louis Waller (Law School, Monash University, 23 October 2013, 25 November 2013).

[27] Jurisprudence, Public Law 1 (Administrative Law) and Criminal Law.

[28] Cowen (n 24) 201–02.

[29] This initiative is described in the following chapter.

[30] Zelman Cowen to Peter Brett, 13 December 1954, Law Dean's Correspondence 1953–1961, University of Melbourne Archives.

[31] Allan Myers, a university medallist from Melbourne who went on to complete a Bachelor of Civil Law at Oxford, said that, 'This would be regarded as heresy by many but I actually thought the teaching I got at the University of Melbourne was on the whole better than the University of Oxford. … I thought that the courses were more comprehensive and the teachers were better teachers': Interview with Allan Myers (Office of Dunkeld Pastoral Co Pty Ltd, Melbourne, 10 June 2014).

[32] See chapters seven to eleven on Alice Erh-Soon Tay.

[33] Brett (n 22).

Law Faculty at the University of Queensland was a conservative institution that was heavily influenced by the profession.[34] In the late 1950s, at the University of Tasmania all members of the law school resigned in protest against the University's treatment of its academics.[35] The Faculty of Law at the University of Adelaide was faring better, but was not yet as large or ambitious as Melbourne.[36]

Brett had therefore arrived at a confident, collegial and well-run law school. Former Attorney-General, Foreign Minister and Chancellor of the Australian National University, Gareth Evans, was a law student at Melbourne in the 1960s. Evans suggests that 'it was probably the best Law School in the country. It had very good lecturers. It had a very vibrant deanship under Zelman Cowen. It was operating at a very high level, competent, classy'.[37] Barrister, entrepreneur and philanthropist, Allan Myers, also a student at that time, referred to it as a 'very fine place' and said that, as in the case of the University of Oxford, 'nothing which [was] second rate [was] passed off as first rate' and that there was 'a definite determination to maintain standards and try to be the best'.[38] In his history of the faculty, Waugh describes this generation of legal academics at Melbourne as 'founding the New Jerusalem'.[39] Dating back to Geoffrey Sawer's time in the 1940s, there was a sense that Melbourne could be as good, if not better, than the greatest law schools in the world.[40] This environment gave Brett the opportunity to dream big and make a strong contribution to the academic foundations of the discipline. He had come to the right place at the right time.

The Makings of a 'Liberal Humane Scholar'

In addition to the opportunities provided by the Law School at the University of Melbourne, Brett's other piece of good fortune was that his interests corresponded with the leading jurisprudential issues of the day. He was also inspired by the law professors who were responsible for the major American jurisprudential movement of the time, the Legal Process School. By travelling to Harvard in 1958 to

[34] See M White, 'History of the Garrick Chair at the TC Beirne School of Law' (2010) 29 *University of Queensland Law Journal* 335.

[35] R Davis, *100 Years – A Centenary History of the Faculty of Law University of Tasmania 1893–1993* (Hobart, University of Tasmania Law School, 1993) 49–52.

[36] See A Castles, A Ligertwood and P Kelly, *Law on North Terrace – 1883–1983* (Adelaide, University of Adelaide, 1983) 62–68; VA Edgeloe, 'The Adelaide Law School – 1883–1983' (1983–85) 9 *Adelaide Law Review* 1, 32–38; D Pearce, E Campbell and D Harding, *Australian Law Schools: A Discipline Assessment for the Commonwealth Tertiary Education Commission* (Canberra, Australian Government Publishing Service, 1987) vols 1–2.

[37] Interview with Gareth Evans (ANU House, Melbourne, 13 June 2014).

[38] Myers (n 31).

[39] Waugh (n 23) 143.

[40] See, eg, Ayres (n 8).

undertake an SJD, Brett came under the influence of three inspiring mentors and giants of American legal theory: Henry Hart,[41] Albert Sacks and Lon Fuller. It is important to recognise that Brett's experience was unique. While Cowen facilitated several other exchanges to America, Brett was the only Australian legal scholar of this era to take a strong interest in the work of Hart, Sacks and Fuller, and to adopt the agenda of the Legal Process School. It is also important to recognise that Brett's experience in America was critical to the contributions he later made in Australia.

What was it about Brett that led to his attraction to the Legal Process School? From even a casual review of Brett's career, two features stand out. First, there is his 'fascination with the interplay between law and morality'.[42] Every person interviewed for this study remarked on this,[43] and it is evident in both his teaching and scholarship. Second, there is his standing as a 'liberal humane scholar'.[44] Myers recalled that Brett 'was someone who was a humanist, who was tolerant of people, although he had clear standards. He didn't want to control people's lives although he did have a strong idea of what was right or wrong'.[45] Several aspects of Brett's background might explain these characteristics. Most obvious is his substantial involvement in the Second World War and close acquaintance with the many atrocities of that war. Brett served continuously in the army from the outbreak of the war until 1946, occupying a range of posts.[46] He was granted a commission as Second Lieutenant in the Royal Army Service Corps, serving in both England and France.[47] He also served with the 5th Auxiliary Group Nigeria Regiment in West Africa, Nigeria and Sierra Leone.[48] Brett also had 'sporadic experience as counsel, and as judge-advocate at military courts-martial' investigating 'illegal absences and desertions of conscript soldiers'.[49] He ultimately attained the substantive rank of Lieutenant and was discharged with the honorary rank of Captain.[50] At the end of the war, he served 'in Germany and Belgium, first at a Brigade Headquarters and then on the staff of a prisoner-of-war camp, until [he] was demobilised in March 1946'.[51] As a Jewish man, the Holocaust and widespread anti-Semitism of the time touched Brett personally. Because he possessed a strong

[41] Where no initials are provided, a reference to Hart should be interpreted to mean Henry Hart, not HLA Hart.
[42] Waller (n 26).
[43] eg, Myers said, 'He was always interested in what's right. He wanted to argue the rights and wrongs of things': Myers (n 31).
[44] Interview with Ian Leader-Elliot (Law School, University of South Australia, 10 February 2014); Myers (n 31).
[45] Myers (n 31).
[46] Peter Brett to the Registrar of the University of Melbourne, 3 September 1954, Law Dean's Correspondence 1953–1961, University of Melbourne Archives.
[47] ibid.
[48] ibid.
[49] ibid.
[50] ibid.
[51] ibid.

intellectual curiosity, his experience and the events of this time no doubt provoked deep questioning of both his own identity and broader concepts of morality and humanity.

Religion played a part in Brett's life in several ways and might also explain his fascination with these subjects. His Jewish background was of course a central component, but Brett's scholarship suggests that he was familiar with both the Old and New Testament.[52] At St Paul's Grammar School in London he would have had a religious education founded in Christian belief. In these ways, he was exposed to a range of different ideas about morality that might have challenged his identity.

By the time Brett arrived in Australia, he was no longer an observant Jew. Two of his sons, Robin and Jonathan, hold slightly different views on why this was so. According to Jonathan:

> He was brought up liberal Jewish in London and basically gave it away largely because he joined the British army. It wasn't a good thing to do to fight in the British army as a Jew, not if you had any chance of getting caught, and it meant nothing to him to be a Jew. I probably am saying things I shouldn't say but I think in hindsight he probably felt bad about having done that. Although I don't blame him at all.[53]

Robin considered that his father's reasons were mixed; that he did it partly to protect his children and partly because of his war experience and a sense that anti-Semitism would continue throughout the twentieth century.[54] As Robin explains, their mother, on the other hand 'was your absolutely classic middle-class Sydney WASP. Church of England. Went to church every Sunday, it's just what you did'.[55] Somewhat curiously, Brett never told his closest friend and colleague, Louis Waller, that he was Jewish. Waller, a practising Jew, only discovered that Brett was Jewish by accident, when he and another colleague, Mary Hiscock, called on Brett's brother, Jim, during a trip to England years into the pair's friendship.[56] Neither Robin nor Jonathan was taught anything about Judaism by their father. Jonathan says that his father had strong Jewish attributes but that he had learned to conceal them 'because he was petrified, as he had a right to be, because Jews didn't get a good time in the 1930s and 1940s'.[57] Why Brett never took up Judaism again (or any other religion) will probably never be known. Waller believes that Brett later became a Freemason because he saw it as a 'sort of spiritual anchor'.[58] One might, however, speculate that being born a Jew, later abandoning his faith, and

[52] The following book review demonstrates that Brett had a strong knowledge of the New Testament: P Brett, 'Book Review: *The Sanctity of Life and the Criminal Law* by Glanville Williams' (1958) 1 *Melbourne University Law Review* 556.

[53] Interview with Robin and Jonathan Brett (RACV Club, Melbourne, 11 June 2014).

[54] Email from Robin Brett to Susan Bartie, 13 October 2015.

[55] ibid.

[56] Waller (n 26).

[57] Jonathan Brett (n 53).

[58] Waller (n 26).

witnessing the terrible treatment of Jews, meant that he wrestled with the question of faith throughout his life and that this later infiltrated his teaching and scholarship. Brett's academic agenda suggests that scientism may have largely filled the void of spirituality.

The 1950s and 1960s were a time of great change, both within the law faculties and in broader Australian society. Brett was not the only one attracted to the interplay between law and morality, and it was not just the Second World War that had prompted such questioning. Common views of what was right and wrong were being debated in all kinds of circles. After decades of sexual repression, followed in the late 1950s and early 1960s by strong moves towards sexual liberation, questions about decency in art, literature and broader society were also fiercely debated. Brett contributed in various ways to these and other debates.[59]

In England, HLA Hart, who held the Chair of Jurisprudence at the University of Oxford, was coming to the fore as the leading jurisprudential scholar, as he re-injected law with a strong philosophical foundation inspired by the fashionable ordinary language philosophy of Wittgenstein, Ryle and others. HLA Hart's seminal work, *The Concept of Law*,[60] was not published until 1961; however, he already had found fame both in England and America through two widely publicised debates that formed the basis of much writing on jurisprudence throughout the second half of the twentieth century. First, there was HLA Hart's debate with English judge, Lord Devlin, over whether it was the function of law to intervene in matters of private sexual morality.[61] Second, there was his debate with Harvard Professor Lon Fuller over whether immoral laws, such as those of Nazi Germany, were in fact law.[62] On the other side of the Atlantic, the writings of Lon Fuller, Henry Hart and Albert Sacks, all of Harvard, formed the dominant American jurisprudential school.

Brett understood both the methods and motivations of all four of these great scholars and very much wanted to be a part of their tradition. Like them, he had lived through and participated in the events of the Second World War and was committed to making the most of the liberty that the allies had won. Like them, he was fascinated with matters of law and morality. Like them, he believed that being a legal academic was a serious vocation. And like them, he believed that

[59] Brett's contribution to these debates is acknowledged in GP Fletcher, 'The Fall and Rise of Criminal Theory' (1998) 1 *Buffalo Criminal Law Review* 275, 277.

[60] HLA Hart, *The Concept of Law* (Oxford, Oxford University Press, 1961).

[61] The debate began when Lord Devlin delivered the second Maccabaean Lecture in Jurisprudence at the British Academy in 1958. HLA Hart responded with various radio broadcasts and lectures in England and America. Many of the ideas raised during the debates were expanded upon in the following publications: P Devlin, *The Enforcement of Morals* (Oxford, Oxford University Press, 1965); HLA Hart, *Law Liberty and Morality* (Oxford, Oxford University Press, 1963).

[62] HLA Hart, 'Positivism and the Separation of Law and Morals' (1958) 71 *Harvard Law Review* 593; LL Fuller, 'Positivism and Fidelity to Law: A Reply to Professor Hart' (1958) 7 *Harvard Law Review* 630. For an excellent re-examination of the debates, see K Rundle, *Forms Liberate – Reclaiming the Jurisprudence of Lon L Fuller* (Oxford, Hart Publishing, 2012) 51–85.

jurisprudence ought to extend beyond examining the concept of law to both the critique of law and law reform.[63] Holding these views, it is therefore unsurprising that as a student at Harvard in 1959 Brett sought out the assistance of Fuller, Henry Hart and Albert Sacks, and drew from their work and that of HLA Hart in his SJD thesis.

It is important, however, to note that Brett was not overawed by Harvard and was not of a mind to try to get Melbourne to adopt the Harvard model of Legal Education. Brett's critical views of Harvard were made plain in a letter to his friend and colleague at Melbourne, Harold Ford:

> I am enjoying life here, but frankly I think that there is a lot to criticise. There is tremendous gulf between student and teacher which I think is appalling, and which no one seems even concerned to discuss, let alone remedy; there are some honourable exceptions. Even the Graduate School programme is not in any real sense organized. I really believe that we at Melbourne could teach them a lot as regards the art of human relations in conducting a law school. … I am also in some measure disappointed at the general quality of the faculty. There are lots of very good technical lawyers and 'gimmick' men, but comparatively few real scholars. This seems odd for a school which has the money and the reputation to buy up the finest legal scholars in the world. Anyway, I suppose each graduate finds that he gets his real learning from one or two members of the faculty who strike a chord with him. So far as I can forecast, I shall derive most from Hart and Fuller, and perhaps from Al Sacks.[64]

A Legal Process SJD

The immediate and most obvious result of Brett's time in America was the monograph he published from his SJD, entitled *An Inquiry into Criminal Guilt*.[65] One of the central arguments was that the purpose of *mens rea* is to distinguish people who are morally blameworthy ('guilty') from those who are not. According to Brett, the role of *mens rea* is to formulate those matters that exonerate a person from guilt. He challenged the prevailing view, adopted by leading criminal law scholar Glanville Williams and others, that the conditions of blameworthiness are formulated by an act directed by the mind. This, Brett believed, was to continue the myth of Cartesian dualism. Instead, he argued that the law should adopt the position of leading Oxford philosopher, Gilbert Ryle. In *The Concept of Mind* (1949),[66]

[63] Lacey explains that this was an aspect of Hart's agenda: N Lacey, *A Life of HLA Hart – The Nightmare and the Noble Dream* (Oxford, Oxford University Press, 2004) 256.

[64] Handwritten letter from Brett to Harold Ford, 26 October 1958, Harold Arthur Ford Papers, University of Melbourne Archives.

[65] ibid.

[66] G Ryle, *The Concept of Mind* (London, Hutchinson University Library, 1949).

Ryle had rejected what he called 'the ghost in the machine', arguing that bodily and mental processes are really part of the one underlying phenomenon.[67] Brett reasoned that this meant it was impossible to formulate conditions of blameworthiness in advance.[68] It was, therefore, impossible to define the contents of *mens rea* precisely.

Brett also invoked Wittgenstein's notion that the meaning of a word can only be understood 'by seeing how the word is used in practice' and that words 'do not bear a constant meaning, but rather a series of different meanings, each apt for a particular purpose, and linked together only by a "family resemblance"'.[69] Brett applied this reasoning to suggest that defining blameworthiness merely by collecting together the 'family resemblances' was both impossible and futile. He said, 'We cannot find the "essence" of blameworthiness in this way, nor can we state any unifying principle for all the cases, except in the most vague and general terms; and these terms will afford us no more than a guide which must be used with common sense'.[70] Brett argued that, in failing to incorporate this learning and instead attempting to precisely formulate conditions of blameworthiness in advance, the law failed to align with contemporary understandings of the mind.[71]

In addition to ordinary language philosophy, Brett's thesis considered many of the leading debates in criminal law, taking a position on behaviourism and explaining the most recent contributions made by psychologists, including why their theories could not be neatly translated into law. While he did not adopt their brand of legal positivism, Brett believed he was continuing the task set by John Austin and Jeremy Bentham. These jurists had sought to expound and improve upon the law by drawing widely on the best learning of their day. They treated law as an object of 'scientific' study. One of the problems that Brett believed was associated with existing approaches to law was that contemporary learning in other disciplines was largely ignored. Because of this, the law was based on 'a seventeenth century philosophy and an eighteenth century psychology'.[72] By reading widely into the social science and philosophical literature, and seeking advice from psychologists and psychiatrists, Brett sought to rectify this position and bring law into line with twentieth-century thinking.

[67] ibid 5.

[68] HLA Hart took a similar position, which he later qualified: see HLA Hart, 'The Ascription of Responsibility and Rights' (1949) 49 *Proceedings of the Aristotelian Society* 171–80, and his later work in HLA Hart, *Punishment and Responsibility: Essays in the Philosophy of Law* (Oxford, Clarendon Press, 1968).

[69] P Brett, *An Inquiry into Criminal Guilt* (Sydney, Lawbook, 1963) 14, citing L Wittgenstein, *Philosophical Investigations* (Oxford, Basil Blackwell, 1953) 66–67.

[70] ibid 42.

[71] ibid.

[72] ibid 213.

Taking Legal Process Seriously

What was it about Brett's thesis that aligned it with the Legal Process School? Although Hart had written on some matters of criminal law, Hart and Sacks's acclaimed set of teaching materials, 'The Legal Process' ('the materials') principally concerned other types of legal and social ordering. Understanding how Brett's work embodied Legal Process sentiment requires some investigation.

Three central tenets of the Legal Process School are well known. First, put simply, for Legal Process scholars, law was a purposive activity that ought to be directed towards promoting social cohesion and curing social ills. Like the American legal sociologists of the early 1900s, Legal Process scholars believed that law should be treated as a policy science to facilitate this social cohesion.

The second premise involved elevating the jurisprudential importance of the question, 'What is the nature of the basic problem and how should we choose among the various procedures of social ordering that might be applied to it?'[73] Hart and Sacks considered that examining and choosing among various means or processes was fundamental to the progress of jurisprudential inquiry.[74] The legitimacy of America's laws was therefore firmly wedded to the institutions used for lawmaking and the procedures that they followed. Hart and Sacks went so far as to suggest that the central importance of these institutions and procedures meant that laws made by them were beyond challenge. Thus, they endorsed the principle of institutional settlement, which is the idea that 'decisions which are the duly arrived at result of duly established procedures [for making decisions] of this kind ought to be accepted as binding upon the whole society unless and until they are changed'.[75]

The final premise underpinning the School is something Hart and Sacks called 'reasoned elaboration'. The instrumental tendencies of the School might suggest that judges had free rein to mould the law to suit their own views of what society needed. Instead, Hart argued that a 'court in making law is bound to base its action, not on free judgment of relative social advantage, but on a process of reasoned development of authoritative starting-points (i.e., statutes, prior judicial decisions, etc)'.[76] An official, such as a judge, interpreting a general directive, such as a statute, must 'elaborate the arrangement in a way which is consistent with the other established applications of it' and 'must do so in a way which best serves the principles and policies it expresses'.[77]

[73] N Duxbury, *Patterns of American Jurisprudence* (Oxford, Clarendon Press, 1995) 233, quoting from L Fuller, 'Mediation – Its Forms and Functions' (1971) 44 *Southern California Law Review* 307.

[74] ibid 235.

[75] Quoted in WN Eskridge Jr and PP Frickey, 'The Making of the Legal Process' (1994) 107 *Harvard Law Review* 2031, 2045, digitalcommons.law.yale.edu/fss_papers/3843/.

[76] ibid 2038.

[77] ibid 2043.

Evidence of Brett's commitment to these tenets can be found in many aspects of his scholarship. However, to fully understand how Brett's SJD thesis embodied the Legal Process School, it is necessary to consider more recent revisionist histories. These revisions help explain Brett's motivations; in turn, Brett's thesis adds weight to the arguments that they advance.

Perhaps the most important revision is Charles Barzun's article on the 'forgotten foundations' of Hart and Sacks.[78] Barzun challenges the central reason advanced by scholars for ignoring the Legal Process: that it is based on 'a narrow form of utilitarianism that has an impoverished conception of the good'.[79] He does so through a close examination of the text of the materials, in which he highlights overlooked passages and explains the relationship between Hart and some of the most important philosophers of knowledge in the early to mid-twentieth century. For example, Barzun explains that Hart and Sacks's line that the fundamental purpose of society was to 'maximize the total satisfaction of human wants'[80] must be read in the context of numerous other passages where they suggest that maximising such wants involves a qualitative evaluation of ends that recognises the 'individual worth of every human being'.[81] He bolsters this interpretation, and brings greater clarity to Hart and Sacks's position, by demonstrating that there is a link between their position and the thinking of prominent philosopher, William James. Barzun explains:

> James argued, in short, that experience was the sole test for ethical truth. There was no good or bad in the 'nature of things,' but that fact did not imply ethical scepticism. Indeed, James refused to accept such scepticism as a real possibility. He thus began by observing that all human beings have feelings, desires, and hence 'demands' upon the world and others. His controversial move was then to say that the mere existence of such demands generated moral obligations by others to respect them. For James, morality only existed insofar as there were sentient beings who had demands, whether physical or emotional. But once such beings came into existence, so did morality.
>
> Two crucial points qualify and clarify this seemingly counter-intuitive claim. First, a person's demands included not just subjective physical needs or satisfactions, but his or her 'ideals' as well. So it seems clear that James was not endorsing a 'desire-satisfaction' brand of consequentialism. Second, the obligations that a person's demand generated could be defeated if, another person had a conflicting demand.[82]

Hart and Sacks's position stands in contrast to other legal theorists of the twentieth century because it does not identify a single-value end, or even ends, from which legal reasoning and processes can be assessed.[83] Again, Barzun

[78] CL Barzun, 'The Forgotten Foundations of Hart and Sacks' (2013) 99 *Virginia Law Review* 1.
[79] ibid 21.
[80] ibid.
[81] ibid 22.
[82] ibid 23.
[83] David Wolitz distinguishes Hart and Sacks from criminal law theorists in this way. D Wolitz, 'Herbert Wechsler, Legal Process, and the Jurisprudential Roots of the Model Penal Code' (2016) 51 *Tulsa Law Review* 633, 635, digitalcommons.law.utulsa.edu/tlr/vol51/iss3/7/.

considers that an understanding of Jamesian thinking provides the intellectual foundation for eschewing the notion of identifying ends in advance. No one, both James and Hart argue, is capable of settling on a set of desirable ends in advance: 'From this unsparing practical ordeal no professor's lectures and no array of books can save us'.[84] Instead, the desirable ends must emerge from a process of trial and error and overall experience. Hart explains that 'it is only through personal, self-reliant participation, by trial and error, in the problems of existence, both personal and social, that the capacity to participate effectively can grow'.[85] Barzun claims that the 'process' in Legal Process should be 'understood to be that of guiding a historical process quite similar to the one James described'.[86] He goes on to explain that '[f]or James, the idea seems to have been that over time, as individuals were faced with dilemmas requiring action of one sort or another, the ethical truth would come out'.[87]

Similarly, Brett's SJD does not identify a single-value end from which the substances of the criminal law or its processes can be assessed. His investigations into criminal guilt led him to conclude that the courts should be left to develop the common law with some appreciation of the limits of language and learning from other disciplines. The idea that lawyers and society should simply wait and see what happens – to see what a decision-maker or official will do – seems to invite a level of trust and passivity that most legal scholars would find deeply problematic. Nonetheless, Brett's SJD demonstrated this same commitment to 'process'. One of the most controversial parts of Brett's thesis, his prescription on how courts should approach the question of guilt, draws from one of the leading philosophers of science of the time, Michael Polanyi. Polanyi's book, *Personal Knowledge* (1958),[88] was published the year before Brett commenced his thesis at Harvard. Polanyi visited Harvard and gave presentations while Brett was a student there, no doubt due to his friendship with Fuller. In *Personal Knowledge*, Polanyi challenged conventional thought by arguing that creative endeavour, such as the creation of new knowledge, is value-laden rather than objective and value-free. He coined the term 'tacit knowledge' to mean knowledge based on intuition, ascertained not through reasoning from premises but from what he called a person's 'indwelling understanding' – the understanding of human motivations and actions that they had gained from their life experience and awareness of that experience.[89] Brett explained that, 'Polanyi urges that in all human mental operations, even those which on the surface consist of articulate logical operations, it is this tacit component of knowledge which plays a decisive role'.[90]

[84] Barzun (n 78) 24–25 (quoting from James).
[85] ibid 25.
[86] ibid.
[87] ibid.
[88] M Polanyi, *Personal Knowledge* (Chicago, University of Chicago Press, 1958).
[89] Brett (n 69) 78.
[90] ibid 78.

Polanyi's theory gave Brett grounds to suggest that the law could abandon its former, ill-conceived quest to define *mens rea* precisely and could rely instead on loose notions of negligence, recklessness and intention without abandoning the claim that the law was scientific – in other words, without losing its moral or intellectual integrity. Values, rather than mere factual observations, were a part of developments in human science. Brett believed that Polanyi's theory supported the notion that when a jury determined the question of guilt they were reasoning in the same manner as a scientist would. Just as, according to Polanyi, scientists draw upon their tacit knowledge to make a creative leap, so too do members of a jury when determining the moral culpability of an accused. Brett argued that jury members draw on their indwelling understanding in attempting to understand why the accused had acted in a certain manner. Consequently, a finding of guilt could only follow where a jury member could say: '"I understand why he did this, but he ought not to have done it; if I had been in his place, I would not – or I hope I would not – have done it myself." If they cannot say this, they should absolve him from guilt'.[91]

Adopting Polanyi's theory, Brett argued that a jury's recourse to their indwelling understanding, while a freewheeling process, was really not that different from how a social or natural scientist advanced knowledge, and therefore should not cause alarm. Moreover, jurors' tacit knowledge helped them to identify the basis of their duty – what Brett described as the 'community ethic'.[92] According to Brett, relying on a jury and deploying the notion of tacit knowledge meant that guilt could be determined consistently with such ethics.

Brett's faith in the jury aligns with Hart and Sacks's principle of 'institutional settlement'; the idea that selecting an appropriately qualified institution improves the chances of good decision-making. Invoking the principle of institutional settlement would not, however, satisfy many critics. As Barzun points out, the obvious question that arises from the coupling of institutional settlement with reasoned elaboration is: how can one treat law as settled when such judgment is based on a prescriptive and highly evaluative assessment? As Barzun puts it: 'how can one endorse a concept as a normative matter without having some sense of what that concept is prior to the endorsement?'[93] Perhaps Barzun's most important claim is that Hart and Sacks did not overlook this challenge to their work and thinking. Indeed, just as these questions are central to current debates on the philosophy of law, they were questions Hart and Sacks took seriously.[94] Brett, following in this tradition, also took these questions seriously.

According to Barzun, Hart and Sacks attempted to answer these central questions of moral legal philosophy by adopting what they considered to be the best thinking on the philosophy and sociology of social (human) sciences. He explains

[91] ibid 77.
[92] ibid 17–18.
[93] ibid 32.
[94] ibid.

that they rejected the analogies traditionally drawn between law and the natural sciences and instead drew from the 'prudential' methodologies of the social sciences.[95] By prudential, Barzun appears to mean:

> a set of intellectual dispositions related to thinking practically about specific choices and actions rather than thinking in purely abstract or theoretical terms. Among the traits typically associated with prudence are: a disposition toward the practically achievable rather than the ideal; thinking in particulars rather than universals; recognizing the limits of one's knowledge and power; sensitivity to complexity in human nature and human institutions; and reliance on experience and common-sense intuition in addition to formalized knowledge or decisional criteria.[96]

Hart and Sacks based their position on a controversial ethical claim that the goal of the social sciences is to improve social institutions.[97] They also referenced the epistemic claim that a social scientist must consider both the means and ends in conjunction, switching from fact to value and back again.[98] This improves our understanding of what Hart and Sacks meant by 'process': 'It refers to the process of "interaction of means and end," of fact and value, of ethics and science, by which society fulfils its purposes. In this way, "process" is more akin to *growth* or *development*'.[99]

Barzun's thesis therefore rejects the longstanding characterisation of the Legal Process School as lacking a strong philosophical foundation. Instead, he demonstrates that Hart and Sacks were pursuing objectives and drawing ideas from the leading philosophers of the day: WV Quine, Morton White, Michael Polanyi, Thomas Kuhn, Ludwig Wittgenstein and Leo Strauss. Rather than returning to Langdellian notions of the objective scientific foundation of law,[100] the Legal Process School emphasised the value-laden and subjective nature of knowledge and reasoning within law and other disciplines.[101]

By drawing on the work of Ryle and Wittgenstein, Brett's approach resembled that of the English scholar, HLA Hart. However, Barzun's thesis suggests that we should not assume that Brett's attraction to ordinary language philosophy came from this Oxford legal scholar. Although Brett was clearly aware of HLA Hart's work, there is little to suggest that he wished to emulate his scholarship. Instead, Brett's thesis is consistent with, and provides support for, Barzun's claim that the Legal Process scholars drew from the best of the philosophy of knowledge at the time. In *An Inquiry into Criminal Guilt*, we find Brett embracing law's subjectivity

[95] ibid 35.
[96] Wolitz (n 83) 666.
[97] Barzun (n 78) 34–35.
[98] ibid 34.
[99] ibid 43 (Barzun's emphasis).
[100] There is evidence to suggest that Langdell did not in fact embrace these ideas: BA Kimball, *The Inception of Modern Professional Education* (Chapel Hill, University of North Carolina Press, 2009) 349–51.
[101] Barzun (n 78) 6.

and arguing that lawyers should abandon their over-reliance on definitions, as modern learning showed that this was liable to lead to further injustices. His thesis embraces the prudential spirit of Legal Process: acknowledging that there might not be a perfect way to determine guilt, but nonetheless proposing a model that could be considered the next best thing.

Brett's adoption of Polanyi's indwelling understanding supports the connection Barzun draws between Polanyi and the Legal Process scholars. It supports the argument that Legal Process scholars highlighted, rather than downplayed, the role of values in legal reasoning and the social sciences. It also illustrates the Legal Process scholars' willingness to embrace the limits of knowledge and intellectual capacity and their preference for experience over pre-configured normative ends. In this way, Brett's work supports Barzun's definition of the 'Legal Process'. By extension, his work also supports, and provides additional insight into, the foundations of the Legal Process School, and reinforces Barzun's argument that these foundations should not be so readily dismissed. As I explain in the next chapter, the Process commitments underpinning Brett's monograph formed the foundations of his approach to criminal law teaching.

Reception

Brett made an impression on his teachers at Harvard. On 16 June 1960, Fuller wrote to inform Brett that he had obtained the SJD, noting that he was the only candidate to have 'made the grade this year'.[102] Professor Livingston Hall regarded him as 'gifted', 'imaginative' and capable of providing 'brilliant' insights.[103] In Administrative Law, Legal Process and the Legal Education seminar, he 'obtained 80% (an A grade being 75 or above) which while not a record is somewhat unusual' at Harvard Law School.[104] Brett's achievements are made all the more remarkable by the fact that his wife and three young children, aged seven, five and four, accompanied him to Harvard. His son Robin remembers that they lived in a 'basement flat in a student building that got incredibly hot with central heating because they turn it up too high. There was a bank down from street level to the entrance of our place that was always covered in snow all winter'.[105] Brett had considerable responsibilities outside his studies, which were lightened somewhat by his wife, Margaret. Robin and Jonathan recall that throughout their childhood she worked very hard as a nurse during school hours and doing all of the home duties.[106] In the preface

[102] Lon L Fuller, Chairman of the Committee on Graduate Studies at Harvard Law School to Brett, 16 June 1960, Peter Brett Papers, National Library of Australia Manuscript Collection.

[103] Attachment to Brett to the Registrar of the University of Melbourne, 26 October 1962, *Law Dean's Correspondence 1962–1965*, University of Melbourne Archives.

[104] ibid.

[105] Robin and Jonathan Brett (n 53).

[106] ibid. On the significant advantages of having a wife like Brett's, see A Crabb, *The Wife Drought* (Sydney, Ebury Press, 2014).

to his book, Brett acknowledged that he would not have been able to complete his studies so successfully were it not for the support and sacrifice of his young family; the book is dedicated to them.[107]

Following his time at Harvard, Brett published many articles and a further monograph based on the conception of law advanced by the Legal Process School.[108] Even his advocacy work and writing for the public was set within the framework of Legal Process thinking.[109] In fact, he continued to breathe life into the Legal Process School long after enthusiasm for it had largely evaporated in the United States.[110] However, of all Brett's publications, the textbook he wrote with Louis Waller (considered in the next chapter) and his initial monograph, *An Inquiry into Criminal Guilt*, had the greatest chance of fulfilling one of Griswold's aspirations for the SJD: to transplant the leading Harvard conception of law to Australia. The reception of these works suggests that this aspiration was only partially fulfilled.

In reviews of *An Inquiry into Criminal Guilt*, scholars found Brett's faith in juries unpalatable. Rather than engaging with the philosophy that Brett adopted to give his prescriptions epistemological strength, they simply rejected them. For example, Graham Hughes, in the lengthiest review, acknowledged that Brett had made his case that current approaches to *mens rea* were wrong, but he rejected Brett's solution of relying on a jury's indwelling understanding.[111] Hughes argued (without providing any theoretical support for his criticisms) that this overestimated the jury's ability to empathise and that, in some abhorrent cases, such as the actions of the Nazi Adolf Eichmann, most juries would reject the possibility of contemplating what they would have done had they been placed in the accused's position.[112] Brett had anticipated this line of argument and had taken a position now commonly attributed to Hannah Arendt and her phrase 'the banality of evil'.[113] He adopted the position that ordinary people are capable of doing extraordinarily evil things. He spoke of the tendency to treat criminals as outcasts and said that this was a myth, arguing that the criminal law 'is a series of restraints on behaviour in which ordinary people would like to indulge for ordinary reasons, at some time or other'.[114] Hughes also considered that the community ethic was not an adequate touchstone, given the variety of different community ethics that exist.[115] To this Brett's answer appears to have been that

[107] Brett (n 69) ix.
[108] See, eg, P Brett, *An Essay on a Contemporary Jurisprudence* (Sydney, Butterworths, 1975); P Brett, 'Free Speech, Supreme-Court Style: A View from Overseas' (1967–68) *Texas Law Review* 668.
[109] See, eg, P Brett, *The Beamish Case* (Melbourne, Melbourne University Press, 1966).
[110] Brett (n 108).
[111] G Hughes, 'Criminal Responsibility' (1964) 16 *Stanford Law Review* 477.
[112] ibid 478.
[113] H Arendt, *Eichmann in Jerusalem: A Report on the Banality of Evil* (London, Faber and Faber, 1963).
[114] Brett (n 69) 147.
[115] Hughes (n 111) 481.

the community ethic is a democratic concept and that, as long as the jury is representative, it will fulfil its aim.[116] Again, this displays Brett's faith in democratic institutions.

Ronald Wertheim, Associate Professor of Law at the University of Virginia, believed that Brett had made a good case that the foundation of the criminal law ought to be updated in light of modern learning. But he also criticised Brett's prescription, pointing to the fact that most jurors would be unwilling to empathise with the accused and that the jury required greater guidance. He said: 'A rule which goes this far to achieve individualisation of justice could easily achieve legitimised lynch law instead'.[117] Another American, Jack Leavitt from the San Francisco Law School, similarly criticised the discretion Brett placed in the jury but went further, maintaining that Brett was giving the jury a licence to determine what conduct ought to be considered criminal.[118] This seems to misrepresent Brett's position. Brett had made it clear that it was the legislature and judges that created legal rules and criminal standards. The jury's determination of guilt was a response to those rules and standards. While the reviews were positive overall, none of the Australian reviewers engaged with the philosophical aspects of Brett's work.[119]

Concluding Remarks

There is little to suggest that the Australian legal academy adopted any of the philosophical foundations of the Legal Process School in either their teaching or scholarship. Modern Australian jurisprudence textbooks make little, and most often no, reference to the School. There are few signs that criminal law scholars beyond jurisprudential circles were interested in engaging with leading thought within the philosophy of knowledge, ordinary language philosophy or Polanyi's work. In some ways, Brett's monograph made the Legal Process School's commitment to considering law alongside the latest philosophical learning more apparent than Hart and Sacks's materials did. However, few engaged with this aspect of his thesis. This might suggest that it was not Brett's endeavour but the nature of the leading Harvard jurisprudential school that compromised its potential to shape legal education beyond the US. Neither Hart and Sacks nor Brett had put forward

[116] Brett (n 69) 77–79, 147.

[117] RP Wertheim, 'Book Review: *An Inquiry into Criminal Guilt* by Peter Brett and *Law, Liberty and Psychiatry* by Thomas S Szasz' (1964) 64 *Columbia Law Review* 980.

[118] J Leavitt, 'Book Review: *An Inquiry into Criminal Guilt* by Peter Brett' (1963) 51 *California Law Review* 1035.

[119] JV Barry, 'Book Rreview: *An Inquiry into Criminal Guilt* by Peter Brett' (1963) 4 *Melbourne University Law Review* 293; C Howard, 'Book review: *An Inquiry into Criminal Guilt* by Peter Brett' (1963–66) 2 *Adelaide Law Review* 139.

a clear and convincing manifesto for the Legal Process School that would attract enthusiasm beyond students who had studied at Harvard. Had Brett attempted to transpose Langdellian, Sociological or American Legal Realist ideas, he might have had greater success, and an elite US conception of law might have subsequently underpinned Australian legal education.

Brett was therefore misunderstood in much the same way as the Legal Process School more generally has been misunderstood. Thinking of his legacy purely in terms of the way he gathered together case law and commentary in his cases and materials book without recourse to his broader philosophy would suggest that he was a black letter scholar, preoccupied with common law reasoning at the expense of other bodies of knowledge. It would ignore the depth of his broader studies and interests. He read widely, keeping up with modern learning, in particular philosophy and psychology. Focusing on the textbook would also ignore Brett's willingness to consider legislative and administrative processes, rather than merely court processes. Brett was a broadly read and intellectually ambitious scholar whose theories were designed to elevate Australia's discipline of law. However, as I explain further in the following chapters, he only partially succeeded.

4

The First Theory for Teaching Australian Criminal Law

Introduction

In this chapter I make a case for recognising Peter Brett and Louis Waller's textbook on Australian criminal law as one of the most imaginative teaching innovations to come out of Australian law schools in the twentieth century.[1] Careful study of the impetus for the textbook, the contents of the first three editions, and the context in which it was written reveals its distinctive qualities and achievements. Brett brought to Australia not only American enthusiasm about reforming the intellectual credentials of law, but also a distinctly American advocacy for educational reform. To Brett, just as it was important to ensure that reform of the criminal law had a strong intellectual basis, drawing the best from the philosophy of science, so it was also essential that law be taught in the classroom using methods that encouraged students to adopt an intellectual and scientific approach to legal reasoning.

Brett and Waller's goal was not simply to produce a competent legal practitioner. The pair wished to foster a sense of moral awareness in their students and to impress upon them the onerous moral responsibilities lawyers faced. They sought to create serious, reform-orientated, critical lawyers. Their textbook represents an ambitious attempt to embody these ideals, while also for the very first time providing an impressive compendium of all the leading Australian criminal cases, with comparative material, largely from England and America. The first four editions ranged from 713 to 904 pages. That the textbook was regarded as an exciting work by international experts – and is remembered fondly by students educated in the 1960s – attests to its strength.

At Harvard, Lon Fuller's main complaint about his students was their 'uncritical attitude towards the substance of law and their lack of interest in ethical

[1] P Brett and PL Waller, *Cases and Materials in Criminal Law* (Sydney, Butterworths, 1962); P Brett and PL Waller, *Cases and Materials in Criminal Law*, 2nd edn (Sydney, Butterworths, 1965); P Brett and PL Waller, *Criminal Law – Cases and Text*, 3rd edn (Sydney, Butterworths, 1971); P Brett and PL Waller, *Criminal Law – Text and Cases*, 4th edn (Sydney, Butterworths, 1978). The work was a 'cases and materials' book, but for convenience will be referred to by the broader descriptor of textbook.

questions'.[2] Brett made the same complaint at Melbourne.[3] In the 1960s, Brett's students were for the most part 'baby boomers', whose lives might have been touched by the Second World War but who had not witnessed its horrors. In contrast to most of the full-time legal academics at Melbourne, who had served in the defence forces, they had not faced the life-and-death conundrums that were of central concern to the criminal law. Brett and Waller's book sought to bring the importance of the criminal law's moral dilemmas into sharper focus.

Working with Waller, Brett devised pedagogical innovations that sat within the US tradition but were more significant than those of the American Legal Realists. The pair drew from the Legal Process School but also added innovations of their own, drawing on other traditions and then tailoring the work to an Australian context. Until now scholars have not sufficiently interrogated the foundation, creation, context or content of this work to reveal its important place within the history of Australian legal education and scholarship. The point of this chapter is not to argue that criminal scholars should adopt Brett and Waller's approach to textbook writing. Instead, I argue for greater acknowledgment of Brett and Waller's sophisticated and intellectually robust theory for teaching criminal law. If current criminal scholars were to follow in Brett and Waller's tradition, they too would draw from what they believe to be the best learning of their age to promote a certain kind of lawyerly practice and, perhaps, more thoughtful citizens.

In this chapter I explore a number of factors that might explain why the early editions of the textbook have not received the recognition they deserve. While the textbook's importance and value were recognised at the time, Brett and Waller's work has not been recognised – at least to the same level – since. While making a case that this was an important textbook, I identify some significant problems with the book. I also suggest that if certain intellectual currents, teaching arrangements and student attitudes had been different, the specific features of early editions of this book – and the concept of law on which it was based – might have become more broadly known throughout Australia. This points to the importance of these factors in any explanation of the trajectory of academic law.

Brett and Waller

On his return from Harvard in late 1959, one of Brett's major ambitions was to reform the teaching of Australian criminal law. At that time, there was no comprehensive textbook on Australian criminal law. Teachers instead used a combination of English textbooks and a small Australian book produced by Melbourne

[2] N Lacey, *A Life of HLA Hart – The Nightmare and the Noble Dream* (Oxford, Oxford University Press, 2004) 181. Lacey compares Fuller to Hart, whose 'main complaint about the Harvard law students was their lack of precision'.

[3] Interview with Ian Leader-Elliot (Law School, University of South Australia, 10 February 2014).

scholars in the 1940s, which had not been intended to provide a complete treatment of Australian criminal law.[4] To achieve his grand plan, Brett, like Henry Hart, needed a collaborator, which he found in the form of a young university teacher named Louis Waller, appointed to the Law School at the University of Melbourne in 1958 after completing a BCL at the University of Oxford.[5] Before that, Waller had completed an undergraduate degree in law at Melbourne. Brett and Waller were similar in that they had both fallen under the spell of an important foreign jurisprudential scholar. Brett, of course, had Henry Hart; for Waller, it was the tutorials conducted by HLA Hart at Oxford that made a lasting impression.[6] The new collaboration provided opportunities for the pair to discuss their foreign mentors,[7] allowing for further cross-fertilisation between English and American traditions. The two industrious scholars completed the book in less than two years.

When Brett approached Waller, he was planning his exit from teaching the criminal law course. Waller was going to teach torts, which, he explained 'I much preferred, not this slimy bloody business about crime'.[8] Waller's low estimation of the subject was influenced, at least in part, by the way it had been taught at Melbourne:

> Criminal Law was taught in a way that I immediately thought was bizarre, with general principles before you started on crimes. There were general principles on *actus reus* and *mens rea*, textbooks like *Kenny on Crime* where you didn't get to homicide until you had read through all this twaddle. I thought straight away (but I'm a young green teacher) how can you expect young students to start to deal with this somewhat spongy and difficult stuff when they have had no exposure to what crimes are other than generalities – 'A Crime is' – and the general definition is circular.[9]

Brett's vision for a new criminal law course represented a significant departure from the old order, and his enthusiasm for his new model infected Waller so much that Waller decided to return to criminal law.[10]

The entire textbook was infused with moral problems and graphic examples of those problems. For example, the book began with a problem based on the

[4] JV Barry, GW Paton and G Sawer, *An Introduction to the Criminal Law in Australia* (London, Macmillan, 1948).

[5] Michael Kirby provides a useful summary of Waller's career in a farewell speech delivered on Waller's retirement in 2000 and later published as M Kirby, 'People in Criminal Law: Louis Waller AO' (2001) 25 *Criminal Law Journal* 215. Waller's contribution to the Law School at Monash is captured in P Yule and F Woodhouse, *Pericleans, Plumbers and Practitioners: The First Fifty Years of the Monash University Law School* (Melbourne, Monash University, 2015).

[6] Interviews with Louis Waller (Law School, Monash University, 23 October 2013 and 25 November 2013). Waller also provided a lengthy tribute to Brett, which offers a vivid account of Brett's personality, motivations and principal achievements: L Waller, 'Peter Brett Remembered' (1975) *Summons* 100.

[7] ibid.

[8] ibid.

[9] ibid.

[10] ibid.

case *R v Dudley and Stephens*,[11] which Fuller had used as a basis for his problem in 'The Case of the Speluncean Explorers'.[12] The legal issue was whether men stranded on a lifeboat who kill and eat one of their crewmates to stay alive ought to be convicted of murder. Fuller's problem concerns the same issue, with the difference that the men are trapped inside a sealed cave. Brett and Waller's problem introduces students to many of the central issues of the criminal law, while demonstrating the difficulty of formulating bright-line rules. As Waller explains:

> Peter had a vision. What he was absolutely fascinated by was the interplay between law and morality which of course was Lon Fuller's *chef-d'oeuvre* which is in all sorts of ways captured in and spewed out by *Dudley and Stephens*. Here are two respectable, experienced, decent men who find themselves in hell and who end up making a life decision: the only way we can stay alive and have – they wouldn't have put it like this – and have minuscule expectation of salvation is by using the most vulnerable and weakest man, he's going to die because he is drinking sea water. … So, what happens to them? Their sentences are commuted to six months in prison. Just six months for murder. So, the whole murky picture – right, wrong, life, death, crime, punishment – it's all there.[13]

This dramatic introduction to the study of criminal law remained in the minds of students.[14] The book ended on a similar note, with a quote from Dostoevsky's *The Brothers Karamazov*,[15] which prompted students to consider whether they would take a utilitarian approach and kill a baby for the sake of improving the happiness and wellbeing of society.[16] It challenged students to consider the circumstances in which crimes are excusable.

Brett and Waller encouraged students to think about the relationship between law and morality through other allegories. Drawing on the technique made famous by Lon Fuller, Brett and Waller's textbook presents students with a transcript from a cocktail party where lawyers, psychiatrists, philosophers and sociologists discuss how the issue of insanity should be addressed by the criminal law.[17] The allegory makes the learning from these other disciplines accessible to students and helps them consider the challenges faced by anyone trying to draw from those disciplines for the purpose of law reform. Through the conversation, some of the central points from Brett's SJD are made in a clear, entertaining and

[11] *R v Dudley and Stephens* (1884) 14 QBD 273.

[12] LL Fuller, 'The Case of the Speluncean Explorers' (1949) 62 *Harvard Law Review* 616.

[13] Waller (n 6).

[14] 'What I do remember is *Dudley and Stephens*, the criminal cannibal case, and all the issues that that raised about what the criminal law was all about, which was quite intriguing. … It was a very intelligent piece of legal education, I think, because it was an extraordinary case that raised all sorts of fascinating issues right across the spectrum. It was a subject matter that was very engaging to a young student audience': Interview with Gareth Evans (ANU House, Melbourne, 13 June 2014).

[15] Book 5, chapter 4.

[16] Brett and Waller (1962) (n 1) 713.

[17] ibid 618–30.

engaging style reminiscent of Fuller's Speluncean judgments. It is important to note, however, that the book otherwise contains very few references to the philosophical and social science thinking that underpins Brett's thesis. Brett considered that an undergraduate law degree did not permit a close consideration of other disciplines.[18] For the most part, students were expected to make their assessment of the 'justice' or morality of law based on the content of cases, statutes and legal commentary, as well as their own intuition, as opposed to material from other disciplines.

Legal Process in the Australian Classroom

Many things could be said about the significance of this book to the shape of Australian law teaching, but what is most important to note here is that it was modelled on Hart and Sacks's materials.[19] At Harvard, Brett took Henry Hart and Sacks's course on 'The Legal Process' and attended education seminars conducted by Elliot Cheatham. For Cheatham's course, Brett completed a paper on how he proposed 'to completely revamp the Criminal Law course at Melbourne'.[20] Brett wrote to Henry Hart to ask permission to adopt the 'Hart–Sacks format' for the textbook,[21] which Hart gave.[22] Brett believed that the textbook 'bears many signs of the impression that [their] all too brief association left with me'.[23] This influence is expressly acknowledged in the preface of the textbook.[24]

The book encouraged students to conceptualise judicial reasoning as a Legal Process scholar would. Given that the book was very well received and was read by a much broader audience than *An Inquiry into Criminal Guilt*, it had far greater potential to encourage Australian law teaching and legal practice to embody a Legal Process mindset.

The idea that Legal Process thinking had a considerable influence on the founding of modern criminal law teaching and the form and nature of Australian law textbooks will no doubt surprise many Australian legal scholars. Most Australian jurisprudential textbooks make no mention of Legal Process thinking, and few contemporary Australian legal scholars know about the central tenets of

[18] Memorandum from P Brett, FKH Maher and J Phillips to the Faculty of Law at the University of Melbourne, 3 July 1969, Graduate LLB Committee, 1969–1971, University of Melbourne Archives.

[19] The materials are explained in chapter three.

[20] Peter Brett to Harold Ford, 23 February 1959, Harold Arthur Ford Papers, University of Melbourne Archives.

[21] Peter Brett to Henry Hart, 2 May 1961, Henry Melvin Hart Papers, Harvard Law School Library, Historical and Special Collections.

[22] Henry Hart to Peter Brett, 23 June 1961, Peter Brett Papers, National Library of Australia, Manuscript Collection.

[23] Peter Brett to Henry Hart, 22 August 1962, Henry Melvin Hart Papers, Harvard Law School Library, Historical and Special Collections.

[24] Brett and Waller (1962) (n 1) vii.

the School. In accounts of Australian legal education, American Legal Realism and Sociological Jurisprudence are usually credited with the greatest influence on judging and teaching. This is largely due to the emphasis placed on Julius Stone's teachings at Sydney Law School.

Even in the US, scholars have been slow to recognise the impact of Legal Process thinking on the criminal law and criminal law teaching. As David Wolitz explains, this appears to be in part because the bulk of criminal law theorising has been underpinned and defined by a normative platform.[25] As the Legal Process School typically eschews theories that revolve around single norms, it is at odds with the bulk of legal theory. To provide a specific example, Wolitz argues that this led to a failure to recognise that Herbert Wechsler (law professor at Columbia and director of the American Law Institute) drafted the US Model Penal Code from a Legal Process perspective. In a complementary vein, Anders Walker argues that Wechsler and Jerome Michael's ground-breaking criminal cases and materials book constitute a Legal Process approach to criminal law teaching.[26]

While I am running a similar thesis to Wolitz and Walker here, it is important to recognise that Brett and Waller's book is materially different from Wechsler and Michael's book and other US textbooks that followed in the Legal Process tradition.[27] There are two reasons for these differences. First, Brett and Waller adapted Legal Process thinking to Australian conditions and concerns, which were different from those in the US. Second, Brett and Waller's book in some ways embodies the philosophical foundations of the Legal Process School, as described by Barzun, to a greater extent than Wechsler's code or Wechsler and Michael's textbook.

Walker's explanation of the ambitions and thinking behind Wechsler and Michael's cases and materials book is fascinating and significant as it starkly reveals one of the underlying normative premises of criminal law teaching in the US. Walker explains that, in writing their criminal law book, the authors hoped to encourage their students to become policy-makers rather than criminal lawyers.[28] He notes the perception among elite American law teachers of the time (and perhaps still) that criminal lawyering was an unsavoury business that was unsuited to their class of students.[29] The material included in the book encouraged a reformist mindset that could be used in drafting new criminal laws and policies – a more fitting role for their students than criminal practice. Walker considers that this approach resulted in criminal law classes becoming highly theoretical,

[25] D Wolitz, 'Herbert Wechsler, Legal Process, and the Jurisprudential Roots of the Model Penal Code' (2016) 51 *Tulsa Law Review* 633, 634–35.

[26] A Walker, 'The Anti-Case Method: Herbert Wechsler and the Political History of the Criminal Law Course' (2009) 7 *Ohio State Journal of Criminal Law* 217.

[27] eg, MG Paulsen and SH Kadish, *Criminal Law and its Processes: Cases and Materials* (Boston, Little Brown, 1962).

[28] Walker (n 26) 217–18.

[29] ibid.

to the extent that the teaching of criminal law could almost be considered a 'liberal arts' course.[30] The format and content of Wechsler and Michael's book constituted a reaction against Langdell's case method and conceptualist thinking. The textbook also exhibited Wechsler's diminished faith in the US judiciary. Along with other elite law professors of his generation, he had been scarred by the way the US Supreme Court had struck down New Deal legislation.[31]

Brett and Waller's cases and materials book was created within and for a very different environment. While many Australian law graduates went on to work in Australian legislative drafting and in Australian politics, such roles did not have the same prestige as working for the US administration. Brett and Waller no doubt appreciated that the bulk of their students would advance careers in legal practice. Even though Brett had worked for the Treasury Solicitor's Office in London, it does not follow that he wanted his students to follow a similar path. Brett was dismayed by most forms of elitism and sought to combat it both within the university academy and the legal profession. He would not, therefore, have shared Wechsler and Michael's view that criminal law practice was unfitting for his students. Indeed, his own efforts to provide expert advice and counsel to men accused of crimes, and his involvement in criminal trials, would suggest that he believed that the practice of criminal law was a noble part of the profession.[32] Moreover, his work educating police officers suggests that he wished to improve all aspects of its application and administration.[33]

Rather than providing an explanation of the central rules and principles emanating from the case and statute law, each chapter of Brett and Waller's textbook provided extracts from primary sources (cases and legislation) and scholarly and newspaper articles. While primarily presenting Australian materials, a substantial proportion of the textbook drew from the US and England. Each chapter began with a legal problem related to the material provided in that chapter. The problem was typical of those faced by superior Australian courts. The problem was then followed by a case that raised the same issue and provided an authoritative pronouncement. Rather than leaving the student with that pronouncement, the book then presented other cases, commentary, newspaper articles and legislative provisions that raised similar legal issues, answered the issues in different ways, and encouraged students to interrogate the reach and appropriateness of the rule or principle of the authoritative pronouncement. Students were therefore encouraged to develop their own interpretation of what the law is or ought to be. Rather than indoctrinate, the book was designed to prompt students to question the law: it was premised on the notion that the criminal law required reform.

[30] ibid 217.
[31] ibid 217–20, 226, 246.
[32] These efforts are explained in chapter five.
[33] Brett's work with the police force is also described in chapter five.

As Ian Leader-Elliot acknowledged, it was the only Australian legal textbook that adopted this format.[34]

The development of the problem method has been hailed as a significant innovation in American legal education. Duxbury suggests that its adoption meant that, by converting the concept of law into a teaching strategy, the Legal Process scholars succeeded where the American Legal Realists had failed:[35]

> Cavers observed … that although certain realists espoused the problem method, they failed to embrace it. '[T]he Realists have fitted their aspirations into the framework of the casebook system.' Emphasis on cases rather than on problems remained their priority. … In *The Legal Process*, by contrast, specific cases are used to illustrate general problems concerning law creation and application. Hart and Sacks were attempting to invoke the pedagogic strategy which realism had only promised.[36]

While Wechsler and Michael's book also consisted of a wide variety of material, they did not begin each chapter with a problem typically faced by the courts. As they wanted their students to become policy-makers not practicing lawyers, they encouraged freewheeling inquiries, unhampered by the consideration of concrete disputes between litigants.

Another important difference from Wechsler and Michael is that Brett and Waller did not believe that the criminal law should be codified. Brett's monograph, *An Inquiry into Criminal Guilt*, was in part a response to Wechsler's argument for codification. Brett specifically referenced Wechsler's view in favour of codification of the criminal law in the opening pages, where he is identified as one of the main targets of Brett's critique.[37] Brett countered that the common law's approach had not reached a significant stage of maturity to be translated to a code. By examining the latest thinking on the mind from a range of disciplines, Brett demonstrated that the common law was based on out-of-date learning. The textbook is clearly grounded in his thinking in *An Inquiry into Criminal Guilt* and draws from the same Legal Process philosophical foundations. Implicit in his thesis is the idea that the experience of judging and reasoning would lead to better principles that could later be codified. The opening passages to Brett and Waller's textbook state their conviction that, over time, Australian courts would develop better and more enlightened principles:

> We believe that the common law consists of principles; and that individual decisions, if inconsistent with these principles (which are to be derived from the whole body of precedent which they permeate, not from isolated instances), must be treated as wrong. …
>
> This seems to be the attitude of Australian courts; although they do not lightly refuse to follow English decisions, or overrule their own, they regard themselves as free to do so if

[34] Leader-Elliot (n 3).

[35] See also L Kalman, *Legal Realism at Yale 1927–1960* (Chapel Hill, University of North Carolina Press, 1986) 229.

[36] N Duxbury, *Patterns of American Jurisprudence* (Oxford, Clarendon Press, 1995) 253.

[37] P Brett, *An Inquiry into Criminal Guilt* (Sydney, Lawbook, 1963) 3–4.

> sound principle so requires. Australian judges would, we think, accept Roscoe Pound's dictum that 'law is experience developed by reason and reason tested by experience'; they certainly seem so to act.[38]

According to Brett and Waller, the common law did not derive its authority from the doctrine of precedent but from the strength of its reasoning processes, judged by how well they adhered to overarching principles. Waller recalls that Brett 'often railed at Frank Maher and me, jointly responsible for the first-year course, ILM [Introduction to Legal Method], that we … brainwashed our students into believing that the doctrine of precedent really mattered'.[39] Brett's aversion to precedent accords with Henry Hart's characterisation of it as an 'inert, remote-from-life notion, summoning up a picture of a desiccated English solution'.[40] By contrast, the type of social ordering Henry Hart envisaged through the development of principle was 'dynamic and vital'.[41] As Duxbury explains, Legal Process scholars believed that 'so long as judges respect the principles of institutional competence, they ought to engage in the reasoned elaboration of principles as actively as possible in order to achieve substantive justice for the parties of any particular dispute'.[42]

This idea that courts would develop their reasoning based on experience is consistent with Barzun's definition of 'process' explained in the previous chapter. It demonstrates a faith in courts over time to develop their reasoning processes in line with the best of modern learning. It is important to note that, although here Brett placed faith in the judiciary rather than the legislature, he was as committed to the 'democratisation of decision-making' as Wechsler. As noted in chapter three, he drew on both the ideas of Polanyi and ordinary language philosophy to make a case for entrusting the jury with ultimate responsibility for determining guilt. According to Brett's thinking, the jury provided representative decision-making.

Brett and Waller's textbook is therefore fundamentally different from Wechsler and Michael's book because it encourages students to adopt a Legal Process mindset to judicial reasoning. Brett and Waller suggested that both judges and lawyers should critically analyse the variety of values that underpin the criminal law and should adapt their arguments and reasons to reflect those underpinnings and produce sound principles. They maintained faith in the Australian judiciary. The differences between these approaches therefore suggest that there is more than one way that Legal Process thinking can be adapted to the criminal law. Moreover, the fact that Brett drew from the leading philosophers of knowledge of his time

[38] Brett and Waller (1962) (n 1) viii.
[39] Waller, 'Peter Brett Remembered' (n 6).
[40] HM Hart Jr, *Legislation Notes* (Summer Term, 1947) 2, quoted in WN Eskridge Jr, and P Frickey, 'The Making of the Legal Process' (1994) 107 *Harvard Law Review* 2031, 2037.
[41] ibid.
[42] Duxbury (n 36) 264.

to make a stand against codification and place greater reliance on the judiciary suggests that both his SJD and his cases and materials book embraced the philosophical foundations of the Legal Process School, perhaps to a greater extent than Michael and Wechsler's book.

Brett and the Australian Judiciary

Brett and Waller's faith in the Australian judiciary's capacity to develop better criminal law principles is perhaps puzzling in light of the opinions Brett voiced outside of the textbook. In a book review in 1960, he said that:

> as a whole the profession in England and Australia has reduced itself to the status of a body of priests performing a ritual without caring what its meaning may be or even whether it has any meaning at all.
>
> ... My own belief is that much of the trouble must be attributed to John Austin, who convinced our lawyers that law and morality were utterly distinct and that the lawyer's task was merely to see that the command of the sovereign is obeyed. I am here speaking of the way in which Austin has been understood by later generations; he was, in fact, well aware that lawyers, as well as legislatures, make the law and thus have a responsibility for its shape, but this part of his message has gone unheeded.[43]

In correspondence with his friend, Melbourne judge Justice Barry, Brett voiced frustration over the narrow view of legal reasoning that Sir Owen Dixon's articulation of complete and strict legalism had encouraged.[44] Rather than teaching students to fit within existing common law moulds and traditions, Brett and Waller were in fact inviting their students to see the judicial task differently from the dominant professional view. Brett was keen to rebut the positivist tendencies that he perceived in his students. In a letter to Henry Hart, Brett spoke of his jurisprudence class and said that he was:

> trying to put over to our students some of the things I learnt at your feet during my year at Harvard. You would detest the class which I have as most of them seem to have been indoctrinated with Austin and look at me as though I am slightly queer when I ask them whether a particular result is just. So I am trying hard to rebut positivism – and you will know where I learnt this attitude.[45]

Chief Justice of the High Court, Sir Owen Dixon emerges as an important character in Brett and Waller's cases and materials book. The pair no doubt recognised

[43] P Brett, 'Book Review: *Legal Education and Public Responsibility* by Julius Stone' (1960) 2 *Melbourne University Law Review* 568.

[44] Peter Brett to Justice John Barry, 16 October 1968, Sir John Vincent Barry Papers, National Library of Australia, Manuscript Collection.

[45] Peter Brett to Henry Hart, 2 May 1961, Henry Melvin Hart Papers, Harvard Law School Library, Historical and Special Collections.

that Dixon was Australia's most prominent and respected lawyer of the time. And they believed that showing Dixon's occasional willingness to depart from precedent and a literal reading of statutory provisions would further their cause of creating reform-orientated lawyers committed to advancing just principles. They cast Dixon not as a narrow formalist or legalist, but as a progressive liberal responsible for maintaining the moral underpinnings of Australia's criminal law. The first edition of their textbook was published at a time when considerable doubt existed about whether all serious crimes required proof of intent. Courts were also grappling with the vexed question of whether it was legitimate or appropriate for courts to read provisions within the context of a larger system of criminal responsibility, where most crimes required a mental element that signalled guilt. A willingness to dispense with the requirement to establish that an accused possessed a guilty state of mind would, as argued by many liberals, erode the moral foundations of the criminal law.

In the first edition of their textbook, Brett and Waller highlighted Dixon's criminal judgments, where he signalled his unease at the prospect of a significant conviction being based on strict liability. In the second edition, they quoted parts of Dixon's judgment in *Parker v R*,[46] where, on behalf of the Court, he rejected the House of Lord's controversial decision in *DPP v Smith*.[47] The House of Lords had suggested that the mental element could be established through an objective assessment of what a hypothetical 'reasonable person' would have thought in the circumstances. The case of *Parker v R* has, of course, been lauded for its role in advancing the independence of Australian law. For Brett, however, Dixon's judgment bolstered his attack on precedent, with Dixon's status helping Brett to convince his students of the superior value of principles and the connections between law and morality. Irrespective of what Dixon had said extra judicially about the nature of judicial reasoning, his judgments in this area suggested that the Legal Process view of legal reasoning – reasoned elaboration – was a plausible account of Australian judging. As Waller points out, these developments shaped the book, and his and Brett's teaching:

> Sometimes you have got to be lucky, and there we were in the first year of teaching Crime. This horrendous judgment of the House of Lords [*DPP v Smith*] formed a wonderful kind of coda for us, and then – as I say again, you've got to be lucky. There is Devlin's Maccabean lecture and Herbert's response in *The Listener*, and then his little book on law and morals and then – how much did that controversy and its manifestation in print affect the High Court in *Parker's* case?[48] When I think back to it, how lucky I was to be doing what I was doing at that time. And everything plays a role in how your scholarship develops.[49]

[46] *Parker v R* [1963] ALR 524 (HCA).
[47] *DPP v Smith* [1960] 3 All ER 161 (HL).
[48] *Parker v R* (1963) 111 CLR 610 (HCA).
[49] Waller (n 6).

Reception

Brett and Waller's cases and materials book drew much more attention and enthusiasm than Brett's monograph. Brett and Waller hoped that their efforts in devising innovative teaching materials based on a particular conception of law would help promote a scholarly approach to the writing of legal textbooks.[50] They also hoped that their textbook would encourage other Australian scholars to think of the task of textbook writing as something more than providing a compendium of authoritative sources.[51] This type of problem method is, of course, a regular feature of Australian legal textbook writing today.[52] Incorporating hypotheticals and probing questions that invite critical scrutiny, in amongst cases, legislation and commentary, is common practice. However, Brett and Waller were the first Australians to use this approach, and the success of their book no doubt encouraged its adoption.

The textbook's success can be measured in a number of ways. First, consider its longevity. In 2009, some 47 years after the first edition, Waller and his co-author Bob Williams (who took up the role a few years after Brett's sudden death in 1975) published the eleventh edition of the work, and then retired as authors.[53] A thirteenth edition was published in 2013 with six new authors.[54] Over its life, the book has changed considerably but its original popularity and success was a product of Brett and Waller's pioneering approach and the hard work that went into making it Australia's first comprehensive criminal law textbook. It remained the only case-book on criminal law in Australian common law states until 1979, when AP Bates, TL Buddin and DJ Meure published *The System of Criminal Law: Cases and Materials – New South Wales, Victoria, South Australia*.[55]

Second, consider its popularity. Students and teachers found the book to be both memorable and inventive. It attracted glowing reviews, and students from the 1960s still remember it fondly, recalling some of its more inventive components.[56] Pat Urban, a former student of Brett's, describes the work as the 'bible' on criminal law.[57]

[50] ibid.

[51] ibid.

[52] Most Australian law textbooks incorporate a materials, commentary and problem question format. See, eg, one of Australia's best-selling introductory textbooks: R Creyke, D Hamer, P O'Mara, B Smith and T Taylor, *Laying Down the Law* (Sydney, LexisNexis Butterworths, 2017).

[53] L Waller and CR Williams, *Criminal Law – Text and Cases*, 11th edn (Sydney, Butterworths, 2009).

[54] T Anthony, P Crofts, T Crofts, S Gray, Arlie Loughnan and B Naylor, *Waller and Williams Criminal Law – Text and Cases*, 12th edn (Sydney, LexisNexis, 2013).

[55] GB Elkington, 'Book Review: *The System of Criminal Law: Cases and Materials* by AP Bates, TL Buddin and DJ Meure' (1981) 9 *Sydney Law Review* 497.

[56] Myers said, 'I enjoyed it. I thought it was interestingly and provocatively written. I actually liked reading it and liked studying criminal law through Brett and Waller. What more can one say'. Interview with Allan Myers (Office of Dunkeld Pastoral Co Pty Ltd, Melbourne, 10 June 2014).

[57] Interview with Pat Urban (by telephone, 17 June 2014).

That the first edition of the book was held in high regard is evident not only from the reviews it received, but also from looking at who was recommending its use. Brett asked the publishers to send a copy of the book to Louis B Schwartz, professor at the University of Pennsylvania. He explained that Schwartz was 'going to visit Cambridge for a year beginning next September to teach a course there, and Dr Glanville Williams suggested to him that the book might be the most suitable vehicle for introducing English students to case method teaching'.[58] In Britain, Professor DW Elliot said that the book put his own work on the criminal law (co-authored with Wood) to shame,[59] while Glanville Williams described it as an 'excellent sourcebook'.[60]

Members of the profession in Australia also commended the book. For example, the Solicitor-General of New South Wales, HA Snelling QC, gave it strong praise,[61] Justice Smith of the Victorian Supreme Court said that he found the book of 'great help',[62] and Chief Justice Bray of the South Australian Supreme Court considered it a 'most valuable work' and referred to it in a judgment.[63]

While none of the reviewers ever associated the book with the Legal Process School, they nonetheless recognised some of the book's chief aims and believed that the authors had largely been successful in meeting them. Rupert Cross of Magdalen College, Oxford, reviewed the book while he was a visiting professor at the University of Adelaide. He believed that Brett and Waller had been successful in their ambitious endeavour to incorporate '[t]hree well recognised instruments of legal education … the hypothetical case, the source-book and the narrative account of the development of the present state of the law'.[64] Cross praised the 'authors' own contributions' as 'uniformly first class'.[65] The only substantial criticism he provided was that the case extracts ought to have been longer.[66] Also, in good humour, he rebuked Waller for his criticism of both Cross and Glanville Williams as 'willing to indulge in elaborate arguments with a view to reconciling the cases'.[67] (Waller had been one of his pupils at Oxford.)

[58] Peter Brett to Editor at Butterworths, 25 January 1965, Peter Brett Papers, National Library of Australia, Manuscript Collection. Louis B Schwartz said that he planned to use the book at Cambridge: Louis B. Schwartz to Peter Brett, 16 February 1965, Peter Brett Papers, National Library of Australia, Manuscript Collection.

[59] DW Elliot to Peter Brett, undated, Peter Brett Papers, National Library of Australia, Manuscript Collection.

[60] Glanville Williams to Peter Brett, 15 July 1971, Peter Brett Papers, National Library of Australia, Manuscript Collection.

[61] HA Snelling to FC Judson of Butterworths, 17 March 1965, Peter Brett Papers, National Library of Australia, Manuscript Collection.

[62] Justice Smith to Peter Brett, 5 February 1965, Peter Brett Papers, National Library of Australia, Manuscript Collection.

[63] Chief Justice Bray to Peter Brett, 11 May 1971, Peter Brett Papers, National Library of Australia, Manuscript Collection.

[64] R Cross, 'Book Review: *Cases and Materials in Criminal Law* by Peter Brett and Peter L. Waller' (1962) 3 *Melbourne University Law Review* 546.

[65] ibid 546.

[66] ibid.

[67] ibid 548.

Cross and another reviewer, EM Bingham from the University of Tasmania, both recognised that the book sought to avoid dogmatism and attempted to instil in students a taste for law reform. Bingham (later Sir Max Bingham QC, Rhodes Scholar and future Chair of the Criminal Justice Commission in Queensland) said that the method employed 'provokes the student to formulate his own solutions … to the problems specifically posed'.[68] Cross referred to the risk that the English approach to instruction 'may make students insufficiently conscious of the need for reform'.[69] By contrast, he believed that this textbook removed that risk.[70]

Brett received similarly high praise for the cases and materials book he published on administrative law at around the same time.[71] In the 1960s, at least, Brett and Waller wrote for an appreciative audience who believed they were making a valuable and engaging contribution to legal education: their work departed from the mere methodical summary and exposition of case law and was of use beyond Australia's shores.

Intellectual and Practical Obstacles

There are a number of reasons to explain why the innovations contained within the earlier editions of the textbook have not subsequently received the recognition they deserve. In this section I describe some of the intellectual and practical obstacles. The practical obstacle is easy to state. Following Brett's death, a new author (Bob Williams) took on responsibility for updating the textbook. In the final edition before Brett's death, the book was already being transformed into a grand treatise that sought to authoritatively expound the major principles of criminal law in all Australian states. While Waller and Williams subsequently retained some of the initial innovations of the first few editions, the Legal Process format had largely gone. This can be attributed to Brett's absence, as well as a belief that some aspects of the problem method did not translate effectively into the classroom. According to Waller, they 'took up too much time'.[72] Waller and Williams did not fall into the trap of some of the English textbooks, where subsequent editions of textbooks and treatises were poor imitations of the original, or were distorted by a subsequent author's efforts to merely 'update' the primary sources.[73] Instead, Waller and

[68] EM Bingham, 'Book Review: *Cases and Materials in Criminal Law* by Peter Brett and Peter L. Waller' (1962) 5 *Tasmanian University Law Review* 762.

[69] Cross (n 64) 547.

[70] ibid.

[71] RW Baker, 'Book Review: *Cases on Constitutional and Administrative Law* by Peter Brett' (1962) 5 *Tasmanian University Law Review* 760; SA De Smith, 'Book Review: *Cases on Constitutional and Administrative Law* by Peter Brett' (1961–2) 3 *Melbourne University Law Review* 544.

[72] Waller (n 6).

[73] Australian scholars of this period were generally critical of the English practice of 'propping up works of long dead colleagues rather than writing new texts': S Bartie, 'A Full Day's Work – A Study of

Williams reinvigorated and devised their own initiatives, and the book changed dramatically over the three decades when the pair authored it.

The intellectual obstacle came in the form of changing expectations around what criminal law teachers ought to teach, a broadening conception of the 'criminal law', and a sense that the criminal law – like other areas of law – embodied and entrenched the interests of a sexist and elitist class. While Waller and Williams were able to address at least some of these concerns in subsequent editions, they were not addressed in the original four editions authored by Brett and Waller.

One strand of thought that helps explain the lack of recognition of Brett's contribution to the criminal law is the trajectory of criminal law theory, both during and after the writing of the textbook. Throughout the second half of the twentieth century, there was growing recognition that, in addition to its doctrinal elements, other components of the criminal law were equally important in the quest for justice; for example, police powers and procedures, customary law in Aboriginal communities, racial prejudice in the administration of justice, pre- and post-trial procedures, and the workings of prisons. In a 1969 book review, Richard Fox argued that the Brett and Waller cases and materials book ought to have paid greater heed to these other matters.[74] While Brett touched on some of them in his Masters thesis and also worked directly with the police,[75] they were not a central concern of his first monograph or the cases and materials book, and he did not consider himself to be a criminologist or a sociologist.[76] As greater attention turned to these broader fields and to the rights and interests of victims as well as minority groups, Brett's writings appeared narrow and out of touch with some of the major problems of the criminal law. As noted earlier, Brett and Waller's book drew from learning in the social sciences and was based on a theory for teaching law graduates, but did not present raw social science or philosophical material to students.

Critics of the Legal Process School argued that Hart and Sacks' approach did not prompt deeper questioning of the social assumptions underlying the law.[77] In this sense, the School appeared to stand in sharp contrast to the Marxist sentiment that was popular in the 1970s and 1980s, and which influenced some components of the Critical Legal Studies movement. Barzun argues, and I agree, that this is a mistaken assumption. Brett's career and a careful reading of the Legal Process

Australia's First Legal Scholarly Community' (2010) 29 *University of Queensland Law Journal* 67, 90, 91. See also D Sugarman, 'Legal Theory, the Common Law Mind and the Making of the Textbook Tradition' in William Twining (ed), *Legal Theory and Common Law* (Oxford, Basil Blackwell, 1986) 26, 52.

[74] R Fox, 'Book Review: *Cases and Materials on Criminal Law and Procedure* edited by ML Friedland' (1969) 7 *Melbourne University Law Review* 146, 146–47.

[75] This is discussed further in chapter five.

[76] Letter from Peter Brett to Zelman Cowen, 15 December 1954, Law Dean's Correspondence 1953–1961, University of Melbourne Archives.

[77] As explained in chapter three.

materials suggest that he and scholars like him were aware of the value-laden nature of the law and its institutions. It is clear from his writing and his broader endeavour that Brett was both very conscious of, and repelled by, the elitism and conservatism both within the law and the universities. He believed that an individual's place in a hierarchy should be earned, not inherited, and that institutions should not proceed on the basis of what he saw as the self-satisfied and self-serving assumptions of certain individuals.[78] On numerous occasions, he sought to expose elitist and complacent practices that worked against the good governance of those institutions.[79] His liberalism meant that he had a faith in these institutions that was at odds with the thinking of the Critical Legal Scholars. But it does not follow that he ignored deeper questions concerning these institutions.

On the other hand, there were areas where Brett was clearly blind to some of the prejudices being perpetrated through the law. In particular, some passages of his scholarship and aspects of his teaching were insensitive to the interests of women and blind to the sexism inherent in law. Brett, like several scholars of his time, did little to quell – and, indeed, did much that probably fuelled – the complaints later made by feminist legal scholars of the criminal law and criminal law scholarship. This is most evident in his teaching and writing on the law of rape. Some students at Melbourne in the 1960s remarked on the way that Brett frequently drew on the law of rape in class, and they suggested he made insensitive jokes on the subject.[80] The chapter on sexual assault in the first edition of the Brett and Waller book contains passages that treat instances of sexual assault in a humorous fashion, implicitly trivialising the effect of such assaults on the lives of women.[81] These passages do not appear in the second or subsequent editions, perhaps indicating that the authors subsequently realised their error of judgment.

During the interviews for this project, Ian Leader-Elliot, a student and then colleague of Brett's at Melbourne, provided thoughtful and incisive comments on the way in which the law of rape was taught at the University of Melbourne. Consistent with other student impressions from the time Leader-Elliot recalls that:

> The crime of rape was taken by Brett, Howard and Norval Morris … as kind of archetypal in terms of analysis of criminal liability. Why rape, the most atypical of all the criminal offences, was treated this way was bizarre. So, if we were giving an example

[78] See P Brett, 'The Allocation of Resources between the Teaching Role and the Research Role of the Universities, between Undergraduate and Postgraduate Education, between Liberal and Vocational Education, between Applied and Fundamental Research' (Paper presented at the Third Australian Universities Conference, August 1970).

[79] Chapter five provides several examples.

[80] In a short magazine produced by the Law Students' Society at the University of Melbourne, students caricatured Brett's teaching of law with descriptions such as: 'According to Professor Brett, (our first-year reporter tells us) 'Criminal Law embraces; murder: rape: arson: rape: burglary: rape: manslaughter: rape etc …': M McInerney and D Marsh (eds), 'Lecturers' Quotes', *De Minimis* (Law Students' Society of Victoria) 6 May 1969.

[81] Brett and Waller (1962) (n 1) 217.

> of a crime, rape would be used as an instructive example in teaching criminal law in the early days. In trying to get a point across to students, we would say 'Now, take rape as an example.' ... Rape was centrally important to a Melbourne criminal lawyer's understanding of criminal liability, and that was true of Norval Morris as well. ... many of us involved in criminal law theory at that time could switch from talking about criminal responsibility in rape to criminal responsibility in illicit drug possession with no apparent awareness of incongruity. To anyone other than a criminal lawyer, this juxtaposition of such very different sorts of crime must have seemed very strange indeed.[82]

Leader-Elliot put forward a number of factors that explain how criminal law and the sex offences were taught at Melbourne. First, '[t]here was then an attitude among some teachers (myself among them) that criminal law dealt with often shocking instances of depravity and students ought to be jolted out of what we assumed to be their complacency'.[83] It is evident from the Brett and Waller textbook that Brett set out to make his Criminal Law course shocking and, according to Leader-Elliot, Brett 'delighted at being shocking in his delivery of the rape classes'.[84] Second, there was also 'a Rabelaisian element of crude humour'.[85] Leader-Elliot recalls:

> When I went to teach at Boalt Hall Law School, Berkeley in 1974–75, my American law students – who were so much more assertive and socially adept than my Australian students – very quickly pulled me up on this and many other things and devoted themselves to re-orienting me.[86]

Third, there was also 'a significant theoretical element in the concentration on rape'.[87] One of the central debates at the time concerned whether it was necessary for the defence to establish that an accused had actual knowledge that a woman had not consented to the sexual act. The requirement of actual knowledge, of course, made it more difficult for the prosecution to establish its case. While Brett's monograph on criminal guilt had generally supported a widening of the scope of defences and stressed the central importance of moral wrongdoing in all crime, he did not suggest that the prosecution must establish actual knowledge on the part of the accused. Brett and Waller's textbook also encouraged students to question the fiction behind the immunity for rape in marriage rather than accept it.[88] Hence, while in several ways his efforts worked against the feminist cause and in fact inadvertently encouraged some of the sexism already proliferating within the Law School, these aspects of his doctrinal prescriptions should not have evoked the ire of later feminists.

[82] Leader-Elliot (n 3).
[83] ibid.
[84] ibid.
[85] ibid.
[86] ibid.
[87] ibid.
[88] Brett and Waller (1962) (n 1) 226; Brett and Waller (1965) (n 1) 298. See K Lesses, '*PGA v The Queen* – Marital Rape in Australia: The Role of Repetition, Reputation and Fiction in the Common Law' (2014) 37 *Melbourne University Law Review* 786, 816, 818.

These parts of the criminal law and the way that the teaching of them fed into a sexist culture hostile to women were, with hindsight, clearly unfortunate. While the historical context provides a partial explanation for the insensitivities of some lawyers and academics, it is nonetheless deeply regrettable that Brett played a part in this chapter of the criminal law and the legal academy. In this, Brett was indeed blind to the plight of women's rights.

It may be that the attitude of feminist legal scholars to this aspect of Brett's work has lessened the influence of Brett's criminal law scholarship more generally. According to Fletcher, 'one should not underestimate the importance of articulate opponents or intellectual enemies in developing the profile of an academic field'.[89] While the enemy in this instance was ultimately the legal system itself, scholars like Brett – by apparently legitimising sexist practices and doctrine and feeding a sexist culture through their teaching – could be deemed complicit.[90]

Brett's attitudes and actions in this area stand in stark contrast to the strong activism and compassion he displayed in other aspects of his career. For example, Brett wrote supporting the rights and interests of Indigenous Australians within the justice system. He wrote publicly against the aversion 'treatment' of homosexuals (also appearing on television to speak against such practices). He supported the right to protest in the context of hostilities over the Vietnam War, and engaged in such protests. In several areas, then, Brett seemed ahead of his time. Perhaps, if he lived longer and entered a new world where women occupied a greater role in law, Brett might have come to better appreciate the way in which his teaching of criminal law subordinated women and contributed to a state of gross inequality. Owen Fiss, a US law professor born 20 years after Brett, in 1938, speaks of coming to a similar realisation. In a book chapter about one of his former students, Catharine MacKinnon, he speaks of feeling both 'appalled' and 'ashamed' by his 'silence and that of … fellow classmates' in the face of the sexist treatment of women pupils in the 1960s by Erwin Griswold and W Barton Leach at Harvard Law School.[91] He asks, '[h]ow could we – how could I have remained silent in the face of practices that so grossly offended the principle of equal treatment?'[92] MacKinnon helped him understand how his views on the treatment of women had been inconsistent

[89] GP Fletcher, 'The Fall and Rise of Criminal Theory' (1998) 1 *Buffalo Criminal Law Review* 275, 281.

[90] In an article on rape in legal scholarship, Ngaire Naffine critiques aspects of the sixth edition of the textbook dealing with rape, particularly the authors' suggestion, without sound evidence, that Hale was correct in his statement that women (both within and outside marriage) could easily make false claims of rape: N Naffine, 'Windows on the Legal Mind: The Evocation of Rape in Legal Writings' (1992) 18 *Melbourne University Law Review* 741, 744–45, 746–47. Brett was not alive at the time when the sixth edition was published. The quote from Hale singled out by Naffine appeared in the first edition; however, it was followed by questions, rather than propositions, about the potential for reform in this area: Brett and Waller (1962) (n 1) 209a–210, 217, 226.

[91] O Fiss, *Pillars of Justice–Lawyers and the Liberal Tradition* (Cambridge, Mass., Harvard University Press, 2017) 118.

[92] ibid.

with his commitment to racial equality.[93] Perhaps Brett, too would have come to recognise that his blindness to the plight of women was grossly inconsistent with his liberal thinking on other matters of inequality.

Student Impressions

Brett was a dedicated teacher. He was not, by any stretch, a professor who neglected his teaching in order to advance his scholarship. Teaching was extremely important to him, as shown by his aspirations for criminal law students and his efforts in devising materials for his students. He was critical of particular colleagues who, he believed, let their own interests override those of students. For example, in a manifesto for the Deanship at Melbourne, Brett opposed the Law School becoming a graduate school, where students had to complete two years in another degree before commencing law, as he believed such proposals were 'educationally unsound; an indulgence of teacher preferences to the detriment of student and community interests and an attempt to export our own problems and difficulties to other parts of the university or other institutions'.[94]

In line with their textbook, Brett and Waller pursued a highly interactive teaching style in class. They adopted a Socratic method, where students were assigned a seat and called on pursuant to a seating chart that Brett and Waller had asked the law school manager to arrange.[95] They sat in on each other's classes and rigorously critiqued each other's performance.[96] Waller considered that the experience was critical to his early development:

> After the first two classes [with Brett attending my lectures] I stopped being terrified, and found his presence a comfort, and at the same time a challenge – to ask the most effective question, put the clearest, most accurate proposition and overall make each class a learning occasion for me and for my students. That's what he tried to do in every class. I learned my craft from watching him and from the discussions we had after each of his and my classes.[97]

Students at Melbourne did not, however, always appreciate Brett's efforts in the classroom. The mixed – and often negative – reception Brett's of teaching is one obvious factor in explaining why his conception of law and reforms for the discipline are not well known.

Although several legal academics at the University of Melbourne experimented with the Socratic method of teaching, many students took exception to the

[93] ibid 121.
[94] Peter Brett to Colin Howard, 16 August 1973, Harold Arthur Ford Papers, University of Melbourne Archives.
[95] Waller (n 6).
[96] ibid.
[97] ibid 101.

approach taken by Brett. Brett's belief that students should question and assemble for themselves an understanding of the principles from the materials presented, which they would then discuss during a lecture, proved too onerous for many.[98] In 1954, Brett's first law dean at UWA wrote of his early academic career:

> I have heard it said by some of his better students that 'he knows all the answers' – and a very occasional criticism that he tends to get impatient if they do not always discover the answers for themselves after he has explained the questions. He is reputed to set very stimulating topics for tutorial classes, but to be a little too ready to indulge in sarcastic comment at the expense of those who do not take an active part in the discussion – and that makes them withdraw still further into their private shells.[99]

Allan Myers said that Brett was 'very tough and had no qualms about embarrassing students who were ignorant or prudish. Some of the things he said and did would now be regarded, I think, as unacceptable'.[100] Myers referred to the fact that Brett would often single out a student. If the student didn't know the answer, they would be ridiculed and made to feel as though they hadn't performed.[101] Gareth Evans said, 'I don't particularly remember him being intimidating. I mean, quite sharped tongued and quite smart, but not brutal in the way in which he dealt with students. He was a good, solid, interesting teacher'.[102]

Despite the negative student reviews, of which Brett was well aware (in some instances, large numbers of students stopped attending his classes),[103] Brett continued to take a robust approach that was designed both to shock students and to impress upon them the seriousness of their future career. Some former students describe Brett's teaching in various critical ways, from fierce and aggressive to scattered and unhelpful.[104]

Comparing correspondence between Brett and a student with his letters to colleagues, lawyers, politicians and others, one is struck by the severity he reserved for students.[105] It seems that the warmth and encouragement he often extended to others were not experienced by most of his students. Some recall Brett's generosity to particular students (for example, taking private tutorials for those who were genuinely struggling), but it seems this kindness was rarely on view to the whole

[98] It is interesting to note that Glanville Williams also failed in his experiment to teach students using the Socratic method: D Sugarman, 'A Special Relationship? American Influences on English Legal Education, c 1870–1965' (2011) 18 *International Journal of the Legal Profession* 7, 25.

[99] Report on Peter Brett, 8 November 1954, Law Dean's Correspondence 1953–1961, University of Melbourne Archives.

[100] Myers (n 56).

[101] ibid.

[102] Evans (n 14).

[103] Interview with Richard Fox (Law School, Monash University, 23 October 2013).

[104] See, eg, S Campbell and D Grace (eds), '"Munchies" Fauna of Australia', *De Minimis* (Law Students' Society of Victoria) 3. Brett is depicted as an aggressive, thick-skinned monkey, who, rather than packaging material for students, expects them to assemble the material for themselves.

[105] See, eg, Peter Brett to Simon Wynn, 21 January 1971, Peter Brett Papers, National Library of Australia, Manuscript Collection.

student cohort.[106] The general view was that Brett was intelligent and witty,[107] but that his dramatic presentation and method were at times too challenging and menacing for his undergraduate classes.[108] By contrast, in a reference based on Brett's teaching at Harvard (where he taught older postgraduate students who were more used to a robust Socratic method), Livingston Hall spoke of the high regard in which students held him.[109]

Few students undertook postgraduate studies at the Law School at the University at Melbourne during Brett's tenure. Two students who had Brett as a supervisor (one for an honours and another for a Masters thesis) were interviewed for this project. Each had very different experiences, again demonstrating that both in undergraduate teaching and in the supervision of doctrinal theses Brett's teaching methods received mixed reactions. One student, Richard Fox, spoke of Brett's general lack of pastoral care and his dogmatism.[110] While at first the exchanges were pleasant, with Brett providing favourable comment on a research topic, Fox became frustrated during the second and third meetings by what he perceived as Brett's dogmatic attitude.[111] During the third meeting, Brett pressed Fox to develop a conclusion for his LLM thesis on the legal concept of obscenity.[112] Fox believed that Brett's approach worked against the basic tenets of university research, those of dispassionate and open inquiry.[113] He also considered that Brett's later treatment of him – ignoring him in corridors and making no further inquiries about his thesis – spoke of a general lack of pastoral care.[114] Pat Urban, a former solicitor with the Legal Services Commission in Victoria, undertook an honours thesis in 1972 under Brett's supervision. In contrast to Fox, she describes him as an 'amazing supervisor' who went out of his way to provide her with opportunities to speak to police officers and scientists working in the field of her thesis – on blood alcohol and drivers.[115] Overall, Urban reflects on her thesis as a very positive, perhaps *the* most positive, aspect of her legal studies.[116] Both Fox and Urban received first class honours.

In Waugh's history of the University of Melbourne, Brett, along with Sawer, was criticised for the way that he treated women in class.[117] Some former women

[106] Waller (n 6); Interview with Robin and Jonathan Brett (RACV Club, Melbourne, 11 June 2014).
[107] One former student wrote to me with recollections of various witticisms Brett delivered during his classes: Catherine Turner to Susan Bartie, 2 October 2014.
[108] Campbell and Grace (n 104) 3.
[109] Peter Brett to the Registrar of the University of Melbourne, 26 October 1962, Law Dean's Correspondence 1962–1965, University of Melbourne Archives.
[110] Fox (n 103).
[111] ibid.
[112] ibid.
[113] ibid.
[114] ibid.
[115] Urban (n 57).
[116] ibid.
[117] J Waugh, *First Principles – The Melbourne Law School 1857–2007* (Melbourne, Miegunyah Press, 2007) 167.

students believe that Brett picked on them. When asked about Brett's treatment of women in class, several former students – all men – suggested that Brett treated both men and women alike, subjecting both to the same harsh treatment.[118] They speculated that women felt picked on because they were not accustomed to having the same expectations placed upon them. While there is evidence of sexism in some of Brett's scholarship (considered earlier), Brett's friendships, admiration for particular women scholars, and the way that he promoted and engaged with clever women students, suggest that he would not have wanted to stunt the progress of bright women at law school or in the law more generally. His actions, however, suggest that he was not sympathetic to – or aware of – the disadvantages that flowed from the minority status of women in law, and that he did little to smooth the road.

Fracturing the Teaching Team

Brett and Waller's joint vision for teaching criminal law at Melbourne and creating a certain kind of graduate was fractured when Waller resigned to take up a professorship at Monash University in October 1964.[119] While the two remained close and were in daily contact, Waller's departure meant that Brett lost his closest collaborator: the teachers of criminal law at Melbourne no longer took a unified approach. Waller might have been replaced by a similarly minded colleague, but that is not what happened. The new Hearn Professor, Colin Howard, took up the role.[120] Friction and intellectual differences between Howard and Brett meant that Howard did not embrace Brett's philosophy for the teaching of criminal law and the pair did not work together to create a new pedagogical vision.

All who knew Brett and Howard recognised that, despite their similar academic interests, the two were not close. There are, however, signs that Brett respected Howard's intelligence and that their relationship was good before Howard's arrival at Melbourne. Writing to Henry Hart in 1963, Brett acknowledged that he had 'a very high opinion of [Howard's] abilities as a criminal lawyer',[121] and asked Hart to make Howard welcome during his year at Harvard.[122] Similarly, in a review of Howard's monograph, *Strict Responsibility*, Brett praised the work as being of the 'highest merit'.[123]

[118] While efforts were made to find former women students to speak to this issue, none came forward.

[119] Louis Waller to Zelman Cowen, 8 October 1964, Law Dean's Correspondence 1962–1965, University of Melbourne Archives.

[120] Colin Howard was Hearn Professor of Law from 1965 until 1990, and Dean of the Law School from 1978 to 1983. He also served as a barrister and was appointed Queen's Counsel in 1996.

[121] Peter Brett to Henry Hart, 20 April 1963, Henry Hart Papers, Harvard Law Library.

[122] ibid.

[123] P Brett, 'Book review: *Studies in Criminal Law* by Norval Morris and Colin Howard, *Strict Responsibility* by Colin Howard and *A Casebook on Criminal Law* by DW Elliott and JC Wood' (1965) 5 *Melbourne University Law Review* 106, 107.

Brett and Howard both studied criminal law and shared concerns about prevailing trends towards strict liability for crime. Brett followed in Jerome Hall's footsteps by strongly refuting Oliver Wendell Holmes's earlier suggestion that fault was not a necessary component of all crime.[124] While Howard was not opposed to Brett's position, he modelled his own criminal law scholarship on that of Glanville Williams, rather than Hall or any of the other Americans who excited Brett.

Rather than turning to modern learning, Howard was fascinated by the logical puzzles in law and sought to break the law down into logical propositions. Leader-Elliot remembers Norval Morris once saying that Brett was the 'poet or mystic' and Howard the 'logician or technician'.[125] Allan Myers, who took on Howard as a pupil when he went to the bar to become a barrister, has similar recollections.[126]

Over the course of almost 10 years of teaching criminal law at the same institution, it is clear that Brett and Howard did little to collaborate. In 1971, Brett published an article in the *Modern Law Review* that heavily criticised the reasoning Howard deployed in suggesting that the High Court of Australia had abandoned strict responsibility in favour of liability for negligence. Brett sought Howard's comments on a draft of the article and was concerned to ensure that his criticisms did not cause offence. The interchange between Brett and Howard is recorded entirely in memoranda, suggesting that at no time did they speak face-to-face about the paper; Howard displayed little sign of wishing to engage Brett in debate.[127]

Some former students and colleagues remember Howard's charisma, and believe that he took greater care than Brett to cultivate certain junior members of staff.[128] His warmer public persona meant that several members of the next generation of legal scholars were recruited to his camp and to his approach to studying criminal law.[129] While Brett had a group of close and loyal colleagues from the Law School,[130] Howard's stronger relationship with junior scholars and students had the potential to diminish the influence of Brett's ideas.

Howard's presence was not fatal to Brett and Waller's initiatives: the pair continued to collaborate and publish new editions of their cases and materials book, and

[124] Brett (n 37) 48–49; L Waller, 'Book Review: *General Principles of the Criminal Law* by Jerome Hall' (1961) 3 *Melbourne University Law Review* 86, 86.

[125] Leader-Elliot (n 3). This was also consistent with the impression of Allan Myers. Brett and Myers became friends while the pair taught in Canada at Osgoode Hall Law School. Howard became Myers's pupil when he went to the bar: Myers (n 56).

[126] Myers (n 56).

[127] See, eg, Memorandum from Colin Howard to Peter Brett, 25 August 1971, Peter Brett Papers, National Library of Australia, Manuscript Collection; Memoranda from Peter Brett to Colin Howard, 17 September 1971 and 20 September 1971, Peter Brett Papers, National Library of Australia, Manuscript Collection.

[128] Fox (n 103); Leader-Elliot (n 3).

[129] Leader-Elliot (n 3).

[130] Brett's sons mentioned the following academics as part of Brett's close circle of friends: Louis Waller, Harold Ford, Frank Maher and Mary Hiscock. Robin and Jonathan Brett (n 106).

the book was prescribed reading for criminal law students at Melbourne, as well as at several other law schools. However, the nature of Brett and Howard's relationship diminished the possibility of further strong Melbourne initiatives in the teaching of criminal law. This meant that not all Melbourne students at this time received an instruction in the criminal law overlaid with legal process sentiment, or were encouraged to see the criminal law as something more than a process of logical induction and deduction. Had Brett and Howard reconciled their differences, or had Waller stayed on, it is possible that more dynamic teaching initiatives would have ensued and the Legal Process sentiment would have become more widely known and appreciated.

Concluding Remarks

Brett and Waller's textbook, based on a Legal Process model, constituted one of several initiatives put in place by their generation of legal scholars to challenge narrow conceptions of judicial reasoning. It did not encourage its students to see judicial reasoning as openly instrumental reasoning. Instead, it encouraged students to engage with the moral dilemmas at the heart of law and to recognise that the common law presented choices rather than single authoritative solutions. This faith in the common law was a result of Brett's concerns about the implications of codifying the criminal law. It also appears that Brett had some faith in Australia's judiciary and, in particular, Sir Owen Dixon. The challenge was not to encourage a departure from Dixon's approach, but to convince Australian lawyers that judicial reasoning in Australia was not as narrow as Dixon had seemed to suggest in extra-judicial comment, or as was commonly believed by Australia's conservative legal profession.

The popularity of the work, and its strong endorsements, suggests that it gained some traction and that judging in Australia (although unknowingly) embraced the Legal Process concept of 'reasoned elaboration' to a greater extent than elsewhere. This also suggests that it influenced Australian lawyering more generally in ways that we cannot measure. Perhaps for this reason, Griswold would have been pleased. The Harvard conception of law helped to bring about a change in judicial reasoning. Australian judicial reasoning in the second half of the twentieth century certainly seems more in line with Legal Process thinking than the instrumental tendencies of the US Supreme Court.[131] Despite these achievements, Brett and Waller's contributions are neither well known nor well understood.

In 2003, Justice Heydon observed that a new class of judges had emerged in Australia: 'a segment of ambitious, vigorous, energetic and proud judges' who

[131] See, eg, the comparisons made in T Josev, *The Campaign against the Courts – A History of the Judicial Activism Debate* (Sydney, Federation Press, 2017).

'think that they can not only right every social wrong, but achieve some form of immortality in doing so'.[132] He argued that this new class arose 'partly because almost all modern judges were educated in law schools staffed by professional law teachers as distinct from practitioners teaching part-time, and a critical analysis of the merits of legal rules was a significant aspect of that education' and also partly because of an increased interest in American law.[133] His gaze was set firmly on Australian judges educated in the 1950s and 1960s. Irrespective of whether Heydon's criticisms are warranted, his comments suggest that the law teachers of this first generation had brought about some kind of change. Scholars have made similar causal connections, albeit in more sympathetic or at least neutral terms, by hypothesising that the Mason court's dynamism was a product of their teachers, in particular Julius Stone, adoption of American Legal Realism and Sociological jurisprudence.[134] I suggest that the story is more interesting, and perhaps more complex, than either of these portrayals.

Two of the leading law teachers who produced one of the most popular textbooks of the time – and the only extensive criminal law textbook until 1979 – did not simply adopt an American conception of what a criminal lawyer ought to be or do. They possessed far greater faith in the courts than their American contemporaries, and thought of their students as future lawyers rather than government advisers. Their views largely accorded with more dynamic readings of Dixon, although they perhaps encouraged their students and lawyers to subject the law to greater scrutiny and engage in greater reflection on its moral qualities. While it is impossible to measure the influence of Brett and Waller's textbook, its prominence suggests that it should be factored into accounts of potential contributors to judicial attitudes. It takes no stretch of the imagination to suggest that Brett and Waller contributed to the change in mood that swept over several elements of the Australian judiciary and profession in the late twentieth century.

[132] JD Heydon, 'Judicial Activism and the Death of the Rule of Law' (2003) 2 *Australian Bar Review* 1, 29.

[133] ibid. In a less critical vein, Weber has argued that the 'rational, systematic character' and 'relatively small degree of concreteness' of the 'legal concepts produced by academic law-teaching' 'result in a far-reaching emancipation of legal thinking from the everyday needs of the public'. M Weber, *Economy and Society* (1978), quoted in D Weisbrot, *Australian Lawyers* (Melbourne, Longman Cheshire, 1989) 123.

[134] A Blackshield, 'The Legacy of Julius Stone' (1997) 20 *University of New South Wales Law Journal* 215, 225.

Portrait of Peter Brett. Image courtesy of Louis Waller

Portrait of Peter Brett. Image courtesy of Louis Waller

Legal team of Robert Peter Tait, 1962: Trial of Robert Peter Tait, Melbourne, Victoria, 1962: [L-R] Mr. J. H. Phillips, Dr. Peter Brett, Mr. John A. Nimmo, QC., Professor David C. Derham PICTURE: Fairfax Photographic, Fairfax Syndication

Peter Brett appearing in trial of Robert Peter Tait PICTURE: Fairfax Photographic, Fairfax Syndication

5

One of Australia's 'Pillars of Justice'?

Introduction

In this chapter, I move beyond Brett's teaching and scholarship to examine his role as a lawyer statesman.[1] In keeping with the activities of his predecessors at Melbourne Law School, Brett believed he had a responsibility to use his expertise to improve the way that institutions (both legal and academic) and lawyers operated. For Brett, these activities were as important as his academic work, as well as an extension of it. His relentless campaigns made him a role model, as he encouraged both lawyers and law students to take responsibility for Australia's legal system and to call out all manner of injustices. No public official was immune from Brett's scrutiny and criticism. In doing so, he challenged what he believed to be a strongly conservative legal and university culture. In this work Brett presented as immensely able – a clear 'can-do' man, who was unfazed by the varying levels of responsibility thrust upon him.

It is possible to view these activities as another product of Harvard's influence. Brett's mentors at Harvard, along with other prominent law professors of his period, involved themselves in efforts to improve the law, casting themselves as supreme legal experts. However, Brett's desire to put his ideas into practice was on display well before his first trip to America. Despite having trained in England, it is doubtful that his enthusiasm for the role of lawyer statesman was inspired by an English model. While English legal scholars such as HLA Hart and Glanville Williams were involved in a number of public campaigns, the extent of Brett's frank and severe criticisms of some Australian public officials and judges sat uneasily with the English deferential tradition.[2]

It seems more likely that Brett's endeavours were a product of his independent mind and spirit and a Melbourne Law School tradition. His association with Zelman Cowen, Norval Morris and Justice Barry appears to have fed both his

[1] The title of this chapter is taken from O Fiss, *Pillars of Justice – Lawyers and the Liberal Tradition* (Cambridge, Mass., Harvard University Press, 2017) 1–2. Brett, standing against the instrumental tendencies of the US Supreme Court would not fit Fiss's definition of a 'pillar of justice'. The question here is whether he might fit the Australian equivalent.

[2] See, eg, HLA Hart's reflections on the deferential nature of the English legal profession in the middle of the twentieth century: D Sugarman, 'Hart Interviewed: HLA Hart in Conversation with David Sugarman' (2005) 32 *Journal of Law and Society* 267, 293.

'readiness for public intervention' and a belief in himself as an intellectual 'who would advance understanding of law, society and government through a variety of media and personal performance'.[3] Historian Mark Finnane has described the many ways that the sense of public obligation to advance the public good felt by Cowen, Morris and Barry prompted them to advance a range of activities.[4] In this chapter I explain how Brett pursued the same agenda with substantial vigour and applied his unique talents to furthering the public good.

Here, again, Brett's career attests to the importance of the institutional climate fostered by Cowen and others as the Australian legal academy was forming. The ethos at Melbourne cultivated the idea that legal academics were in a privileged position relative to other lawyers. Freed from the pressures of attracting and serving clients, they had a duty to contribute to society and show moral leadership within the profession. The early law professors are portrayed in far more altruistic terms then other practising lawyers of the time.[5] Their intellectual prowess, along with their public duties, places them in a class alongside the better judges. This chapter reveals how Brett made the most of this privileged position.

Orr

One of Brett's most significant, yet largely unacknowledged, achievements came about in the 1960s when he served as President of the Federation of Australian Universities' Staff Association (FAUSA) at a very turbulent time. FAUSA was involved in attempts to broker a settlement between one of its members (philosophy professor, Sydney Sparks Orr) and the University of Tasmania, in what became known as the 'Orr dispute'. The matter is of immense significance in the history of Australian universities. At its heart was the protection of academic freedoms, which, it seemed, the University of Tasmania had been eroding for some time. Orr's treatment was viewed as an attempt to silence one of the University's fiercest critics. As a representative body for university staff across Australia, Brett's role as President of FAUSA was to represent the interests of both Orr and his former colleagues.

The Orr dispute has been the subject of scholarly and popular commentary.[6] Here, the essential details are recounted along with an explanation of Brett's role – something that is not fully revealed in the existing accounts. In 1954, Orr wrote a

[3] M Finnane, 'Law as an Intellectual Vocation' (2015) 38 *Melbourne University Law Review* 1060, 1060, 1061, 1062, 1076.

[4] ibid.

[5] See, eg, the negative portrayal of Victorian lawyers in R McQueen, 'Together We Fall, Divided We Stand: The Victorian Legal Profession in Crisis 1890–1940' in WW Pue and D Sugarman (eds), *Lawyers and Vampires: Cultural Histories of Legal Professions* (Oxford, Hart Publishing, 2003) 293.

[6] Several books are devoted to the subject: see, eg, WHC Eddy, *Orr* (Brisbane, Jacaranda, 1961); C Pybus, *Gross Moral Turpitude: The Orr Case Reconsidered* (Melbourne, Heinemann, 1993).

letter to the Tasmanian Premier and Minister for Education outlining his concerns over the poor governance of the University of Tasmania. He pointed to the lack of academic representation on university boards, and to generally poor standards of governance. As a result, he suggested, the University was not fulfilling its responsibilities. Orr was particularly concerned that academics did not have the final say over academic matters, such as entry standards. This letter was the impetus for a Royal Commission into the University in 1955 that made findings largely in accordance with the dissatisfaction felt by Orr and many of his colleagues. The existing regime, however, was slow to implement the findings, prompting more activism by Orr and others. One example of the University's defiance of the Commission's findings occurred on 15 December 1955, when it sanctioned the continuation of the University Council in its previous form, as opposed to implementing measures that would encourage greater academic involvement in governance.

The Orr dispute arose out of allegations that Orr had affairs with four female students, which amounted to sexual misconduct and breached the University's code of conduct. The timing of the allegations – brought by the Vice-Chancellor just one day after legislation securing the continuation of the old governance model was passed in the Tasmanian Parliament – led to suspicions that Orr was being framed to prevent him raising further objections to the University's management. Following investigations by the University Council and Vice-Chancellor, Orr was summarily dismissed on 16 March 1956. He challenged the dismissal in the Supreme Court of Tasmania. The Court found that Orr was liable for sexual misconduct with respect to one of the students, and the University was entitled to dismiss him. A special leave application was then made to the High Court of Australia, which found no reason to interfere.

The saga continued as various people voiced their support for Orr and accused the University of unfair dealings. There was a large public campaign, with both students and staff moving in protest. Staff Associations from universities around Australia took up Orr's cause; even the Presbyterian Church launched an investigation, which concluded Orr was innocent. In September 1960, FAUSA became involved and passed a resolution that the University of Tasmania had failed to afford Orr natural justice, that it had insufficient evidence to dismiss Orr on the basis of sexual misconduct, and that it had conducted its litigation against Orr in a manner that was unfitting for a university. It resolved that, unless the University entered into negotiations with FAUSA for the speedy resolution of the matter, a censure would be imposed whereby FAUSA would inform all members of academic staff, as well as international associations, of its position on the University of Tasmania's conduct. FAUSA's request was rejected and the censure imposed, resulting in long-term damage to the University's reputation and culture.

Brett's time as President of FAUSA coincided with the conclusion of the Orr dispute and it seems that he played a significant role in bringing the matter to an end. Despite the seemingly intractable nature of the dispute, Brett was able to obtain assurances from the Vice-Chancellor of the University of Tasmania that the University would conclude a settlement amount with Orr.[7] After almost a decade of conflict between the parties, a satisfactory settlement was reached shortly after Brett's negotiations took place. Brett also obtained the Vice-Chancellor's agreement to implement a set of tenure rules that would give academics at the University security and would hopefully prevent or at least reduce the risk of future cases of unfair dismissal.[8] Brett played a part in amending previously proposed tenure rules (to ensure that the bar for dismissal was set sufficiently high, with the primary grounds being 'gross misconduct') and in implementing procedures to ensure that decision-makers had a sufficient level of impartiality.[9] If the University agreed to the tenure rules, FAUSA would lift the censure that was damaging the University's reputation and deterring academics from seeking employment there. Brett secured the Vice-Chancellor's agreement and the censure was lifted.[10] He was also instrumental in arranging for the University to make a public statement to clear Orr's name. Brett later revealed that he was particularly concerned that any settlement between the University and Orr be reached quickly: Orr was in poor health, suffering from a heart condition, and any potential libel action against the University would cease following his death.[11]

Despite his quick action and attempt to keep all interested parties informed of his various strategies and dealings, Brett faced criticism from members of the University of Tasmania Staff Association and others of Orr's supporters who considered that they had not been sufficiently consulted.[12] They were concerned that the heads of agreement would be reached in the absence of any settlement of Orr's grievances.[13] The matter had become so embittered and seemingly intractable that tempers were high. Brett's correspondence throughout this period speaks of high-level diplomacy skills. Both strategic foresight and a strong level of restraint can be detected in Brett's correspondence, as he responds to strong criticisms with gentle reason rather than strong reproach. He was quick to caution against any action he believed would undermine the potential for a settlement. A confidential memorandum addressed to 'all executives of Staff Associations' noted that, 'Professor Brett's achievement, on December 10th in association with

[7] Peter Brett to Professor SW Carey, Chairman of the Staff Association at the University of Tasmania, 20 September 1965, Brett Staff Association (Orr Case), University of Melbourne Archives. Cassandra Pybus has also detailed aspects of Brett's involvement in her history of the Orr dispute: Pybus (n 6) 193–7.

[8] ibid.

[9] ibid.

[10] Confidential Memorandum to 'All Executives of Staff Associations', 14 December 1965, Brett Staff Association (Orr Case), University of Melbourne Archives.

[11] Brett to Carey, 25 July 1966, Brett Staff Association (Orr Case), University of Melbourne Archives.

[12] See, eg, IR McPhail to Peter Brett, 29 November 1965, and Carey Brett, 4 October 1965, Brett Staff Association (Orr Case), University of Melbourne Archives.

[13] ibid.

Dr Rodda, in assisting the parties to this stage and getting evidence of the bona fides of the University of Tasmania and its assurances to us deserves the highest respect'.[14] It was also Brett's efforts that led to the University making a public statement to clear Orr's name.[15]

Nonetheless, Brett received further criticism for failing to take steps to secure a new position for Orr in an Australian university.[16] It was Brett's view that the Association should only intervene if asked to do so by Orr. There was no reason to believe that Orr was incapable of winning a position on his own merit; any approach by the Association might suggest otherwise.[17] Orr died on 15 July 1966 without superannuation, and his family was left with nothing (the settlement money had gone to paying his existing debts). This led to further animosity and may have suggested to some that Brett and the Association should have done more to protect Orr's interests. Brett attempted to obtain money for Orr's family, but there was little he could do.

Brett's dealings indicate that he was an able president of FAUSA, someone who was willing to enter into a bitter political fray and subject himself to personal criticism to advance the solution that he believed was the best given difficult circumstances. The energies he expended on the matter demonstrate again his immense industriousness and dedication to improving the state of Australian universities.

Tait, Beamish, Ratten

Tait

Like his colleague Norval Morris, Brett had a 'lifelong interest in the fate of the incarcerated',[18] and his most public and notable work as a lawyer statesman arose in connection with prisoners. In the 1960s and 1970s, Brett became involved with three high-profile murder cases. In the first, he intervened to prevent the execution of Robert Tait, who had been convicted of the brutal murder of an 82-year-old woman.[19] Brett had previously written about capital punishment and strongly

[14] Confidential Memorandum to 'All Executives of Staff Associations', 14 December 1965, Brett Staff Association (Orr Case), University of Melbourne Archives.

[15] Peter Brett to James Grieve, Australian National University Staff Association, 1 July 1966, Brett Staff Association (Orr Case), University of Melbourne Archives.

[16] See, eg, James Grieve, Australian National University Staff Association, to GWF Smith, Executive Secretary of FAUSA, 22 June 1966, Brett Staff Association (Orr Case), University of Melbourne Archives.

[17] See Peter Brett to WJ Ginnane, Honourable General Secretary AAP, The School of General Studies, 2 June 1966, and Peter Brett to James Grieve, Australian National University Staff Association 1 July 1966, Brett Staff Association (Orr Case), University of Melbourne Archives.

[18] Finnane (n 3) 1061.

[19] For an exposition of the case, see C Burns, *The Tait Case* (Melbourne, Melbourne University Press, 1962).

condemned the prevailing practice in Victoria where the fate of a convicted murderer depended on whether a State Labor or Liberal government held power. While statute mandated the death penalty for murder, it was the practice of Labor governments to commute all death sentences, while the Liberal government did not.[20] Brett objected to the unfairness that this contingency created. The large public outcry and protests following the announcement of Tait's impending execution suggested that a large proportion of the Victorian public did not support the death penalty. Nonetheless, neither Liberal nor Labor governments had been willing to bring the matter before parliament and risk a debate over the reform of the legislation that would polarise their voters.

Within days of Tait's scheduled execution, various applications were made to the Supreme Court of Victoria, and then the High Court, to have Tait's death sentence commuted on the grounds that the common law provided that the State could not execute an insane man. While the Crown and Tait's experts agreed that he had various mental illnesses, they disagreed over whether he was insane in the legal sense. The proceedings were carried out in an atmosphere of heightened drama, with courts sitting at short notice and into the night as the executive pressed on with its intention to execute Tait within a matter of days. When Tait's counsel was called away on another trial, Waller suggested to Tait's legal team at Corr and Corr[21] that David Derham and Peter Brett should be briefed, as senior and junior counsel respectively, to appear before the High Court. Waller thought 'we needed some heavy artillery'.[22]

On the eve of the day set for Tait's execution, the High Court made an order to restrain the executive from dealing further with Tait until the Court had sufficient time to form and deliver its judgment on the matter. A few days later, without explanation, the executive commuted Tait's sentence to life imprisonment. It was clear that the government viewed the court proceedings as an illegitimate form of political protest. Some observers saw the later execution of Ronald Ryan, the last man in Australia to receive the death penalty, as a matter of the Victorian Liberal government reasserting its authority.[23] Whether the litigation was a successful piece of political advocacy therefore remains in doubt.

Beamish and Ratten

In the 1960s, the nation was struck by a series of rapes and murders in Perth, Western Australia. The crimes continue to capture the imagination of residents,

[20] P Brett, 'Conditional Pardons and the Commutation of Death Sentences' (1957) 20 *Modern Law Review* 131, 144.

[21] Interview with Louis Waller (Law School, Monash University, 23 October 2013 and 25 November 2013).

[22] ibid.

[23] Z Cowen, *A Public Life – The Memoirs of Zelman Cowen* (Melbourne, Miegunyah Press, 2006) 214–15.

some of whom are now authors. In the celebrated Australian novel, *Cloudstreet* (1991), Tim Winton imagines Perth in the 1950s and 1960s:

> The city is howling with outrage. They're talking of bringing in the army, bringing across the Sydney homicide squad, Scotland Yard. The whole city goes mad with fear and outrage.[24]

A generation later, Craig Silvey's award-winning *Jasper Jones* (2009) conjures a 'fever of panic against an unseen evil, as though Perth were Gotham City itself'.[25] It is now generally accepted that corrupt police officers framed suspects in order to close cases and quell public hysteria.[26]

Brett's involvement in a second murder trial, the *Beamish* case in Western Australia, was far more extensive than the time he spent on the *Tait* case. He adopted the role of activist and expert counsel. Over a number of years, he was largely responsible for drawing the matter to public attention and for Beamish's eventual release from prison. The case concerned the conviction of a deaf and intellectually disabled man, Darryl Beamish, for the brutal murder of Ms Jillian Brewer, a wealthy Perth socialite. Beamish was sentenced to death, with his sentence commuted. While he was in prison, serial killer Eric Edgar Cooke confessed to Brewer's murder. Following Cooke's confession, Beamish's solicitors were successful in their petition to have the matter brought before the Western Australian Supreme Court for a second time. The Court did not, however, order a retrial.

Brett was so incensed by the various injustices he believed to have been committed by the police, prosecution and justices in handling the case that he was moved not only to assist Beamish's counsel, but to also write a short pamphlet about the case. Among other things, Brett's pamphlet criticised the police for the way that they interrogated and elicited a confession from someone with Beamish's level of disability;[27] the Crown for failing to bring forth medical evidence that would have strengthened the accused's case;[28] and the Western Australian Supreme Court for the way that it handled the law and facts, its confused interpretation of principle, and its bias.[29] He alleged that, by hearing the case a second time, the Court had participated in hearing an appeal against its own decision and, further, that the judgments demonstrated actual bias.[30] Brett concluded his pamphlet on a note of strong condemnation, which left the reader in no doubt of this belief that the legal officials had infringed both the law and morality: 'The judges, Crown Law officers,

[24] T Winton, *Cloudstreet* (Melbourne, Penguin, 2007) 373.

[25] C Silvey, *Jasper Jones* (Sydney, Allen & Unwin, 2009) 106.

[26] B Christian, *Presumed Guilty: When Cops Get it Wrong and Courts Seal the Deal* (Melbourne, Hardie Grant, 2013).

[27] P Brett, *The Beamish Case* (Melbourne, Melbourne University Press, 1966) 7–8, 57.

[28] ibid 23, 24, 52, 56, 57.

[29] ibid 16, 18–19, 21, 22–23, 56, 57.

[30] ibid.

and police who participated in the sorry proceedings which I have described can be left to live with their own consciences'.[31] The publication received the attention that Brett hoped for, with copies of the pamphlet selling out and newspaper articles about the piece appearing all over Australia.

In 1970, Brett's reputation for intervening in miscarriages of justice earned him an invitation to assist another man, Leith Ratten, who had been convicted of murder in Brett's home state of Victoria. The request for assistance came from a politician, Don Chipp, then Federal Minister for Customs in the Liberal-Country Party government and later the first leader of the Australian Democrats. On 7 May 1970, Ratten's wife, who at the time was eight-and-a-half months pregnant, died of a gunshot wound. Ratten did not deny that he had fired the shot, but argued that it was a result of his carelessness rather than an intentional act. He said he had been cleaning his double-barrelled shotgun at the time. He called the police as soon as the incident occurred. The Crown's case consisted of circumstantial evidence which, they argued, proved Ratten's act was deliberate. The prosecution also argued that Ratten had a motive: an affair with Jennifer Kemp, who had told her husband that she was leaving him and had placed her house on the market. The Crown suggested that Ratten believed his wife's death would enable him to begin a life with Kemp, free of moral condemnation. Ratten was sentenced to death, which was later commuted to 25 years' imprisonment.[32]

In both the *Beamish* and *Ratten* cases, Brett mastered the legal and factual points and devised strategies to have the matters challenged both in the courts and through appeals to the government. Papers from this time read a little like a Sherlock Holmes novel, with Brett discovering arguments and avenues that Ratten's lawyers had not.[33] Brett's relationships with various scientists and medical researchers, as well as his own interest in science, helped him scrutinise the Crown's case, in particular their claim that Ratten's account of events could not be reconciled with expert evidence.[34] Brett also engaged in an extensive media and political campaign. He wrote to politicians, published newspaper articles and, in one instance, was interviewed on television. He kept both causes alive.

In the *Beamish* case, Brett's efforts were, in one sense, successful. When a Labor Government was elected in Western Australia in 1971, Brett wrote to the new Premier, John Tonkin, to remind him of his pledge to release Beamish.[35] The Premier was true to his word and Beamish was released; however, he was placed on parole rather than granted a pardon. Beamish's parents believed that

[31] ibid 57.

[32] For a further exposition of the case, see T Molomby, *Ratten: The Web of Circumstance* (Melbourne, Outback Press, 1978).

[33] See collection of correspondence in the Peter Brett Papers, MS 5603, Box 5, File 25 Beamish Case, National Library of Australia, Manuscript Collection.

[34] Brett sought assistance from one of Australia's leading pathologists, Dr KM Bowden, and a specialist in anatomy at the University of Melbourne, Professor LJ Ray: Report from Peter Brett to DL Chipp, 29 October 1971, Peter Brett Papers, National Library of Australia, Manuscript Collection.

[35] See collection of correspondence in Peter Brett Papers, MS 5603, Box 5, File 25 Beamish Case, Tonkin, National Library of Australia, Manuscript Collection.

this meant that the stigma on Beamish remained.[36] It also meant that Beamish's ongoing liberty was less assured. Their fears were not unwarranted. When, a year later, Beamish was charged with a minor offence, his parole was revoked and he returned to prison to serve the remainder of his sentence. He was finally released in 1976, a year after Brett's death.

Brett's efforts in the *Ratten* case were ultimately in vain (Ratten served out his sentence). Yet, his innovative strategies kept the matter alive. He was successful in his application to the Attorney-General to have Mrs Ratten's body exhumed,[37] and he led others to believe in Ratten's innocence, or at least to doubt his guilt. This was important. As Ratten wrote to Brett from prison:

> After you visited, something awakened in me again. It was not so much the fact of your efforts and report, but the knowledge that not all of humanity was against me, and that in you I could find saneness in a seemingly mad world.[38]

Similarly, in the *Beamish* case, Brett had considerable success in turning public opinion.

Brett's dedication to these various causes is also reflected in numerous letters he wrote to both Ratten and Beamish and their families and the visits he made to prison.[39] In these dealings he displayed a great deal of compassion. He deployed a deliberate strategy aiming to give hope while keeping expectations in check. He also responded individually to a mountain of correspondence (hundreds of letters) from members of the public, both thanking them for their support (where provided) and providing clarification on matters where correspondents were confused.[40] He continued to write, campaign and provide expert advice, even while he was in America and Canada on sabbatical and following his heart attack in late 1973. During the months before his death, Brett wrote to Ratten with constructive advice on how to deal with the Surveyor Board's decision to suspend Ratten's surveyor's licence.[41] He also wrote to the Solicitor-General, Daryl Dawson, requesting permission to give Ratten a lie detector or polygraph test.[42] The request was refused.[43]

[36] Mr and Mrs Beamish to Brett, 4 May 1971, Peter Brett Papers, National Library of Australia, Manuscript Collection.

[37] GO Reid, Attorney-General of Australia, to MR Reese, 17 April 1972, Peter Brett Papers, National Library of Australia, Manuscript Collection.

[38] Leith Ratten to Peter Brett, 8 July 1972, Peter Brett Papers, National Library of Australia, Manuscript Collection.

[39] See, eg, Memorandum by Peter Brett regarding his visit to Ratten in Pentridge Prison, 2 March 1972, and Brett to Mr and Mrs Beamish, 1 July 1971, Peter Brett Papers, National Library of Australia, Manuscript Collection.

[40] See folder of correspondence in Peter Brett Papers, MS 5603, Folder 4, Correspondence with Public, National Library of Australia, Manuscript Collection.

[41] Peter Brett to Leith Ratten, 21 April 1975, Peter Brett Papers, National Library of Australia, Manuscript Collection.

[42] Peter Brett to Daryl Dawson, Solicitor-General of Victoria, 9 April 1975, Peter Brett Papers, National Library of Australia, Manuscript Collection.

[43] Daryl Dawson, Solicitor-General, to Peter Brett, 10 April 1975, Peter Brett Papers, National Library of Australia, Manuscript Collection.

A Mixed Reception

In 1990, legal scholar David Weisbrot in a book entitled *Australian Lawyers* suggested that the relationship between the profession and legal academics was strongly divided and unhealthy. He thought that this was, at least in part, because legal academics 'have been far more actively involved in progressive legal and social issues than the profession'.[44] He also considered that Australian legal scholars were largely shut off from shaping the legal system.[45] In light of these comments, it is worth considering how members of the profession reacted to a legal academic's attempt to criticise judges, lawyers and police officers and to hold them to account.

Brett received encouragement and support, in the form of letters and offers of assistance, from members of the profession[46] as well as the legal academy. Many held him and his efforts in very high esteem. In 1966, Julius Stone, Chair of Jurisprudence and International Law at the University of Sydney, wrote to Brett:

> Your thoughtful gift of the important and exciting Beamish piece accelerates the intention that I already had to write and congratulate you on the public service you are doing by reopening the question of miscarriage of justice. I trust that the parliamentary move in Western Australia is followed through and has some result.[47]

Chief Justice of the High Court, Sir Owen Dixon, said that he admired 'the great industry and hard work of Professor Brett',[48] while the Dean of the Law School at Harvard, Erwin Griswold, said:

> I expect that you will get some violent and unhappy reactions, particularly from some of the more conservative members of the bar. It is very good, though, that there are persons like you who are willing to dig into these matters, and to speak up about them. Keep up the good work.[49]

Griswold's predictions and understanding of the likely reaction of the Australian legal profession were soon borne out. A member of the Western Australian Bar and legal academic at UWA, Douglas Payne, was so affronted that he wrote a long review essay of Brett's pamphlet, issuing a blistering attack on its central argument as well as Brett personally.[50] Payne accused Brett of failing to disclose the work he

[44] D Weisbrot, *Australian Lawyers* (Melbourne, Longman Cheshire, 1989) 146.

[45] ibid 147.

[46] See, eg, RE McGarvie to Peter Brett, 12 October 1966, Peter Brett Papers, National Library of Australia, Manuscript Collection.

[47] Julius Stone to Peter Brett, 25 August 1966, Peter Brett Papers, National Library of Australia, Manuscript Collection.

[48] Sir Owen Dixon to Peter Brett's publisher, Mr Ryan, 15 August 1966, Peter Brett Papers, National Library of Australia, Manuscript Collection.

[49] Erwin Griswold to Peter Brett, 18 August 1966, Peter Brett Papers, National Library of Australia, Manuscript Collection.

[50] D Payne, 'Book Review: *The Beamish Case* by Peter Brett' (1966) *Western Australian Law Review* 583.

had undertaken to advise Beamish's counsel in the second trial, suggesting that Brett was himself biased. He stated that the 'pamphlet reveals a disposition not to accept the ordinary processes of the law which is reminiscent of the *Tait* and *Orr* cases'.[51] It was clear that Payne represented the strong conservative element within Australia's legal profession which believed that open criticism of judges and the working of the system served to erode its legitimacy. Brett found Payne's position puzzling:

> It defeats me why an academic should decide to enter the lists on behalf of judges who sit on appeal from themselves. And since he chose to make some unpleasant personal references to me, I had no compunction in replying with vigour.[52]

Little did Payne know that his public condemnation of Brett would only serve to further Beamish's cause. Brett published a reply and then Payne added a rejoinder, all of which were picked up by the press, helping Brett to gain further publicity for the case as well as public support. Journalist Syd Donovan also took on Beamish's cause and Channel TVW in Perth invited Brett to participate in an hour-long panel discussion, along with Payne and others. It is clear from the transcript that Brett prepared well for the discussion. Payne, who had been reluctant to appear in the first place, appears to be the least knowledgeable member of the panel and his contributions come across as hesitant and a little muddled. By contrast, Brett seems both confident and authoritative. Brett's own assessment of his performance was that he 'emerged easily the victor'.[53] The television channel shared Brett's view. Donovan told Brett that his appearance was met

> with overwhelming approval of you and your point of view. Peter, my telephone has run hot at the office and at home – with people wanting to tell me how much they enjoyed the programme and how convincingly you argued your case. You will be interested to know that a number of them have been lawyers who, without exception, were loud in their praise of you. … TVW managing director Jim Cruthers was elated with the whole deal and considers it probably the most important programme TVW have undertaken.[54]

The managing director of TVW Limited wrote to Brett to inform him that because 'a number of people, including the Premier, did not see the full programme, we are repeating it this coming Sunday night'.[55]

Some police officers took issue with Brett's criticisms of the police force. However, Brett had the support of some of the force's most senior members.

[51] ibid 604.

[52] Peter Brett to Frank Beasley, 30 June 1967, Peter Brett Papers, National Library of Australia, Manuscript Collection.

[53] Peter Brett to Frank Beasley at the University of Singapore, 30 June 1967, Peter Brett Papers, National Library of Australia, Manuscript Collection.

[54] SJ Donovon to Peter Brett, 1 June 1967, Peter Brett Papers, National Library of Australia, Manuscript Collection.

[55] JW Cruthers, Managing Director of TVW Limited to Peter Brett, 2 June 1967, Peter Brett Papers, National Library of Australia, Manuscript Collection.

When an officer wrote a negative review of Brett's pamphlet on Beamish in the Victorian publication of 'Police Life', describing it as 'sensational', the Acting Chief Commissioner of Victoria wrote a formal apology to Brett which concluded: 'I look forward to a lifetime of friendship, and hope that you will defend our police force when warranted in the future'.[56] This letter suggests that Brett's voluntary efforts to educate police officers were highly valued.[57] Nonetheless, Brett, concerned that the review would damage Beamish's cause, wrote to the editor of the magazine suggesting that the publication was libellous. In the course of the letter he explained his motivations:

> Those of us who wish to see law and order maintained by effective police operations are also anxious that in the process of maintaining it the innocent should not be wrongly convicted. We are, therefore, vigilant to ensure, so far as we can, that police investigation techniques are of the highest quality. We accordingly think it right to criticize those techniques whenever they appear defective. We do so because we believe that in the long run this will improve the reputation of the police and aid them in the execution of their duties. If reasoned criticism of police action in a particular case is met with violent or inadequately considered criticism of those who advance it, there is real danger of calling into existence the restrictions of police powers in order to curb possible abuses. Such a result would be regrettable; but I am sure you will appreciate that thoughtful citizens concerned with the preservation of civil liberties will react against placing wide discretionary powers in the hands of men who display an immature – indeed, I would say an exaggerated – antipathy to the slightest hint of criticism of their work.[58]

Brett therefore made clear that his aim – consistent with the ethic he attempted to instil in his criminal law students – was to help to constructively reform the law and its operation.

In 1998, investigative journalist Estelle Blackburn published a book about the serial killer, Eric Edgar Cooke.[59] Based on the material she had gathered, Blackburn convinced lawyers Tom Percy and Jonathan Davies to make an application to reopen Beamish's case. A Full Court of the Western Australian Supreme Court, Justices Steytler, Wheeler and McLure, found that the Beamish's conviction was unsound as evidence relevant to the jury's deliberation had been excluded from the Court's consideration. His conviction was overturned. In 2011, the State Government of Western Australia announced that it would make a $425,000 *ex gratia* payment to Beamish, who was then 69 years of age.[60]

[56] CH Petty, Acting Chief Commissioner of Police, to Peter Brett, 28 September 1966, Peter Brett Papers, National Library of Australia, Manuscript Collection.

[57] ibid.

[58] Peter Brett to CH Petty, 27 September 1966, Peter Brett Papers, National Library of Australia, Manuscript Collection.

[59] E Blackburn, *Broken Lives* (Melbourne, Hardie Grant, 2001). T Percy, 'John Button and Darryl Beamish Cleared of Murder Four Decades after Serial Killer's Execution', *Justice Denied* (online) 6 June 2011, justicedenied.org/wordpress/archives/1204.

[60] 'Ex Gratia Payment for Wrongly Jailed Man', *Sydney Morning Herald*, 2 June 2011, www.smh.com.au/national/ex-gratia-payment-for-wrongly-jailed-man-20110602-1fhq6.html.

For her part in having the matter reopened, Blackburn received both official and professional recognition: she received a Medal of the Order of Australia and a Walkley Award for excellence in journalism for her investigations and the book. In 2007, the lawyers, Percy and Davies, were awarded the Australian Lawyers Alliance West Australian Civil Justice Award for exposing the injustices in that case. The saga continued to promote interest with a further book on the police corruption by Brett Christian published in 2013,[61] and a series covering the *Beamish* case, entitled 'Wrongful', aired on ABC Radio National in 2017. What is missing from these accounts is an explanation of Brett's extraordinary early efforts to attempt to remedy the legal system's failings.

Concluding Remarks

While Brett became a very public figure, it does not appear, from reading correspondence of the time, that he was motivated by fame or fortune. He was pursuing matters of principle in a very determined fashion in order to attempt to right a wrong. While he had an extremely strong political constitution,[62] it is clear that his activism took a very heavy emotional toll. In a letter to Don Chipp he somewhat uncharacteristically thanked him for the personal support he had provided and the way he 'consoled [him] during some of the darker periods last year'.[63] Brett proved himself to be an admirable advocate for social justice. He was someone to be relied upon for the protection of the disempowered and vulnerable. He cut a powerful, although sometimes unpopular, figure.

Brett contributes to nascent understandings of what it meant to be an Australian legal liberal in the 1950s and 1960s. His time in the US, the culture at Melbourne, Dixon's looming presence, and perhaps also his war experience, led him to place faith in repairing the legal system rather than condemning it. The leadership described in this chapter provides some insight into the hard and harrowing work this repair involved. Brett did not believe he was advancing a political cause; indeed, he discouraged political activism among academics. Instead, he thought of his activities as a matter of restoring the legal system to good health. Nor did his efforts involve placing faith in the courts to bring about social change. What he wanted was for the courts and public instrumentalities to check themselves against traditional notions of justice and to acknowledge what he believed were some obvious and gross failings.

[61] Christian (n 26).

[62] Brett's son Jonathan attested to his strong political constitution, saying 'Dad liked the politics' in academia: Interview with Robin and Jonathan Brett (RACV Club, Melbourne, 11 June 2014).

[63] Peter Brett to DL Chipp, 28 February 1973, Peter Brett Papers, National Library of Australia, Manuscript Collection.

6

A Professor of Jurisprudence

The Last Professor of Jurisprudence at Melbourne

Peter Brett was the last Professor of Jurisprudence at the University of Melbourne. Notwithstanding his considerable achievements, at the end of his career (and life) Brett had not made a sufficient case for continuing the position or for making jurisprudence compulsory within the law curriculum. In this final chapter on Brett, I consider the significance of this role and his final ambitious attempt to influence how jurisprudence was taught and studied.

The Chair in Jurisprudence at Melbourne was created in 1927 at the instigation of William Harrison Moore, a graduate of Trinity College, Dublin, where he studied both philosophy and law. In 1927, Kenneth Bailey was the first person appointed, but he was no jurisprude. When funding was found for a second professor in 1931, Bailey gladly relinquished the position to take up the Chair of Public Law.[1] His successor, George Whitecross Paton, was the longest standing jurisprudential Chair,[2] and, of the three preceding Brett's appointment, was the most distinguished in the area of jurisprudence. In 1954, Paton was awarded the Swiney Prize for his *Textbook of Jurisprudence* and, with Bailey, he designed a curriculum that was 'directed more towards the social and theoretical context of law'.[3] Rather than aspiring to advance and enhance law's academic credentials, the work is more in the nature of a comprehensive textbook that catalogues, with great clarity, all of the major schools of jurisprudential thought and includes Paton's commentary. Paton's successor, David Derham, had been a top student at Melbourne, but had no real profile or publications in the area of jurisprudence at the time of his appointment to the Chair.[4] Derham updated Paton's textbook and developed an interest in the Scandinavian Realists, but did not otherwise advance a strong jurisprudential agenda.[5]

[1] J Waugh, *First Principles – The Melbourne Law School 1857–2007* (Melbourne, Miegunyah Press) 111.

[2] Paton was Chair in Jurisprudence from 1931 to 1951 with a short interruption for service in the Second World War.

[3] Waugh (n 1) 112.

[4] ibid 155.

[5] D Derham, *George Paton's A Textbook of Jurisprudence*, 3rd edn (Oxford, Oxford University Press, 1964).

Before Brett's appointment, two of the three previous appointments to the Chair of Jurisprudence had been made on the basis of the candidate's academic ability rather than their interest or reputation as jurisprudential scholars. When a vacancy arose following Derham's departure, Cowen viewed it as an opportunity to recruit a new professor of strong potential and had his mind set on Colin Howard. The fact that Howard had not demonstrated an interest or reputation in theory or jurisprudence did not concern Cowen. He said, '[s]o far as special skills in jurisprudence are concerned, these can be developed. When we took David [Derham] he had done no special work in jurisprudence and he developed into a splendid teacher'.[6] The fact that the number of law professors was limited by legislation no doubt influenced Cowen's view that the emphasis should be on appointing the most able legal academic rather than the person whose credentials best fitted the Chair.[7] The primary reason Brett was moved from the Hearn Chair to the Chair of Jurisprudence was because the standing committee believed Howard to be unsuitable for a jurisprudential role.[8] By taking up the Chair of Jurisprudence, Brett vacated the Hearn Chair and made way for Howard's appointment.

Brett attached considerable importance to the Chair, but it seems that he was alone in this belief. A Chair was valued simply because it brought with it the opportunity to become a professor. Several colleagues wondered why someone like Brett, who had already been appointed to a professorial role, would wish to move sideways.[9] The idea that the Chair of Jurisprudence would provide a beachhead for legal theory, would distinguish the academic from the professional lawyer, and establish the discipline's academic credentials was central to Brett's thinking, but was absent from the minds of his colleagues. In the late 1940s and 1950s, Australian scholars, including Derham, had predicted the growth of jurisprudence in law schools. Indeed, it had been a compulsory subject. Between 1967 and 1969, however, jurisprudence became optional at Melbourne.[10] When Brett died in 1975, the new professor appointed to fill the vacancy created was made a Professor in Law, not a Professor in Jurisprudence. The role effectively ceased.

'The Most Urgent Contemporary Task'

The Melbourne Law School's decision to discontinue the role of Professor of Jurisprudence can be viewed in a number of different ways. First, it constitutes another

[6] Zelman Cowen to Harold Ford, 13 May 1964, Harold Arthur Ford Papers, University of Melbourne Archives.

[7] Brett explained the importance of named Chairs in Australia in a letter to Cecil A Wright, Dean of the Faculty of Law at the University of Toronto, dated 24 March 1964. Peter Brett Papers, National Library of Australia, Manuscript Collection.

[8] Zelman Cowen to Harold Ford, 1 May 1964, and Ford to Cowen, 7 May 1964, Harold Arthur Ford Papers, University of Melbourne Archives.

[9] Robyn Campbell, Interview with Harold Luntz (University of Melbourne, 19 February 2003).

[10] Waugh (n 1) 172.

way in which Australian law discontinued its ties with English legal traditions in the second half of the twentieth century. The history of the Chair outlined above suggests that the role never sat comfortably in the Australian context. Melbourne needed the flexibility to appoint professors of strong academic merit, irrespective of their interest in jurisprudence. Moreover, none of the jurisprudential professors at Melbourne was given special reverence simply because they held the post of Professor of Jurisprudence. Second, the decision might suggest that none of the Australian legal academics believed that a law professor from Melbourne, or Sydney, could hold the same command over the discipline as their Oxford (or US) counterparts. It might indicate that they believed that the major trends and models within the discipline would be created within England or the US. However, this possibility runs contrary to evidence of their strong ambitions. Third, the decision might support the notion that Australia's discipline of law was more egalitarian than in England. None of the law professors was to be elevated above the others on the basis of their subject of study. Fourth, it might point to Australian scepticism over what the UK professors of jurisprudence – and in particular the analytical philosophers – had achieved, and thereby signal a desire that Australian law professors should take prudential or applied, rather than abstract, approaches to the study of law. Fifth, it suggests that university legal education was moving away from its original emphasis on a 'gentlemanly', liberal education, which focused on the relationship between society, law, lawyering and morality.

It is important to emphasise that Brett did much to live up the status he gave to the role of Professor of Jurisprudence. The demise of the role was therefore not due to a lack of effort on Brett's part or a failure to appeal to attributes associated with the English model. Brett's scholarship fitted the mould of his contemporary Oxford jurisprudential professor, HLA Hart, in that he sought to maintain a close relationship between law and philosophy. Brett was interested in the social sciences but believed that philosophy remained the mater discipline. Further, like both Hart and Dworkin, he clearly conceptualised his job as one of advancing a concept of law on which both law teaching and legal practice could be based. This is made plain in a report Brett wrote in 1968 while on a period of study leave in the US:

> For many years now the dominating concept in American legal education has been the functional approach to the formation of legal doctrine. This is no doubt due to the great influence wielded by Dean Roscoe Pound, whose sociological jurisprudence has come in the United States to hold the same dominating position as was held (until recently) in English law by analytical jurisprudence. The American law teachers have viewed law as a tool whereby social objectives are to be obtained and they have correspondingly neglected and, indeed, on occasion, derided, the careful use of analysis of legal concepts as a means of deciding cases. The results, I think, are now beginning to make themselves felt in decisions emanating from the Bench and notably from the United States Supreme Court. While one would not cavil against the view that legal concepts are not in themselves a sufficient basis for the administration of justice it has gradually become clear, in my view, that it is equally insufficient to speak merely of adjusting competing claims made by various members of society. Some basis has to be found for adjusting

> those claims, and in the absence of a generally accepted political and ethical philosophy adjustment becomes exceedingly difficult. … There seems to be a growing feeling of uneasiness in the United States over this and it is reflected in the renewed interest being displayed in Jurisprudence as a discipline in the law schools. It would seem that one of the most urgent contemporary tasks is the formulation and acceptance of a basic philosophy of law suitable for a pluralistic society. This in turn may lead to a re-examination and re-assessment of the law school curricula and teaching methods.[11]

Despite being on the other side of the globe, in the final years of Brett's career he sought to contribute to this 'urgent contemporary task'. The most obvious manifestation of his efforts was a monograph completed at the very end of his career. As his friend and colleague Waller explained in the foreword to the book:

> When he finished he told his secretary, Miss Muriel Bennett, that he was immensely pleased about it, that it was almost as if he had waited to complete it. He died suddenly the next day.[12]

Published in 1975, *An Essay on a Contemporary Jurisprudence* consisted of two central arguments. First, Brett mounted an argument based on institutional settlement. He argued that modern learning from the philosophy of science demonstrated that law was a dynamic, open and hierarchical system that interacted with other similar systems, such as the moral and the economic. Law, he maintained, could not be separated from morality. He put forth a conceptual apparatus devised by Karl Popper and complemented by Konrad Lorenz's writing on the mind and human and animal behaviour, to demonstrate the type of multifaceted study required to truly understand the law, its effects, and to fashion reform.[13] He believed that the study of law could be equated with a scientist's study of biological systems. Based on the complexity associated with understanding and monitoring the effects of law reform, he argued that courts were not suited to law reform functions. Their law-making responsibilities, therefore, ought to be kept to a minimum.

Brett also sought to solve the primary challenge confronted by Legal Process scholars and made more acute by the Warren Court: how to reconcile their progressive beliefs and desire for law reform with their counsel for judicial restraint. Brett's response was that by injecting greater intellectual muscle into non-judicial law reform bodies, by making legislative and administrative reform a matter of serious jurisprudential study and attracting great minds to their advancement, constructive and rapid law reform would follow.

[11] Draft report on study leave by Peter Brett (undated) Faculty Correspondence 1968, University of Melbourne Archives.

[12] P Brett, *An Essay on a Contemporary Jurisprudence* (Melbourne, Butterworths, 1975) vii.

[13] Brett (n 12) 35–8. Writing to the playwright and paleoanthropologist Robert Ardrey to thank him for his hospitality in Rome, Brett said, 'I envy you your visit to Konrad Lorenz who, from his writings, must be all that you found him to be': Peter Brett to Robert Ardrey, 23 July 1974, Peter Brett Papers, National Library of Australia, Manuscript Collection.

The second component of Brett's thesis was that judicial method, in particular the reasoned elaboration propounded by Legal Process scholars, was analogous to the scientific method as then explained by the philosophers of science. Rather than precedent, Brett believed that judicial method was based on a science-like 'hypothetical-deductive process' consistent with the understanding of science advanced by Popper and others.[14] Following Brett's analogy, judges draw a hypothesis when reading cases. They then rigorously test that hypothesis by scrutinising it against the existing case law and by questioning how the hypothesis might apply to future cases. As with the method expounded in Brett and Waller's casebook, and consistent with the concept of 'reasoned elaboration', judicial method involves searching out and critically examining principles. According to Brett, the fact that this is not an entirely logical process does not diminish its scientific credentials, as the scientific process itself does not follow purely logical lines. Science, after all, involves making subjective judgements.

Brett drew support from Lorenz's theory about perception, particularly the idea that humans perceive wholes rather than individual items – something he called 'Gestalts'.[15] Neither the scientist (according to Lorenz) nor the judge (according to Brett) works through a process of inductive or deductive logic, but rather perceives 'Gestalts'.[16] For judges, these are guiding principles or impressions formed from a collection of data or case law that they then scrutinise for error. So long as judging is neither wholly formalistic nor wholly instrumental, it is akin to a scientific process.

In this small monograph, Brett therefore sought first to challenge the American resurgence of sociological jurisprudence and the naked instrumentalism of the Warren Court and, second, to demonstrate the scientific nature of reasoned elaboration and encourage the upcoming generation along a new theoretical path: the jurisprudence of non-judicial law reform bodies. He sought to strengthen the discipline with new intellectual credentials.

Brett's career is full of examples of his strong commitment to ensuring that law kept up with the best of modern learning and thereby maintained – or regained – its intellectual credentials. When fashioning prescriptions for law reform, he drew from a range of social scientists, particularly psychiatrists and sociologists and their work on the mind. Many of Brett's friends within the university were natural or social scientists and he sought out their assistance and advice for various projects.[17] He was a member of scientific associations, delivered papers at scientific

[14] Brett (n 12) 49–71.

[15] ibid 52–3, 59–62.

[16] ibid.

[17] Brett put his honours student Pat Urban in touch with Dr NEW McCallum, then a Reader in Chemical Pathology at the University of Melbourne; Dr J Birrell, Police Surgeon, Victoria; Miss A Raymond, Research Officer, Australian Road Research Board; Mr LK Turner, Director, Police Forensic Science Laboratory, Victoria; and Professor SH Lovibord, Department of Psychology, University of New South Wales: Interview with Pat Urban (by telephone, 17 June 2014). He also sought the

conferences,[18] and taught alongside a member of the medical school.[19] In a paper delivered to an annual conference of Australian and New Zealand psychiatrists, Brett said:

> an institution or system of social control that disregards or turns its back on the method of science is likely to wither away. For it is the method of science that provides the basis for our trust in its powers, and we are not likely to continue to endure an institution in which we can no longer place our trust.[20] … Science is the dominant feature of our age, and its methods account for its success and consequent pride of place. *If we wish our legal system to achieve similar success and public respect, we should adopt its methods and established teachings wherever we can.*[21]

Giving advice to a father who wanted to know which subjects his son should take to prepare for a career in law, Brett said: 'The lawyer of the future ought to have some understanding of how the scientist goes about his work'.[22]

Reviews of Brett's final monograph suggest that scholars, both domestic and international, either did not appreciate what his aims were or were sceptical of the idea of incorporating new learning from the philosophy of science. Baron Lloyd of Hampstead, a legal scholar at the University of London, who had himself written textbooks on jurisprudence, summarised the essence of Brett's thesis well and considered it a stimulating work.[23] He was not, however, convinced by Brett's suggestion of taking up more of the philosophy of science, saying instead that Brett was 'prone to overstate both the novelty of invoking the "new science" in the field of jurisprudence, and the extent of the contribution such forays are likely to achieve'.[24]

Brett's thesis therefore provoked scepticism – was it science or an aversion to the Warren Court that drove his prescriptions? GHL Fridman, a professor at the University of Western Ontario who had begun his career at the University of Adelaide, concentrated on what the work proposed with respect to judicial

assistance of his science friends at Melbourne to scrutinise the evidence in the *Ratten* case (described later in this chapter). Interviewees mentioned Brett's friendship with professor of physiology Roy Douglas ('Panzee') Wright and psychologist Elwyn Aisne Morey, and noted that at lunch Brett would move beyond the circle of lawyers at Melbourne and sit with his friends from the sciences.

[18] See, eg, P Brett, 'The Law and the Changing View of Man' (1971) 5 *Australian and New Zealand Journal of Psychiatry* 78.

[19] Brett taught a course in forensic medicine with Norman E W McCallum, then a Reader in Forensic Medicine at the University of Melbourne. The pair compiled a detailed set of lecture notes, which they had reviewed by Dr AW Burton C St J, MBBS, LLB, FACMA, Medical Secretary of the Victorian Branch of the Australian Medical Association; Dr JFJ Cade, Superintendent Psychiatrist, Royal Park Psychiatric Institutions; and Dr Vernon Plueckhahn, Director of Pathology, Geelong: P Brett and NEW McCallum, 'Lecture Notes on Forensic Medicine (Excluding Forensic Pathology)' (1972), Peter Brett Papers, National Library of Australia, Manuscript Collection.

[20] P Brett, 'The Implications of Science for the Law' (1972) 18 *McGill Law Journal* 170, 172.

[21] ibid 204–05 (emphasis added).

[22] Peter Brett to Dr JRW Bryce, 6 October 1972, Law Dean's Correspondence, University of Melbourne Archives.

[23] Lloyd of Hampstead, 'Book Review: *An Essay on a Contemporary Jurisprudence* by Peter Brett' (1976) 39 *Modern Law Review* 742, 742.

[24] ibid 743.

decision-making, ignoring Brett's larger proposals about re-orientating the study of jurisprudence so that law was conceptualised as one system among many.[25] He characterised Brett's alleged focus on judicial law-making as old-fashioned, and suggested that a better approach would be to construct a new jurisprudence encompassing what legislatures, administrative bodies and governmental or corporate agencies were actually doing. He seemed to miss Brett's point that the new jurisprudential project he was advocating would focus attention on precisely these things. Lloyd and Fridman's reviews suggest that neither was familiar with the philosophy of science that Brett was expounding.

Given this lukewarm reception, one might say that Brett's most enduring legacy was not a grand jurisprudential theory but rather his contribution to an Australian textbook tradition that invited students to engage with materials and discover and evaluate principles for themselves. While this was no small achievement, and may well have contributed to a Legal Process attitude among the Australian students who studied law in the 1960s, it did not mark Brett out as a leading jurisprudential scholar, either within Australia or globally. It also did not encourage the teaching of jurisprudence within Australian law schools.

Conclusion – Peter Brett

As a founding member of Australia's first community of legal scholars, Brett made a significant and lasting contribution to the Australian legal academy that was inspired by his Harvard Legal Process mentors, in particular Henry Hart. Brett's vision was for the Australian legal academy to be a large, confident and reformist enterprise that would act as conscience to the Australian legal profession and produce morally aware practitioners. In this he was continuing the early cultural mission of Australian law schools. Whereas previous generations considered that this mission would be achieved largely through a liberal education, Brett believed that the law curriculum could serve the same purpose. Like the elite American professors, he adopted and advanced a coherent vision for both law schools and graduates. The textbook he co-wrote with Waller provided a vehicle for exporting this attitude to other Australian law schools and law graduates. Future legal practitioners would not so easily see law as divorced from the moral conundrums at its core. Future Australian legal academics were challenged to take an intellectual approach to teaching law, where the material and exercises were fashioned to encourage students to adopt a particular conception of law and to critically question doctrine. Brett's scathing criticism of aspects of the administration of justice and his advocacy work signalled to the public and profession alike that Australian scholars would not emulate the perceived deference of their

[25] GHL Fridman, 'Book Review: *An Essay on a Contemporary Jurisprudence* by Peter Brett' (1976) *Canadian Bar Review* 220, 222–23.

English counterparts.[26] His monographs demonstrates that Australian scholars could engage with the leading legal thought of the age and to engage in debate over what the correct intellectual capital and credentials for their discipline should be.

In the early twenty-first century, we largely take for granted the capacity of legal academics to assume roles that were so passionately and imaginatively pursued by Brett. But in the 1950s and 1960s, the emergence of an academic-lawyer-statesman was challenging. Many of his peers did not approve. Brett therefore helped smooth the road. He created the model of a constructive legal theorist whose privileged position obliged him to both 'venerate' and 'freely criticise'[27] the law and work towards the betterment of Australian society. He is an early example of an Australian liberal lawyer and legal scholar: his career enriches our currently impoverished understandings of what it has meant to be a liberal legal scholar within Australia.

In Brett we find a clear correlation between his life, the times and the academic agenda he pursued. During the Second World War, he had risked his life to conquer fascist regimes. The moral fibre of a society was important to him and explains why he was so devoted to defending those most vulnerable to injustices. It is not surprising, therefore, that, like Hart and Sacks, he found the philosophers of science, who were attempting to bridge the gap between science and morality, so fascinating. In Brett we also find that many of his activities were fuelled by his appraisal of what the discipline required in order to perform an important social function. His attempt to advance legal knowledge was both an intellectual and moral strategy born of the responsibilities he felt were inherent in his post. His role in history and the infant status of the academy were both central to his thinking. He was a dedicated, courageous and highly intelligent scholar whose contribution ought to be better known.

[26] See S Bartie, 'A Full Day's Work – A Study of Australia's First Legal Scholarly Community' (2010) 29 *University of Queensland Law Journal* 67, 90–93.

[27] P Brett and PL Waller, *Cases and Materials in Criminal Law* (Sydney, Butterworths, 1962) v.

PART B

Alice Erh-Soon Tay

Portrait of Alice Ehr-Soon Tay. Greg Weight Photography

7

Morality and the Legal Academy

Introduction

Professor Julius Stone is a name well known among Australian legal academics, lawyers and even the current generation of law students. It has even been suggested that the High Court's approach to legal reasoning in the 1980s and 1990s was, at least in part, a product of Stone's teaching.[1] Stone's students were encouraged to abandon strict legalism in favour of his own version of American legal realism, captured most readily in his phrase 'leeways of choice'.[2] Stone is often depicted as Australia's foremost jurisprudential scholar and the greatest Australian contributor to international law.[3] By contrast, we know little about his successor, Alice Erh-Soon Tay (1934–2004), holder of the Challis Chair of Jurisprudence at the University of Sydney and the subject of this part.[4]

Tay's considerable list of accomplishments makes this relative lack of attention all the more puzzling. Her appointment as Professor of Jurisprudence in 1975 was a momentous event in the trajectory of the Australian legal academy, even when viewed purely as a matter of gender and cultural divergence. She was born in 1934 to Chinese parents, undertook just four and a half years of formal school education (her schooling in Singapore was cut short due to illness and the Japanese occupation) and qualified as a lawyer through the Inns of Court in London rather than a University. In 1975 she rose to become the first woman to hold a Chair of Jurisprudence at an Australian university and the first person from Singapore/China, and second woman, to become an Australian law professor.[5] She did not apply

[1] See, eg, M Kirby, 'Review Essay: HLA Hart, Julius Stone and the Struggle for the Soul of the Law' (2005) 27 *Sydney Law Review* 323, 334; H Patapan, *Judging Democracy: The New Politics of the High Court of Australia* (Cambridge, Cambridge University Press, 2000) 20–23, 32, 180.

[2] This is a theme that Stone advanced throughout his career. See, eg, J Stone, *Legal System and Lawyers' Reasoning* (Stanford, Stanford University Press, 1964) 202, 234, 304, 321.

[3] Stone 'can lay claim to being one of this country's greatest writers, teachers and public figures in law': R Shelly, 'Book Review: Leonie Starr, *Julius Stone an Intellectual Life*' (1993) 16 *University of New South Wales Law Journal* 601, 601.

[4] eg, there is no entry on Tay in 'Australia's pre-eminent dictionary of national biography', the *Australian Dictionary of Biography* (Melbourne, Melbourne University Press, 1966). Writing about Professor Claire Palley, Fiona Cownie considers it unsurprising that so little had been said about her, as most biographies have been written about men: F Cownie, 'The United Kingdom's First Woman Law Professor: An Archerian Analysis' (2015) 42 *Journal of Law and Society* 127, 128.

[5] At the time of her appointment there were only two other women professors at the University of Sydney and one other law professor (Enid Campbell) in the whole of Australia: 'First Woman Professor in Faculty of Medicine' *Sydney News* (Sydney) 7 June 1983, 87.

for the Chair but was instead sought out. Her work departed from the dominant analytical jurisprudential tradition and she was recognised globally in elite philosophical, sociological and jurisprudential circles. In 1985 she was made Member of the Order of Australia for contributions to teaching and research in law and in 1990 she, along with a colleague, Klaus Ziegert, established the Centre for Asian and Pacific Law at the University of Sydney (CAPLUS). In 1998 she was appointed President of the Human Rights and Equal Opportunities Commission (HREOC).

While many of the threads of Tay's career are fascinating, this part (as with the previous part devoted to Peter Brett) concentrates primarily on the novel ways in which Tay contributed to the discipline of law in Australia. From an extensive review of Tay's scholarship and an analysis of the transcripts from 18 interviews, it became apparent that the most interesting and significant aspect of Tay's career is that she subscribed to a particular scholarly model and sought to elevate the intellectual credentials of Australia's discipline of law in accordance with that model. She believed that there were certain values and environments that should be fostered within universities in order to equip academics with the courage and independence required to perform their important role. According to Tay – at least in the context of law, philosophy and sociology – academics were important because of their capacity to provide free and frank criticism of government, ideologies and each other. She believed that this capacity sprang not only from their intelligence, but also from their commitment to a strong set of scholarly – and moral – values.

In essence, Tay believed, first, that scholars should take their lead and draw inspiration from the world's leading intellectuals; second, that they should refuse 'to bow to the demands of fashion, convenience or authority';[6] and, third, that they should favour conflict over coherence. Finally, they should aspire to lead 'perilous and fighting lives'.[7] Ultimately, Tay believed that being a legal academic was a high calling and should be pursued with due seriousness and devotion.

The motivations and moral principles underpinning Tay's model of a legal scholar were a product of her upbringing as well as a peculiar mix of academic mentors: Professor of Philosophy at the University of Sydney, John Anderson; intellectual historian (and Tay's husband), Eugene Kamenka; Marxist philosopher, Yevgeni Bronislavovich Pashukanis; and social scientist, Ferdinand Tönnies.[8] In this chapter I explain how each school of thought initially contributed to Tay's thinking, and how her personal characteristics – her upbringing, tough constitution and strong sense of self-belief – resulted in a strong commitment to reform the legal academy. Ultimately, she was a formidable character who advanced a

[6] E Kamenka, 'Australia Made Me – But which Australia is Mine?' (John Curtin Memorial Lecture, Australian National University, 16 July 1993) 21.

[7] This was a mantra associated with John Anderson. See M Weblin (ed), *A Perilous and Fighting Life: From Communist to Conservative, The Political Writings of Professor John Anderson* (Melbourne, Pluto Press, 2003).

[8] While her scholarship contained relatively few citations, Tay frequently referred to Pashukanis.

robust critique of the Australian legal academy and provided an example for other legal scholars to follow. Her career raises interesting questions about the strengths and shortfalls of Australia's legal academy, and Tay's contributions to it.

The Makings of an Academic Warrior

> I just don't think you can understand what is being written unless you understand the person and that person and his or her environment is what really creates that person. So you referred in the questions you sent me to what scholarship or scholars influenced [Tay] most. I think it is her life and her first husband's life.[9]

Two of the most frequent remarks made about Tay's constitution by interview participants were that she was a fighter and that her career was her life.[10] For Tay the professional and personal bled into one another. Her early experiences fed her intellectual agenda and shaped her concept of the model legal scholar, which she later embodied. This intellectual agenda also dominated her later life. Tay fought against a number of institutions and practices but her primary enemies were governments – first the government of Singapore, then the USSR, then China and then Australia. The most obvious impetus for this fighting spirit was her childhood experience as a member of an oppressed minority in Singapore.

Tay was born in Singapore on 2 February 1934.[11] Her parents were from Guangdong Province in Southern China.[12] Her father had been a civil servant, a clerk for the Australian Water Pipe Company, but was stripped of his professional standing and job when the Japanese, who occupied Singapore, interned his employers.[13] While Tay spoke of happiness in her childhood,[14] it was in many ways grim. The memory of the experience of prejudice, and being denied opportunities and a comfortable existence, stayed with her throughout her life. Tay spent much of her childhood not at school but working as a seamstress to support the family.[15] One of her sisters was given up for adoption to a childless couple, as without her

[9] Interview with Participant A (11 June 2014).

[10] Interview with Martin Krygier (Law School, University of New South Wales, 7 February 2014); interview with Christopher Birch SC (Garfield Barwick Chambers, Sydney, 28 July 2014); interview with Klaus Ziegert (Law School, University of Sydney, 5 February 2014); interview with Wojciech Sadurski (Law School, University of Sydney, 31 July 2014); Participant A (n 9); interview with Gabriel Moens (by telephone, 30 September 2014); interview with Hamish Redd (by telephone, 5 August 2014); interview with Ron McCallum AO (by telephone, 4 November 2014).

[11] Curriculum Vitae of Alice Erh-Soon Tay, 1965, Alice Erh-Soon Tay Staff Files, Australian National University Archives.

[12] J Horne, 'The Cosmopolitan Life of Alice Erh-Soon Tay' (2010) 21 *Journal of World History* 419, 430.

[13] J Horne, 'Alice Erh-Soon Tay, The Making of an Intellectual' in G Doeker-Mach and K Ziegert, *Alice Erh-Soon Tay – Lawyer, Scholar, Civil Servant* (Stuttgart, Franz Steiner Verlag, 2004) 16–17.

[14] ibid 17.

[15] ibid 17.

father's wage her parents could no longer afford to support her,[16] and died of bone cancer while still a child.[17]

Tay spent just four and a half years at Raffles Girls' School in Singapore.[18] Her formal education was cut short as her father refused to have his children educated within a school system operated by their Japanese oppressors.[19] After the Japanese occupation, Tay spent a year hospitalised with what was then a 'horrible' and 'shameful' disease: tuberculosis.[20] After the War, her mother was nonetheless determined to ensure that her children gained independence through education,[21] and the family provided the financial support needed for Tay to complete her training to become a lawyer at the Inns of Court in London.[22] Tay explained:

> When I was a child, growing up in a family that knew little English and not much of Western tradition or of culture in China, deprived for four years of food, books and schooling by a brutal Japanese occupation, I was quite clear what I and my family admired – a concept of culture, of the significance of literature and philosophy, history and art, of the possibility of transcending one's situation.[23]

In the few short years Tay did spend at school she demonstrated strong intellectual abilities, and was awarded a scholarship to study in America for a short period.[24] She undertook additional studies to make up for her year in hospital, but did not have the correct subjects needed to study her first choice, medicine.[25] Studying at the Inns meant that she could qualify for practice in a much shorter period of time than at a university – just 18 months – and thereby reduce the financial burden on her family.[26] Tay's upbringing was largely free of privilege but she made the most of the few opportunities she was given. She was intelligent and she was tough.

When Tay returned to Singapore from London in the mid-1950s, it was with a view to shaking up its legal and political system. It is therefore no coincidence that she went to work for David Marshall as a barrister. Tay joined Marshall in 1957, a year after he resigned office as Singapore's first Chief Minister in a government formed by coalition.[27] Singapore was then a British colony, and Marshall's primary agenda had been to demand Singapore's self-governance.[28] When talks in London

[16] S Humphrey, 'Alice Tay's Top Brain in Law's Wonderland', *The Australian* (Sydney) 15 March 1984, 10.
[17] ibid.
[18] Horne (n 13) 18.
[19] Horne (n 12) 430–31.
[20] Humphrey (n 16).
[21] ibid.
[22] ibid.
[23] A Tay, 'Women, Culture and the Quality of Life' in L Sandell and EE Schmidt (eds), *Women of the Year – A Collection of Speeches by Australia's Most Successful Women* (Boorowa, NSW, The Watermark Press, 1987) 23, 27.
[24] Horne (n 13) 18.
[25] Humphrey (n 16).
[26] ibid.
[27] A Tay and E Kamenka, 'Singapore-City State' (1960) 20 *Current Affairs Bulletin* 146, 156; Tay (n 11).
[28] ibid.

failed to deliver this outcome, he resigned and returned to the bar.[29] Marshall, a Singapore-born Iraqi Jew, was a very successful barrister, known for winning a majority of cases.[30] However, Tay soon became frustrated with the work she was performing, finding it dull and repetitive and believing that it would be many years before she would be able to lead more exciting superior court proceedings.[31]

Academia, by contrast, provided opportunities for even junior scholars to take on grand causes and level criticism at both Singapore's legal system and government. Tay was angered by the persecution of the Chinese in South-East Asia.[32] Her family's treatment under the Japanese occupation was just one example of the many instances of hardship inflicted on the Chinese diaspora population.[33] In an article published in 1962 she quoted the Chinese Foreign Minister who, at a press conference in Taipei in 1957, said '[w]e Chinese … are being looked on as the Jews of Asia'.[34] Tay endorsed this sentiment and added that just as 'the anti-Semite saw only the rich Jew, so the South-East Asian nationalist speaks only of the rich Chinese'.[35] The worst example of prejudicial treatment she cited was in West Java, Indonesia, where a decree

> meant the expropriation of some 300,000 Chinese shopkeepers from villages. Officially, they were given eight months to sell their businesses … Military authorities in West Java not only cut short the period, but interpreted the decree to prohibit Chinese from living in the countryside altogether. Chinese were driven to the main towns and placed in camps. Violence flared up in several areas. In Tjimahi, near the Afro-Asian peace and friendship town of Bundung, Indonesian troops entered the village at 5am and began rounding up Chinese. Two Chinese women were shot and killed. Chinese who now 'wished' to leave Indonesia were encouraged to do so; they were forbidden to take either property or cash.[36]

Turning to Singapore, Tay cited policies requiring strong English language skills for employment and an education taught in English as drastically reducing the employment prospects of most Chinese people.[37] She also documented the numerous fundamental rights and freedoms eroded by the radical People's Action Party, elected in 1959.[38]

Tay's movement into academia in 1958, as an assistant lecturer at the newly created Department of Law at the University of Malaya (now the National University of Singapore), meant that she could freely and publicly criticise Singapore's government. Her one independently authored publication while at the

[29] ibid.
[30] ibid.
[31] D Wild, 'The Law is No Fossil, says a New Professor', *The Australian* (Sydney) 21 January 1975, 3.
[32] A Tay, 'The Chinese in South East Asia' (1962) 4 *Race* 34.
[33] ibid.
[34] ibid 41.
[35] ibid 41.
[36] ibid 36.
[37] Tay and Kamenka (n 27) 155.
[38] ibid.

University of Malaya was a doctrinal analysis of the Preservation of Public Security Ordinance.[39] Tay argued that the ordinance gave the government too much power and discretion to detain people without transparent grounds, gave citizens little scope to challenge detention orders, and denied them natural justice. In another article, co-authored with her colleague JMH Heah, the pair boldly criticised the local judiciary, suggesting that its jurisprudence was unremarkable and inferior to that of the great judges of the common law world, including Sir Owen Dixon and Benjamin Cardozo.[40] In both articles, criticisms are expressed frankly and reveal a sense of frustration with Singapore's governance, legal system and laws.

The single most important event in Tay's early career was her introduction to a young Australian scholar, Eugene Kamenka. He was then aged 30 and she was 24. Kamenka had moved to Singapore from Canberra to take up a position as a lecturer in philosophy. At the time, he was two-thirds of the way through a PhD at the RSSS at the new ANU. His thesis, supervised by Australian philosophy professor, Percy Herbert Partridge, was entitled 'The Ethical Foundations of Marxism'. Tay and Kamenka's relationship began when he sought her help, asking her 'for examples of legal situations and cases for his students to explore their logical validity'.[41] Friendship, and then romance, soon followed.

Tay's relationship with Kamenka initially brought turmoil, imposing considerable personal and professional costs. Kamenka had arrived in Singapore with a wife and two children. While he was only six years her senior, the age difference between them and the fact that he was married meant that the relationship was considered taboo and she was labelled a 'scarlet woman'.[42] Their colleagues considered the liaison to be immoral, and they were summoned by the Vice-Chancellor of the University of Malaya and asked to explain themselves.[43] This led to their resignation from the University and departure from Singapore, and dramatically, if temporarily, removed their financial and professional security. At the time, neither Tay nor Kamenka held doctoral qualifications. (Kamenka had been granted an extension in 1958 to allow him to take up the appointment at the University of Malaya, and did not submit his PhD thesis until March 1961, some time after the couple left Singapore.)[44] From Singapore, Tay and Kamenka sought refuge in London.[45] Kamenka's strong writing skills enabled him to write for the press, and this provided them with an income.[46]

[39] A Tay, '"Conditional Release" under the Preservation of Public Security Ordinance' (1959) 1 *Malayan Law Review* 341.
[40] A Tay and JMH Heah, 'Some Notes on the Malayan Law of Negligence' (1960) 9 *Cleveland Marshall Law Review* 490.
[41] Horne (n 13) 25.
[42] Horne (n 12) 434.
[43] ibid.
[44] Minutes of the Faculty of the Research School of Social Sciences, 21 March 1961, Research School of Social Sciences, Faculty Board Minutes, 15 February 1961–10 December 1964, Australian National University Archives.
[45] Horne (n 13) 25.
[46] ibid.

While they may have held other ambitions, they ultimately looked to Canberra for refuge, and as a place where they could salvage their academic careers. Kamenka had a network of friends and colleagues at the RSSS. He applied a number of times for a position there but was initially rejected.[47] He eventually obtained a short-term contract as a Research Fellow,[48] and throughout the early 1960s the couple survived on the scholarship money that Tay received to complete a PhD at the RSSS and Kamenka's income from a series of short-term junior appointments.[49] Money was especially tight as Kamenka sent money overseas to support his two children.[50] It was not until 1965 that he was granted some permanency as a Senior Fellow.[51]

The turbulence of Tay's childhood therefore continued into her early career. Her departure from the University of Malaya, coupled with her frustration with its political system, erased any fond memories of Singapore. Once in Australia, she renounced her Singaporean citizenship.[52] While the experience of leaving Singapore brought hardship, it also brought a level of freedom and a broader perspective. Tay and fellow immigrant Kamenka were later regarded as 'citizens of the world',[53] and much of their scholarship was written from the perspective of critical outsiders. The experience perhaps cemented in Tay the idea that success in life was the product of struggle and that an individual cannot rely on the support of others or expect to be treated fairly. Instead, she believed, one must fight.

An Open Mind – John Anderson

Tay's relationship with Kamenka played a critical role in shaping her academic agenda. He introduced Tay to several intellectuals who influenced her scholarly beliefs and the work she performed throughout her career. One of her central beliefs was that scholars should devote themselves to studying 'big ideas … important ideas'.[54] She said, 'You don't work on some Wagga Wagga scientist, you

[47] See, eg, Eugene Kamenka to the Registrar of ANU, 3 December 1960 and 28 June 1961, and Registrar of ANU to Kamenka, 16 February 1961, Eugene Kamenka Staff Files, Australian National University Archives.

[48] Minutes of the Board of the Faculty of the Research School of Social Sciences, 20 September 1961, Australian National University Archives.

[49] Kamenka to the Registrar of ANU, 21 October 1964, Eugene Kamenka Staff Files, Australian National University Archives.

[50] Kamenka to the Registrar of ANU, 3 December 1960, 19, Eugene Kamenka Staff Files, Australian National University Archives.

[51] Minutes of the Board of the Faculty of the Research School of Social Sciences, 8 September 1964, Australian National University Archives.

[52] Horne (n 12) 434.

[53] J Passmore, 'Citizen of the World Whose Gift was Liberty', *The Australian* (Sydney) 21 January 1994, 11; JA Moses, 'Eugene Kamenka 1928–1994 – The Great Cosmopolitan Australian' (1994) 40 *Australian Journal of Politics and History* 295. Horne argues that Tay, too, should be described as cosmopolitan: Horne (n 12) 426, 427.

[54] Horne (n 13) 18.

work on Marx, Darwin, Lenin – if you must, although I don't like him – people like that. You open your mind, you don't close it'.[55] This was, perhaps, a lesson that Tay learnt from Kamenka, who was grateful for his Australian schooling and teachers who had introduced him to the leading thinkers of great civilisations.[56] It was also something Kamenka's chief academic mentor, John Anderson, had instilled in him, by encouraging his students to concentrate on older philosophical traditions rather than 'bow to the demands of fashion, convenience or authority'.[57] From Anderson Kamenka said he had learnt that the 'first-class academic measures himself against first-class minds, against Plato, Hume, Hegel, Marx, Freud, Maitland, Keynes'.[58]

Tay had not completed an undergraduate degree, and so had not been formally instructed about any particular contemporary school of thought. While she may have conducted her own independent studies (although there is no clear evidence of this), the absence of a strong intellectual mentor suggests that she would have been open to advice – such as that she received from Kamenka, drawing on his mentor Anderson – on who and what was worth studying. Seeking refuge in grand intellectual traditions would also help Tay in her quest to wage war against the radical changes in governance and the general malaise she perceived in the societies that she studied. Looking to the intellectual elite of an earlier age not only represented an escape from provincialism, but also provided an important weapon against oppressive politics, propaganda, complacency and mediocrity. For Tay, it represented the key to both widening horizons and lifting standards.

Tay and Kamenka's relationship was no marriage of convenience. Those close to the couple speak of the relationship as one of affection and love. Kamenka clearly 'adored' Tay,[59] and Tay was devastated when Kamenka died in the early 1990s.[60] Yet, for each of them the professional and private were so closely intertwined that it is necessary to speak of both a personal and intellectual alliance. They no doubt saw in each other an intellectual equal. While Kamenka's chief interest was in philosophy rather than law, his studies of societies and the philosophical foundations of social policies and attitudes required some consideration of law. Tay could provide such knowledge and could also provide an insight into the culture and attitudes circulating within South-East Asia and China. Kamenka's decision to take up an appointment at the University of Malaya suggests that he wanted to learn more about the region.

What Kamenka offered Tay was a path into an intellectual tradition that rewarded lived experience as opposed to formal learning. Kamenka's studies were motivated by a sense of injustice similar to that felt by Tay over the treatment of her family and Chinese migrants more generally. Kamenka was born in Cologne,

[55] ibid.
[56] Kamenka (n 6) 14.
[57] ibid 21.
[58] 'A Man who Learnt a Hell of a Lot', *Canberra Times* (Canberra), 27 February 1975, 3.
[59] Krygier (n 10); Ziegert (n 10).
[60] Ziegert (n 10).

Germany, in 1928 to Russian Jews.[61] In 1937, due to the pre-war treatment of Jews in Germany, his family migrated from Berlin to Sydney, Australia.[62] The Second World War and the persecution and genocide of Jews had a lasting impact on his scholarship. It ignited in him an interest in world politics, governance and social structures and ideas.[63] Coming from a minority culture that was subjected to strong and sustained attack and prejudice was an experience that the pair had in common, and this paved the way for the political and social histories that they later wrote together. Moreover, the legacies of Bolshevik Revolution played a central role in Kamenka's early life, leading to his fascination with Marxism.[64]

Kamenka's experience was, however, different from Tay's, in that for much of his adolescence he lived in Australia, where he was shown kindness and given opportunities that he believed were absent in Europe and, according to Tay, Singapore.[65] Unlike Tay, he had an academic mentor in John Anderson, and was part of an exclusive club that later became known as the 'Andersonians'.[66] Anderson published very little – his ideas instead being bestowed primarily on his students through his teaching – with the result that it has been difficult for non-Andersonians to understand and interpret his ideas.[67] Kamenka identified a set of academic values that he received from Anderson's teaching and it is evident from Tay's career and scholarship that he passed these on to Tay. They served as a motivating force. One of the clearest enunciations of these values is found in the following passages from a speech Kamenka delivered shortly before his death in 1994.

> We, who then called ourselves 'Andersonians', believed in free thought, in criticism and enquiry, in enterprise, in the natural cooperativeness of social and moral goods, in the integrity and independence of universities and academic institutions. We were pluralists. We elevated conflict, rejecting compromise and the illusion of a common interest. We fought censorship (whether religious, sexual or political) as well as government interference. We rejected both bourgeois commercialism and socialist planning. We repudiated obscurantism, the attempt to conceal or to palliate social and intellectual conflict by glossing over difference and distinctions. We rejected 'essentialism' and 'reductionism' as the attempt to reduce complex states of affairs to one fundamental essence, principle, or material base. We rejected 'atomism' as the elevation of pure particulars – there were none – and 'holism' as the attempt to make organisms or systems logically primary and what goes on in them always subordinate and derivative. We pitted – or thought we pitted – sound logic and good argument against all appeals to the fashionable, the 'accepted, the comforting'.[68] …

[61] Kamenka (n 6) 4–5.
[62] ibid.
[63] ibid.
[64] M Krygier, 'Four Visions of Post-Communist Law' (1994) 40 *Australian Journal of Politics and History* 104, 104.
[65] Kamenka (n 6) 9–10.
[66] ibid 18–19.
[67] CM Cole, 'John Anderson', in EN Zalta (ed), *The Stanford Encyclopedia of Philosophy* (Winter 2012 edn, plato.stanford.edu/archives/win2012/entries/anderson-john/). See also J Franklin, *Corrupting the Youth* (Sydney, Macleay Press, 2003).
[68] Kamenka (n 6) 19.

> [Anderson's] outstanding characteristic was a clear-minded intellectual intransigence, a refusal to bow to the demands of fashion, convenience or authority. To use the language these sought to impose – the language of politicians, educational administrators, social reformers – was to already give the game away. Education was not the imparting of skills, business was not service but the search for profit, advertising was not the provision of information but the attempt to influence, by any, means.[69]

We can see these values reflected in various aspects of Tay's career.

Another important intellectual influence that emerged in the course of Tay and Kamenka's Soviet studies was Marxist philosopher, Yevgeni Bronislavovich Pashukanis. In the very first article that the pair wrote together, published in 1959, they drew liberally from Pashukanis's concept of Western law.[70] Much later, during a trip to the USSR, Tay and Kamenka were given a copy of one of Pashukanis's books that had been hidden away by a Russian academic.[71] One colleague, Klaus Ziegert, noted that Pashukanis 'was one of those rare people who was not just a functionary in the machinery of Soviet law but also an accomplished legal theorist before and after the Sovietisation of Russia'.[72] Tay and Kamenka admired him for his serious attempt to examine, rather than caricature, Western law, and for his integrity. Pashukanis refused to adopt the political propaganda that Stalin and his minions, most notably Andrey Vyshinsky, advanced to replace scholarly thinking about law.[73] He paid for his convictions with his life – he was executed under Stalin's orders. While ultimately unsuccessful, Pashukanis represented the potential for academics and their ideas to provide important opposition to governments. Studying Pashukanis firmed up Tay's belief that ideas were important – that intellectuals were important. Like Kamenka, she believed that 'ideas and ideologies have consequences and are major contributors to socio-political change'.[74]

Possession

Tay's PhD thesis provides the first piece of tangible evidence of Anderson's influence on her career. In 1962, she was awarded a scholarship by the RSSS and began her thesis under the supervision of Sam Stoljar, one of two legal academics in the Department of Law.[75] Tay chose to write on 'The Concept of Possession in the

[69] ibid 21.

[70] A Tay and E Kamenka, 'Karl Marx's Analysis of Law' (1959) 1 *Indian Journal of Philosophy* 19.

[71] Horne (n 13) 20.

[72] Ziegert (n 10).

[73] See, eg, A Tay and E Kamenka, 'The Life and Afterlife of a Bolshevik Jurist' (1970) 19 *Problems of Communism* 72, 73.

[74] NA Rupke and DW Lovell, 'Introduction' (1994) 40 *Australian Journal of Politics and History* 1, 1.

[75] The other was, of course, Geoffrey Sawer. Minutes of the Faculty of the Research School of Social Sciences, Research School of Social Sciences, Faculty and Faculty Board Minutes, 15 February 1961–10 December 1964, Australian National University Archives.

Common Law'.[76] Many jurisprudential scholars from the common law world had been attracted to the problems thrown up by the law of possession. In Australia, the Professor of Jurisprudence at Melbourne University, George Paton, had written on the topic,[77] and it was something that the great legal writers Salmond, Pollock, Goodhart, DR Harris, Bentham, Dias and Hughes had studied in depth.[78] It was not, however, an emerging area. By choosing this topic – and in accordance with Andersonian beliefs – Tay was placing herself within an older tradition, rather than looking to developments in modern learning.

One of the dominant intellectual traditions of Anderson's age was ordinary-language philosophy. Anderson was, for example, a direct contemporary of Gilbert Ryle. Anderson, nonetheless, rejected this school of thought in favour of older approaches to philosophy.[79] When Tay wrote her thesis, HLA Hart's scholarship, which drew liberally from the linguistic tradition, had become prominent within the common law world. Hart believed that his 'jurisprudential predecessors, in seeking to illuminate the meaning of terms of legal art such as a "corporation" through definition, had been both asking the wrong question and using the wrong methods to answer it'.[80] As Nicola Lacey explains, Hart instead 'counselled a return to Bentham's and Frege's insight that such words can only be understood in the context of sentences in which they have meaning'.[81] At that time, an emerging scholar with jurisprudential ambitions, attracted to the elite, and looking to investigate a central common law doctrine would, surely, have considered adopting Hart's approach to their study of possession. Yet Tay did not follow his lead. Her approach suggests quite a different influence.

The aim of Tay's thesis was, in the words of Sir John Salmond, to attempt a 'complete theory of possession', that provided 'an analysis of the conception itself' and an 'exposition of the manner in which it is recognised and applied in the actual legal system'.[82] While Salmond and the other great jurisprudential scholars had attempted such a theory, Tay argued that their efforts had fallen short. Her argument was that the concept of possession 'enters the law not as a technical term but as an infra-jural relation of fact, recognised and protected by the law and used by it as the basis for obvious but important rights and obligations'.[83] By 'infra-jural relation' she meant something that 'exists in fact independently of its recognition by law and which the law can only adopt as a fact (to which it then ascribes certain

[76] A Tay, 'The Concept of Possession in the Common Law' (PhD Thesis, Australian National University, 1964).

[77] GW Paton, *A Text-Book of Jurisprudence* 2nd edn (Oxford, Clarendon Press, 1951) 454.

[78] Tay (n 76) 5–7.

[79] Cole (n 67).

[80] N Lacey, *A Life of HLA Hart – The Nightmare and the Noble Dream* (Oxford, Oxford University Press, 2004) 156.

[81] ibid.

[82] GL Williams (ed), *Salmond – Jurisprudence*, 10th edn (Sweet and Maxwell, 1947) 287, quoted in Tay (n 76) 3.

[83] ibid.

legal consequences)'.[84] From an extensive analysis of case law dating back to the 1400s she deduced that 'the concept of control ... provides a basis and an explanation for the important uses of "possession" in the common law'.[85]

Tay's thesis was therefore based on what she described as a conceptualisation, rather than on linguistic analysis. Her work was an intellectual history of doctrine in the context of various common law legal systems (English, Australian, Canadian) over many hundreds of years. She sought to challenge existing approaches by treating possession as an enduring logical concept, one of many 'fundamental "rational" principles' lying at the heart of the common law.[86] In this respect she rejected the dominant view of the leading scholars of her age, who suggested that such rational analysis was not possible.[87] Tay's approach had much in common with the work of German legal scholar Friedrich Carl von Savigny, whose seminal work *The Law of Possession* (1803) was based on a historical study of the Roman Law of possession from which he, like Tay, developed his own concept of possession.[88] Tay's method of attempting to define the concept on the basis of an intellectual history is very similar to Savigny's method, and her ultimate concept of possession – based on control – bears some resemblance to his concept of possession as resting on an intent to possess.[89] At the time when Tay was writing her thesis, Savigny's work was out of vogue. Rudolph von Jhering (1818–1892), another German legal scholar who is best known for his advocacy of instrumental approaches to law which gained particular traction in America in the first half of the twentieth century, had challenged this older body of thought.[90] In the course of his career, Jhering came to reject Savigny's methods and theories, believing that they placed too great a faith in logic.[91] Jhering came instead to see private rights such as possession as ultimately resting on social needs, not logical analysis.[92] Tay passed over the instrumental school in favour of Savigny's historical method. She preferred the old greats to popular writers.

In her work on possession Tay presented as a confident scholar who was frank (perhaps to a fault) in her attitude towards other scholars. Nothing was held back. At this time – the 1960s – her criticism of her leading contemporaries would have been interpreted by the legal academy as blistering. Perhaps the bluntness of her attack could be attributed to her 'feisty' personality, another of her often remarked upon qualities.[93] However, the confidence with which she challenged the established, old, predominantly white and male, guard and boldly proclaimed a better

[84] P Keenan, 'Finders, Occupiers and Possession' (1983) 10 *Sydney Law Review* 180, 185.
[85] Tay (n 76) 342.
[86] ibid 7.
[87] ibid.
[88] For a recent interpretation of Savigny's approach, see DM Rabban, *Law's History* (Cambridge, Cambridge University Press, 2013) 94–97.
[89] ibid 96.
[90] ibid.
[91] ibid 109.
[92] ibid 106–14.
[93] This clearly has gender connotations. The appropriateness of this descriptor is considered in chapters ten and eleven.

view must also be attributed to the influence of Kamenka and Anderson. Following these intellectual influences, she 'elevated conflict', 'reject[ed] compromise and the illusion of a common interest' and 'pitted … sound logic and good argument against all appeals to the fashionable, the "accepted", the comforting'.[94]

Parts of Tay's thesis were published in several prestigious law journals.[95] Her condemnation of fellow scholars embodied in these articles did not go unnoticed. Harris, a Fellow of Balliol College, Oxford, made specific reference to how Tay had assigned him (and the other scholars she critiqued) to the 'intellectual ice age' and branded him as 'an adherent to "nihilism"'.[96] He argued, among other things, that Tay had begun with a false preconception, approaching 'the problem with the tacit assumption that there must be a unitary concept to explain the various uses of the same verbal symbol, "possession"'.[97] He therefore believed that her approach was liable to oversimplify rather than elucidate the concept of possession. While her larger doctrinal thesis suggested that she had in fact comprehensively investigated and tested her assumption, Harris's remarks show that she was nonetheless brave to submit such a controversial work. One of her examiners, David Derham,[98] shared Harris's 'prehistoric' mindset (to use Tay's characterisation) and was therefore opposed to her central thesis.[99] By contrast, her second examiner – the highly regarded English scholar, Glanville Williams – gave the thesis a favourable review.[100] Given Williams's stature, this must have provided Tay with a strong vote of confidence.[101] Her thesis passed without the need for amendments.[102]

The Sociological Tradition

Once Tay had completed her PhD, she abandoned the jurisprudential 'greats' in favour of a school of thought that sat outside the discipline of law: the sociological tradition. This was Kamenka's chief interest. In a reference written for Kamenka, Anderson spoke of his protégé's talents in the history of ideas rather than

[94] Kamenka (n 6) 19.

[95] A Tay, 'Bailment and the Deposit for Safe-Keeping' (1964) 6 *Malaya Law Review* 229; A Tay, '"Bridges v Hawkesworth" and the Early History of Finding' (1964) 8 *American Journal of Legal History* 224; A Tay, 'The Concept of Possession in the Common Law: Foundations for a New Approach' (1964) 4 *Melbourne University Law Review* 476; A Tay, 'Possession and the Modern Law of Finding' (1964) 4 *Sydney Law Review* 383; A Tay, 'Possession, Larceny, and Servants – Towards Tidying up a Historical Muddle' (1965) 16 *University of Toronto Law Journal* 145; A Tay, 'Problems in the Law of Finding – The US Approach' (1964) 37 *Australian Law Journal* 350; A Tay, 'The Essence of a Bailment – Contract, Agreement or Possession?' (1965) 5 *Sydney Law Review* 239.

[96] DR Harris, 'Comment' (1963–64) 4 *Melbourne University Law Review* 498, 498.

[97] ibid 498.

[98] Minutes of the Faculty of the Research School of Social Sciences, 13 March 1964, Research School of Social Sciences, Faculty Board Minutes, 15 February 1961–10 December 1964, Australian National University Archive.

[99] Horne (n 13) 27.

[100] ibid 27.

[101] ibid 27.

[102] Minutes of the Faculty of the Research School of Social Sciences (n 98).

analytical philosophy.[103] Unlike other Andersonians, Kamenka wished to combine learning from the social sciences with philosophy, and was particularly drawn to Ferdinand Tönnies. As one of the fathers of modern social science, Tönnies was, according to Anderson's criteria, a worthy subject of study as well as a worthy intellectual mentor. Tönnies was a German sociologist and philosopher who, despite having a lesser reputation than Max Weber, is said to have provided 'arguably the first systematic sociological account to sketch an evolution from ancient to modern society'.[104]

Tönnies's interests and methodologies fitted the interests and lives of Tay and Kamenka. Their intellectual paradigms legitimised theorising about societies based on observation. They suggested that these were robust and valuable ways to study political currents. We can guess that Tay, having studied neither law nor philosophy at a university, was attracted to a scholarly tradition that gave credence to a person's lived experience and allowed for the study of a society. With sociology she did not have to start from scratch, and could instead draw on the curiosity and frustrations that had beset her childhood and adolescence. As a former doctoral student of Tay's astutely observed: 'If you look into the life and theories [of Weber and Tönnies], they are the closest to the way in which Alice Tay and Kamenka conducted their life'.[105]

Tay's subsequent studies combined doctrinal studies of particular laws and constitutions of the Chinese and Soviet legal systems with an intellectual history of Marxist thought and political history. Paradoxically, after leaving the RSSS Tay sat squarely within the social sciences, drawing connections between changes in politics and values within a society and their mode of governance. By prompting her to firm up her views on the common law and consider the concepts underlying the property law doctrine that was the antithesis of Marxist studies, her PhD helped shape some of her later sociological and comparative studies (discussed in the following chapter). However, it was not an obvious transition. This suggests that she initially sought to explore an issue that accommodated the traditional legal methods that she had learnt as a practitioner.

While Tay and Kamenka did not subscribe to Marxist philosophies, their methods nonetheless resembled those of Marx, whose elucidation of the 'distinctions between feudal law, bourgeois law and the regulation of human affairs under communism' constituted 'an important example of the macro sociological approach'.[106] Tay's studies sat outside those of her colleagues in Australian law schools. As she and Kamenka noted, common lawyers have 'traditionally been

[103] John Anderson to the Registrar of ANU, 11 January 1961, Eugene Kamenka Staff Files, Australian National University Archives.

[104] M Deflem, 'Ferdinand Tönnies (1855–1936)' *Routledge Encyclopaedia of Philosophy* (online), (Taylor and Francis, 2001) www.rep.routledge.com/article/R048.

[105] Participant A (n 9).

[106] A Tay and E Kamenka, 'Beyond the French Revolution: Communist Socialism and the Concept of Law' (1971) 21 *University of Toronto Law Journal* 109, 110.

ill at ease with the macro sociology of law'.[107] Her intellectual partnership with Kamenka therefore encouraged her to adopt an intellectual agenda that was different from other modes of study within Australian law schools.

The Australian Legal Academy

Joining the law faculty at the ANU in 1965 made very little impression on Tay.[108] Later in life she painted her colleagues in narrow terms, suggesting that they were part of a boys' club.[109] There were no other full-time women in the faculty and Tay did not feel that she belonged. As explained in a later chapter on Sawer, the faculty did not have the interdisciplinary focus of the RSSS and had very little contact with the research school where Tay had completed her PhD. She did not, however, consider her differences to be a disadvantage. A significant part of her tenure at ANU was spent abroad: in Russia and America studying Soviet law, and visiting leading universities around the globe (for example, Toronto and Cologne). While at ANU she taught across the curriculum and enjoyed her teaching.[110] She did not seek friendship, reward or recognition from her colleagues but instead sought to build her profile and reputation through prestigious publications and international connections.[111]

When reading about Tay's achievements, it is easy to forget that she was a young woman, of Chinese descent, in a sea of white, mostly Anglo-Australian, men. Tay never drew attention to this fact or suggested that it limited her horizons. Others noticed. Former High Court justice, Michael Kirby, for example, said that when he stood to defend his Masters thesis in front of his examiners, Tay and Kamenka, she commanded his respect and also instilled an element of fear.

> First of all, remember we are talking about 1967 or thereabouts. At that time feisty women were thin on the ground in the law. It was a very unusual experience for me to be interrogated in such an assertive, confident, upfront and dynamic way by a then still quite young person who was a woman. Secondly, the times were still in the midst of White Australia, so not only did I have to grapple in my psyche with the fact that my interrogator was a woman, she was an Asian woman. She was not in the least lacking in confidence because of that. On the contrary, she was assertive and obviously in charge of the examination. Thirdly, she was someone whom I had not met before and was somewhat different to the quiet, reflective, contemplative atmosphere of the Jurisprudence Department at the University of Sydney.[112]

[107] ibid 109.
[108] Tay was made a part-time tutor in 1965, senior tutor in 1966, lecturer in 1967 and senior lecturer in 1970.
[109] Horne (n 13) 27, 30.
[110] ibid 31.
[111] ibid 27.
[112] Interview with Michael Kirby (by telephone, 14 March 2015).

Tay's endeavour was not shaped by a sense that she ought to fit in or conform to scholarly norms within Australia. Her attitude would suggest that her minority status, rather than being a disadvantage, provided her with a unique vantage point from which she could appraise disciplinary practices and avoid any compromises that might come from a sense of group belonging. She was a tough, independently spirited woman whose academic mentors and partners no doubt buoyed her confidence and belief that scholars should scrutinise existing conventions and modes of governance rather than join them.

At least until 1975, it therefore appears that the Australian legal academy had very little influence on her formative development and subsequent career. Tay's later career suggests that if it had any influence at all it was to encourage Tay to stand apart from, rather than fit in with, her colleagues.

Concluding Remarks

In many ways, Tay's early life was difficult. It is staggering that a woman born and raised in Singapore, and in poverty, could achieve such prominence both in the Australian legal academy and the world of legal theory. The success she achieved points to both a sense of resilience and strong intelligence. Her life and early mentors explain why she set such store on her career, why she wished to embody and advocate for a strong set of academic values, and why she had such a strong aversion to complacency.

The scholarly values that she developed in this early formative period sustained Tay's career and fed into what I consider to be her greatest contribution to the Australian legal academy: the governance of the Department of Jurisprudence at the University of Sydney. It is to that contribution that this book now turns.

8

Tay and the Department of Jurisprudence: Reigniting Hostilities

Introduction

Identifying Alice Tay's contribution to the Australian legal academy during the remaining 26 years of her academic career raises some controversial questions. These stem primarily from her appointment as Challis Professor of Jurisprudence at the Faculty of Law at the University of Sydney in 1975. At a time when Sydney's Department of Jurisprudence (the Department) was under threat, Tay as its new head chose to fight for its survival. It is tempting to align Tay's contribution to the legal academy with that of the Department. Yet, this is problematic because those who opposed the Department's existence have argued that the Department itself contributed little, either to the University of Sydney or to the Australian legal academy.[1] While they acknowledge Tay's significant achievements, critics nonetheless attribute these to her personal attributes and position as Professor of Jurisprudence, rather than to the culture and community of the Department.[2] Similar arguments are made about the achievements of her colleagues in the Department. If we accept this view, then equating Tay's contributions to the legal academy with those of the Department itself would mean that she contributed very little. Others, most obviously those who were formerly part of or associated with the Department, suggest that Tay's leadership was critical to their contributions and successes.[3]

In one sense, I sympathise with those who supported the continued existence of the Department. In this and the following chapters, I argue that the Tay's leadership of the Department both enabled her to make important contributions to the legal academy and explains many of her contributions. Of course, appointment to such an esteemed position as the Professor of Jurisprudence at Sydney – and becoming Julius Stone's successor – might have encouraged anyone to strive to live up to the role by publishing strong works of scholarship. However, by giving Tay

[1] This chapter provides a detailed account of such views.

[2] Interview with Jeremy Webber (by telephone, 22 October 2014); interview with James Crawford (by telephone, 25 November 2014); interview with Ron McCallum (by telephone, 4 November 2014).

[3] See chapter ten.

the autonomy to work with a small, carefully chosen group of scholars, the responsibility for a small but compulsory part of the law curriculum, and the ability to host accomplished academic visitors, the Challis Professorship empowered her to drive initiatives and shape the Faculty of Law in ways that may not have been possible as an ordinary Professor of Jurisprudence. Rather than working as an individual, she now had the authority and resources to advance initiatives directed by the scholarly beliefs identified in the previous chapter.

Even if such additional effort was not the natural consequence of heading the Department, it is the natural response of someone who believed their Department to be under threat. Within the first three years of Tay's tenure at Sydney, the precarious position of the Department was made very clear to her. As a consequence, in the first 15 years of her leadership much was done to drive ambitious teaching and scholarly initiatives, promote the Department and win allies. While securing the Department's survival was not Tay's only motivation, there is evidence to suggest that it was central to her thinking. In this sense, the existence and context of the Department played a crucial role in enabling and motivating Tay to make a number of important contributions to Australia's legal academy.

This chapter shows that Tay made a conscious choice to maintain and run the Department throughout her tenure, and that she did so knowing that her decision would reignite divisions and hostilities within the Faculty of Law. Her choice to head the Department, coupled with her subsequent efforts to ensure its survival, suggests that Tay believed that the Department had special qualities that were of value to her, her colleagues and the legal academy.

Reigniting Decades of Division

The First Challenge

The Department of Jurisprudence and International Law was created in 1947, shortly after Kenneth Owen Shatwell was appointed Dean of the Faculty of Law at Sydney.[4] As will be explained later in this chapter, there had been significant friction between the previous Dean of Faculty, Professor James Williams, and Stone. In an effort to avoid further conflict, Shatwell approached the Vice-Chancellor, Sir Stephen Roberts, with a proposition to divide the Faculty into two separate departments, the Department of Law and the Department of Jurisprudence

[4] WL Morison, 'Professor KO Shatwell 1947–73' in J Mackinolty and J Mackinolty (eds), *A Century Down Town – Sydney University Law School's First Hundred Years* (Sydney, Sydney University Law School, 1991) 105, 116; B Bilinsky, 'Shatwell, Kenneth Owen (1909–88)' in *Australian Dictionary of Biography* 18 (Melbourne, Melbourne University Press, 2012).

and International Law.[5] Shatwell believed that providing Stone with autonomy over his sphere of academic activity (both teaching and research) would reduce the potential for conflict between Stone and other members of the Faculty.[6] The Vice-Chancellor acquiesced.[7] However, contrary to Shatwell's intentions, tensions between Stone and the rest of the Faculty remained throughout the ensuing decades and in some ways were transformed from a conflict between personalities to a conflict between the two departments.

Tay took up her appointment as Professor of Jurisprudence on 10 January 1975,[8] and it soon became clear to critics of the Department of Jurisprudence that she would embody and honour some of Stone's central beliefs and attributes. Before her appointment, it had been proposed that the departmental structure should be abolished upon Stone's retirement.[9] Three years later, in 1978, the Vice-Chancellor, Bruce Williams, returned to the issue of whether the departmental structure ought to be maintained.[10] He commissioned a report by the Deputy Vice-Chancellor, Professor O'Neil, who recommended that the Department of Jurisprudence and International Law should be changed to a Department of Jurisprudence.[11] Williams accepted the recommendation.[12]

Tabling the Vice-Chancellor's recommendation at a meeting of the Faculty of Law provided an opportunity for those who wanted to abolish the Department of Jurisprudence, and those whose relationship with Stone had been strained, to make themselves known to Tay. Professor PH Lane tabled a motion that the Vice-Chancellor 'delay the implementation of the recommendation until the Faculty had an opportunity to discuss the separation fully' and noted the 'Vice-Chancellor's omission to seek the Faculty's formal view on this separation'.[13] David Johnson (the Professor of International Law who was appointed shortly after Tay) was Acting Dean and Chair of the meeting. He ruled the motions out of order, stating his view that the Vice-Chancellor 'had acted properly within an area which was solely within his competence for the balance of his recommendations'.[14] A motion was made for Johnson to vacate the Chair, which he did, and John Mackinolty was elected Chairman for the purpose of presiding over the question of whether Johnson's ruling was appropriate.[15] William (Bill) Morison then put a case for

[5] ibid.
[6] Morison (n 4) 116.
[7] ibid.
[8] Professorial Board Minutes, 18 November 1984, University of Sydney Archives; 'Appointments', *The University of Sydney News* (Sydney), 5 March 1975, 30.
[9] Starr suggests that it was proposed in early 1972: L Starr, *Julius Stone – An Intellectual Life* (Oxford, Oxford University Press, 1992) 242.
[10] Faculty of Law Minutes, 8 December 1978, University of Sydney Archives.
[11] ibid.
[12] ibid.
[13] ibid.
[14] ibid.
[15] ibid.

returning to Lane's original motion and the Faculty redrafted it. On the critical question of whether to invite the Vice-Chancellor to reconsider his recommendation, the votes were tied, with 16 for and 16 against.[16] In the absence of a clear majority, the motion was lost and the meeting adjourned. At the following meeting the central part of the motion (to question the Vice-Chancellor's decision) was carried, 15 votes to 13.[17] The Vice-Chancellor did not, however, reconsider his decision and the Department of Jurisprudence remained in existence for another two decades.

Although Tay was present at both meetings, there is no record of any views expressed by Tay concerning the motion. The first of Tay's new academic appointments to the Department of Jurisprudence, Martin Krygier, remembers the motion as an important moment in the continuation of divisions between the two departments. He and Morison argued over the matter,[18] and Krygier recalled that at around that time Tay 'had completely lost faith in Morison and the others on grounds of, as she put it, "academic principle"'.[19] It was the first time they had quarrelled.[20] Krygier also believed that the attempt to abolish the Department weighed heavily on Tay at that time and, despite her tough disposition, 'she almost broke' and 'was much more fragile'.[21]

Morison's long history within the Faculty and at the University of Sydney had begun as a student in 1937. He graduated with a Bachelor of Arts in 1940 with first class honours and the university medal in both history and philosophy, before graduating in 1944 in law, again with first class honours and a number of scholarships and prizes.[22] In 1946, following time as an articled clerk and work in the Department of External Affairs during the war, Morison was appointed a lecturer in law at the University of Sydney, where he remained until his retirement in 1985.[23] In 1949 he accepted a scholarship from ANU to conduct a doctoral thesis into tort law at Lincoln College, Oxford.[24] Returning to Sydney in 1951 he taught in the Faculty of Law at the University of Sydney from until 1985. Morison was appointed a professor in 1959, and wrote scholarship in the fields of torts, jurisprudence, evidence and procedure.[25]

Like Eugene Kamenka, Morison had studied philosophy under John Anderson and acknowledged Anderson as a significant ongoing influence in his work.[26]

[16] ibid.
[17] ibid.
[18] Interview with Martin Krygier (Law School, University of New South Wales, 7 February 2014).
[19] ibid.
[20] ibid.
[21] ibid.
[22] Curriculum Vitae of William Loutit Morison (Professor WL Morison Memorial), www.nealemorison.com/wlmorison/cv.html.
[23] ibid.
[24] ibid; J Robatham, 'Obituary for WL Morison', *Sydney Morning Herald* (Sydney), 14 April 2000, 32.
[25] Curriculum Vitae (n 22); Jeremy Webber, 'In Memoriam – William L Morison' (Professor WL Morison Memorial), www.nealemorison.com/wlmorison/webber.html.
[26] Webber (n 25).

He was a man of obvious intellectual ability with a strong interest in philosophy and history that perhaps either equalled or surpassed his interest in law. He was admired by many of his colleagues, including Australian torts scholar Professor Carolyn Sappideen, formerly his research assistant, who described Morison as 'the most outstanding intellectual and scholar I ever met'.[27]

Several interviewees for this book attested that the personal and professional animosity between Morison and Stone carried forward into his relations with Tay.[28] It is therefore worth considering the reasons for this animosity. Krygier recalled Morison 'bitterly' telling him that he had come to 'Sydney hoping to teach jurisprudence and Stone blocked him on the grounds that he was an Andersonian'.[29] Given Morison's strong interest in both history and philosophy, one would have thought he would have earned a place in Stone's department; yet he remained in the Department of Law teaching jurisprudence within a first-year introduction to law subject. There are some signs that when Morison joined the Faculty in 1946, and over the ensuing decade, he was on good terms with Stone, with Stone approaching Morison for his views on various topics and putting him forward for some teaching opportunities.[30] Yet it is equally clear that the pair had quite different views on jurisprudence and that Morison objected to the division of the Faculty into two departments, describing it as a 'pioneer in unintelligible developments, which subsequently spread over the tertiary educational system of the State generally'.[31] There is also some suggestion that Stone treated Morison badly. For example, Morison describes an incident where the former Professor of Jurisprudence at Oxford, Arthur Lehman Goodhart, visited the University of Sydney and delivered to Morison a note from HLA Hart that read '[s]ay a word of encouragement to WL Morison, I think Stone bullies him'.[32] In print, at least, Morison maintained that he did not feel that Stone treated him any worse than anyone else.[33]

Starr's 1992 biography of Stone quotes Morison as saying that his colleagues' criticisms of Stone were merely 'academic' commentary.[34] However, students and others characterised these arguments as intensely personal.[35] When Starr compiled her biography, several of Stone's adversaries in the Faculty were still employed at Sydney. This would have made it difficult to fully investigate the dispute between Stone and Morison and between the two departments. Over 20 years later, comments made by some of the interviewees for this study suggest

[27] C Sappideen, 'Eulogy for WL Morison' (Professor WL Morison Memorial), www.nealemorison.com/wlmorison/sappideen.html.

[28] Krygier (n 18); Crawford (n 2); interview with Christopher Birch SC (Garfield Barwick Chambers, Sydney, 28 July 2014).

[29] Krygier (n 18).

[30] Morison (n 4) 114, 119, 122.

[31] ibid 116.

[32] ibid 126.

[33] ibid.

[34] Starr (n 9) 110.

[35] ibid.

that Starr's biography does not convey the full extent of the hostility over the departmental structure that existed throughout Stone's tenure.[36]

The staff meeting in 1978 and Lane's motion reignited the previously strained relationship between the departments. From that moment, Tay was in no doubt that the position of her Department was anything but secure. Not only did this recreate divisions between the two departments but this sense of being under threat also fed back into Tay's agenda for her Department. While Tay and Morison had Anderson in common,[37] it appears that her decision to maintain the Department brought a strain to that relationship as well.[38] In these respects her position at Sydney and the precarious situation of the Department began to mirror the conditions under which Stone had operated for many decades.[39]

Origins of the Division

The divisions can in fact be traced to before Stone's time. In the 1940s and 1950s the Faculty of Law at Sydney University showed little sign of becoming a liberal ambitious law school like Melbourne, with its Jewish Dean, and great enabler of the people, Zelman Cowen, and strong American ambitions. Speaking of the 1930s and 1940s former judge of the Supreme Court of New South Wales, Rae Else-Mitchell made the following comparison:

> This was a period of stimulating influence in the University of Melbourne which manifested a spirit of liberal thought not equalled by the other universities and law schools in Australia. At a time when law teaching in Sydney was dominated by Peden's black-letter conservatism and attempts were made to muzzle John Anderson as an atheist and anti-imperialist, students in Melbourne were being introduced by teachers like Kenneth Bailey and 'PD' Phillips to Holmes and Pound, both of whom were hardly known in Sydney.[40]

From 1910 to 1940 Sir John Peden had been Dean at Sydney. Generally feared by students[41] and considered strongly parochial,[42] Peden's principal interests lay in

[36] Birch (n 28); Crawford (n 2).

[37] Morison even published a chapter in a book edited by Tay and Kamenka: WL Morison, 'Frames of Reference for Legal Ideals' in E Kamenka, R Brown and A Tay (eds), *Law and Society* (Melbourne, Edward Arnold, 1978).

[38] Krygier (n 18).

[39] In the late 1980s the division was also reflected in an assessment of the discipline of law in Australia commissioned by the Commonwealth Tertiary Education Commission. The committee suggested abolishing the Department of Jurisprudence: D Pearce, E Campbell and D Harding, *Australian Law Schools: A Discipline Assessment for the Commonwealth Tertiary Education Commission* (Canberra, Australian Government Publishing Service, 1987) lxxxvi.

[40] R Else-Mitchell, 'Introduction' in L Zines (ed), *Commentaries on the Australian Constitution – A Tribute to Geoffrey Sawer* (Sydney, Butterworths, 1977) xix, xxi.

[41] J Mackinolty, 'Learned Practitioners – Professor John Peden 1910–41' in J Mackinolty and J Mackinolty (eds), *A Century Down Town – Sydney University Law School's First Hundred Years* (Sydney, Sydney University Law School, 1991) 57, 77.

[42] ibid 76.

the technical doctrinal aspects of law and he did not attempt to write or publish any strong works of scholarship.[43] He was a practitioner teacher rather than a scholar. He had connections to both bench and Bar and was a member of the Legislative Assembly.[44] For Peden, one of the principal roles of the law schools was to ensure that future practitioners had an accurate understanding of the law.[45] Perhaps, as a consequence, his lectures were considered dull.[46]

Peden's only full-time colleague, Archibald Charteris, appointed to the new Challis Professor of Jurisprudence and International Law in 1920, was in many ways Peden's opposite. Charteris had spent his formative years overseas, as a student then teacher at various Scottish universities. He was interested in the broader aspects of law and wrote and published in a literary style.[47] He was charismatic and his teaching appealed to students whose faces were said to 'light up with affection and admiration at Charteris's name'.[48] He did much to advance the study of international law in Australia and, at a time when overseas travel from Australia involved long and difficult journeys, attended several international conferences in places ranging from Japan to Canada.[49] He also became a public figure, being a regular and very successful radio broadcaster.[50] He has been described as 'one of the most colourful legal and academic figures in Sydney: "a great scholar and a very lovable man"'.[51]

It would have come as quite a surprise to these two men that throughout the twentieth century caricatured versions of Peden and Charteris – the narrow technocrat and the broad-minded theorist – came to represent some aspects of the central division within the Faculty of Law. In the late 1940s Sawer noted the friction he observed between Stone and Shatwell, then the Dean of the Faculty of Law at Sydney, during one of the Australian Law Schools Association (ALSA) conferences.[52] He astutely observed that 'one of the curses of the Sydney Law School has been the inability of the senior professors to get along with one another'.[53] While only a brief sketch of the various conflicts can be outlined in a study devoted to Tay's role in the Faculty post-1975, it is nonetheless worth noting some of the key events and attitudes, as they help explain the task that lay ahead of Tay once she decided to maintain the Department.

[43] ibid 77–78.
[44] ibid 57, 76.
[45] JM Ward, 'Peden, Sir John Beverley' (1871–1946) in *Australian Dictionary of Biography* 11 (Melbourne, Melbourne University Press, 1998).
[46] ibid.
[47] ibid 77.
[48] ibid 77.
[49] JG Starke, 'Charteris, Archibald Hamilton' (1874–1940) in *Australian Dictionary of Biography* 7 (Melbourne, Melbourne University Press, 1979).
[50] ibid.
[51] ibid.
[52] M Pratt, Interview with Geoffrey Sawer (Oral History Interview, Canberra, 16 November 1971), https://nla.gov.au/nla.obj-214869908/listen.
[53] ibid.

The more unseemly aspects of this division began in 1941 when, under a cloud of controversy, Stone was given the Chair. Starr has documented the objections to Stone's appointment that were made by members of the profession as well as Peden, who resigned from the Senate following the appointment.[54] She explains that their motivations included anti-Semitism and conservatism over Stone's particular brand of sociological jurisprudence.[55] While Stone and his supporters, including many of his future students at Sydney,[56] triumphed and he took up his appointment in 1942, the animosity did not dissipate. James Williams (the professor appointed at the same time as Stone and succeeding Peden as Dean), objected to Stone's presence in the Faculty of Law for personal reasons, including some that were overtly racist:[57] Williams did not want to work with a Jew.[58]

The two were also divided on matters of governance. Stone hoped to build a large academic enterprise where teaching was conducted by full-time, career academics with the time to devise inventive teaching initiatives.[59] Williams, on the other hand, even after the war, was content to leave matters largely as they had been, with much of the teaching being conducted by legal practitioners who taught part-time.[60] His loathing of Stone also meant that he sought to avoid him wherever possible.[61]

While Williams did not stay long at Sydney – resigning in 1945 following further animosity and tension with Stone[62] – the division between the theoretical and technical teaching of law, which had begun with Peden and Charteris and then transferred to Williams and Stone, continued over the following decades. As noted above, there were signs of friction between Stone and a subsequent Dean, Shatwell, and there were also signs of tension between Morison and Stone. Rather than harmonising the Faculty and limiting the potential for tension between professors within the Faculty as Shatwell had planned, dividing the Faculty into two departments was instead viewed as an arrangement that privileged members of Stone's Department.[63] In 1953, Shatwell and Stone had taken steps to ensure that

> the spheres of the Professor of Law and the Professor of Jurisprudence and the International Law be finally and authoritatively defined on the basis of the complete separation and the autonomy of each Professor in his respective field.[64]

[54] Starr (n 9) 56–67.
[55] ibid 59–60.
[56] ibid 63.
[57] ibid 64.
[58] ibid 64. Starr quotes correspondence from Williams: 'I don't want to be plagued by a Hebrew for the rest of my life'.
[59] ibid 79–80.
[60] ibid.
[61] ibid 80.
[62] ibid 103–7.
[63] Members of Tay's Department said that arguments for it to be abolished were sometimes based on the suggestion that those in the Department had lighter workloads and benefited from greater autonomy in their affairs: Krygier (n 18). Interview with Klaus Ziegert (Law School, University of Sydney, 5 February 2014).
[64] Starr (n 9) 112.

What, perhaps, could not have been anticipated at this time was that Stone's scholarly reputation would grow in strength, particularly among his students who went on to become leading members of Australia's legal profession, and the division, at least in the 1960s, began to represent the demarcations between the enlightened (Stone's Department) and the technocratic (the Department of Law).[65] Moreover, the small size of Stone's Department meant that he and a few, handpicked colleagues could more easily pursue their own goals. Stone's Department therefore took on an appearance of elitism and privilege.

The lingering tension between the two parts of the Faculty is illustrated by the fact that Stone's retirement from the university was almost as controversial as his appointment. As Starr has dealt extensively with the disputes that erupted at that time, the detail will not be repeated here.[66] Ructions within the university arose from two key matters. First, as previously mentioned, there was a suggestion that Stone's Department should be abolished following his retirement.[67] Second, Stone was excluded from the meeting of the Professorial Board in 1974 where the decision concerning the appointment of a new Professor of Jurisprudence and International Law was to be made. This exclusion spoke of yet another instance of anti-Semitism. The Professorial Board's meeting was deliberately scheduled on the 'Jewish Day of Atonement, the most sacred day of the religious calendar, on which no secular work can be undertaken by any practising Jew'.[68] The bitterness was compounded by the fact that the university did not offer Stone an office or honorary position that would have allowed him to continue his association with Sydney in retirement.[69]

Tay's Appointment

At the controversial Professorial Board meeting that Stone could not attend, the Board decided to appoint Professor Clive Parry to Stone's former Chair. When Parry declined the offer,[70] the Board decided to split the Professorship and advertise for both a Professor of Jurisprudence and a Professor of International Law. In response to these advertisements, the university received four applications from scholars with an interest in the jurisprudential role.[71] Two of the applicants had formerly been part of Stone's department and one, Tony Blackshield, was shortlisted for the position.[72] His referees included Julius Stone along with a

[65] See, eg, M Kirby, 'The Graduating Class of Sydney Law School 1962: Talented, Lucky, Unquestioning' (2012) 36 *Australian Bar Review* 189, 196, 199–200.
[66] ibid 243–50.
[67] ibid 243.
[68] ibid 244.
[69] ibid 249–50.
[70] ibid 248.
[71] Professorial Board Minutes, 21 October 1974, 1004, G2/1, University of Sydney Archives.
[72] ibid. For an account of Blackshield's accomplishments, see M Kirby, 'AR Blackshield and Realism in Australian Constitutional Law' (2013) 11 *Macquarie Law Journal* 7.

number of strong foreign scholars.[73] The appointment committee, however, did not appoint Blackshield but instead sought an application from Tay.

Tay and Blackshield were both strong candidates with impressive international referees, so there is nothing particularly odd about the committee favouring Tay over Blackshield. However, the fact that Tay did not initially apply, but was approached at a time when references had been sought in relation to Blackshield's application, suggests that some members of the university might have taken steps to prevent the appointment of a member of Stone's camp. Perhaps they disliked Stone or opposed the Department; perhaps they believed that such an appointment would only have furthered the bitterness between the two departments. Some might also have feared that Blackshield's history with Stone would make him less amenable to merging the two departments. As someone who was not closely associated with Stone, Tay presented as a safer bet on all these fronts.

Tay was appointed Challis Professor of Jurisprudence in 1975, while David Johnson, from the London School of Economics, took up his new role as Professor of International Law in 1976.[74] Securing the appointment of Tay and Johnson could have signalled the end of conflict and divisions within the Faculty of Law. Johnson decided to abandon the notion of maintaining a separate department, which left Tay to decide whether to do the same. Starr speculates that Johnson's decision was 'possibly because of his belief that his lifelong struggle to have his subject recognised as an academic discipline would be enhanced by association with black-letter law subjects'.[75] It is rumoured that certain members of the Faculty believed that Tay, like Johnson, would be more amenable to a merger and, as a young woman, she seemed to represent a soft target. On the one hand, the rumours seem plausible. Tay and Kamenka were known to the Faculty of Law. In the first half of 1974 they had both spent a semester teaching jurisprudence at Sydney to fill part of the gap created by Stone's retirement.[76] Tay's networking skills might have helped her establish rapport with members of the Faculty during this time. One of the leading opponents to Stone's Department, Morison, was a known Andersonian and so it seems likely that he would have appreciated Tay's link with Kamenka and may have believed that their shared outlook meant that Tay would be more amenable to the merger that Morison wanted. Krygier believes that Tay had been prepared to close the Department when she joined the Faculty, but then changed her mind.[77]

On the other hand, the sexism implicit in this theory – that as a young woman she was weak and therefore an easy target – seems less likely. Tay had already spent six months teaching at Sydney, so the Faculty would have become acquainted with her personality. Almost everyone interviewed about Tay for this project

[73] ibid.
[74] ibid 248–49.
[75] ibid 249.
[76] Professorial Board Minutes, 18 March 1974, University of Sydney Archives.
[77] Krygier (n 18).

commented on her strong disposition. They referred to Tay's scathing frankness[78] and 'fierceness'.[79] Klaus Ziegert, Tay's colleague in the Department, said that she never conveyed a sense that she 'felt intimidated or inferior or any of these, let's say, female attributes'.[80] Shortly after Tay's appointment to the Professorship a Sydney newspaper, *The Daily Mirror*, began an article with:

> Professor Alice Tay is tiny, dainty and possibly the toughest woman in the southern hemisphere – and that includes the Philippines' Steel Butterfly, and Vietnam's Dragon Lady.[81]

Tay's confidence and strength were evident long before she arrived at Sydney.[82] She was anything but demure.

If part of the thinking that led to Tay's appointment was that she would acquiesce to the closure of the Department, her appointees could not have been more wrong. Not only did Tay decide to relentlessly defend the existence of her Department, but she did so in a way that was destined to reinforce divisions within the Faculty. Perhaps the appointment committee did not realise that she possessed several of Stone's attributes and values. This meant that, rather than erasing memories of Stone's presence, many of the characteristics of Stone's Department were, to a large extent, reincarnated. It is to these attributes and values that the following chapter turns.

[78] Ziegert (n 63); Interview with Wojciech Sadurski (Law School, University of Sydney, 31 July 2014).
[79] Interview with Michael Kirby (by telephone, 14 March 2015).
[80] Ziegert (n 63).
[81] 'Brains-and-beauty Alice Has Her Life All Mapped Out', *Daily Mirror* (Sydney), 28 April 1975, 12.
[82] Kirby (n 79).

9

Tay and the Department of Jurisprudence: Stone's Successor

Introduction

Many connections can be drawn between Tay and Stone's leadership of their respective Departments. It ought to be recognised from the outset that Tay was not merely Stone's successor in name. While Tay's scholarship was markedly different from Stone's – her work sat within a different tradition and although she wrote many articles and book chapters, she never published any weighty tomes like Stone – she carried on Stone's legacy in a different way, through her management of the Department. She embedded in the Department many of the characteristics that Stone had pioneered, and there is evidence to suggest that she looked to Stone's model for guidance. By leading the Department for a further two decades, Tay extended this aspect of Stone's legacy.

Controversy over the Department and its importance to the Faculty of Law at Sydney has meant that this connection between Tay and Stone has not been properly acknowledged. In this chapter, by outlining Tay's scholarly agenda, and drawing comparisons and contrasts with Stone, I make these connections clear. I also explain that there were good reasons for maintaining the Department as a 'beachhead' for jurisprudence, and that its existence ensured that Sydney law students were introduced to broader ways of thinking about law. I detail two of the key aspects of Stone's Department that Tay preserved: its diversity and international orientation. Finally, I suggest that during the later period of Tay's tenure some of the reasons for opposing the Department changed and that these changes made it more difficult for Tay to defend its existence.

Tay's Credentials

When applying for the Chair, Tay's resume and scholarly record spoke of her strong intelligence and international reputation. Her referees – Harold Berman of the Law School at Harvard, John N Hazard of the Law School at Columbia University, Colin Howard of the University of Melbourne, and H Whitmore, the Dean of the

University of New South Wales – were each loud in their praise.[1] Commendations included: '[in] her combination of legal scholarship, linguistic ability, capacity for handling abstract ideas and power of analysis, she is unique in this country'; she 'brings to her studies not only a thorough knowledge of Soviet and Western literature but also a very keen mind both in the analytical and philosophical sense'; she is 'a very good lawyer and at the same time is capable of stepping back from legal analysis to examine its philosophical implications'; she is an 'excellent speaker and teacher who is patient with students, but demanding, and she succeeds in getting a very good response from them'; and 'she has contributed a great deal to faculty discussion on such matters as course content, curriculum revision and faculty management'.[2]

Berman and Hazard were highly accomplished scholars who had written much in what was at that time Tay's primary field of interest. In the decade following the completion of her PhD (1965–75), the focus of her studies was to provide a framework for comparative lawyers, so that the unstable and seemingly alien Soviet and Chinese legal systems could be compared with those of the West. Tay had begun this task with Kamenka during her first trip to Russia in 1965. In addition to her lived experience, described in chapter seven, the trip served as a kind of apprenticeship.[3] Soon after, she began to study China on her own.[4]

Tay and Kamenka's work on Soviet and Chinese legal systems contained descriptive, prescriptive and comparative elements. At the base of their work sat a critique of the grand narratives that had previously been used to describe the central features and trajectories of legal and social orderings in Soviet, Chinese and Western societies. They viewed themselves as 'empiricists and realists' who thought of philosophy as 'the analysis of confused ideas – not the recognition of the dictates of Higher Reason'.[5] This empiricism and realism was largely historical in nature, involving an analysis of the social and intellectual developments and orderings of Russia, China and the West. Tay spoke of her study of China in lofty terms. It involved

> a number of unrelated skills: a knowledge and appreciation of Chinese history and culture, an understanding of Marxism and Communist ideology, a close acquaintance with Soviet institutions and law and more than a dash of sociological insight and imagination.[6]

[1] Professorial Board Minutes, 21 October 1974, University of Sydney Archives.

[2] ibid. We can assume that the final two comments are from Whitmore who had previously been Tay's Dean at ANU.

[3] In his letter to the Registrar of ANU, Kamenka said that Tay would 'want to be given an intensive course in Russian language and considerable aid and guidance in her researches into Soviet law and jurisprudence': Eugene Kamenka to the Registrar of ANU, 21 October 1964, Eugene Kamenka Staff files, Australian National University Archives.

[4] A Tay, 'Law in Communist China – Part 1' (1969) 6 *Sydney Law Review* 153. The work was part of a trilogy, with 'Law in Communist China – Part II' (1971) 6 *Sydney Law Review* 335 and '"Smash all Permanent Rules": China as a Model for the Future' (1976) 7 *Sydney Law Review* 400.

[5] A Tay and E Kamenka 'The Law as Reasonable: Applying Perelman's Dictum to Common Law and to Continental Civil Law' (1993) *Australian Society for Legal Philosophy Bulletin* 1, 2.

[6] Tay (1969) (n 4) 154.

Tay and Kamenka presented themselves as hard-working intellectuals, doing their best to make sense of the world and its legal orderings by drawing from a rich and wide body of knowledge. At the time Tay applied for the Chair at Sydney, her scholarship provided good evidence to suggest that this was no empty claim. However, as time went on, her scholarship gave reason to doubt that her inquiries were those of an open-minded and curious scholar.

Tay and Kamenka argued that existing approaches to studying Soviet and Chinese law, by scholars sitting on the outside, did not allow for adequate comparisons – either between those systems or with the West – and did not permit the recognition of signs of convergence. For example, Tay said that Jerome Cohen, then a Professor of Law at Harvard, treated the study of Chinese law as something to be explained through the history of China, while Hazard bundled China up with other Marxist socialist legal systems, with the implication that it could be understood through the Soviet legal model and its Marxist communist foundations.[7] According to Tay, Cohen placed too much emphasis on the continuity of traditions in China, and Hazard's approach ignored the differences between soviet systems. Two of Tay's early articles on Russia – one on inheritance laws and the other on the law of Torts – point to her early realisation that existing theorising was inadequate. She explained that Soviet law in these fields did not neatly align with Marxist theorising and that its characteristics were a product of a range of different cultural factors and moral commitments.[8] Attempts by Western scholars to draw conclusions about the relationship between law and society by drawing these types of neat causal connections were, she argued, fundamentally flawed.[9]

By contrast, Tay and Kamenka believed that any apparatus for understanding the different strains within legal systems and their relationship with law and morality ought to embrace the complexity between law and other parts of the society that their own empirical (historical) studies bore out. Tay said:

> Social pluralism is not the recognition that society is made up of many atomic indivisible interests, individuals, institutions. It is on the contrary the recognition that each of those interests, individuals and institutions is in turn infinitely complex. This is equally true of law. The legal world is not made up of a finite set of specific atomic legal systems, each totally distinct from the other. On the contrary each legal system contains many strains pulling in different directions. These strains transcend any one legal system; they recur in quite foreign and different systems, creating the possibility of unexpected alliances between the native and the foreign and conflicts between different aspirations in the native. It is impossible to understand either the spread of Marxism or that of Western law if one takes a mechanical view of the monolithic native as confronted by

[7] Tay (1971) (n 4) 337–38.

[8] A Tay, 'The Law of Inheritance in the New Russian Civil Code of 1964' (1968) 17 *International and Comparative Law Quarterly* 472; A Tay, 'The Foundation of Tort Liability in a Socialist Legal System: Fault Versus Social Insurance in Soviet Law' (1969) *University of Toronto Law Journal* 1.

[9] ibid.

> the monolithic foreign. The ultimate point of any sensible doctrine of legal pluralism is to help us see the conflicting and competing strains within any one society and within any one legal system or culture.[10]

Tay's attitude towards opening up these cultures and legal systems is captured neatly by Marx's favourite moral principle and motto: 'Nothing human is alien to me'. She and Kamenka quoted it in several of their works.[11]

Tay and Kamenka identified four key strains within legal systems which, they argued, would provide a stronger conceptual apparatus for evaluating and comparing Russian, Chinese and Western legal systems and their relationship with society: *Gesellschaft*, *Gemeinschaft*, 'administrative-bureaucratic' and 'domination-submission'. The strains were not original, in the sense that Tönnies had devised *Gesellschaft* and *Gemeinschaft* as conceptual tools, and the administrative-bureaucratic strain was drawn from Weber. Similarly, the way they conceptualised each of the strains for the purposes of analysis was nothing new. Following Weber rather than Tönnies, they treated the strains as 'ideal types' that did not exist anywhere in reality but rather attributed tangible qualities and meanings to subjective values.[12] Tay's principal contribution was to describe and emphasise the distinctive legal characteristics of each strain and to turn to the Russian philosopher Pashukanis to explain the legal dimensions of the *Gesellschaft*. In doing so, she rejected HLA Hart's and Austinian positivism as a valid descriptor of Western law. She agreed with Pashukanis that the element of state compulsion was *not* the defining element of law and that this explained why

> army regulations, rules, binding elements of an order of the priesthood, the authoritarian prescriptions of a family head or elder do not constitute or become *law* if or merely because they are sanctioned by the external authority, be it even that of the state.[13]

Tay and Kamenka's studies of the political history of Russia and China helped them to fill out the distinctive characteristics of each of the four types, drawing from primary and secondary sources and, to a lesser extent, from their own observations while living within these societies. Given their emphasis on, and preference for, *Gesellschaft*, it is worth quoting one of their explanations of this type in full:

> [*Gesellschaft*] assumes a society based on individual as opposed to organic solidarity, made up of atomic individuals and private interests, each in principle equivalent

[10] A Tay, 'China and Legal Pluralism' (1984) 8 Bulletin of the Australian Society of Legal Philosophers 23, 37.

[11] See, eg, A Tay, 'Introduction' in A Tay (ed), *Australian Law and Legal Thinking between the Decades* (Sydney, University of Sydney, 1990) viii; A Tay, 'The Role of the Law in the Twentieth Century: From Law to Laws to Social Science' (1991) 13 *Sydney Law Review* 247, 248.

[12] SH Kim, 'Max Weber', *The Stanford Encyclopedia of Philosophy* (EN Zalta (ed), Fall 2012 Edition), http://plato.stanford.edu/archives/fall2012/entries/weber/ quoting from Max Weber, 'Objectivity in Social Science and Social Policy' in EA Shils and HA Finch (eds), *The Methodology of the Social Sciences* (Glencoe, Free Press, 1904).

[13] A Tay and E Kamenka, 'Beyond the French Revolution: Communist Socialism and the Concept of Law' (1971) 21 *University of Toronto Law Journal* 109, 132–33.

> to the other, capable of agreeing on common means while maintaining their diverse ends. It emphasizes formal procedure, impartiality, adjudicative justice, precise legal provisions and definitions, and the rationality and predictability of legal administration. It is oriented to the precise definition of the rights and duties of the individual through a sharpening of the point at issue and not to the day-to-day *ad hoc* maintenance of social harmony, community traditions, and organic solidarity; it reduces the public interest to another, only *sometimes* overriding, private interest. It distinguishes sharply between law and administration, between the public and the private, the legal and the moral, between the civil obligation and the criminal offence. Its model for all law is contract and the *quid pro quo* associated with commercial exchange, which also demands rationality and predictability. … It is enshrined, at least in part, in the concept of the *Rechtsstaat* and the rule of law.[14]

The opposite of *Gesellschaft*, *Gemeinschaft* is grounded in 'a community based on dedication to a common order and on familial and social ties rather than on contracts and individual rights and duties'.[15] Tay and Kamenka said that Tönnies' two ideal types (the *Gesellschaft* and the *Gemeinschaft*) were a product of the nineteenth century that ignored 'the ever-increasing scope and power of the state and its bureaucracies, that have become so evident in the twentieth century'.[16] They therefore developed their third ideal type to reflect this emerging power of the state, drawing in part on a fundamental theme in the work of Max Weber, who had written at length on the phenomenon of bureaucratisation.

Tay and Kamenka's final type was extra-legal. 'Domination-submission' was devised to help explain the parameters of their conception of law and its potential to be manipulated. The difference between this category and the other ideal types was, according to the pair, that it did not require 'a structural system of regulation incorporating certain values and moral and socio-political assumptions'.[17] They considered that a society governed by domination and submission is not law because it 'requires the obedience to rules rather than the determination of rights'.[18] Domination-submission can, therefore, be found within all of the other ideal types, but it is particularly prevalent in – and can strongly manipulate – the *Gemeinschaft* and bureaucratic-administrative types.

Analysing the political and intellectual history of Russia, China and the West by searching for these four ideal types allowed Tay and Kamenka to contribute new understandings of the competing strains existing within each society. They also evaluated and advanced prescriptions for law. In the remaining decades of Tay's scholarly life she exalted the importance of the *Gesellschaft* type which, while a part of all of the legal systems she studied, presented most strongly in Western

[14] ibid.

[15] A Tay and E Kamenka, 'The Life and Afterlife of a Bolshevik Jurist' (1970) 19 *Problems of Communism* 72, 78.

[16] A Tay and E Kamenka, 'The Sociology of Justice' in AR Blackshield (ed), *Legal Change: Essays in Honour of Julius Stone* (Sydney, Butterworths, 1983) 107, 112–13.

[17] Tay and Kamenka (n 13) 137–38.

[18] ibid 132–33.

law due largely to the common law. It seemed that, despite her broad-ranging studies over decades, Tay remained assured of the superiority of the common law – a belief she had held since her early life as a barrister and then junior academic in Singapore. For example, in the 1990s, during presentations in Korea and the United States, she argued that

> the Western legal tradition has a specially developed and self-conscious appreciation of the tasks of law, of the requirements of doing justice, and of the social role of a legal tradition and legal profession. Precisely for that reason, it is becoming the legal tradition of humankind.[19]

Tay's prescriptions and unyielding faith in the *Gesellschaft* and common law systems appear inconsistent with her emphasis on the complexity of the different political, intellectual and social currents that need to be understood in order to appreciate the type and role of law in any one society. Her analysis of Russia and China showed, for example, that the presence of a strange mix of ideal types, sometimes operating in a confused tandem, had allowed domination-submission to prosper. Tay and Kamenka argued that their studies suggested that *Gesellschaft* provided the greatest resistance to tyranny. Yet, distilling their pluralistic and cultural analysis down to a case strongly endorsing the *Gesellschaft* type seems at odds with their opening ambitions to challenge grand narratives and provide a complex accounting of the role of law in society that drew on contextual factors. Were their claims really so different from those who had attempted to fit the history of modern legal systems within a trajectory that moves from naïve collectivism to a more sophisticated individualism? And was their position really so strong that they could ignore critiques of Western systems of the time, most notably Duncan Kennedy's work on the irrationality of the common law?[20] The elevation of Western law by Tay and Kamenka seems just as overly deterministic as the older studies that had encouraged them to take different approaches.

The frequency and severity with which they critiqued work that sought to undermine or weaken the *Gesellschaft* reads like dogmatism rather than scholarly exploration. It suggests that they had nailed their colours to the mast long before they had conceived and applied their comparative apparatus. This cast a shadow over the strong early contributions that their appraisal and comparative apparatus had made.

Tay is often referred to as a human rights scholar. It is important to recognise that Tay's writing on human rights did not represent a new turn in her scholarship. Rather, her arguments again turned on the importance of maintaining

[19] A Tay, 'The Role of Law in the Twentieth Century: From Law to Laws to Social Science' (1991) 13 *Sydney Law Review* 247, 251.

[20] D Kennedy, 'Form and Substance in Private Law Adjudication' (1976) 89 *Harvard Law Review* 1685.

the *Gesellschaft* and the common law system, as these were, in her view, the best protectors of human rights. For example, she said:

> There is probably no country in the world in which human rights, whether of individuals or groups, are more extensively or better protected than they are in the Commonwealth of Australia. This state of affairs, however, owes more to the inherited tradition of British liberalism, strengthened by Australia's own history and economic circumstances than to any formal system of constitutional guarantees.
>
> Economic circumstances have helped to maintain a social system in which respect for human rights is high. The absence of extreme disparities of wealth and a general living standard better than that of any country in the world … have tended to preserve a mutual tolerance, and to reduce the bitterness of political conflict. It is probably that the high degree of racial homogeneity has also assisted in the preservation of social attitudes favourable to civil liberties. With this heritage, Australians have never felt the need to express in formal documents the fundamental human rights which their system of government in fact protects. The expressions 'constitutional guarantee' and 'fundamental rights' are unfamiliar to most Australians.[21]

As Human Rights and Equal Opportunity Commissioner, Tay later favoured education as the means to bring about cultural change, considering that too much emphasis had been placed on the potential of law.

Tay's faith in the *Gesellschaft* and common law was tested most when confronted with the position of Indigenous Australians in Australian society. Tay had explained that extreme inequality posed a major threat to the *Gesellschaft* which limited its potential to govern effectively:

> *Gesellschaft* law works best where the fiction of legal equality and interchangeability is accompanied by a reasonable approximation to social equality and interchangeability, where parties do confront each other as relatively independent, 'free', and equal actors. It is seriously threatened by major and relevant inequalities of power, education or social position which undermine the *Gesellschaft* conception of legal capacity as well as of the equality of the parties.[22]

The displacement of Indigenous Australians from their land, their marginalised and oppressed position in Australian society, and their comparatively poor health and living standards was something Tay acknowledged in her scholarship and had witnessed as a part-time commissioner with the Australian Law Reform Commission. At the invitation of James Crawford, she assisted with the inquiry into the recognition of Aboriginal Customary Law, which involved, among other things,

[21] A Tay and E Kamenka, 'Human Rights and "The" Australian Tradition' (Canberra, Australian National Commission for UNESCO, 1981) 1, 10 quoting from G Sawer, 'Protection of Human Rights in Australia' in (1946) 1 *Yearbook on Human Rights* 31.

[22] A Tay and E Kamenka, 'Beyond Bourgeois Individualism: The Contemporary Crisis in Law and Legal Ideology' in E Kamenka and RS Neale (eds), *Feudalism, Capitalism and Beyond* (Sydney, Edward Arnold, 1975) 126, 140–41.

visiting remote Aboriginal communities. In one piece on the state of human rights protections in Australia she said:

> Only in the case of the Aborigines is the problem genuinely urgent and one that does call for specific and dramatic action both at the practical and symbolic level – a matter for which probably no Australian politician has the requisite combination of boldness and commanding statute and public support.[23]

The significant inequalities experienced by Indigenous Australians in Australian society did not, however, lead Tay to question the dominance of the *Gesellschaft* ideal type in Australia. The position of Indigenous Australians, and the poor and confused treatment of customary law, did not, in Tay's view, point to a larger failing of Australia's legal or political system. Rather, they called for exceptional measures within the existing framework. As Tay did not carry out a detailed intellectual and political history of Australia's legal system that incorporated the diverse experience of Australians, it is difficult to understand how she drew this conclusion. This points to a major weakness of her work.

From the 1980s, Tay's work did not investigate the history of societies as her previous work had done. She did not, for example, document Australia's political and legal history, including the treatment of Aboriginal and Torres Strait Islander people, in the same way as she had investigated China and Russia. Instead, her work consisted of recycling prior propositions and ideas, and advancing arguments and prescriptions designed to convince others of the primary importance of maintaining the present balance between strains/types within Australia's legal system. This arguably weakened the analysis and arguments she made about the state of Australian law. It is difficult to know why she abandoned her earlier, more rigorous, approach. Perhaps it was because she believed that her previous studies provided sufficient evidence for the positions that formed the basis of her subsequent arguments. Or perhaps her new role heading the Department, running symposia and government commissions, meant she simply did not have the time to engage in that type of empirical and historical work.

Tay and Stone – Different Sociological Traditions

Stone also wrote on Soviet legal systems and has been described as sitting within the school of 'sociological jurisprudence'. His school of sociology was, however, different from Tay's. Stone took his lead from Dean Pound, a pioneer of the school of sociological jurisprudence with whom he had worked at Harvard. As Paton argued,

> it is unfortunate that the term 'sociological' was ever used in this connection – to speak of the functional method would have been more accurate and less confusing.

[23] Tay and Kamenka (n 21) 16.

> The fundamental tenet of this school is that we cannot understand what a thing is until we study what it does.[24]

Tay followed within the more appropriately named 'sociology of law' tradition. Again, Paton's definition proves useful:

> its main difference from functional jurisprudence is that it attempts to create a science of social life as a whole and to cover a great art of general sociology and political science. The *emphasis of the study is on society and law as a mere manifestation*, whereas Pound rather *concentrates on law* and considers society in relation to it.[25]

Tay and Stone's methodologies were therefore very different in orientation. While both sat outside the dominant Western analytical tradition, Tay followed in the sociological traditions founded by Weber and Marx, and Stone took his primary lead from Pound. Moreover, Tay's respect for John Anderson (through Kamenka) and the fact she had adopted some of his central scholarly tenets also distinguished her from Stone.[26]

At the time of his appointment to the Challis Professorship, Stone was also more accomplished than Tay and had stronger academic credentials. He had studied at some of the world's leading universities (both Oxford and Harvard), held a philosophy degree as well as a postgraduate degree in law, and had published several significant works of scholarship. Tay had published 27 articles and book chapters, but no books. It would have been difficult – perhaps even impossible – to find a scholar of similar standing to replace Stone. Nonetheless, Tay shared some of Stone's qualities and her résumé suggested that she had potential. Like Stone, she was an outsider with lofty ambitions. While she was not Jewish, she was, at the time of her appointment, a young Asian woman married to a Jewish immigrant and had experienced considerable turbulence and hardship in her life. Like Stone, being a scholar mattered to her: it was her vocation. It is therefore unsurprising that both Stone and Tay believed that the Department could provide them with an opportunity to create an environment where broader thinking about law could flourish.

A 'Beachhead' for Jurisprudence

Before Tay's arrival, the dispute between Stone's Department and the Department of Law, was – following on from Peden and Charteris – partially depicted as a division between the technocratic and theoretical aspects of law. The jurisprudential camp feared that merging the departments would result in the contraction of legal theory. Concerns included a fear that jurisprudence would be mainstreamed in a

[24] GW Paton, *A Textbook of Jurisprudence* (Oxford, Clarendon Press, 1946) 18.
[25] ibid 22 (references omitted) (emphasis added).
[26] L Starr, *Julius Stone – An Intellectual Life* (Oxford, Oxford University Press, 1992) 167.

way that diluted its potency, with half-hearted attempts to consider the theoretical sides of law merely labelled 'jurisprudence'.[27] Or perhaps, without this 'beachhead', jurisprudence would simply be 'washed away'.[28] If there was nothing in the institutional makeup to preserve jurisprudence, and if the jurisprudence teachers formed a small minority at Faculty meetings and were outnumbered by personalities who either disliked Stone or were suspicious of legal theory, then it is easy to appreciate why, without a Department, the teaching and advancement of jurisprudence would be at risk. These provided good reasons for preserving Stone's Department.

Some viewed his Department as an essential 'antidote' to the narrow technocratic and conservative elements of the Department of Law. Michael Kirby, who began as an undergraduate law student at Sydney in the late 1950s and became a research assistant to Stone, believed that the Department played a crucial role in ensuring that Sydney law students – many of whom went on to fill the highest legal and political offices in the country – were encouraged to think more broadly about the study of law:

> I think it is necessary to have such a Department particularly in a country which has the common law tradition, in a community that has long taught law as a positivist isolated activity divorced from social impact and unconcerned with the deep values which inform decisions that are made in that discipline. I think it is necessary as an antidote. There is a similar debate on the issue of statutory interpretation. Do you teach it as a separate topic or do you simply teach it where it is relevant in particular legal categories? For me the problem of the latter approach is that so busy will you be in teaching the categories that you just don't have time to stop and teach either what are the values that underline the categories or whether they are good values or out-dated values or values that should be reformed; that you don't end up ever thinking about such issues.[29]

Others believed that the Department had become an exclusive club that promoted a particular brand of jurisprudence and excluded other Sydney legal scholars who regarded themselves as 'jurisprudes'. Depicting Stone's Department as an 'antidote' implies that something was missing from the Department of Law. In this way, the Department's very existence might be seen as denigrating the Department of Law and its members.[30] Hiving off a small minority of academics and providing them with a special department also seemed undemocratic and elitist. There were, therefore, also strong arguments for changing the human architecture of the Department.

[27] Some perceived that for a short period after the abolishment of the Department in 1998 this dilution occurred: interview with Martin Krygier (Law School, University of New South Wales, 7 February 2014); interview with Christopher Birch SC (Garfield Barwick Chambers, Sydney, 28 July 2014); interview with Klaus Ziegert (Law School, University of Sydney, 5 February 2014).

[28] Krygier (n 27).

[29] Interview with Michael Kirby (by telephone, 14 March 2015).

[30] This formed part of the thinking that led to the abolishment of the Department: interview with Jeremy Webber (by telephone, 22 October 2014); interview with James Crawford (by telephone, 25 November 2014).

The risk that jurisprudence would be marginalised and diluted if left to mix with the larger Faculty remained an issue until at least 1998, when Tay left to become President of the Human Rights and Equal Opportunity Commission (HREOC). Each of the three former Sydney Deans interviewed for this study acknowledged that, even in the 1990s, components of the Faculty of Law were narrowly technocratic and insular. James Crawford (Dean from 1990 to 1992) suggested that in the late 1980s and early 1990s some members of the Faculty believed that academics were 'subservient to the profession'.[31] Jeremy Webber (Dean from 1998 to 2002) offered a similar view:

> My sense at Sydney was that Sydney's ambitions were too framed by service to the bar, service to the profession. While that was an extraordinarily important dimension of what any law school should do, we shouldn't see ourselves as relating to the profession exclusively in a training role but should be contributing to the development of legal knowledge in the Australian context.[32]

Reflecting on the focus of the Faculty when he joined in 1993, Ron McCallum (Dean from 2002 to 2007) agreed that Sydney's orientation was narrow:

> Sydney was not a happy law school. … I can't speak about jurisprudence but what was seen to be good for promotion was getting an article in the *Australian Law Journal*, which was not refereed. I think Sydney had appointed too many of its own and hadn't looked internationally enough.[33]

There is, therefore, evidence to suggest that the need for an antidote to the parochial and technocratic elements of Sydney persisted throughout Tay's tenure.

The Antidote

In several ways, Tay responded to her environment in a similar manner to Stone. Like Stone, one of Tay's primary concerns was to counter the perceived deficiencies in the Department of Law, and she approached this task by reinstating several of Stone's early initiatives. First, she recruited scholars from diverse backgrounds, something that stood in stark contrast to the parochial aspects of the Department of Law.[34] Her Department was tiny. As Klaus Ziegert, a sociologist who worked with Tay for over 24 years and acted as Head of the Department for much of Tay's time, explained:

> At the height of our budget we had three permanent staff and often only two because Alice was always somewhere in the world and the rest of us went on sabbatical leave

[31] Crawford (n 39).
[32] Webber (n 30).
[33] Interview with Ron McCallum (by telephone, 4 November 2014).
[34] As Krygier explained, in contrast to other elements of the Faculty of Law, Tay 'was never parochial': Krygier (n 27).

> every seven years. We filled the places with temporaries and casuals, but we never had enough money to have more than [the equivalent of] around four full-time permanent staff.[35]

The attributes of the core staff of the Department were therefore critical to its shape and contribution.

The three full-time members of the Department recruited by Tay – Martin Krygier, Klaus Ziegert and Wojciech Sadurski – were (at least initially) primarily interested in ideas outside analytical jurisprudence, the dominant British legal theory of the time. Tay recruited two of these scholars during her trips abroad (Ziegert from Germany[36] and Sadurski from Poland)[37], and recruited many international doctoral students. Tay also gave the Department a strong interdisciplinary quality and rewarded learning from outside the discipline of law. Krygier, for example, held a doctorate in the history of ideas, but only an undergraduate qualification in law, while Ziegert did not have a law degree but had a doctorate in the sociology of law.

Tay had, therefore, created a department of interdisciplinary outsiders that resembled Stone's. Stone had recruited to his Department a range of foreign scholars, including 'Ilmar Tammello, an Estonian, Giovanni Tarello, an Italian, Charles Boasson, an Israeli, Charles Alexandrovitz, a Pole, Bob Moffat, an American, Stevan Glichitch, a Yugoslav, René Marcic, an Austrian, and Upendra Baxi, an Indian'.[38] Both Stone and Tay's Departments were able to create a diverse teaching agenda that introduced students to a range of ideas on law, extending beyond Australia's territorial boundaries and its English and common-law heritage.

The second way that Tay was similar in her approach to Stone was in sharing his belief that diversity in the Department allowed for a broadening of the curricula.[39] One of the most remarkable features of Stone's career is the change in attitude of eminent members of Sydney's legal profession towards him. At the beginning of Stone's tenure, judges and senior practitioners were among those who strongly opposed his appointment.[40] At the end of his tenure, members of a large part of this same demographic – his former students who were now leaders of the profession – were his closest allies.[41] His teaching, and that of his Department, was largely responsible for this considerable change of heart. In the 1990s, leading Sydney practitioners and judges believed that it was important for law students to have sound instruction in matters of theory and supported the broadening of Sydney's curricula to accommodate greater theoretical study.[42] Some donated

[35] Ziegert (n 27).
[36] Ziegert (n 27).
[37] Interview with Wojciech Sadurski (Law School, University of Sydney, 31 July 2014).
[38] Starr (n 26) 116.
[39] ibid.
[40] ibid 58–63.
[41] Jeremy Webber referred to several practitioners and judges who supported his intention to reclaim Stone's legacy: Webber (n 30).
[42] Two Deans at the University of Sydney in the 1990s spoke of conversations they held with various members of the profession who supported the widening of the curricula and orientation of the Faculty to embrace more legal theory: Crawford (n 30); Webber (n 30).

substantial funds to create a research institute in Stone's name.[43] That Stone and his Department convinced high achieving graduates of the importance of theory was no small feat and demonstrated his commitment to students.

A third similarity lay in connecting the Faculty of Law and Australian legal academy with the larger world of ideas, and publicising it to that world. This would remain a central platform of the Department under Tay's leadership. Again, like Stone, Tay had numerous international connections to build on. She also drew upon existing links to Stone's Department, as well as Kamenka's networks. During Tay's time as Professor of Jurisprudence she was twice elected President of the International Association for Philosophy for Law and Social Philosophy (IVR), and in 1988 was the first Australian elected a full member (*Académicienne Titulaire*) of the Paris-based International Academy of Comparative Law.[44] She travelled frequently and extensively, always with the purpose of furthering her work. She also took measures to ensure that particular colleagues benefited from her international connections and, by establishing opportunities for them to present papers or teach overseas, she encouraged them to broaden their studies beyond Australia's territorial borders.[45]

Tay also promoted the Department in a way that made it attractive to foreign scholars and students, so they would be more likely to come to Australia to attend conferences or workshops or as visiting scholars. Several of Tay's former students and colleagues said that when travelling overseas they learnt that Tay was in regular contact with international scholars. Sadurski recalled that,

> I went to my first academic conference in 1984 and it was a conference held at Bologna in Northern Italy on legal reasoning sponsored by the University of Bologna … What struck me was that everyone I spoke to, no matter where they came from in the world, whether it was Iceland, Argentina or Poland to name just three, all knew Alice and knew her quite well and said 'I just sent Alice a letter the other day' or something like that. This was before email or they would be emailing her all the time.[46]
>
> It is interesting now to think about it, that these were years when there was no internet and so the way you contacted someone was through letters to them and the letter arrives maybe two weeks after, so the response might come a month after. But she managed to maintain these incredibly thick continuous contacts with the outside world.[47]

Ziegert explained that, despite his initial reluctance, comparativist colleagues at the Max Planck Institute talked him into coming to Australia. Tay and Kamenka

[43] eg, former Judge and President of the New South Wales Court of Appeal and Supreme Court, Dennis Mahoney.

[44] 'International Role for Professor Tay', *The University of Sydney News* (Sydney) 1 March 1988, 8.

[45] Allars recalls that Tay invited her to teach in the Masters of Law programme that Tay established with Friedrich Schiller Universität Jena, Germany and that through that exercise she was encouraged to look at other aspects of European law: interview with Margaret Allars SC (Law School, University Sydney, 1 August 2014).

[46] Birch (n 27).

[47] Sadurski (n 37).

had spent long periods of time at the Institute and were well known to the scholars there. Their positive views of Australia were in part attributable to Tay's networking:

> They were great admirers of Australia. They had been there. Alice was clever in hosting a conference of comparative lawyers in Sydney. All my German comparativist colleagues came because Australia in Germany is a big thing.[48]

Not only did international scholars come to conferences and workshops in Australia arranged by Tay and Kamenka, they also occupied visiting posts. Copying a scheme implemented by Kamenka in the History of Ideas unit at the RSSS, Tay kept one of the full-time posts at the Department free. She kept the post filled with visiting scholars, who contributed to teaching and delivered papers at events arranged for both the Faculty and broader scholarly community. Short and longer term visitors to the Department included a range of internationally acclaimed scholars: Chaim Perelman, William Twining, Joseph Raz, Bernard Rudden, Neil MacCormick,[49] Pierre Ryckmans (who used the pen-name Simon Leys), Jan Broekman and CB Macpherson.[50] In 1981 Tay arranged for MacCormick, Regius Professor of Public Law and Law of Nature and Nations at Edinburgh University, to spend three months teaching in the Department.[51] He indicated a willingness to teach across the curriculum[52] and his correspondence speaks of affection for both Tay and Kamenka.[53] In 1989 he organised for Tay to receive an honorary LLD (*honoris causa*) from the University of Edinburgh. Tay and Kamenka's posts and the Department's strong reputation provided an incentive for foreign scholars to come to Australia.[54]

Tay therefore followed closely in Stone's footsteps and developed a strong and diverse Department with a rich network of elite, foreign and theoretically inclined scholars. Her vision for the Department was based on her desire to enrich the education of Sydney law graduates.[55]

New Protagonists

In these various ways, then, Tay maintained these parts of Stone's legacy for another two decades. The environment within the Faculty of Law nonetheless changed over this time, which made Tay's arguments for maintaining a separate

[48] Ziegert (n 27).
[49] 'Neil MacCormick Visits the Department of Jurisprudence', *The University of Sydney News* (Sydney) 7 July 1981, 13.
[50] Interview with Roger Wilkins AO, (Attorney-General's Department, Canberra, 19 August 2014); Birch (n 27); interview with Gabriel Moens (by telephone, 30 September 2014).
[51] Neil MacCormick to Alice Tay, 21 January 1981.
[52] ibid.
[53] See, eg, MacCormick to Tay, 19 February 1981 and 23 October 1981.
[54] See, eg, J Passmore, 'Citizen of the World Whose Gift was Liberty', *The Australian* (Sydney) 21 January 1994, 11.
[55] This is considered further in chapter ten.

department weaker. One of the most significant changes was the emergence of new protagonists with different agendas. Rather than representing the traditional components of the Faculty, these new protagonists were motivated by a desire to change the culture of the Faculty at Sydney, so that the antidote supplied by Stone, then Tay, would no longer be needed. During Tay's time as Professor of Jurisprudence, three Deans – Colin Phegan, James Crawford and Jeremy Webber – each sought to abolish the Department. The first two Deans were met with strong opposition from Tay and were ultimately unsuccessful. Webber, who began his tenure the year when Tay left for HREOC, succeeded.[56]

Rather than marginalising legal theory, Phegan,[57] Crawford and Webber aimed to change the culture of the Faculty in a way that would mainstream and increase its importance. Crawford expressed his reasons for merging the departments as follows:

> My view was that Law was better off having Jurisprudence as part of its activity and Jurisprudence was better off having Law as part of its empire, so to speak. That was an English view of things. I'm a believer in unitary law departments, so I'm a believer in the connection between public international law and private international law. Obviously, one makes distinctions and subjects have their own provenance and methodology, but they should learn from each other and they are part of a tradition of universal thinking about law which is very important.[58]

Webber largely shared Crawford's motivations and views.

> One of the problems that I became increasingly concerned with, in relation to the departmental structure, was that there were people who were seriously committed to legal theory and were doing very strong work in legal theory who were not part of the department and so were structurally defined away from legal theory precisely at a time when legal theory had become an essential mainstream function of any decent law school – one which had to be woven into substantive areas of law. The structure tended to treat legal theory as though it were a separate thing that should be hived off – not something that needed to pervade the way we dealt with law …[59]

In a report to Faculty, Webber said that he saw:

> [T]he chief benefit in a single-unit structure to be an expansion, not a contraction, of the presence of legal theory within the Faculty. I am strongly committed to the maintenance of rigorous legal theory within both the research and teaching missions of the Faculty.[60]

Crawford and Webber were both scholars who took a keen interest in legal theory and whose scholarship departed from the traditional model. Their diverse scholarly

[56] This was achieved following a consultative process with the whole of the Faculty.
[57] 'Law Meeting on Jurisprudence', *The University of Sydney News* (Sydney) 1 August 1989, 170.
[58] Crawford (n 30).
[59] Webber (n 30). Webber made similar comments in his report to faculty: 'Dean's Report to Faculty', 11 August 1998, Faculty of Law Minutes, University of Sydney Archives.
[60] Dean's Report (n 59).

interests, and the fact that they had not been educated in law at the University of Sydney, suggest that they were sincere in their desire to change the intellectual culture of the Faculty of Law and Sydney and to improve – rather than restrict – the profile of jurisprudence, or at least legal theory, within the Faculty. They both suggested that senior members of the legal profession supported their effort to rejuvenate the Department of Law so that it would embrace broader concerns.[61] Their positions seem more enlightened than the objections and agendas of some of the Department's earlier opponents. It was also clear by that point that some strong jurisprudential scholars (in addition to Morison) were precluded from teaching jurisprudence.[62] For these reasons, Crawford, and then Webber, presented an argument that was more difficult for Tay and her colleagues in the Department to rebut.[63] Throughout the twentieth century there had been good reasons to support the desire to insulate the Department from the wider Faculty. Now, the presence of Deans who were themselves outsiders and who sought to broaden the horizons of the larger Faculty, by encouraging the spread of legal theory throughout the curricula, made the Department's position less tenable. Rather than an antidote, this insularity began to present as an obstacle to the reconciliation and enlightenment of the Faculty as a whole. This cast doubt over the wisdom of continuing this part of Stone's legacy into the twenty-first century.

Whether abolishing the Department has achieved, or will achieve, the aims pursued by Phegan, Crawford and Webber is difficult to measure or predict. Some certainly hold the view that Sydney is now a very different place. What is clear, however, is that, even if the merger was able to achieve the goal of 'mainstreaming jurisprudence', Tay believed that the integration would simply place current and future jurisprudential scholars at Sydney on the mediocre and compromising path which she feared most Australian academics were encouraged to follow. This attitude is described further in the next chapter.

Concluding Remarks

As another 'outsider' leading the Department of Jurisprudence, it might seem that Tay's position was stronger than Stone's. She did not face the anti-Semitism that he had faced throughout his career. If some of Tay's colleagues held prejudices against her on account of her Asian background or the fact that she was a woman, this was

[61] Crawford (n 30); Webber (n 30).

[62] For example, even though Margaret Allars had obtained a PhD in jurisprudence at Oxford studying under Joseph Raz, she was employed in the Department of Law and so did not teach in the jurisprudence streams: 'Removing the departmental structure would have been advantageous in that people like myself would have been able to teach jurisprudence, so I saw it as a negative in that sense, but I felt some sense of loyalty to Alice in terms of preserving her empire.' Allars (n 45).

[63] At the time of the consultations and meetings that led to the abolishment of the department, Tay was at HREOC and therefore not included in the discussions.

not something to which Tay drew attention[64] or something that was noticed by others close to her. At least externally, she seemed unaffected by prejudice.

However, in other ways, the Department was more vulnerable during Tay's tenure than Stone's. New law Deans outlined strong arguments for closing the Department, and university management increasingly favoured large faculties over smaller entities in order to increase their ability to standardise and measure performance.

Tay sought to preserve Stone's legacy in the face of considerable opposition from Deans and other law professors at Sydney. She made deliberate choices to maintain and defend the Department that guaranteed that her tenure at Sydney would be turbulent. But by doing so, she ensured that Sydney graduates throughout the remainder of the twentieth century would reap the benefit of some of the central initiatives that Stone had instilled in his Department. The fact that many of these graduates went on to serve in high office suggests that, in this way, Tay performed a considerable service to both the profession and society. Whether the Department ought to have continued into the 1990s remains open for debate. There were good reasons to propose its abolition, in spite of its success.

[64] J Horne, 'The Cosmopolitan Life of Alice Erh-Soon Tay' (2010) 21 *Journal of World History* 419, 436.

Unveiling of Portrait of Alice Erh-Soon Tay, Sydney University Archives, G3_224_2778

Alice Erh-Soon Tay (left) with her research assistant Conita Leung, Sydney University Archives, G77_1_2053

10

Tay and the Department of Jurisprudence: An Academic Entrepreneur

Introduction

Alice Erh-Soon Tay's greatest contribution to the legal academy was, perhaps, the creation of a department that embodied, and was governed solely by, academic values. Tay believed that for a discipline to have integrity and strong intellectual credentials scholars must be situated in an environment that provides them with the confidence and security to say what they think; they must also be able to progress knowledge and education for its own sake. Moreover, she believed that, to be deserving of such conditions, scholars must exercise their own self-scrutiny and self-criticism. They must have the courage and freedom to offer intellectual criticism of their colleagues and to acknowledge their own shortcomings. Tay believed that Australian universities did not provide these conditions and that the situation was becoming worse. Her contribution to the legal academy lies in fostering a department that stood in opposition to the management trends which, she believed, were preventing scholars from fulfilling their important role of combating harmful ideologies and governance. In this chapter, I explain Tay's approach to creating such a department, detailing her motivations and identifying some of the central innovations and achievements that resulted from her distinctive academic agenda. Tay's experience – in conjunction with that of Julius Stone – raises important questions concerning the role of academic imperatives and how disciplines should be run.

As this aspect of Tay's contribution consists largely of intangible qualities and is based primarily on her engagement, networking and the impressions she made on others, this chapter draws heavily from interviews. As Klaus Ziegert astutely observed:

> I believe … an explanation of [Professor Tay] cannot be found on the personal or psychological level. One has to look further and to the social dimension; that is, to the interactions that Professor Tay commanded with the people she worked with, communicated with, supervised, advised, challenged and confronted. The closest category that comes to mind, and which could cover the phenomenon in this respect, is 'institution' – if it were sociologically possible that a person 'is' an institution. In this wider

sense, then, the Department of Jurisprudence of the Faculty of Law at the University of Sydney, which formed the launching-pad for her work and life, was not the institution where she worked: she was the institution which energised the work of the Department and radiated far beyond the boundaries and into the world.[1]

The Rise of an Academic Entrepreneur

The mere existence of the Department did not guarantee its independence or autonomy. Tay, however, seemed well qualified to create the conditions required to engender these attributes in the Department. One of her most distinctive and most remarked upon qualities was that she assumed the role of academic entrepreneur.[2] By building a strong network of distinguished lawyers, academics and judges, as well as competent and talented teachers, Tay was able to insulate the Department from external threats. She did this by building strong initiatives, by making more with less, and by signalling to adversaries that they would have to contend with some of the profession's and academy's eminent leaders if they attempted to abolish the Department.

It is telling that Roger Wilkins – someone who has occupied several high posts in both government and its bureaucracy, including Director-General of the New South Wales cabinet office and head of the Attorney-General's Department – acknowledges that he learnt a great deal from Tay:

> Most of the other things [Tay] did [beyond teaching and scholarship] was as an entrepreneur who really got other people to do stuff. I don't use the term entrepreneur glibly because she really was an entrepreneur. I learnt a lot about how to get things done and how to manage things from her. *I probably learnt more from her about how to handle bureaucracy than I did from working in the bureaucracy*. …
>
> She got into the business of selling the Department. She developed … debate and juristic thinking but not directly herself. She got other people in and put them together. … she would bring all these people from the judiciary and legal practice and academics into this and she would organise it or get you to organise it. She would organise the money and she would organise the terrific dinners and organise the infrastructure. Around this, dialogue and teaching happened.[3]

[1] KA Ziegert, 'AEST – An Attempt at Explaining the Phenomenon' in G Doeker-Mach and KA Ziegert (eds), *Alice Erh-Soon Tay – Lawyer Scholar, Civil Servant* (Stuttgart, Franz Steiner Verlag, 2004) 7, 7.

[2] Interview with Roger Wilkins AO (Attorney-General's Department, Canberra, 19 August 2014) (emphasis added). Other interviewees strongly supported this view: interview with Martin Krygier (Law School, University of New South Wales, 7 February 2014); interview with Wojciech Sadurski (Law School, University of Sydney, 31 July 2014); interview with Gabriel Moens (by telephone, 30 September 2014); interview with Hamish Redd (by telephone, 5 August 2014); interview with Michael Kirby (by telephone, 14 March 2015); interview with Christopher Birch SC (Garfield Barwick Chambers, Sydney, 28 July 2014); interview with Klaus Ziegert (Law School, University of Sydney, 5 February 2014).

[3] Wilkins (n 2) (emphasis added).

Ziegert explained that Tay 'combined … vision and … leadership with an eminent sense, not usually found in academics, for the practicalities of translating a design into a programme and the persistence to convert the programme into practice. … The characteristic is the entrepreneurial spirit'.[4]

Hamish Redd, her former assistant at HREOC, recalled that she approached politicians privately to advance the Commission's agenda:

> [S]he would write letters to the Attorney General, Daryl Williams, and she would ask me to draft letters. I remember her telling me, 'I want the tone to be concealed irritation' – so, yes, she was definitely a canny political operator. She maintained connections that she thought she needed to maintain. I think she enjoyed – and why the hell not, a lot of people do – having friends in high places.[5]

Several of Tay's qualities suited her to the role of academic entrepreneur and 'maven'.[6] She was an attractive woman who stood out and could be extremely charming. Many people found her interesting and felt that she was interested in them.

Tay hosted many functions at her home for students, colleagues, members of the profession and international scholars. By doing so, she created a level of intimacy. Her cooking was legendary. Redd conjures up an endearing image:

> She was an amazing cook, an absolutely amazing cook. She used to stand on a little wooden block so that she was the right height above the wok. … She was a beautiful cook of Chinese Malay food. She would hand-make dumplings and cook Hainan chicken, all kinds of exotic things.[7]

Wilkins confirmed that he learnt from Tay that both cooking and charm helped enormously in handling bureaucracy.[8]

In addition, Tay designed her life in a way that best accommodated her networking. For much of her time in Sydney she chose to live in a place that was both central and attractive to visitors: a famous apartment in a building in the heart of the city, known as 'The Astor'. There she held many cocktail parties on the roof, as well as smaller lunches in her dining room during the week. A former student of Tay's, John Atkin, said that 'in the late 1970s it was the only sort of swish apartment block in the city and so to think that your professor had an apartment there and then you were invited there for cocktail parties on the roof of the Astor – it was impressive'.[9]

Tay's strong personal skills and enthusiasm for networking differentiated her from her predecessor. While Stone also hosted social events and developed international networks, he was less of a social being and his relationships were less

[4] Ziegert (n 2) 8.
[5] Redd (n 2).
[6] An expression used by Roger Wilkins: Wilkins (n 2).
[7] Redd (n 2).
[8] Wilkins (n 2).
[9] Interview with John Atkin (by telephone, 29 October 2014).

personal. Michael Kirby, who had been a student and research assistant of Stone's as well as a friend of Tay's, noted that 'they had commonalities of belief but Stone was truly the God professor and a remote figure'.[10] He explained that Stone

> was very conscious of his status as an important figure in global jurisprudence in the English-speaking world, therefore a mere student, even one who was advancing through the rather suspect ranks of student politics at the University of Sydney like me was a very small player on a field that he dominated. Alice was more democratic in that sense. She knew her status and was also a professor, but she was vivacious and voluble, talkative, excitable. Julius Stone was controlled and reserved and formal, conscious of his high status and so they were just different personalities and of course they came from different ethnic backgrounds.
>
> … people admired and respected Julius Stone rather than engaged with him. Alice's personality was more outward going and more engaging.[11]

In addition to these differences in personality, Stone's greater formality and reserve might also have been a product of the prejudice and exclusion he suffered from being Jewish. By contrast, Tay's outsider status gave her an attractive exotic quality. Her outspokenness, charm and stylish dress drew people to her. The fact that she stood out worked for, rather than against, her. Wilkins said:

> She used her feminine charm. She was a really beautiful woman and she used her charm and she used her rather exotic attributes because it was exotic the way she dressed, the fact that she was this little Asian woman, she used all of that to her great benefit in terms of getting things done. She was always dressed immaculately. Her hair and makeup was also immaculate.[12]

Tay's charm and networking skills allowed her to form strong relationships with Vice-Chancellors of the University of Sydney, senior members of the profession and academics with relative ease. Many of them became allies. At the same time, some visitors to the Department were less impressed by Tay's persona. For example, Isaiah Berlin, who spent some time as a visiting scholar in Kamenka's department, provided the following criticisms of both Tay and Kamenka:

> Kamenka, my boss, is a disarming, affable, know-all, with a rather pedantic ambitious Chinese wife who lacks the higher attributes very conspicuously: she works hard & is not sympathetic: Herbert [Hart] thinks highly of her.[13]

Tay therefore drew a mixed reception.

[10] Kirby (n 2).
[11] ibid.
[12] Wilkins (n 2). Similar remarks were also made by interviewees in the following interviews: interview with James Crawford (by telephone, 25 November 2014); interview with Margaret Allars SC (Law School, University Sydney, 1 August 2014); Sadurski (n 2); Ziegert (n 2); Birch (n 2); interview with Participant A (11 June 2014); Moens (n 2); Kirby (n 2).
[13] H Hardy and M Pottle (eds), *Affirming – Letters 1975–1997 by Isaiah Berlin* (London, Chatto and Windus, 2015) 9.

Motivating Principles

It might seem surprising that a Professor of Jurisprudence should possess such entrepreneurial qualities and be widely known for them. This could point to a weakness and suggest that Berlin was right in his assessment. While there is no doubt that Tay worked extremely hard, engaging in so many entrepreneurial and networking activities meant that she had less time to devote to scholarship.[14] The nature of her later scholarship and the fact that she spoke of, but never published, a monograph suggests that her scholarship did play a lesser role and was not as developed as it might otherwise have been. She published many articles but even at the end of her career her scholarship did not resemble – and had not attracted the same attention as – Stone's.

Does Tay's emphasis on enterprise therefore point to a deficiency, and did it diminish her contribution to the Australian legal academy? Before making a final assessment based on traditional notions of what amounts to a 'great jurisprudential scholar', it is important to recognise both Tay's motivations and what she hoped to achieve through these pursuits. At one level, it seems clear that she devoted so much energy to these activities because she enjoyed entertaining and was good at networking. There are, however, other dimensions to these activities that are evident from her larger academic agenda. As one of Tay's former PhD students and research assistants explained, Tay was a woman of principle and in several ways these activities can be viewed as an extension of her scholarly values introduced in the previous chapter:

> What Tay constantly told me – and in a way I suffer in today's environment from what I learned from her – is that if you can't stand for principles, you are not a human being. Full stop.[15]

Tay's tenure as an Australian academic coincided with dramatic changes to the way Australian universities were governed. She entered the legal academy at a time when the Commonwealth government began to increase funding for universities and enlist them into 'nation building' efforts. The two major federal policy waves that altered the university governance in the second half of the twentieth century caused Tay great alarm. The first, beginning in 1965 with the creation of the Australian Research Grants Council, did not noticeably affect the legal academy until at least the 1990s. As historian Stuart Macintyre has pointed out, the existence of the Council encouraged social scientists to organise themselves into groups to vie for funding as a way of establishing their importance within society. Australia's legal academy largely ignored the Council during the early decades, and Tay was one of the few law professors to obtain research grants in the 1980s. Most of her colleagues still believed that law was a teaching, rather than research, institution, and that law teachers carried out doctrinal scholarship for their

[14] Wilkins (n 2).
[15] Participant A (n 12).

students that did not fit into the realm of research. The second policy wave, beginning in the 1980s, was more strongly felt in law schools. The Commonwealth government continued to place emphasis on research funding and redoubled its efforts to impose external regulation and control, to identify certain research priority areas, and to dismantle disciplinary based knowledge.[16] At the same time, new management models grounded in thinking from elite business schools swept through Australian universities.[17] This led to research and teaching being evaluated by market-based models. In the ensuing decades, legal academics and managers of law schools began to think more in terms of fulfilling expectations based on the new policy and models. As university management increasingly governed according their interpretation of what this new environment required, linking staff and student recruitment and promotions to university benchmarks and international rankings, it seemed that law could no longer hold itself out as exceptional. These changes continue to be felt within Australian university governance.

During the early years of her career at Sydney – as well as at the very end – Tay painted a vivid picture of what was wrong with Australian/Western universities. In 1985, she identified the 'three great enemies of university achievement'.[18] The first and most worrisome was economic rationalisation: 'using one yardstick to measure everything, discounting that which is not quantifiable'.[19] She said that 'the ideal of economic rationalisation meant that the spirit and interaction of small departments and units was swept away' and that it was 'in the interests of creating an allegedly cost-effective larger whole in which there is no spirit, no sense of involvement and personal responsibility but increased tension and jockeying for position'.[20] Another was 'the belief that the university, culture, education and research are all justified only insofar as they serve some goal that is not their own'.[21] The final enemy of the university was the 'shallow demand that they elevate the community and their students into sacred cows, make them feel good and demand from them neither effort nor self-criticism'.[22]

At the end of her career, and shortly before she died, Tay put the matter even more forcefully:

> The scramble of universities to join the corporate world, the commercialisation of so-called education in the last 20 years, has made a mockery of the university. The dishonesty of the corporate world has taken hold of university management and scholarship. …

[16] S Bartie, 'The Social Sciences in Australia and the Experience of Law' (2012) 34 *Sydney Law Review* 371, 374.

[17] ibid.

[18] 'Academics Identify Some of the Problems Facing Universities', *The University of Sydney News* (Sydney) 12 March 1985, 37.

[19] ibid.

[20] ibid.

[21] ibid.

[22] ibid.

> Today, in universities everywhere, not only is there failure of the rules of natural justice, but academic corruption, which flourishes as a result of the former. Academic corruption, like all other forms of corruption, is a highly contagious disease. It is worse, because it does not usually involve money, only false, unearned, inflated CVs and hence it excuses tolerance of inflated standards. Only exposure to the light can curtail the disease. But, alas, there are so many dark holes and corners in universities.[23]

One of the most enduring aspects of Tay's scholarly agenda was to describe and explain the way that different governance models were linked to the freedom and prosperity of citizens. While initially her studies concentrated on the USSR and China, eventually her gaze, along with Kamenka's, turned to the West, concentrating on Australia.[24] The comparative apparatus designed by the pair, consisting of the ideal types described earlier, enabled them to contrast the three. Their studies extended beyond legislatures and judiciaries to political policies, ideas and ideologies. Most obviously, Tay and Kamenka were interested in the way that Marxist thinking influenced communist regimes. Their studies therefore included consideration of the independence and influence of intellectuals. They suggested that part of the reason Stalin's and Mao's tyrannical regimes had prospered was because intellectuals – scholars who raised arguments that opposed existing modes of governance – were marginalised and all too frequently paid with their lives. According to Tay and Kamenka, intellectuals supported by those governments were in the business of propaganda rather than theory. They saw parallels in the West and endeavoured to fight against them. In an address at a graduation ceremony Tay said:

> [I]n an egalitarian society with weakly developed cultural traditions and independent institutions in which everyone expects the government to provide for them and in which only money has universal respect, it takes great *courage and institutional self-confidence* to resist whatever goals and procedures are being elevated at the moment, no matter how bad, and to examine critically the cleanliness of the hand that feeds you.[25]

The Department of Jurisprudence at Sydney was therefore designed and preserved by Tay as a protest against these external agendas, as well as a bastion of traditional university values. In other exchanges, to signal the point of difference, she described herself as an 'old-fashioned scholar'.[26] By preserving her Department and contrasting it with the Department of Law, she sought to prove that a small department organised around a set of scholarly values could provide a far greater service to society than a large faculty organised to achieve economic efficiency and

[23] Tay, quoted in P Sheehan, 'No Credit in Devalued Degree', *Sydney Morning Herald* (online) 8 January 2003, http://www.smh.com.au/articles/2003/01/07/1041566407260.html.

[24] The first sign of this change in direction in Tay's scholarship was in the following article: A Tay, '"Smash all Permanent Rules": China as a Model for the Future' (1976) 7 *Sydney Law Review* 400.

[25] 'Academics Identify Some of the Problems Facing Universities' (n 18), 37 (emphasis added).

[26] See, eg, G Leech, 'Tay a Law unto Herself', *The Australian* (Sydney) 31 July–1 August 1993, 6. This was also an expression Participant A used to describe Tay: Participant A (n 12).

to work *with* government. Although the Department was not entirely independent or autonomous – it relied upon university funding – Tay acted as if it were,[27] and projected both confidence and courage. The relationships she established through her networking engendered the patronage of those who could discourage or prevent the two departments from being merged. Tay used her networking and management skills to encourage others to contribute to the Department in various ways. The academic elite of the legal theory world always filled the post she left open within the Department for visiting scholars. She also sought to raise money for the Department. At a time when few legal scholars were seeking grants, she attracted several from both the Australian Research Grants Committee (now the Australian Research Council) as well as the Human Rights and Equal Opportunity Commission (now the Australian Human Rights Commission). She also obtained funding through teaching initiatives, such as teaching in the profession's Law Extension Committee course.[28]

A further strategy Tay deployed was to publicise the Department. Throughout her tenure she featured, along with other members of the Department, in articles in Sydney's major daily newspapers, Australia's legal philosophy journal and the University's newsletter, *The University of Sydney News*. By comparison, few articles in *The University of Sydney News* mentioned the achievements of the Department of Law.

These activities were central to the Department's independence and longevity. They explain why the Department continued to exist for another 23 years following Stone's retirement. For Tay, this was an important achievement. She took the abolition of the Department very personally and had no lingering affection for the University of Sydney.[29] Recent literature on the corporatisation of universities and the move towards 'mega faculties' also gives force to the strength of her achievement in maintaining such a small department.[30] As several of the people interviewed for this study attest, academic departments like Tay's no longer exist in Australia.

The Heart of the Department

Academic Considerations

Having created an autonomous and independent department, Tay became responsible for its culture and agenda. It fell to her to decide on a vision for the

[27] Crawford (n 12).

[28] This is considered further below.

[29] Ziegert (n 2); Participant A (n 12); Birch (n 2); Moens (n 2).

[30] See, eg, M Thornton, *Privatising the Public University: The Case of Law* (Abingdon, Routledge, 2012); S Macintyre, 'Universities' in C Hamilton and S Maddison (eds), *Silencing Dissent: How the Australian Government is Controlling Public Opinion and Stifling Debate* (Sydney, Allen & Unwin, 2007) 41; J Lancaster, *The Modernisation of Legal Education: A Critique of the Martin Bowen and Pearce Reports* (Sydney, Centre for Legal Education, 1993).

Department that might contribute to the ideals of a university. Under Tay's stewardship the Department distinguished itself from other Australian law schools and resisted external agendas that seemed to her to undermine rather than further the main goals of the university. It was led by academics and academic values. In 1989, in response to a proposal by then Dean Colin Phegan to dissolve the Department, she said that the proposal would 'not solve any problems' and that her Department 'always treats academic considerations as more important than administrative ones'.[31] According to Tay, those who did otherwise were acting immorally.[32]

For Tay, the central mission of a university was teaching. The Department would therefore give priority to teaching and provide an environment where academics were free to pursue their own agendas, provided that they worked hard and took their teaching seriously. Sadurski described the teaching priority as a 'perfectly noble motivation'.[33] He elaborated:

> I mean she was a university person, she believed in education and she believed in teaching and she believed in putting students first. That was her passion. She was very passionate about students and about her teaching mission. I don't think I even discussed it with her. It may have been something more important to her than her research. This is a perfectly legitimate priority for a person at a university. She was an extremely passionate teacher and a person who would spend a lot of time preparing classes, delivering classes and marking essays.[34]

Within the Department, she attempted to promote academic freedom among its members who were united not by a particular brand of jurisprudence, but by the common goal of providing law graduates at the University of Sydney with a strong liberal legal education.

Tay's different approach did not mean that the Department failed to meet external requirements. Even though it would never subject itself to such measurements, the Department would probably have performed extremely well on any research or teaching assessment exercise. Tay and her colleagues brought exceptional scholars to Australia and built a strong scholarly community that extended beyond the full-time members of the Department.

A Community of Scholars

Ziegert, Sadurski and Krygier are all now acknowledged to be strong intellectuals, and some of Australia's finest legal academics – certainly among *the* finest in terms of Australian legal theorists. Each would no doubt have been successful, irrespective of the Department and Tay. However, all three say that Tay and Kamenka

[31] 'Law Meeting on Jurisprudence', *The University of Sydney News* (Sydney), 1 August 1989, 170.

[32] This was made clear in the early parts of her career (as described earlier) and she explicitly drew a connection between academics and morality: Leech (n 26) 6.

[33] Sadurski (n 2).

[34] ibid.

played a significant part in setting up their initial scholarly careers and that, were it not for Tay and Kamenka's efforts, they would never have taught in an Australian law school. One of Tay and the Department's initial contributions to the legal academy in Australia was therefore to recruit these scholars to Australia's discipline of law.

Before his meeting with Tay and Kamenka, Ziegert had been reluctant to come to Australia, and considered the idea of teaching law at an Australian law school very unappealing.[35] Sadurski, similarly, had not previously contemplated coming to Australia.[36] He met Tay and Kamenka during one of their trips to the University of Warsaw in Poland, when he was asked by the Faculty of Law to take charge of their stay.[37] For Ziegert and Sadurski, the decision to move to Australia to work in the Faculty of Law was made only after they had spent a year as visiting lecturers at Sydney.[38] Both formed very favourable impressions of the Department and say that Tay and Kamenka provided them with considerable assistance.[39] They found it to be a very friendly and happy place.[40] It was young and vibrant, with most of the Department's members in their 20s or 30s.[41] Both thought that the Department stood in contrast to the rest of the Faculty, which seemed 'to be fossilised – old-fashioned, conservative and traditional with all sorts of eccentrics'.[42]

Before he was offered a position in the Department, Krygier was hoping to pursue a path in either political science or sociology. Once he had completed his doctorate, he intended to apply for a Harkness Fellowship at Harvard so that he could study half of Leon Trotsky's archive, which was soon to be made available to the public.[43] Tay convinced him to join the Department instead.[44] She explained that writing a reference to support his application for a Harkness Fellowship would be difficult as she hoped that he would join her in the Department.[45] His relationship with and loyalty to Tay and – more strongly – Kamenka, who had been his PhD supervisor, made the invitation attractive and so, rather than Cambridge, he moved to Sydney.[46] His first impressions of the Faculty of Law at Sydney were not as favourable or as strong as Sadurski's or Ziegert's. Almost as soon as he arrived, Krygier became embroiled in the dispute over the Department's existence.[47] Nonetheless it was he, along with Tay, Lauchlan Chipman,

[35] Ziegert (n 2).
[36] Sadurski (n 2).
[37] ibid.
[38] Ziegert (n 2); Sadurski (n 2).
[39] ibid.
[40] ibid.
[41] ibid.
[42] Sadurski (n 2).
[43] Krygier (n 2).
[44] ibid.
[45] ibid.
[46] ibid.
[47] ibid.

Roger Wilkins, Chris Arnold and PhD student Gabriel Moens, who made the Department such a happy and vibrant place.[48]

Tay created a very social and largely collegial environment. She often invited members of the Department to dinner, arranged lunches and sought to get to know her colleagues on both a personal and professional level.[49] The fact that she drew no real distinction between her personal and professional life meant that she largely expected her colleagues to do the same.[50] Tay's former PhD student and part-time colleague Christopher Birch recalls that, in many ways, it seemed like an ideal academic environment, with members of the Department spending much time in the corridor and in each other's offices discussing various ideas and issues.[51] Speaking of his time as a postgraduate student and Tay's research assistant, one interviewee reflected: 'I met a lot of people but the most important thing was the enjoyment. I spent six years in Sydney and it was the best time I have ever had'.[52]

The frequent presence of international visitors meant that members of the Department could speak informally with some of the greatest legal theorists. This proved to be a considerable advantage to PhD students, who derived some of their greatest inspiration from these visitors.[53] For Tay, it seems that these informal conversations were a very important part of the Department; they were part of the reason she kept one post free for visiting appointments, to which she invited scholars who held a variety of interesting opposing views. Tay wanted a broad-minded Department that drew from the very best of legal ideas and strived to match them. By mixing with international visitors as well as judges and barristers, the Department created a kind of intellectual elite within Sydney.

In addition to 'charming' on the one hand and 'fierce' on the other, a word that was often used by interviewees when speaking of Tay was 'energy'.[54] Part of the reason Tay was able to create such a diverse network of scholars and lawyers was that she appeared to have an abundance of energy that she devoted solely to her career. People were attracted to her energy and it meant that she got things done. One interviewee recalled that, when he was her research assistant, the pair would sometimes work from 8.30 am until 9 pm without eating because they were so engaged in their work.[55] He also spoke of professors in China asking after Tay and being very surprised on learning of her death: 'She was so energetic, no one would think she would pass away at 70'.[56] Redd said:

> She continued to work right until the end. Her health was deteriorating because of the cancer; there were secondary cancers on her brain. She was having a lot of radiotherapy

[48] Sadurski (n 2).
[49] Sadurski (n 2); Krygier (n 2); Birch (n 2).
[50] Sadurski (n 2).
[51] Birch (n 2).
[52] Participant A (n 12).
[53] Birch (n 2); Participant A (n 12).
[54] Sadurski (n 2); Moens (n 2).
[55] Participant A (n 12).
[56] ibid.

> and chemotherapy and tumours were popping up all over her but she was a workaholic, so I think she needed the work to feel that she was still alive.[57]

She therefore set a strong example for both her postgraduate students and colleagues to follow. She expected her colleagues and assistants to work hard.[58]

One of the Department's central contributions was to create a strong collegial environment where members were encouraged to seek inspiration from a broader world of ideas. Tay was largely loyal to her colleagues and postgraduate students and helped them advance their careers. As a result, the University of Sydney had the benefit of several high performing legal scholars – along with a strong international network of scholars – who would not have been associated with the Australian discipline of law were it not for Tay and the Department.

Some people in the Department did, however, find it oppressive at times. Few wished to integrate their personal and professional lives to the same extent as Tay, and they sometimes resented the amount of personal time they felt obliged to spend with Tay and other members of the Department.[59] While they were devoted to their careers, they wished to set limits. The Department was like a family. Sadurski said that Tay 'wanted to be very much like almost a mother of a big family'.[60] And like many families, the amount of time and personal intrusions meant that several relationships soured over time. Krygier was one of the first to leave the Department, largely due to personal differences.[61] Other formerly very close relationships also broke down over time. Tay's frankness in all things – but especially academic matters – caused strain among even her closest colleagues and friends.

Tay and Women

The composition of Tay's Department – as well as her list of friends – suggests that she had a closer affinity with men than with women. Some of her colleagues speculated that she preferred the company of men. A few women did join the Department, but none lasted for very long. For example, when Tay arrived, Lyndel Prott was a member of the department. She had previously been a member of Stone's Department of Jurisprudence and International Law. Some have suggested that there was friction between the two. Prott was a strong scholar, but her research agenda did not fit neatly with the vision that Tay was advancing for the Department. As the only other senior person in the Department, Prott might, perhaps, have expected a greater say in how it was run. Prott eventually left.

[57] ibid.
[58] Birch (n 2).
[59] Sadurski (n 2); Ziegert (n 2); Krygier (n 2).
[60] Sadurski (n 2).
[61] Krygier (n 2).

Tay's tendency to favour certain colleagues and PhD students with invitations and opportunities is also said to have caused friction within the Department and Faculty of Law.[62] Much of the favouritism was directed at men. Tay was one of the few women in Australia in a senior position in either the academy or the law. Her leadership position might suggest that she had a responsibility to do more to promote women within both spheres.

Some of Tay's PhD students were women and, judging by the acknowledgment sections of their theses, she treated them well;[63] however, the vast majority of her postgraduate students were men. Former female research assistants and female junior academics within the Department declined the invitation to be interviewed for this project. Tay's own advancement might have led her to believe that it was not necessary to take special measures to assist women. Perhaps she appointed men on the basis that they represented the established tradition and were typically considered respected authorities.[64] In other words, this played to her conservative inclinations. Other possible reasons might be that she preferred the company of men, and that being one of very few women meant that she stood out.

Tay's running of the Department therefore had its limitations. She was pluralistic and open in her approach to ideas but clearly sought to favour those she believed to have stronger intellects and who would, presumably, make for better company.

Putting Students First

The most obvious benefactors of the community of scholars and networks that Tay created through the Department were students at the University of Sydney. Members of the Department devised a number of teaching initiatives that were firsts for Australia and provided Sydney students with new opportunities. The high-profile international visitors who spent a semester in the Department were typically asked to teach aspects of both undergraduate and postgraduate units. Tay also taught abroad and, along with other colleagues, taught Jurisprudence in the Legal Admission Board course (now the Law Extension Committee) to students who, for reasons of time and/or money, could not qualify as lawyers through traditional university education.[65] Again, Tay led the academy into new spaces where law could be studied as a larger global enterprise.

[62] Participant A (n 12); Allars (n 12).

[63] One Indian PhD student, Sakuntala Kadirgamar-Rajasingham, who, went on to become a Senior Advisor to the United Nations, in her thesis thanked Tay for 'her unwavering patience, guidance and support' and 'sympathetic ear'.

[64] Ziegert made a similar suggestion: Ziegert (n 2).

[65] A student who completed the course was eligible for admission as a solicitor.

Tay's dedication to her students is evident both from the initiatives she devised and the time and energy she devoted to them. Even after she became the President of HREOC, she continued to teach part-time at Sydney as well as abroad. She also delivered speeches to various groups on the importance of education.[66] Christopher Birch recalled that during this time she would mark all of the Jurisprudence exam papers for the Law Extension Course:

> So, for a number of years I took all the lectures and Alice would mark all of the exam papers. There would be 50–60 students a session and they would each write four or five answers, so you can multiply it all out. It was horrendous. I used to say 'Alice, it must be unbearable having to mark all of those papers', and she said she didn't mind as it helped her keep in touch with what young students were thinking. …
>
> … It always struck me as very unusual that Alice was like this, that she didn't have this view that, 'I've reached this highly elevated position in the profession so teaching in the Diploma of Law course or marking exam papers is beneath me, so I just wish to spend my life in select seminar groups in Oxford or Princeton'. She was quite happy to roll up her sleeves and do all this kind of hard academic work.[67]

While President, Tay continued to travel to England annually to teach in University of Notre Dame's summer programme in Law in London. Gabriel Moens made the introductions that led to her involvement in the programme. He said that she 'liked it very, very much'.[68] This all provides further evidence for the fact, succinctly expressed by Redd, that 'Alice loved teaching'.[69]

Tay devised a number of teaching initiatives. One of the first was an arrangement that allowed students to choose one jurisprudence subject out of four streams. This meant that, while jurisprudence was a compulsory part of the law degree at the University of Sydney, students could choose the subject that best suited them. Interestingly, some students chose Tay's stream on the basis of a perception spread by other students that it was the more 'black letter' of the four subjects and therefore sat more comfortably with what they had already learnt.[70] With the help of other members of her Department (particularly Ziegert), Tay also arranged for exchange programmes in China, Vietnam and Germany – mostly at Masters level. Her second husband, Guenther Doeker-Mach, organised the German exchange programme with Friedrich Schiller Universität Jena; this became a first for an Australian law school.[71] Many other exchanges followed. To provide teachers for

[66] See, eg, A Tay, 'Graduation Address' (Speech delivered at Brisbane Grammar School, Brisbane, 18 November 1998); A Tay, 'Address' (Speech delivered at the Council for Equal Opportunity Limited, Grace Hotel, Sydney, 26 August 1998).

[67] Birch (n 2).

[68] Moens (n 2).

[69] Redd (n 2).

[70] Ziegert (n 2); interview with Justice Julie Ward (Judges Chambers, Supreme Court of New South Wales, Sydney, 8 December 2014).

[71] Birch (n 2).

these programmes, she drew from her contacts in the profession, including former students, as well as other members of the Faculty.[72]

Tay made numerous trips to China throughout her career. During her time as Professor of Jurisprudence Tay was part of government delegations to both China and Tibet.[73] She taught in China while President of HREOC, lecturing alongside Chinese professors. In the 1990s, the Department established the Centre for Asian and Pacific Law at the University of Sydney (CAPLUS), at the instigation of Ziegert. One of Tay's central platforms was to make China's laws, legal system and culture accessible to the West. In the 1970s, at the time when she and Kamenka first travelled to China, this was a considerable task: China's laws and legal system were shrouded in secrecy,[74] and being a lawyer was a vocation that required a high degree of secrecy.[75] At that stage, the rule of both Mao and the Gang of Four had ended and Deng Xiaoping was in power. After a decade of closure during the Cultural Revolution, Chinese universities had reopened and both staff and students were 'hungry for knowledge'.[76] Tay and Kamenka toured throughout China and their speeches were published in newspapers and journals distributed throughout the country.[77] They were considered 'big names' and lectured 'on topics that the Chinese lecturers wouldn't be discussing'.[78] Their understanding of communist, Soviet and Western legal systems meant they were ideally placed to speak to the Chinese about the trajectory of their legal system and reforms that might prevent some of the atrocities of the past. Of course, the new environment did not mean that the Chinese were receptive to a Westernisation of their laws or to strong criticisms of their mode of governance, but it appears that Tay and Kamenka were able to speak with an openness not permitted either in earlier or later times. As one interviewee explained to me, there was a general attitude that they were foreigners and permitted to have their views.[79] He was not surprised that Tay found that Chinese students and academics took to and understood the ideal types far more readily than Westerners, who

[72] eg, Allsop, Birch and Allars all taught in the programme. Interview with Chief Justice James Allsop (Federal Court of Australia, Sydney, 29 July 2014); Birch (n 2); Allars (n 12).

[73] eg, in 1981 she spent five weeks in China as a guest of the Chinese Academy of Social Sciences: Faculty of Law Minutes, 13 March 1981, 15, G3/2, University of Sydney Archives. She returned in 1986: 'Fellow of the Academy of Social Sciences', *The University of Sydney News* (Sydney) 4 November 1986, 18; Leech (n 26) 6. In 1991, Tay and Kamenka were part of an Australian delegation to both China and Tibet. A trip planned for the following year was cancelled by the Chinese government: E Kamenka and A Tay, 'International Law, International Justice and the Autonomy of Tibet' (1993) 18 *Bulletin of the Australian Society of Legal Philosophy* 36, 44–50.

[74] This is something Tay acknowledged: A Tay, 'Law in Communist China – Part 1' (1969) 6 *Sydney Law Review* 153, 154.

[75] Participant A (n 12).

[76] ibid.

[77] ibid.

[78] ibid.

[79] ibid.

never warmed to the ideal types or attempted to study law in a similar way.[80] He explained:

> For those who had gone through the 10 years of the 'Cultural Revolution' the whole teaching was Karl Marx or the Chinese version of Marxism. Someone who saw what was going on in the Soviet Union and the Western democratic system providing a sort of conception and notion of justice and equality, those kinds of things, you thought this is someone who knows all this and can give you a precise summary of what all those notions are about and you have all these eager and hungry people trying to understand, then of course your immediate impression is that they understand it much better than Australians. Australians take it for granted – election, equality, justice, etc – whereas people over there thought these are the things you need to fight for and sometimes fight for your life and for it to be defined in that precise format (they only had an hour also to talk about this). You can imagine the response from the audience, that they were suddenly so enlightened, 'Oh, ok, that is what we are trying to fight for'. We didn't have any guidance on what to do, now we have understanding.[81]

It was an important, not to be repeated, time in the history of Chinese universities and gave Tay and Kamenka an ideal opportunity to bring what they had learnt to those who would benefit from it the most. At least in part, it fulfilled one of Tay's primary goals: to bring greater understanding between the East and West. The various teaching programmes Tay established in China and Asia during her tenure at Sydney can therefore be viewed as initiatives also pursued in furtherance of these goals. Of course, they were not naïve in their understanding of how the Chinese might make use of Western law. In one piece Tay had said: 'Like many Chinese attempts at legal reform, it is largely directed at reassuring the foreign investor and creating the conditions for a more decentralized economic boom'.[82]

It was while Tay was on bereavement leave after Kamenka's death in 1994 that Ziegert decided to propose CAPLUS. He believed that the Centre would give Tay a new focus and that it would provide some consolation and a refuge if the Department were ever abolished.[83] As Ziegert predicted, Tay soon agreed and began devising new initiatives for teaching and research in and about China. Both Ziegert and Redd suggested that her attributes – an older Chinese woman now living in the West – meant that she had a unique vantage point:

> She played this hypocrisy of communism perfectly. She could always criticise them openly for their lack of Rule of Law and legal procedure and was still respected despite kicking ass. That is something only Alice could do because if she had been an American male white law professor and told the Russian law professors that their law

[80] A Tay and E Kamenka, 'Elevating Law in the People's Republic of China' (1985) 9 *Bulletin of Australian Society of Legal Philosophy* 69, 92.

[81] Participant A (n 12).

[82] A Tay, 'The Struggle for Law in China' (1987) 21 *University of British Columbia Law Review* 561, 562.

[83] ibid.

> was deficient, he would not have been invited back and would have been kicked out, but not Alice. She went back to Russia and she made good friends and she also gained strong support in China and Vietnam.[84]

For Tay, these teaching opportunities meant she could attempt to influence present and future lawyers in both China and the USSR/Russia.

The content of Tay's teaching largely replicated her scholarly interests. Her interest in property law flowed through to her teaching, as did her interest in Soviet systems and Marxist ideas. Wilkins, who took tutorials and sat in on Tay's classes, recalled that:

> She was looking at some of the stuff on Reich that was written in the 1930s in Germany on the role of property in a social system. She was interested in Glendon's stuff on welfare and whether it was going to be hypostasised or transformed into some kind of right. This is on the edge of, I suppose, some of the, you might say, more ideological areas of law in terms of property. So, she was certainly alive to that sort of Marxist critique. It wasn't Marx so much. So, in legal history terms she was sort of interested in EP Thompson and people like that and that sort of analysis of legal systems and laws.[85]

Tay was one of the very first Australian legal scholars to write about human rights and she also taught in that subject.[86]

Tay's teaching style could be dramatic and she would sometimes attempt to shock her audience. One interviewee said that there was a lot of interaction: 'You discussed the most serious legal issues in the most relaxed way'.[87] She also sought to instil in students an open mind:

> For each of the subjects she taught she would always have guest lecturers either from the judiciary or international scholars so that you got different perspectives and so you could see that there was no right or wrong. She always said there was no black or white or right or wrong answers in law.[88]

While she did not inspire all of her students, for some her impact was immense.[89] Atkin believed that she had an aura and said that, 'What you did get a sense of was her very strong intellect'.[90] The current Chief Justice of the Federal Court,

[84] ibid. See also Redd (n 2).

[85] Wilkins (n 2).

[86] Tay's scholarship and teaching in the field of human rights constitutes yet another very important contribution to the discipline of law in Australia which cannot be fully explored here. Much of her work could be described as working towards the prevention of human rights abuses and, as indicated in the appendix that contains Tay's publication list, she began publishing articles, book chapters and papers with 'human rights' in the title in the 1980s. She also specifically considered how human rights ought to be taught in Australia. In the 1980s, she was part of an organising committee for a national seminar on teaching and research on human rights at tertiary and adult education levels sponsored by the Australian National Commission for UNESCO.

[87] Participant A (n 12).

[88] ibid.

[89] Chief Justice Allsop attests to this: Allsop (n 72).

[90] Atkin (n 9).

James Allsop, gave strong praise to Tay's teaching, saying that she awakened him to the academic side of law and that it later encouraged him, as a judge faced with hard cases, to draw inspiration from the writings of great jurisprudential scholars.[91]

As with her colleagues, Tay sought to establish personal connections with students and on occasion would organise social events for her classes, including at times offering invitations to students to attend events on the rooftop of the Astor.[92] Chief Justice Allsop said that the small classes were personal; she demanded attention but was never threatening.[93] Instead, she would joke and try to encourage students to participate.[94] He believed that she liked people and she liked students.[95] Hamish Redd, who attended a number of Tay's classes, said that she 'formed views very quickly about who the bright students were and who wasn't. She would focus on the bright students'.[96] She kept in touch with some students and also offered kind words of encouragement and advice.[97]

Those who have the fondest memories of Tay and on whom she made the greatest impression were her doctoral students. At times she could be extremely tough and expected a great deal from them. She perceived a certain undesirable 'easy-goingness' in her undergraduate law students[98] that she would not tolerate in her postgraduates. Both Moens and another interviewee recall Tay describing an early draft of their thesis as 'rubbish'.[99] In Moens's case she accentuated the point by throwing his thesis into the bin.[100] Despite the harsh treatment, both of them believe that they owed her a great debt and that she was a very good supervisor.[101] Tay encouraged her PhD students to become academics and, with her assistance, several of them achieved very high positions early in their career and also took up governance positions in law schools.[102] She hoped to instil in them the scholarly values that drove her career. One interviewee, who later became the Head of School at an Australian university, said that there were moments in his career when he realised that Tay was still 'working on him'.[103] Her legacy therefore extended beyond her scholarship to the set of scholarly values she applied to the management of the Department.

[91] Allsop (n 72).
[92] Atkin (n 9); Moens (n 2); Participant A (n 12).
[93] Allsop (n 72).
[94] ibid.
[95] ibid.
[96] Redd (n 2).
[97] Allars (n 12); Allsop (n 72).
[98] Leech (n 26) 6.
[99] Moens (n 2); Participant A (n 12).
[100] Moens (n 2).
[101] Moens (n 2); Participant A (n 12).
[102] eg, both Participant A and Moens quickly became professors and both acted as Heads of School. Another PhD student, John Mo, became Dean of the Faculty of International Law at the China University of Political Science and Law and is now Dean of Law at Macao University.
[103] Participant A (n 12).

Concluding Remarks

I suspect that many scholars, or at least those sitting outside the sciences, may read these chapters about Tay's Department with a sense of wistfulness and wonder. What would happen if universities abandoned the idea of mega-faculties and corporate imperatives and instead used Tay's Department as a model? Would it lead to complacency, inefficiency, nepotism and elitism? Or might it attract and produce more scholars of the diversity and calibre of Krygier, Sadurski and Ziegert? Might it provide a solution to the fragmentary nature of disciplines? Could it add strength to universities, injecting excitement and creativity by yielding power to strong disciplinary leaders? Tay's example might lead the charge for more academic entrepreneurs and smaller departments.

Irrespective of the model, Tay's career suggests that the critique, reform and management of the discipline of law are jobs worthy of great jurisprudential scholars, and that legal scholars – who have built careers around the study and advancement of reason and the examination of governance structures – are ideally placed to lead a change in the culture of universities. Her experience also suggests that the ideas of scholars, based on theoretical and historical assessments of the role of their discipline in society, should again play a central role in the governance of universities.

Some might say that Tay was exceptional – one of a kind – and that no academic today could advance the agenda or wield the same power she once did. Tay was certainly pessimistic about the future, but I sense that she would not mind if a few scholars proved her wrong.

11

Critic of Australia's Legal Academy

Introduction

One of the most obvious advantages of Tay's largely independent and autonomous Department was that she was able to act as both fierce critic of and conscience to Australia's legal academy. She moved beyond a larger institutional critique to issuing criticisms that called individual Australian legal academics to account. Rather than despairing at the personal frictions that had been created in Stone's time and continued throughout her tenure, Tay played this tension to her advantage in several ways. Moreover, with her friendships and loyalties sitting largely outside the Department of Law, she was free to say what she liked about those within it.[1] In fact, there are few signs that she ever integrated fully into Australia's legal academy. One of Tay's main contributions, therefore, was to draw strength from a vantage point that was both within and outside the legal academy, which allowed her to challenge practices and intellectual currents that she believed went against the true spirit of the scholar and traditional university values. She blamed these negative trends on the external pressures imposed by governments as well as the pervading culture within Australian universities and, more particularly, law schools.

In this final chapter on Alice Erh-Soon Tay, I examine two key factors which alienated her from the academy: her position on emerging Australian legal scholarship in the 1970s and 1980s (including feminist legal scholarship); and the perception that she was deeply conservative at heart. While both factors limited the extent of her own intellectual contribution, I argue that the greatest legacy of Tay's career and the Department was to provoke greater thinking about university governance and the moral questions that sit at the heart of both the discipline and university.

Critique of Australian Legal Education and Scholarship

Tay wrote passionately about the state of Australian legal education and scholarship, and with such passion came criticisms that were bound to alienate her in

[1] Tay acknowledged such freedom during an interview with a journalist. G Leech, 'Tay a Law unto Herself', *The Australian* (Sydney) 31 July–1 August 1993, 6.

certain academic circles. In the 1970s and 1980s, her primary attacks were directed at junior scholars who, she believed, had let their emotions (such as pity for the less fortunate) dominate their thinking at the expense of the careful study required to provide a strong intellectual grounding in the discipline. According to Tay, the role of the law school was to teach a complement of doctrine and general and informed thinking about law which takes into account its history, social context and the experience of other cultures.[2] She considered that this was not occurring in Australia, where doctrinal studies were being replaced with 'half-baked sociology, vociferous compassion, strident protest or the belief that the simple and direct evaluation of policy is an adequate substitute for knowing and understanding the structure and development, the problems and complexities of law and the legal tradition'.[3] She condemned, often to the point of personal insult, colleagues who had adopted this approach:

> Because such empty postures come most readily to unintelligent and unimaginative minds, it is striking that university law courses with the most radical titles normally contain the most conventional and traditional material, failing to bring into genuine relation the complexities of the past and the demands for the future.[4]

These new 'pseudo-individualist' trends not only prospered in areas such as human rights, but also crossed into the heart of Tay and Kamenka's interests: the study of Marxism. For them, Marxism had been commandeered by radical scholars who wished to attack the

> multinational corporations in the world economy, the 'imperialist' and anti-communist role of the United States' 'ruling classes' (implicitly treated as power elites), and the limits that these world protagonists and the unplanned world economy place on the capacity for action by social democratic or socialist national governments anywhere in the world.[5]

Tay and Kamenka did not object to this new reincarnation of Marxism per se but to the way in which this new breed of 'amateur academics'[6] (to use their label) used the parts of Marxism which suited them best and 'were happiest ignoring, or knowing as little as possible about, social ideology, law and legal theory in the communist countries'.[7] They believed that, because these radicals were unconcerned with either Marxism as a theory, 'unproblematic science' or the 'body of general laws', and preferring instead to 'choose sides, against the power of capital and the profit motive and to support the cause of peace, community, and "rational" social relations, they were left with themes rather than laws'.[8] They characterised

[2] A Tay and E Kamenka, 'New Legal Areas, New Legal Attitudes' in A Tay and E Kamenka (eds), *Law Making in Australia* (London, Edward Arnold, 1980) 247, 259–60.
[3] ibid 259.
[4] ibid 259.
[5] ibid 607–08.
[6] ibid 613.
[7] ibid 611.
[8] ibid 612.

these scholars as irresponsible and self-serving academics, who advanced their scholarship in order to promote their own careers and sense of worth, rather than to better society.[9]

What concerned Tay and Kamenka most was that these 'emotional' crusades were being advanced in the absence of a careful and balanced appraisal of the *Gesellschaft* – in their view the ideal type of Western law[10] – and that, in their ignorance, this new band of scholars had sought to erode and dismantle it. Through their Soviet studies Tay and Kamenka had concluded that the *Gesellschaft* was best equipped to achieve justice and to fend off tyranny.[11] Combined with Tay's convictions about the intellectual integrity and coherence of the common law formed during her study of property law,[12] their colleagues' new zeal must have seemed naive and unwise. Indeed, Tay and Kamenka saw it as a 'crisis' in Australian/Western law.[13] Much of what Tay and Kamenka wrote in this new chapter of scholarship served to bring forth the strength of the *Gesellschaft* and, in particular, the common law, which they characterised as the paradigm form of the *Gesellschaft*.

Though they endorsed traditional conceptions of the common law, Tay and Kamenka were not narrow formalists or positivists. They accepted the realist critique of law, beginning with Rudolf von Jhering, that discounts 'the internal coherence and historical integrity of law, its claim to mould society and to represent specifically legal traditions, procedures and ideals'.[14] In a co-authored article they also explicitly endorsed Julius Stone's position on legal reasoning.[15] However, they did not accept that law should be 'a neutral, flexible and totally characterless instrument responsive to or serving uncritically elevated goals and ends alleged to have logical priority over that law'.[16] They believed that the common law had always been capable of protecting diverse interests, that it 'assumed' a plurality of interests,[17] and was inherently flexible. Failings of the common law to protect such interests in the past were due not to 'the rigidity of the common law, but the rigidity of judges' minds'.[18]

[9] ibid 613. A Tay and E Kamenka, 'New Marxism for Old: Contemporary Radicalism and Legal Theories' (1988) 1 *University of California Davis Law Review* 605, 636.

[10] A Tay, 'China and Legal Pluralism' (1984) 8 Bulletin of the Australian Society of Legal Philosophers 23, 27.

[11] ibid.

[12] See chapter six.

[13] See, eg, A Tay and E Kamenka, 'Beyond Bourgeois Individualism: The Contemporary Crisis in Law and Legal Ideology' in E Kamenka and RS Neale (eds), *Feudalism, Capitalism and Beyond* (London, Edward Arnold, 1975) 126, 127.

[14] A Tay and E Kamenka, 'Social Traditions, Legal Traditions' in E Kamenka and A Tay (eds), *Law and Social Control* (London, Edward Arnold, 1980) 3, 3.

[15] A Tay, 'The Sense of Justice in the Common Law' in E Kamenka and A Tay (eds), *Justice* (London, Edward Arnold, 1980) 79, 91.

[16] Tay and Kamenka (n 14) 3.

[17] Tay (n 10) 27.

[18] A Tay, 'Law and "Legal Culture"' (1983) 27 *Bulletin of Australian Society of Legal Philosophy* 15, 24.

Tay clearly believed that the Western desire to elevate the *Gemeinschaft* over the *Gesellschaft* was a product of insularity and ignorance, where scholars 'have no eye for a comparison with other countries and political systems'.[19] She said:

> [T]he *Gesellschaft* strain keeps re-emerging and, at the formal level, the Chinese government is moving to increased emphasis on aspects of the *Gesellschaft* conception of law and its role in modern society, even if its practice, like that of the Soviet Union, is more and more bureaucratic-administrative. Those in the West who are excited about other people's legal systems and traditions nearly always elevate the *Gemeinschaft* conception. Those of [us] who are not white and have lived under *Gemeinschaft* conception have long voted the other way – some with guns and some with their feet.[20]

Feminist Legal Scholarship

Tay's criticisms of the new band of critical legal scholars emerging in the 1970s and 1980s extended to feminist legal scholars. Tay was perhaps the first Australian legal scholar to write an article of feminist legal scholarship:[21] a critique of the treatment of women in Russia, published in 1972.[22] However, despite this early start, Tay did not become part of the feminist legal movement that grew in momentum over the next two decades. Her position on feminism in law was consistent with her strong commitment to liberalism exhibited in her other work: she believed in equality within the liberal paradigm. Tay was not a feminist legal theorist and was highly critical of the radical feminist theory on which several of the most well-known theories were based. She judged this work in the same way that she judged other aspects of critical legal scholarship: it posed a threat to the *Gesellschaft* conception of law; it was largely emotive; and it had disturbing Marxist characteristics. In one piece she outlined some of her central objections.

> The problems of women as women can be the subject of interesting intellectual investigation. Some of the nonsense taught in this area, both by detractors of women and by women's study courses, like some of the nonsense taught in nationalist ideology, in military academies or so-called peace research, cries out for philosophical examination. But this does not provide a basis, in my view, for women gathering together as women to talk some special form of 'female' philosophy or 'female' culture. There is, I believe, no such thing as a 'female' philosophy – analogous, say, to Christian philosophy except for the fact that it does not invite male converts. … We require, on the contrary, a sense of historical development, of interrelation and interaction, a readiness to shuffle

[19] A Tay, 'Legal Education, Legal Research and Legal Reform in Poland' (1980) 54 *Australian Law Journal* 142, 142.

[20] Tay (n 10) 34.

[21] S Bartie, 'Studying Women Legal Scholars: The Challenges of Life History' (2018) 25 *International Journal of the Legal Profession* 279.

[22] A Tay, 'The Status of Women in the Soviet Union' (1972) 20 *American Journal of Comparative Law* 662.

> backward and forward between principles and consequences, a sense of traditions as being the stuff of which social arrangements and beliefs are constituted, and a recognition that people have not one need or character but many.[23]

Several of Tay's criticisms were aligned with those made by feminist legal scholars themselves.[24] However, her early negative impressions of the genre appear to have closed her off from subsequent work. In the ensuing decades, she did not revisit or qualify her views on feminist legal theory in light of new work and ideas, and it seems unlikely that she read much of the literature.[25] Tay had made up her mind that these new scholars took a wrongheaded and overly Western critique of law that did not fit with her worldview or intellectual commitments. Their positions and arguments would only harm the characteristics of law that she held most dear.

Conservative or Liberal?

Tay and Kamenka's forthright – and sometimes very personal[26] – criticisms served to alienate them from parts of the legal academy.[27] In one very scathing article, Tay went so far as to say that the strength of Australian law schools came from the fact that students were required to read the judgments of great Australian judges, and that the 'legal mind in Australia is better outside the law schools than within them'.[28] She also believed that her education in the Inns of Court in England brought advantages that she could not have received at an Australian law school. Moreover, she felt that law schools in Australia ought to not only serve society, but also transform it.[29]

These aspects of Tay and Kamenka's scholarship – along with Tay's talk of being an 'old-fashioned scholar'[30] – also earned them reputations as conservatives. Most of those interviewed for this project agreed that Tay had conservative inclinations.[31] Some disputed the idea that this went beyond her scholarship to

[23] A Tay, 'Women, Culture and the Quality of Life' in L Sandell and EE Schmidt (eds), *Women of the Year – A Collection of Speeches by Australia's Most Successful Women* (Boorowa, NSW, The Watermark Press, 1987) 25.

[24] Bartie (n 21) 18–19.

[25] This point is also made in ibid 18–19.

[26] See, in particular, A Tay, 'Aimless Perspectives – A Comment on Chapter One of the CTEC "Discipline Assessment" of the Australian Law Schools' (1987) 11 *Bulletin of the Australian Society of Legal Philosophy* 154, 154.

[27] Some simply did not accept Tay and Kamenka's central thesis that there was a crisis in legal ideals: see D Nelken, 'Is There a Crisis in Law and Legal Ideology?' (1982) 9 *Journal of Law and Society* 177.

[28] Tay (n 26) 155.

[29] ibid 156.

[30] See Leech (n 1).

[31] Interview with Roger Wilkins AO, (Attorney-General's Department, Canberra, 19 August 2014); interview with Wojciech Sadurski (Law School, University of Sydney, 31 July 2014); interview with Klaus Ziegert (Law School, University of Sydney, 5 February 2014).

Australian politics. One former student had given the matter some thought and had questioned Tay on her position.

> Alice Tay was highly respected by Labor and was in a good relationship with the Hawke and Keating governments. She chaired the Prime Minister's committee on science under the Hawke/Keating government. … That is a question I directly asked her, whether she was into the Labor or Liberal government. She said 'No, to the contrary, I don't like either of the bastards but they both appoint me which is fine with me but I'm not on either side'.[32]

At her dinner and cocktail parties she would bring together lawyers and scholars from both sides of Australian politics.

Significantly, once he had got to know Tay and Kamenka and their work a little better, Michael Kirby revised his initial impression of the pair, formed when they had examined his thesis.

> I think they thought I was a bit of a lefty and I thought they were a bit right-wing. But the truth probably is that we were all fairly conservative in fundamentals. We were quite self-satisfied with the overall structure of our democratic parliamentary system with its independent courts and uncorrupted judges and therefore there wasn't a great deal of difference between us and, as Alice and I got to know each other better in the years after our respective appointments in 1975,[33] our relationship warmed and my original suspicion of them both as anti-communist ideologues was meted by an appreciation that they were simply contributing on the left-right spectrum a perspective that came from their own background, which was entirely legitimate and useful. Including useful to me.[34]

Being labelled a 'conservative' in a law school can mean a number of different things. In some ways, given the often-static nature of the fundamentals of a law school curriculum, it can be argued that many legal academics possess conservative inclinations. Tay was not a member of the law and economics movement, which in the United States is often associated with conservatism in light of its opposition to state intervention in markets.[35] While the *Gesellschaft* type suggested a commitment to the free market, Tay did not concentrate on this characteristic. As Steven M Teles notes in his critical history of the law and economics movements, several leaders of this movement are 'quite liberal and motivated primarily by a

[32] Interview with Participant A (11 June 2014). Sadurski speculated: 'I don't think that they could have had a great sense of sympathy for Liberals because of this Liberal snobbishness type of born to rule and here you had two relative outsiders, a Russian Jew who established himself in Australia and a Chinese woman. They didn't fit the old boy network of the Liberal party, especially of that time'. Sadurski (n 31).

[33] Kirby was appointed Deputy President of the Australian Conciliation and Arbitration Commission and a member (later Chairman) of the Law Reform Commission at around the same time Tay was appointed Professor of Jurisprudence. Interview with Michael Kirby (by telephone, 14 March 2015).

[34] ibid; M Kirby, '*Festschrift* for Professor Alice Erh-Soon Tay – The Future of Human Rights – Does it Have One?', www.michaelkirby.com.au.

[35] SM Teles, *The Battle for Control of the Law* (Princeton University Press, 2008) 90.

desire to make law an empirical discipline, rather than an instrument of conservative libertarian ideology'.[36] Tay was, similarly, a liberal who wanted to make a case for the *Gesellschaft* by drawing from broader studies of society. This case did not extend to condemning the dynamic judging practices of the Mason High Court and, as explained earlier, her position on judging largely matched that of Julius Stone. She was conservative by comparison with the radical and critical legal scholars who emerged in the 1970s and 1980s. And her views on the importance of great thinkers from prior ages, and commitment to bringing well-known and highly accomplished scholars to the Department, speak of elitism. Some might construe her arguments for the *Gesellschaft* as bordering on propaganda, and in this sense a conservative strain can be detected. However, her opposition to the neo-liberal currents sweeping universities gives further force to the idea that the conservative label is either misplaced or should be tempered. Her arguments and oppositions were based on a strong liberal foundation that was a product of her history, background and intellectual mentors.

Limiting Tay's Legacy

Tay's frank and divisive criticisms demonstrated that, given autonomy and independence, academics could act as critic and conscience to the legal academy. She could speak freely because she did not seek approval from the broader legal academy, and her promotion within the academy did not depend on it. Rather than placate, compromise or negotiate, Tay's preferred course was to fight for academic ideals and call to account those who failed to live up to her standards. If colleagues were not working hard enough or sought easy acclaim, she wanted to make them feel uncomfortable. In many ways, this noble and courageous objective points to Tay's strong moral constitution and furthers the case for the existence of a department like hers.

On the other hand, Tay's criticisms at times spoke of her own poor judgment and intemperate nature. Unlike Brett, her frank criticisms sometimes moved beyond the professional and academic and became deeply personal and insulting. In both print and in everyday life she was known to be 'capable of a very cutting turn of phrase and a personal attack'.[37] Tay acknowledged that her frank criticisms of colleagues were likely to offend.[38] She would no doubt argue that she was entitled to form opinions and express them forcefully. For Tay, this was a personal matter – a true academic lives and breathes their vocation. However, her direct personal criticism of named individuals (in particular) spoke of a lack

[36] ibid.

[37] Interview with Hamish Redd (by telephone, 5 August 2014). Others made similar comments: Sadurski (n 31); Ziegert (n 31).

[38] Leech (n 1) 6.

of balance and made her arguments much easier to dismiss. It also prompts the question whether her own scholarship attained the high standards she expected of others.

For those who believe Australian law schools needs more critical historical studies of the role of law in society, Tay's limited legacy and failure to encourage more Australian sociological studies of law seems regrettable. It represents a missed opportunity to widen the way in which the law is taught and studied. Today, most Australian jurisprudence textbooks emphasise the analytical tradition, with some chapters devoted to critical legal schools, especially feminist legal studies (a field again on the rise) and critical race theories. History and context do not feature very much at all in these textbooks, nor do aspects of the law and society movement or the sociological tradition. History is largely marginalised in the curriculum (and faculty) of most Australian law schools.[39] American Legal Realism is often described in ways that emphasise its shortfalls as an explanation of legal reasoning, viewed through an analytical lens. While both Tay and Stone contributed to the Australian Society of Legal Philosophy, their efforts did not lead many Australian legal theorists to abandon their preference for analytical jurisprudence, nurtured first through their undergraduate studies in philosophy. Tay was not wholly opposed to analytical philosophy – her department offered students the option to take analytical jurisprudence which was taught by part-time practitioners/academics with expertise in the field – but she believed that broader contextual historical studies provided greater insights into the role and function of law.

Conclusion – Alice Erh-Soon Tay

Tay's contributions and career provide another insight into what it meant to be a liberal legal scholar in Australia during the second half of the twentieth century. Brett and Tay's shared faith in the Western legal system encouraged them to contribute constructively to society by applying their legal expertise to achieve the goals of any liberal legal system. They shared a strong sense of confidence and self-belief, buoyed by their liberal commitments, courageously occupying a number of significant roles that drew criticism and controversy. When Tay stepped out of the classroom and into bureaucracy, as Human Rights and Equal Opportunities Commissioner, she was well equipped to criticise and take action against the government, while also drawing on her networks and political connections to apply pressure through the back door. She instigated a number of court

[39] See M Kirby 'Is Legal History Now Ancient History?' (2009) 83 ALJ 31; H Lücke, 'Legal History in Australia: The Development of Australian Legal/Historical Scholarship' (2010) 34 *Australian Bar Review* 109.

proceedings, most notably the court interventions against the Howard government following the MV *Tampa* affair. In this highly politicised and publicised saga, which shaped the next decade of Australian politics, the Commission supported the argument, among others, that by refusing to allow a ship carrying over 400 refugees rescued from a sinking boat to dock within Australian waters, the government had arbitrarily detained and breached the rights of the refugees. Similarly, Tay's delegation and foreign teaching work within CAPLAS drew heavily on her liberal convictions and faith in the rule of law.

The departments led by Stone and Tay both made distinctive and innovative contributions to the legal academy. Their existence ensured that, in contrast to several other Australian law schools, jurisprudence remained part of the law curriculum at Sydney. It brought scholars from diverse backgrounds, committed to interdisciplinary study, into the Australian legal academy. It made a case for the importance of faculties and schools to be led largely by academic values, and set an example of how this could best be done. It created a working environment where legal theorists flourished and developed considerable international reputations. Tay's decision to continue the Department therefore brought considerable benefits. Acknowledging the richness of Tay's Department does not, however, lead to the conclusion that those who opposed it, or advocated for its closure, were narrow-minded or wrong.

I have, of course, thought about what Tay would make of this aspect of my book – finding merit in the arguments of those who both opposed and defended the Department. Were she alive to read this, she might say that I have tried to reconcile the irreconcilable; that I am attempting to please everyone and smoothing over the cracks. That is something I might simply have to accept and leave for others to judge. Throughout this study, I have been mindful that biographers often develop a strong bias towards their subjects. Therefore, I have sought to develop the richest and most informed view of Tay based on a thorough review of all the evidence available to me. This included interviewing a range of Tay's associates, who expressed a variety of opinions about her and the Department, and who had interacted with her in different ways. Not all people falling within this category were willing to be interviewed. Nonetheless, balance was achieved in other ways. The interviews revealed that many of Tay's closest colleagues and friends were well acquainted with her shortcomings, and several had argued with her at one time or another. The interviews conducted for this study also revealed that even members of the Department could see merit in some of their adversaries' arguments.

The Faculty of Law (now named Sydney Law School) at the University of Sydney continues, of course. It attracts more student applications than there are places and is one of Australia's most highly regarded law schools. Now that it has moved onto the University's campus and is housed in an iconic architectural structure, it has no doubt become even more appealing to academics. It includes a small group of jurisprudential scholars with strong reputations (including Sadurski, who at the time of writing holds the Chair of Jurisprudence), who identify themselves as primarily jurisprudes. The Julius Stone Institute, created at the instigation of Jeremy Webber in 1998 to help with the task of maintaining and mainstreaming a strong jurisprudential presence at Sydney,[40] provides another forum in which Sydney scholars can advance this area of study. By providing other outlets for jurisprudence and involving a larger number of people from across the faculty in the teaching of theory-based subjects, these features perhaps cast doubt on Tay's arguments and motivations and the wisdom of her initiatives, at least into the 1990s.

The closing of the Department therefore should not be used by those in favour or against legal theoretical inquiry as a sign of its marginalised place or reduced importance within the Australian academy. Nor does it support a case for the simple dichotomy between theory and practice. Members of the profession were some of the strongest proponents of the Department, and Tay believed that legal academics should engage more, rather than less, with the profession. The simple academic versus practitioner binary, which has become such a common element in assessments of Australian legal education and the discipline, simply does not make sense in this context. I would go further and suggest that it does not make sense more generally: we need better, more nuanced explanations and analysis to understand the history, ideas and values that have made the discipline of law in Australia. The importance of Tay's leadership of the Department, and its closure, instead rests with the questions it raises about the way Australian universities are currently run – promoting competition rather than collegiality, prioritising short-term financial gain and rankings over scholarly values. Tay's advocacy and leadership made a strong case for the immorality of such governance.

[40] Interview with Jeremy Webber (by telephone, 22 October 2014).

PART C

Geoffrey Sawer

12

Politics, Law and Society

Introduction

Geoffrey Sawer is the father of modern Australian constitutional law teaching and scholarship. In the second half of the twentieth century, he pioneered a distinct brand of constitutionalism,[1] and advanced significant bodies of scholarship that provided strong foundations for studies in Australian public law and politics. Of particular relevance to this project is what Sawer did to move both the discipline and the legal profession, incrementally, away from the idea of law as an autonomous entity and towards the social sciences – a task he undertook as a full-time legal scholar in a research school, rather than a law school. It is important to recognise that, although he did not draw attention to the fact, Sawer was as much a legal theorist as a constitutional lawyer.[2] The grouping of Sawer with Peter Brett and Alice Erh-Soon Tay can be supported purely on this basis alone. However, there are other attributes that these three scholars have in common. All three professors advanced ambitious scholarly agendas that responded to their legal, political and academic environments, and to what they believed was required to strengthen the discipline of law.

Over the course of Sawer's career, both the discipline of law and Australian society changed dramatically. Sawer studied and practised law during the Depression; began his academic career as the Second World War raged; commenced as the first Professor of Law at the newly created Research School of Social Sciences (RSSS) at the Australian National University (ANU) on the eve of the creation of a full-time Australian legal academy; built an international reputation within the School while the social sciences grew; and retired during the ferment caused by the Critical Legal Studies movement of the 1970s. He accepted his first academic

[1] Former Chief Justice of the High Court of Australia, Sir Anthony Mason, described Sawer as a 'constitutionalist': see A Mason, 'Geoffrey Sawer: The Priceless Professor', *Canberra Times* 21 December 1990, 7; interview with Sir Anthony Mason (Sir Anthony Mason's Chambers, Sydney, 9 December 2014).

[2] When Sawer died in August 1996, several obituaries referred to his sociological approach, but did not describe Sawer as a legal theorist. See 'Obituaries: Geoffrey Sawer 1910–1996', *Sydney Morning Herald* 12 August 1996, 34; N Stephen, 'Constitutional Lawyer and Gardener', *Canberra Times* 10 August 1996; J Nethercote, 'Lawyer Offered an Authoritative Insight into Federalism', *Australian* 12 August 1996, 13; Z Cowen, 'Academic Shaped Legal Scholarship', *Australian* 12 August 1996, 13; R Else-Mitchell, 'Scholar's Life on Public Record', *Age* 30 August 1996, B2.

appointment at the University of Melbourne in 1940,[3] when constitutional law had not yet become an organised body of law and ended his tenure shortly after the dramatic political and constitutional events of 1975, when Australia's Governor-General, Sir John Kerr, dismissed the Prime Minister, Gough Whitlam.[4] While Sawer spent many sabbaticals overseas, he did not hold the usual Oxbridge qualifications of an Australian legal academic: his formal studies had taken place at the University of Melbourne.[5] Sawer drew his ideas and inspiration largely from the Australian environment and, as with Tay, part of his agenda included bringing Australian law and legal scholarship to the attention of the rest of the world.

In the twenty-first century, the notion of a full-time legal scholar, working in a research institution for social scientists, studying law in context, is largely (although not entirely) unexceptional. However, both at the time of his appointment and throughout his career, Sawer's position and ideas about law were controversial. As one reviewer remarked, Sawer's work was 'distinctly provocative constitutional writing' that was 'addressed … to open-minded professionals'.[6] At the beginning of his career, some members of Australia's legal profession interpreted Sir Owen Dixon's concept of complete and strict legalism to mean that politics had no place in law and that law's integrity – at least in the judicial sphere – rested on its autonomy.[7] Further, there was no obvious or natural connection

[3] G Sawer to the Registrar of the University of Melbourne, 20 February 1940, GW Paton Legal Education 1932–1945, University of Melbourne Archives; G Sawer, 'Outline Biography', Geoffrey Sawer Papers, National Library of Australia, Manuscript Collection, 6.

[4] He retired in December 1975, a month after the dismissal. At Kerr's invitation, Sawer had run two small confidential advisory tutorials with the Governor-General and members of ANU staff on the question of the Governor-General's powers. Realising the potential imminent real-life consequence of the matters discussed, Sawer put an end to the tutorials: J Hocking, *Gough Whitlam – His Time*, vol 2 (Melbourne, Miegunyah Press, 2012) 304–05. See also Sawer to Sir John Kerr, 16 May 1975, and a string of correspondence around this time, Geoffrey Sawer Papers, National Library of Australia, Manuscript Collection. See also G Sawer, 'The Governor-General of the Commonwealth of Australia' (1976) 52 *Current Affairs Bulletin* 20; G Sawer, 'The Whitlam Revolution in Australian Federalism – Promise Possibilities and Performance' (1976) 10 *Melbourne University Law Review* 315; G Sawer, 'Towards a New Federal Structure?' in G Evans (ed), *Labor and the Constitution 1972–75* (Richmond, Victoria, Heinemann, 1977) 1; G Sawer, *Federation under Strain: Australia 1972–75* (Melbourne, Melbourne University Press, 1977).

[5] Sawer graduated from the Law School of the University of Melbourne in 1933 with an LLB, and then in 1934, due to his strong honours performance, was awarded an LLM. He also obtained an Arts Degree while a full-time academic at Melbourne. His full-time teachers of law at Melbourne, George Paton and Kenneth Bailey, both held degrees from the University of Oxford. See Sawer, 'Outline Biography' (n 3); J Waugh, *First Principles – The Melbourne Law School 1857–2007* (Melbourne, Miegunyah Press, 2007) 125–26.

[6] LF Crisp, 'Book Review: Geoffrey Sawer, *Modern Federalism*' (1969) 3 *Federal Law Review* 305.

[7] A leading Australian constitutional law scholar and friend of Sawer's, Geoffrey Lindell, spoke of the various interpretations that have been made of Sir Owen Dixon's complete and strict legalism. He explained that there are 'the narrow Dixons', who 'saw in him high legal techniques' where judges 'avoid reliance on values, policies and societal aims', and the 'wider Dixons', like Sir Anthony Mason, who 'interpreted Dixon as advocating a "more dynamic approach"': interview with Geoffrey Lindell (Woodbridge Community Centre, Tasmania, 23 March 2015).

between good lawyering and university legal studies. Plenty of good lawyers and judges had not studied law at university. Proposals to expand the size of law schools and employ more full-time staff had been met with resistance in some quarters. In the early 1950s, all Australian law schools were small, although student numbers were growing. Given that the concept of university legal education remained controversial – and the fact that many lawyers did not believe that the quality of legal practice was improved by university legal education or scholarship, especially that which ventured beyond law – the existence of a research-only Department of Law (the Department) situated in the RSSS was a strange proposition.[8]

Fittingly, given his field of study, Sawer's elevation to the Chair of Law at the RSSS meant that his career took on a political quality. Sawer's task was not merely to pursue scholarship that had recourse to the social sciences, but also to demonstrate that it was both valuable and desirable to have a legal academic within a social science research school. This prompted Sawer both to develop a theoretical position on the role of law and legal academics, and to engage in exercises of public relations to help the community understand the role of the Department. While he did not entirely succeed in his aim of convincing others of the special nature of the Department, he did provide an important Australian account of law's role within the social sciences and within society, which is relevant to both the intellectual underpinnings of the discipline of law and, more generally, the trajectory of law within Australia.

University Life and Politics

Reviewing the archival material that relates to Sawer's early life and career alongside his later large body of scholarship, signs of a natural progression can be detected. The attitudes he later adopted to jurisprudential schools and theories, the relationship between law and society, and how the two ought to be studied, can be traced to some of his more significant formative influences. In this section, I explain these important aspects of Sawer's early life.

Throughout Sawer's childhood and adolescence, there were clear indications that he was a person of obvious intellectual ability. Sawer described himself as always being a 'swot' at school, noting that he preferred reading to sporting and social clubs.[9] While still at school, he spent a large amount of time at the library,

[8] Even Sawer 'doubted whether a university properly so called could be established on the basis of pure research', and 'could not see a viable undergraduate institution being established in the remote bush village of Canberra'. He suggested that the government instead build up a 'series of postgraduate research institutions closely linked with existing universities in the six state capitals'. Sawer, 'Outline Biography' (n 3).

[9] M Pratt, Interview with Geoffrey Sawer (Oral History Interview, Canberra, 16 November 1971) https://nla.gov.au/nla.obj-214869908/listen.

reading and noting the leading books in history and economics as well as philosophy. He generally took up the suggestions of his teachers but sometimes strayed into more controversial territory, reading George Bernard Shaw, Henry Louis Mencken and Karl Marx. He considered that it was his hard work rather than any 'genius' qualities that accounted for his strong academic performance.[10] The extent of his achievements suggests that Sawer's self-analysis is, at least in part, a product of his modesty.[11] In 1928, he graduated from Scotch College, an exclusive private secondary school in Melbourne, as equal dux;[12] in 1933, he graduated from university with first class honours in law and won the Supreme Court and Nunn Prizes.[13] While he had a strong aptitude for undergraduate legal studies, Sawer's greatest interest at university was politics.[14] The scholarship he won to attend university prevented him from completing his preferred degree in Arts,[15] thereby depriving him of the opportunity of gaining a broader liberal education.[16] He made up for this deficiency in other ways. Through his membership of student political bodies and the Historical Society, and by attending lectures on contemporary political issues, he became well acquainted with a wide array of political issues and processes.[17] He devoted his greatest efforts to the university's Labor Club and, along with the woman who later became his wife, engaged in various activities including editing and writing for its magazine, *Proletariat*.[18] Sawer began his university studies on the eve of the Depression.[19] Amid growing poverty and unemployment, the interest of many intellectuals in Australia turned to Marxism and the USSR. Members of left-wing political groups were confronted with the question of whether they ought to subscribe to Marxist philosophies. As Sawer explained:

> The University Labor Club suddenly became the focus of intense and continuous debate and social activity. This was partly because of the social and political drama of the

[10] Pratt (n 9).

[11] Lindell (n 7); N Stephen, 'A Recollection of Geoffrey Sawer' (1980) 11 *Federal Law Review* 261, 261; N Stephen, 'War Crimes Trials and the Future' (Speech delivered at the Inaugural Geoffrey Sawer Lecture, Centre for International and Public Law, The Australian National University, 21 May 1998).

[12] Sawer, 'Outline Biography' (n 3) 2.

[13] ibid; Waugh (n 5) 25.

[14] Sawer (n 10) part 15, 1.

[15] As Michael Coper explains, Sawer's guardian, Rose Bowman, successfully applied on Sawer's behalf for a McCaughey Scholarship. The terms of the trust limited recipients to studies of a 'technical' nature. Sawer was summoned before the trustees during his first year of his Arts degree and told that he would need to reconsider his studies: M Coper, 'Geoffrey Sawer and the Art of Academic Commentator: A Preliminary Biographical Sketch' (2014) 42 *Federal Law Review* 389, 393–94. Sawer was able to count his first-year arts subjects towards his law degree. He went back and completed his Arts degree in 1947 as he felt 'insufficiently acquainted with culture and things of that sort': Pratt (n 9).

[16] Sawer (n 10) part 14, 3.

[17] ibid part 15.

[18] Sawer, 'Outline Biography' (n 3) 3; Sawer (n 10), part 15, 3; Pratt (n 9).

[19] Sawer, 'Outline Biography' (n 3) 2. Sawer believed that there were signs of difficulty as early as 1927 – a year before he began his university studies – even though officially the Depression is said to have begun in Australia in the 1930s: Pratt (n 9).

> Great Depression and the accompanying unemployment, anger and despair, and partly because a link was created between the Labor Club, its members and University activities, and two communist-created and maintained centres in the city – the Workers' Art Club and the Friends of the Soviet Union.[20]

Initially, Sawer took an interest in Marxism and attended lectures on the topic by the Marxist scholar Guido Baracchi.[21] However, as he learnt more about Marxism and was exposed to the radical elements of the Labor Club, he became disenchanted with both; he decided to join the social democratic wing of the Labor Club.[22] While Sawer found Baracchi 'a charming man and delightful companion',[23] he also considered him a dull lecturer,[24] and came to believe that Marxism was more in the nature of religious dogma than a philosophical movement.[25] He considered that the radical intellectuals who pursued a Marxist agenda showed little regard or understanding for the underprivileged sections of society whom they believed they represented.[26] Reflecting on his experiences at university, Sawer described his attitude towards Marxism as follows:

> So far as I could see, Marxism was the creation of middle-class intellectuals – Marx, Engels, Lenin, Stalin, Trotsky and later Mao Tse Tung, Castro and Che Guevera; no sociology or plan of social action could be valid which did not at least admit a leading role for the intelligentsia as well as the proletariat.[27]
>
> …
>
> My private conclusion is this: No one has a right to express opinions on the conduct and opinions of revolutionary parties until he has 1. lived like a worker for some time, 2. taken part in at least one big strike, 3. taken part in some anti-eviction riots. I don't, of course, attribute any mystical significance to such activities. It is simply a matter of common sense – these are typical activities of the worker, and he who would advise the worker, while he must have a first-class education, must also be in the struggle.[28]

Sawer's own turbulent and humble beginnings provide some explanation of why he believed that his contemporaries, along with the founding Marxist thinkers, did not fully understand or relate to the plight of the proletariat. While Sawer's adult life was one of privilege, it was obtained not by virtue of family wealth (of which there was little[29]) but thanks to the scholarships for war orphans he had received to study at Scotch College and then the University of Melbourne. Sawer

[20] Sawer (n 10) part 15, 1.
[21] Sawer, 'Outline Biography' (n 3) 3.
[22] Pratt (n 9).
[23] Sawer (n 10) part 15, 9.
[24] ibid. Sawer wrote that Baracchi 'tried to teach me Marxism and gave me a distaste for it'. Sawer, 'Outline Biography' (n 3) 4.
[25] Sawer (n 10) part 15, 1.
[26] ibid part 15, 9.
[27] ibid.
[28] ibid part 15, 5–6, quoting a letter from Sawer to Professor John Anderson.
[29] Sawer said that when his father and mother died he did not inherit anything: Pratt (n 9).

was born in Burma in 1910 and his family moved to Adelaide in 1914, 'to assist with the "Kitchener scheme" for setting up the Australian system of compulsory military training'.[30] The family was told that the change of climate would improve Sawer's poor health.[31] While his health did subsequently improve, he nonetheless suffered several tragedies in his early life. His father, Edgar Sawer, had been born into a family business of wool broking. He did not, however, succeed in advancing the business, and he cut his losses and enlisted in the Army.[32] He married Sawer's mother, Edith (Peg) Langman, who at the time was a nursery governess. Sawer learnt little else about his mother's background.[33] Edgar Sawer became a decorated soldier, but died in 1917 when Sawer was just seven years old,[34] leaving Sawer's then pregnant mother as a sole parent.[35] Sawer's brother, Derek, was born shortly after. Following his father's death, Sawer's family was supported by various pensions for spouses of war veterans, which she supplemented through a range of enterprises that brought in modest additional amounts.[36] On a happier note, the circumstances of his father's death also brought unexpected support from a new entourage of adults.

Sawer's father spent his final days in hospital in Melbourne,[37] and in order to visit him, Sawer and his mother stayed at a nearby boarding house.[38] At this house they met a group of kindly women who went on to play a crucial role in Sawer's upbringing.[39] The women, whom Sawer referred to as his 'aunts' or members of his 'ongoing committee of management',[40] convinced the young family to move from Adelaide to Melbourne so that they could ease the burden his mother now faced of raising two children on her own.[41] They became part of Sawer's family and in 1924, when Sawer's mother died from cancer, one of the 'aunts', Rose Bowman, took Sawer and his brother, Derek, into her care.[42] Sawer spent his childhood surrounded largely by women, and seemed to both enjoy and prefer their company to that of other children and the men in his life.[43] Bowman was the daughter of French Huguenot migrants and was married to a house painter.[44]

[30] Sawer, 'Outline Biography' (n 3) 1.
[31] ibid.
[32] ibid 1.
[33] ibid 1; Sawer (n 10) part 1, 1.
[34] Sawer's father adopted the assumed name of Edgar Geoffrey Wayne when he enlisted in the army: ibid 1–2. Coper details Sawer's father's military service and the circumstances that led to his death: Coper (n 16).
[35] Sawer (n 10) part 5, 2.
[36] ibid part 8, 1.
[37] ibid part 5, 1.
[38] ibid.
[39] ibid part 5, 1–2.
[40] ibid part 5, 1.
[41] ibid part 5, 1–2.
[42] Sawer, 'Outline Biography' (n 3) 2.
[43] Sawer (n 10) part 9, 3.
[44] ibid, part 5, 1; Pratt (n 9).

Her brother, Fritz, ran a vegetable shop in a 'working class area'.[45] Sawer spent many weekends helping out in the shop and enjoyed Fritz's company.[46] Although Sawer attended a private secondary school, by then he had already 'picked up a Victorian state-school lingo'.[47] It is perhaps this absence of elitism and privilege in his early life that later fuelled his scepticism about the motives and theories of Marxist intellectuals.

According to Sawer, this 'disenchantment with Marxism' as well as his exit from student politics were driven largely by actions taken by his radical colleagues in the Labor Club.[48] When Sawer was editor of the *Proletariat*, the Professor of Philosophy at the University of Sydney, John Anderson (also Eugene Kamenka's mentor), submitted an article that contained criticisms of the Communist Party and some Australian party members.[49] Anderson was a member of the party and had previously written two significant articles about communism that had been published in previous editions of the *Proletariat*.[50] Anderson had addressed his latest submission to Sawer 'as Editor, but … it was intercepted by [a Communist Party member] Silver, and by him returned to Anderson on the specious ground that it was too late to be included'.[51] While Sawer himself had significant intellectual concerns about aspects of the article, he was dismayed by this act of intellectual sabotage and believed that the incident illustrated some of the general dishonesty of his communist colleagues.[52]

The incident is interesting not only for what it tells us about Sawer's motivations and ethics, but also his disposition and ideas. The letters exchanged between Sawer (as editor) and Anderson provide clear evidence that Sawer had thought carefully and read broadly on the subject of Marxism and formed some firm views on the subject. While Sawer said that, when he returned to his letters decades later, he was 'appalled at their bumptiousness' and said that he 'still regretted … accusing Anderson of lying',[53] they nonetheless also speak of the young Sawer's intellectual confidence and the intensity with which he approached student politics. To provide a better sense of Sawer's character and convictions, it is worth quoting a few of the passages from his letters to Anderson at length. In the first letter, he criticises members of the Communist Party, and part of Anderson's thesis, in very strong and personal terms:

> I think your remark about 'bourgeois eugenics' is puerile. It is an unfortunate but undoubted truth that the troubles of revolutionary parties and individuals are frequently psychological; I have met several strong 'individualistic' revolutionaries who object

[45] Sawer (n 10).
[46] ibid.
[47] ibid part 3, 2.
[48] ibid part 15, 4.
[49] Sawer (n 10) part 15, 4.
[50] ibid.
[51] ibid.
[52] ibid.
[53] ibid.

> strongly to Communist Theories of Art and Communist disciplines generally, and who were obvious victims of incipient paranoia – persecution complex and all complete. Also, I question your ability to criticise the labour theory of value. Alice Stewart, B Com, a brilliant economics graduate of this University, approves of it – indeed, she says that Taylor's classic bourgeois textbook practically proves it.[54]

In a second letter, he made a serious accusation against Anderson and complained about the methods and motives of the Communist Party:

> I must congratulate you again on your able pamphlet on the Communist Party. It is a pity that in the introduction to the pamphlet you had to *tell lies* and make *significant omissions*.[55]
>
> It is a source of considerable pain to me that this business should have occurred. A philosophic critic with a respect for accuracy and a contempt for the dialectic methods of Ignatius Loyola is badly needed by revolutionary parties today. I had regarded you as a prophet in this respect, though the preface to your pamphlet gives me doubts. The difficulty is, will they listen to you unless you are in the party? Yet it does seem disturbing that the only revolutionary party not shot through with corruption seems to have a *complete disbelief in the existence of objective fact*. This curious coincidence between the political thought of Communism and the Roman Church is stressed in Thomas Mann's curious book, *Magic Mountain*.[56]

It is startling that a 22-year-old should feel so well equipped to criticise a professor of philosophy in such strong terms. The correspondence provides clear evidence that Sawer had thought seriously about Marxism. It is also significant in that it points to where his later studies of law in context would begin. While Sawer did not subscribe to the views of the radicals, he was interested in the issues that their activism raised and he remained a progressive. His upbringing and leftist inclinations suggest that he, too, was concerned with ways to liberate the proletariat and bring about equality. Much later in life he said that he thought 'that unbridled capitalism is worse than muddling along social democracy' and explained that he 'voted Labor in every succeeding state election, except one' where there was no Labor candidate.[57]

This interchange and the influence of Marxism on Sawer's career are critical to any understanding of his subsequent studies. It demonstrates that early in his life Sawer became disillusioned with radicalism and with theories that attempted to provide a complete explanation of social phenomena. It also demonstrates that he developed an early interest in the relationship between politics and society and how the two ought to be studied. As explained later in this part, these matters became some of the central pillars of Sawer's career and shaped his major contributions to the disciplines of law and politics.

[54] ibid part 15, 5–6, quoting a letter from Sawer to Professor John Anderson.
[55] ibid part 15, 8, quoting a letter from Sawer to Professor John Anderson, dated 29 December 1932.
[56] ibid part 15, 8 (emphasis added).
[57] ibid part 15, 10.

At the University of Melbourne, Sawer was surrounded by men (and they were virtually all men) destined to become leaders in Australian law and politics. In various ways they formed an important elite network, bringing significant opportunities that facilitated Sawer's subsequent strong scholarly career. Sawer liked people and made friends easily. At the same time, people of prominence drew upon and respected his intelligence.[58] When Sawer graduated in 1933, Australia remained in the grip of the Depression. So, while he became first a solicitor and then a barrister,[59] he also pursued various activities beyond the practice of law to increase his earnings. These activities helped him add more names to his already broad net of associates. For example, he made friends through the tutoring work that he provided to articled clerks – men wanting to gain professional qualifications in law but without the means to pursue university education – to assist them to pass the Supreme Court examination.[60] Sawer also taught workers' education courses in Ballarat to various professional men,[61] and in the mid-1930s joined the Melbourne branch of the Round Table, an organisation initially established to strengthen colonial ties with Britain but which, during Sawer's time, simply attempted to preserve 'some special friendship among the countries which had been deeply influenced by British institutions, politics and culture'.[62] This helped Sawer get to know various eminent figures, including one of Australia's first constitutional law scholars, Sir Robert Garran, and the future Vice-Chancellor of ANU, Sir Douglas Copland.[63]

While Sawer held strong views, as illustrated by the interchange with Anderson above, he managed to cultivate friendship with men of different political persuasions and attitudes. For example, he said that he both liked and respected his father-in-law 'notwithstanding his Liberal-voting, Masonic and business connections' and said 'we differed amiably about politics'.[64] Sawer was an atheist in an age where Christianity was the norm, yet this never seemed to work against him. He was a lifelong member of the Rationalist Society from the 1930s and, while he had attended Sunday school as a child, he believed the Bible contained 'only stories, on the same level as King Alfred burning the cakes, and William the

[58] Over the course of Sawer's career, numerous politicians and scholars sought his advice. He gave advice to both the Labor and Liberal governments, to members of the Attorney-General's Department, and frequently corresponded with judges and eminent international scholars. In 1962, he was invited to travel to Nigeria to give constitutional advice to the government on whether they had the power to establish a state bank and also to assist with litigation concerning the delegation of executive powers. A political crisis erupted while Sawer was in Nigeria. Sawer provided a summary of his time in Nigeria in a letter to Oxford law professor, Rupert Cross: Sawer to Rupert Cross, 14 June 1962, Professor G Sawer Correspondence, Australian National University Archives.

[59] Sawer, 'Outline Biography' (n 3), 3. See also Sawer (n 10) part 22, 1; Pratt (n 9).

[60] ibid.

[61] Sawer (n 10) part 21, 3–4.

[62] ibid part 19, 2–3.

[63] ibid part 19, 2.

[64] ibid part 34, 1.

Conqueror starting England, and Queen Victoria and her great Generals putting down the Indian Mutiny'.[65] Nor did anyone take issue with the fact that Sawer did not serve in the Second World War. Sawer participated in the type of sexist humour typical of boys' clubs of the time and this no doubt helped him to curry favour; however, he later acknowledged how this culture served to subordinate women.[66] Perhaps due to his orphan status, it seems that he was able to easily cultivate close familiar relationships with others. When he graduated from law, Sawer became a resident tutor at Ormond, an exclusive Melbourne University college, which brought about further introductions to soon-to-be prominent men.[67] Again, this arrangement came about through Sawer's connections.[68] The following letter of recommendation written by DK Picken MA, the Master of Ormond College, in support of Sawer, is indicative of the deep affection many expressed for him:

> [Sawer] has proved himself, in his own way (and this must always be a man's 'own way') one of the best men we have ever had at our 'High Table.' He is a man of personality and character: learned, original, and – in a very real sense of the term – cultured; a man with a very fine mind, and an extraordinarily nice fellow. We have all – including the members of my own household – a very real affection for him; and I think it is in those terms that we invariably think of him.[69]

Following Sawer's death, former student Michael Coper referred to his old mentor as a model of 'courtesy and generosity.'[70] His mother and the entourage of adults had brought him up well.

Sawer had a high-pitched voice, a very casual and unassuming manner, and eschewed pretence. It is clear that, through his time at Scotch College and at university, Sawer became part of an elite Melbourne network and drew considerable benefit from all of the privileges this entailed. However, it is equally clear that he never forgot his origins and the 'ordinary people' who helped him and his family by offering friendship and support through some of their most difficult times. While confident – and perhaps even arrogant – in his youth, he was never snobbish. This no doubt added to his appeal. These qualities also helped with his journalistic activities and partly explain his later desire to communicate with broader audiences, to become a public intellectual.

A significant relationship was fostered during his university days, when Sawer was introduced at a party hosted by Guido Baracchi to a justice of the High Court of Australia, Herbert Evatt (whom Sawer called 'Bert').[71] Evatt invited

[65] ibid part 9, 1.
[66] ibid part 24, 3–4.
[67] ibid part 18, 4.
[68] ibid part 18, 4.
[69] DK Picken to Kenneth Bailey, 13 April 1940, Faculty of Law Historical and Centenary Papers, University of Melbourne Archives.
[70] Coper (n 16), 418.
[71] Sawer (n 10) part 18, 2–3.

Sawer to his chambers to converse about the matters of the day and later involved Sawer in both legal and political affairs.[72] Sawer accompanied Evatt and his wife on many outings, including visits to their adopted son, with whom Sawer also became friendly.[73] Sawer always admired Evatt and 'hero-worshipped' his judging.[74] The two became good friends, although Sawer noted that Evatt's temper led him to bully staff.[75] Sawer lost respect for Evatt following the allegations he made, as Leader of the Opposition, against the then Prime Minister, Robert Menzies, in the Petrov Affair.[76] Sawer was, of course, not alone in condemning Evatt for his actions in the affair and the consequences it had for the Australian Labor Party.

Sawer's liberal tendencies are also reflected in his choice of wife. On 6 January 1940, he married Beatrice Mabel Pitcher (Mamie), whom Sawer described as a beautiful and intelligent woman with progressive ideas.[77] By the end of their first year of marriage, Sawer noted that she had become a 'much more highly decorated scholar than her husband; he was only a Master of Laws whereas she was a Bachelor of Arts, Bachelor of Laws and a Diplomatist of Education'.[78] He knew Mamie from his time in the Labor Club as well as through the Law School, where for one semester he lectured her in constitutional law. Both were liberal in their political views and the way in which they conducted their lives. For example, Mamie held a driving licence and, like Sawer, had had several sexual partners before the pair met.[79] Sawer explained that,

> [Mamie] was of medium height, buxom, golden hair, blue eyes, fair complexion, liked any sporting activity and in particular played a good game of social tennis. She was interested in but not obsessed by the life of the mind and spirit – like myself somewhat sceptical about ideologies, though also like myself she had at first been attracted to the element of adventure and dedication among the University Communists, and the physical beauty and sexual drive of at least two of them.[80]

Sawer went so far as to suggest that what stood out from his university days was not 'teaching and the law, but revolutionary politics, music and sex – especially sex'.[81] Mamie's sexual liberation had, unfortunately, led to friction within her family: before meeting Sawer, she had undergone an abortion, which caused ongoing tension in her relationship with her mother.[82] In Sawer's unpublished

[72] ibid.
[73] ibid part 18, 2.
[74] ibid part 18, 3.
[75] ibid part 18, 4.
[76] For a book-length account of this famous Cold War spy incident, see R Manne, *The Petrov Affair* (Melbourne, Text Publishing, 2004).
[77] Sawer (n 10) part 22, 2–3, part 26, 1.
[78] ibid part 26, 3.
[79] ibid part 22, 3, part 26, 1. On the role of women motorists in the suffrage movement, see G Clarsen, *Eat My Dust: Early Women Motorists* (Baltimore, John Hopkins University Press, 2008).
[80] ibid part 22, 3.
[81] ibid part 15, 1.
[82] 'She and Mamie had never been close, because of Mamie's early love affairs and their consequences': ibid part 49, 2.

biography, he describes how his first lover, a Russian woman he had met at university, had educated him about the challenges that young women at that time faced when confronted with unplanned pregnancies. After hearing these stories, Sawer 'made modest contributions to a fund for enabling girl students to have abortions, though I had no responsibility for their condition, and after acquiring a motor car I once lent it to a student friend as transport for his girlfriend to [an] … abortionist'.[83] Sawer's progressive attitude extended to other aspects of life; for example, he came to the view, through friendships with several gay men, that a same-sex 'partnership can be just as long-lasting and faithful as heterosexual'.[84]

For Sawer, marriage brought both companionship and happiness as well as a need to seek further financial security. Mamie wished to stay home and raise their children.[85] Their son, Michael, was born on 24 January 1942; on 2 March 1946, they had a daughter, Elizabeth. While there are clear signs before joining the Law School that Sawer held academic ambitions – teaching part-time and publishing the occasional article – his decision to accept a position as a full-time senior lecturer at the University of Melbourne was partly financial: the job provided him with a secure income.[86] Probably due to his orphan status, Sawer took an interest in ensuring his financial security from an early age. His intelligence and hard work, along with the scholarships he received, largely insulated him from the impact of the Depression had that left many of his contemporaries without an income.[87] He witnessed its effects, seeing 'unemployed people trying to hawk a few pitiful wares from house to house' and 'many beggars, by day and prostitutes by night in the entries to shops and public buildings'.[88]

In 1934, Sawer took articles with Stewart and Dimelow, a practice that mainly did conveyancing; the following year, he accepted employment with Herman Coltman, a large litigation firm which acted for insurance and hire-purchase companies. He was admitted to the Victorian Bar in 1937 and received a steady flow of briefs, and even made one appearance in the High Court.[89] Sawer enjoyed practice. This is demonstrated through his willingness to conduct opinion work throughout the course of his academic life. However, he believed he lacked the 'fighting instincts which a successful Bar career required' and was put off by the job insecurity faced by most barristers.[90] Many members of the profession no doubt viewed Sawer's move into the academy as a backwards step.[91]

[83] ibid part 16, 1.
[84] ibid, part 26, 1.
[85] ibid part 26, 3.
[86] ibid part 25, 4–5.
[87] Sawer's scholarship also served as a form of insulation: ibid part 16, 4.
[88] ibid part 16, 4.
[89] Sawer, 'Outline Biography' (n 3) 3; Sawer (n 10) part 23, 1.
[90] Sawer (n 10) part 25, 5.
[91] eg, Sawer noted that Evatt was critical of his moving from practice to academia: Sawer, 'Outline Biography' (n 3) 4.

Initially by choice, and later by necessity, when she became ill, Mamie did not return to paid work, although she sometimes edited Sawer's publications.[92] At least up until Mamie suffered a stroke on 9 April 1957, which devastated Sawer,[93] he had a very happy marriage and home life. After the *Bank Nationalisation Case* in the late 1940s, Mamie accompanied him on most overseas trips, because Sawer enjoyed her company and also because he did not wish her to be burdened with looking after the children alone in his absence.[94]

Sawer's early life was therefore characterised by both privilege and good fortune of various kinds as well as tragedy. His experience made for a well-rounded, down-to-earth intellectual who had a strong drive and took responsibility for the advancement of law and politics and the betterment of society. His early forays into politics made it improbable that he would take a radical stance; they also firmed up some of his thinking on matters of politics and society as well as the ethics of the academy.

Traditional Underpinnings

A question that must be addressed in any attempt to understand Sawer's intellectual contribution is how he reconciled his strong progressive political interests with conventional common law teaching and reasoning at that time. As explained in this chapter, Sawer took on several roles and advanced scholarship within the mould of a traditional legal scholar. He respected the intellectual tradition embodied in common law reasoning and remained wedded to it throughout his career. At the same time, his learning and interests were much broader than those of a mere doctrinal scholar. In this section I detail the various ways in which Sawer's scholarship followed a conventional pattern.

As noted above, while Sawer's scholarly record in law was exemplary, at university it was student politics rather than law that engendered his excitement. Apart from the teachings of the only full-time law teachers, Professors George Paton and Kenneth Bailey, Sawer found the teachers within the Law School largely unremarkable.[95] He said that he 'could have passed exams without attending lectures'.[96] The bulk of the law curriculum was taught by full-time legal practitioners employed by the School on a part-time basis, so that most of Sawer's instruction in law consisted of doctrinal exposition and case analysis. Paton and Bailey taught the jurisprudential and public law subjects. This perhaps points to

[92] See, eg, acknowledgement in G Sawer, *Australian Federal Politics and Law 1929–49* (Melbourne, Melbourne University Press, 1963); G Sawer, *Cases on the Constitution of the Commonwealth of Australia* (Sydney, Law Book Company, 1948).

[93] This is explained further in chapter fourteen.

[94] Sawer (n 10) part 37, 2.

[95] ibid, part 15, 1; Pratt (n 9).

[96] Sawer (n 10).

the reason Sawer later associated full-time legal academics with these fields and the reason they became the mainstay of his career. He said that Bailey and Paton had given him 'respect for the intellectual discipline of the law combined with a good deal of scepticism about older professional intellectual habits and [the] impulse to reform both procedure and content of the law'.[97] Sawer also said that he had learnt from Bailey the 'meaning of rigorous thought' and how to 'pursue something to its conclusion'. He also appears to have adopted Bailey's 'careful measured way of considering a thing'.[98]

Sawer's early scholarship, written both before and after his appointment as senior lecturer at Melbourne Law School, does not, however, speak of the influence of Bailey or Paton. Rather, it was influenced by the professional work he undertook, first as solicitor and then as a barrister, and by his professional mentors.[99] In the five years between Sawer's graduation from law and his appointment to the faculty at the University of Melbourne, he published eight articles, with the majority (five) published in the *Australian Law Journal* and the remainder in the Melbourne Law School student journal, *Res Judicatae*. All but one of these articles[100] addressed topics in the field of private law (property, torts, equity, contracts, wills and estates, conflicts of law and bankruptcy); they were all short and doctrinal in nature, ranging from half a page to four pages in length.[101] Lacking introductions or rhetorical flourishes, they were not literary pieces. Rather, his writing style was one of precise economy, with each article written solely to assist the practitioner to think about a doctrinal point rather than engage the reader. Sawer began several of these articles abruptly with a proposition of law or case. For example, one article begins, 'Section 95 of the Commonwealth Bankruptcy Act, 1924–1933, provides …'.[102] A brief perusal of their prosaic titles ('Accession in English Law', 'Ejectment without Cause from a Place of Entertainment,' 'Non-feasance in Relation to "Artificial Structures" on a Highway', and so on) gives the reader the flavour of what is to follow. It is the kind of work that Frederick Pollock pioneered[103] and that the American Legal Realist, Fred Rodell, mocked and despaired of.[104]

[97] Sawer, 'Outline Biography' (n 3) 3.
[98] Pratt (n 9).
[99] It is notable that in some of these early articles he thanked practitioners, rather than scholars, for their assistance.
[100] The exception being G Sawer, 'Legal Realism' (1939) 2 *Res Judicatae* 68.
[101] G Sawer, 'Accession in English Law' (1935) 9 *Australian Law Journal* 50; G Sawer, 'A Trustee May Not Set Off a Gain in One Transaction Against a Loss in Another (1936) 1 *Res Judicatae* 106; G Sawer, 'Competitions Involving Chance and Skill (1937) 11 *Australian Law Journal* 114; G Sawer, 'Non-feasance in Relation to "Artificial Structures" on a Highway' (1938) 12 *Australian Law Journal* 231; G Sawer, 'Proper Law of Contract – Intention of Parties – Moratorium Legislation' (1938) 11 *Australian Law Journal* 332; G Sawer, 'Bankruptcy Act, s 95 – Preference to Sureties' (1939) 13 *Australian Law Journal* 13; G Sawer, 'Bankruptcy Act, 1924–33 – Relation Back and Protection to Purchasers' (1940) 13 *Australian Law Journal* 438.
[102] Sawer, 'Bankruptcy Act, s 95' (n 102) 13.
[103] N Duxbury, *Frederick Pollock and the English Juristic Tradition* (Oxford, Oxford University Press, 2004) 316–22.
[104] F Rodell, 'Goodbye to Law Reviews' (1936) 23 *Vanderbilt Law Review* 38.

During Sawer's decade as a full-time legal scholar at Melbourne (1940–50), his scholarship changed so that it became less like the work of a mere technocrat. While many of his articles remained largely doctrinal, they were longer and several were published in the prestigious *Law Quarterly Review*.[105] In a reference written on Sawer's behalf, Professor Kenneth Bailey said that he knew 'from personal discussion how much Goodhart, the Editor of the *Law Quarterly Review*, appreciated the short articles Sawer had sent him and how welcome more work from his pen would be in that quarter'.[106] In the case notes he wrote for Goodhart, Sawer became an ambassador for Australian common law, promoting Australian cases and condemning the English courts for failing to cite relevant Australian precedents.[107] Sawer also wrote and contributed to several books, including a collection of constitutional law cases,[108] a short criminal law textbook,[109] and a small book on media law for journalists.[110] His constitutional law casebook was the first of its kind and provided an important foundation for shaping constitutional law teaching in Australia. Over the course of his career, Sawer produced three editions of the book and it remained the leading teaching resource for constitutional law. In 1981, responsibility for the book passed to two other leading Australian constitutional law scholars: Leslie Zines and Geoffrey Lindell.[111] Lindell considered that it was an honour to be chosen. Sawer also published a short book on Australian Government for the general reader which proved especially popular.[112] In 1977, it went into its twelfth edition with sales of over 150,000 and earned Sawer royalties of $25,000.[113] In addition to his publications and teaching duties, Sawer spent time gathering material for a doctoral thesis on the topic of accession (the Roman property law concepts of *occupatio, accessio* and *commixtio*). He never completed the doctorate.[114] As with Alice Erh-Soon Tay's

[105] G Sawer, 'Injunction, Parliamentary Process, and the Restriction of Parliamentary Competence' (1944) 60 *Law Quarterly Review* 83; G Sawer, 'Contract between the Crown and Its Civil Servants (1946) 62 *Law Quarterly Review* 22; G Sawer and G Paton, 'Ratio Decidendi and Obiter Dictum in Appellate Courts' (1947) 63 *Law Quarterly Review* 161.

[106] Minutes of Council of the University of Melbourne, 7 July 1947, University of Melbourne Registrar's Correspondence, University of Melbourne Archives.

[107] See n 106.

[108] Sawer, *Cases on the Constitution* (n 93). The Australian Law Schools Association (ALSA), founded by Sawer and Paton, suggested and supported Sawer's compilation of this book. Sawer opted for a casebook, anticipating that constitutional law doctrine would undergo significant change over the next decade. Again, this is indicative of Sawer's measured approach: Pratt (n 9).

[109] JV Barry, GW Paton and G Sawer, *An Introduction to the Criminal Law in Australia* (Melbourne, Melbourne University Press, 1948).

[110] G Sawer, *A Guide to Australian Law for Journalists, Authors, Printers and Publishers* (Melbourne, Melbourne University Press, 1949).

[111] L Zines and GJ Lindell, *Sawer's Australian Constitutional Cases* (Sydney, Lawbook Co, 1982).

[112] G Sawer, *Australian Government Today* (Melbourne, Melbourne University Press, 1948).

[113] 'Sawer book sales top 150,000', *Canberra Times* 29 September 1977, 9. In total 13 editions were published.

[114] Waugh (n 5), 138. In 1982 he was, however, awarded an honorary Doctor of Letters by the ANU. 'Honorary ANU Degree for Professor Sawer', *Canberra Times* 2 October 1982, 3.

thesis on accession, he probably chose the topic as it fell within the province of a classical English jurisprudential scholarship of the time.

This early scholarship illustrates that Sawer was a strong doctrinal scholar and someone with powerful analytical skills. On the whole, however, the bulk of this work provides no indication of broader pondering about the role of law in society, nor that he was inclined to draw from learning outside the law.

Sawer maintained a fascination with judges and their judging which meant that he kept up with doctrinal developments. It also prompted him to write to both Australian and overseas judges on many occasions to offer critiques of their judgments, to ask for clarification of their reasoning processes, and to seek explanations of how they decided cases. Within Australia, regular correspondents included Justice Kriewaldt of the Northern Territory Supreme Court, Justice Rae Else-Mitchell of the Supreme Court of New South Wales,[115] Justice Vincent Barry, Justice Fox of the Supreme Court of the Australian Capital Territory, Chief Justice Garfield Barwick of the High Court of Australia, and Chief Justice Sir Owen Dixon. Sawer also corresponded with various Canadian justices, such as Chief Justice Bora Laskin of the Supreme Court of Canada. Lord Denning, then Master of the Rolls of the Court of Appeal in England, gave Sawer unsolicited praise for his work and issued a personal invitation to visit him in London.[116] To Sawer, judges were both phenomena to be understood and a key part of his professional and intellectual circle. The letters to judges, while perhaps not as severe as his correspondence with John Anderson, do not suggest an attitude of deference but indicate clearly that Sawer considered himself an equal. As his close friend and mentee, Professor Geoffrey Lindell, said:

> I don't think he showed [judges] any special reverence or I don't think he showed them any special disrespect either. I think he thought of himself as an equal in a way that was less explicit than I've seen in others in my time.[117]

Sawer believed that legal scholars should have a role in critiquing the judiciary. For example, speaking of the High Court's constitutional jurisprudence up to 1968, Sawer said that the 'present interpretation of s 92 is a fantasy resulting from conservative minds brooding over the words of the section'.[118] In several articles and speeches, Sawer voiced his belief that it was critical for any legal academic to have a connection with the courts and profession.[119] This was not a matter of subordinating one to the other, but rather a question of maintaining relevance to society.

For Sawer, the most obvious way to demonstrate the relevance and value of a law school to society was by educating future legal practitioners.[120] According to

[115] Sawer described Else-Mitchell as a 'great friend': ibid.

[116] Lord Denning to Sawer, 7 March 1972, and Denning to Sawer, 20 March 1972, Geoffrey Sawer Papers, National Library of Australia, Manuscript Collection.

[117] Lindell (n 7).

[118] G Sawer, *Australian Federalism in the Courts* (Melbourne, Melbourne University Press, 1967) 206.

[119] G Sawer, *The Place of a Lawyer in the Social Sciences* (Melbourne, Melbourne University Press, 1953) 14.

[120] G Sawer, 'Law at the Australian National University' (1959) 5 *Journal of the Society of Public Teachers of Law* 20, 25.

Sawer, this connection and relevance diminished the further that a legal scholar moved away from teaching towards research because, he believed, the practising profession could exist and perform competently without it.[121] In several articles he stated that the Department of Law at the RSSS was disadvantaged because it was located in Canberra where the legal profession was very small. He argued that most *Australian* postgraduate students were better off studying at the state law schools where they could gain access to larger legal systems and a greater pool of lawyers.[122] How, exactly, this access would assist students in their doctorates was not made clear; however, the fact that he singled out domestic over international doctoral students suggests that he was thinking specifically about the future composition of Australia's legal academy. A postgraduate student who was entirely divorced from the practice of law and legal practitioners might present as someone who could not make it in practice. In other words, it might play to the argument that legal academics were failed practitioners and therefore of little value and lowly status. This was clearly of concern to Sawer. In an article about his role in a research school of social sciences, he said:

> The repute of general jurisprudence has suffered among lawyers from the subject coming to be regarded, particularly in Europe and South America, as the last refuge of a Struldbrug incapable of earning a living in the tough practice of the law. Hence my emphasis on the necessity for the academic lawyer in a research school of social sciences doing the best he can, even in an isolated community like Canberra, to retain a close connection with law in action.[123]

A 'Struldbrug' is a character from Jonathan Swift's book *Gulliver's Travels*.[124] These immortal creatures live at the expense of the state, providing nothing in return. Sawer was determined not to become a Struldbrug. His desire to maintain a connection with law in action is perhaps what prompted him to become a part-time magistrate.[125] It is interesting to note that Sawer considered that the appointment was 'a step in my scholarly experience'.[126]

Concluding Remarks

The left-leaning moderate stance Sawer took in his early student politics days was clearly reflected in his developing career. Sawer was a competent legal practitioner and doctrinal scholar with an interest in judging and judges. This meant

[121] ibid.

[122] G Sawer, 'An Australian National School of Law' (1951–53) 2 *University of Western Australia Law Review* 483, 487.

[123] Sawer (n 120) 14.

[124] J Swift, *Gulliver's Travels into Several Remote Nations of the World* (London, George Bell and Sons, 1892).

[125] Coper has detailed the circumstances of Sawer's appointment as a special magistrate in Canberra, see Coper (n 16).

[126] Sawer (n 10) part 49, 4.

that he never abandoned the traditional concerns of the legal academy. In fact, he believed that interacting with the profession was important, as it ensured the relevance of the academy to society and improved its standing. However, this was just one aspect of Sawer's scholarly agenda. The following chapter shows how Sawer's formative influences led him to become one of the first major and distinctively Australian exponents of law's heteronomy.

13

A Case Against Law's Autonomy

Introduction

At least two myths about the discipline of law in Australia are put to an end in this chapter. First, I refute the claim that, until at least the 1980s, Australian legal scholars did not develop their own jurisprudential schools of thought.[1] As I explain in this chapter, Sawer created and advanced a distinctively Australian legal theory that laid the foundation for strong contextual constitutional law scholarship. Sawer's theory responded to several existing strands of foreign jurisprudence without adopting any one school. He advanced a constructive jurisprudence that urged scholars to begin by seeking a sound understanding of the facts and broader context of constitutional law decision-making. Such facts could then support a range of jurisprudential theorising. He developed and advanced a Constructive Legal Realism that responded to the Australian environment as well as American and English thought. It responded to Sir Owen Dixon's strict and complete legalism and the conservative tendencies that Sawer believed this had encouraged within Australia's legal profession. It also responded to the project of analytical jurisprudence, which he considered interesting but ultimately of limited value. Sawer favoured the moderate American Legal Realist critiques of the analytical jurisprudes.

Second, I counter over-generalisations that the first community of Australian legal scholars was made up of short-sighted doctrinal scholars.[2] I argue that such over-generalisations ought to be abandoned in favour of a more robust exploration of the complex factors and influences that led Australian legal scholars to shape the discipline in various ways. Perhaps Sawer's most important contribution to the discipline and practice of law was to make a case against law's autonomy.

[1] In a general account of Australian legal scholarship published in 1987, Chesterman and Weisbrot argued that, 'It is not yet really possible to identify any distinctively Australian academic jurisprudence, or even to identify local versions of major overseas school of thought: eg, law as science (Langdell at Harvard); economic analysis of law (Posner at Chicago); law as social science (Lasswell and MacDougal at Yale); legal realism (Llewellyn); the now abandoned law and development (Galanter and Trubek); or the recently emerged critical legal studies (Under, Kennedy, Abel)': M Chesterman and D Weisbrot, 'Legal Scholarship in Australia' (1987) 50 *Modern Law Review* 709, 724.

[2] ibid 714; N James, 'A Brief History of Critique in Australian Legal Education' (2000) 24 *Melbourne University Law Review* 965, 968.

He believed that it was high time that all Australian lawyers abandoned the fairy tale of mechanical jurisprudence. He made this case both by way of example and through explicit advocacy.

By setting his substantial works of scholarship alongside his advocacy, I reveal that Sawer delivered a consistent message and did not tailor it to placate dominant schools of thought. Sawer believed that the discipline needed to be liberated incrementally from the narrow views of law that had been circulating in the 1950s and 1960s, and that such liberation should not come at the expense of the existing body of common law and legal scholarship. In other words, he believed that the law should both reflect and lead social change but that stabilising ideas and institutions should not be lost in the process. Here, I suggest that Sawer advanced a consistent and well-informed strategy for advancing Australia's legal profession and legal academy, one that he believed would strengthen Australia's legal system and laws.

A Smorgasbord of Legal Theory

Sawer's early interest in politics and Marxist thought provides the first clear indication that he was attracted to matters of law, politics and governance. During the course of his scholarly career, he did many things that moved the discipline away from its traditional orientations. Some of these activities can be explained by his curiosity about Marxism, but the rest was a product of his early jurisprudential study and, in particular, the teachings of George Paton, Professor of Jurisprudence at the University of Melbourne from 1931 to 1951.

There are clear signs that Paton's teachings in jurisprudence made an impression on Sawer, and that in his early career he did much to learn about the major theoretical schools. Paton helped Sawer to build his career in many ways, including inviting his protégé to co-author an article and contribute to a monograph.[3] Paton also put Sawer forward for promotion[4] and travel opportunities.[5] With Bailey, Paton was willing to appoint Sawer to a permanent full-time position within a law school, even though he did not possess the typical qualification of an Australian legal scholar – an overseas degree. The generosity both men showed to Sawer meant that he became the first Australian legal scholar to demonstrate that the

[3] G Sawer and G Paton, 'Ratio Decidendi and Obiter Dictum in Appellate Courts' (1947) 63 *Law Quarterly Review* 461; JV Barry, GW Paton and G Sawer, *An Introduction to the Criminal Law in Australia* (Melbourne, Melbourne University Press, 1948).

[4] Thanks to Paton, Sawer was the first person to be appointed an associate professor in an Australian law school. G Sawer, 'Partly Unreliable Memoir', Geoffrey Sawer Papers, National Library of Australia, Manuscript Collection, part 33, 2.

[5] Paton organised a Carnegie Grant for Sawer to visit the United States, believing that this would put Sawer in a stronger position to apply for the Chair of Public Law. G Sawer, 'Outline Biography', Geoffrey Sawer Papers, National Library of Australia, Manuscript Collection, 18.

Australian context and a local university could provide sufficiently strong intellectual stimulation and the foundation on which to build an impressive academic legal career.

Sawer's attitude to Marxism suggests that he was sceptical of theories that claimed to hold the answers to law's major problems and provide a definitive way of studying them. This scepticism extended to all of the major jurisprudential schools. In his formative years, Sawer showed interest in American Legal Realism, but did not fully subscribe to its tenets, and rejected its more radical components.[6] He respected the analytical jurisprudential tradition and the contributions of HLA Hart, but later in his career voiced strong views which suggest that he believed such contributions had fatal limitations[7] and were 'merely' 'abstract' studies.[8] Similarly, he thought that sociological jurisprudence and empirical legal studies both held promise, but did not consider that either had stronger academic credentials than the analytical school (by which he meant the tradition laid down by scholars such as Austin and revitalised by HLA Hart).[9] Sawer borrowed from both the analytical and sociological schools and at times adopted the sentiment of American Legal Realism, but did not wholly embrace any of them. He believed that these schools contained valuable ideas and it is clear that aspects of each influenced his scholarship; however, for Sawer a legal scholar's relationship with jurisprudence was not a matter of swearing allegiance to a particular model. Sawer also hoped that others would take a similar view of the various jurisprudential schools as providing nourishment rather than all-embracing philosophies. As Geoffrey Lindell explained:

> [O]ne thing about Geoff is that he never engaged in labels anyway. He never talked in labels, he just plucked things from all these streams of thinking. For example, when talking to students he wouldn't say this is natural law and positivism. He didn't talk that way at all. What he would want is for them to be exposed to all those different ways of thinking. He would bring up a problem and you and I would think that is the natural law approach, and then he'd bring up another example which you and I would think is the positivist approach.[10]

For Sawer, law was not a narrow autonomous discipline, nor could it be explained through one body of knowledge or theoretical school. Instead, it was a rich intellectual discipline that transcended disciplinary boundaries.

[6] eg, in an early article he provided an account of what teaching law would be like if law teachers followed Jerome Frank's theories. It is clear from the tone of the article that Sawer believed Frank had gone too far: G Sawer, 'Legal Realism' (1939) 2 *Res Judicatae* 68. In his article on Sawer's contribution to the social sciences, Ross Cranston also recognised Sawer's refusal to accept the radical elements of legal realism: R Cranston, '"Lawyer in the Social Sciences" – Geoffrey Sawer' (1980) 11 *Federal Law Review* 263, 264.

[7] G Sawer, 'Conscience as Objection in the Law' in TP Grundy (ed), *Conscience in the '70s* (Canberra, Australian National University Centre for Continuing Education, 1972) 66, 71.

[8] G Sawer, 'The Jurisprudence of Ombudsmen' (1971) 30 *Public Administration* 221, 222.

[9] This is the argument Sawer made in the first chapter of his book: G Sawer, *Law in Society* (Oxford, Clarendon Press, 1965).

[10] Interview with Geoffrey Lindell (Woodbridge Community Centre, Tasmania, 23 March 2015).

Sawer's Constructive Legal Realism

The incremental and constructive nature of Sawer's approach to liberating the study of law from its former narrow confines, drawing from a range of different jurisprudential traditions without firmly joining any of them, is demonstrated in many of his works. Even though Sawer rarely engaged in abstract theorising, he was recognised internationally as a legal theorist. In 1962, HLA Hart, the Professor of Jurisprudence at the University of Oxford, said that he found Sawer's writing on the sociology of law 'more illuminating than anybody else's',[11] and invited Sawer to write a book on the subject for the prestigious Clarendon Law Series. Hart's *The Concept of Law*[12] had earlier been published as part of this series. In his letter to Sawer, Hart referred specifically to a book chapter by Sawer on the Marxist scholar Karl Renner[13] as a work sitting within the sociology of law, and told Sawer that he believed it to be a 'model of its kind'.[14] Hart's invitation raises further questions about the nature of Sawer's work, in particular how much of it ought to be classified as part of the 'sociology of law', whether he was at heart a jurisprudential scholar or legal theorist, and what it was that caught Hart's attention.

It must be remembered that, during the first two decades of Sawer's scholarly career, substantial Australian textbooks or monographs on public law did not exist. Similarly, there were few works of Australian jurisprudence (Paton's textbook on jurisprudence being an obvious exception). Some of the full-time legal scholars of the pre-war era had been strong liberal scholars, but they had done little to advance a uniquely Australian legal theory. Julius Stone was a strong legal theorist, but others have suggested that his scholarship was never really an Australian product.[15] His inspiration was forged during his time in America and, perhaps to a lesser extent, England.[16] In this environment, Sawer believed that his contribution ought to be careful and cautious. Stone also recognised the need for careful, detailed study rather than grand, far-reaching work. At a constitutional law symposium at which Sawer presented his thoughts on advancing constitutional law scholarship, Stone issued a caution, stating that he doubted 'whether we have as yet a sufficient foundation of research technique or

[11] HLA Hart to Sawer, 11 March 1962, Professor G Sawer Correspondence, Australian National University Archives.

[12] HLA Hart, *The Concept of Law* (Oxford, Oxford University Press, 1961).

[13] G Sawer, 'Law as Socially Neutral" – Karl Renner' in G Sawer (ed), *Studies in the Sociology of Law* (Canberra, Australian National University, 1961) 137.

[14] Hart (n 11).

[15] 'Despite Stone's involvement in wartime national planning, in the politics of the Law School, and with his students, it has been said that the focus of his intellectual interests remained in the United States and that he never got to know the "real" Australia': L Starr, *Julius Stone – An Intellectual Life* (Oxford, Oxford University Press, 1992) 116.

[16] ibid.

accumulated findings to justify us in embarking even upon speculation on some of the matters that have been raised in this discussion'.[17] Stone went on to suggest that it would be a mistake for Australian legal scholars to embark on the type of work the Americans had undertaken until they had first completed detailed studies of particular aspects of Australian constitutional law.[18] Sawer, though still cautious, was a little more ambitious in the agenda he outlined to an audience of mostly senior legal academics, along with one of the Australian Constitution's early architects, Sir Robert Garran, and a superior court judge, HS Nicholas. He made it clear that he had his sights set on Australia developing an American-style analysis of constitutional law – one that would

> take into account doctrinal analysis of the usual legal character, criticism of results in terms of sociological and ethical standards, and a detailed examination of the personal character and actions of each of the individual judges who have taken part in the relevant decisions and of the 'group psychology' (assuming it to exist) of the courts as collectivities. An approach to critical assessment of this kind has been begun in the USA.[19]

Sawer spoke of the need to find permissible value judgments that could guide the court, being judgments that were neither grossly political nor which subscribed to mechanical notions of reasoning.[20] He referred to Australian legal scholarship at that time as 'only just beginning to develop legal scholarship of this standard, and a periodical legal literature above the level of a practice note'.[21] This could be taken to be a reference to his own scholarly trajectory from 1952.

Rather than provide dazzling ambitious sociological theories, Sawer's purpose was to set the discipline on a path that would contextualise constitutional reasoning and principles, and evaluate their appropriateness to Australian society.

A Response to the Realist Dilemma

In several ways, Sawer's legal theory can be construed as a response to the central question posed by the realists: how can law be predictable and certain, if judging is largely, or in part, a product of the personal characteristics of judges?[22] Unlike the Legal Process scholars, who downplayed the importance of the doctrine of precedent in judicial decision-making, Sawer's response was to defend its

[17] J Stone, 'Commentary' to G Sawer, 'The Record of Judicial Review' in G Sawer (ed), *Federalism: An Australian Jubilee Study* (Melbourne, Cheshire, 1952) 211, 250.
[18] ibid.
[19] G Sawer, 'The Record of Judicial Review' (n 17) 211, 212–13.
[20] ibid 215–16.
[21] ibid 215–16.
[22] One of Sawer's primary intellectual mentors, George Paton, clearly explained the dilemma in his textbook on jurisprudence: GW Paton, *A Textbook of Jurisprudence* (Oxford, Clarendon Press, 1946) 19–21.

ongoing relevance. He suggested measures to strengthen the role of precedent and facilitate a deeper analysis of the types of consideration at play in High Court decision-making and its relationship with federal politics. In essence, Sawer's legal theory was constructive. He believed in the importance of maintaining the integrity of the courts, and his ultimate aim was to encourage Australian legal scholars and students to appreciate the broader context of law and to support wider conceptions of judging, without abandoning the discipline's traditional orientations. He wished to carefully build the edifice of Australian constitutional law and legal theory, beginning with the essential facts that underpinned both constitutional law and politics. Based on a review of all of Sawer's scholarship, those aspects of his work that seek to address the realist dilemma and lay the foundation for a contextual approach to constitutional law studies are identified in this section.

Sawer learnt from Paton that American Legal Realism could be divided into a number of distinct camps. Paton had said that, while there was a 'nihilist tendency in the writings of certain authors [for example, Jerome Frank] who exaggerate the element of uncertainty and under-estimate the part played by the structure of legal rules', 'some of the work is extremely balanced [for example, the work of Karl Llewellyn]'.[23] According to Paton, American Legal Realism formed the 'left-wing'[24] faction of what he described as the 'functional school', being the school founded by Roscoe Pound.[25] Typically, Sawer favoured the left-wing moderate position of the functional school. He rejected its radical elements,[26] but accepted the proposition that the personal characteristics and beliefs of judges played some part in judicial decision-making.[27] Sawer's view that judging can sometimes – but not always – be explained as a process of logical deduction and induction (and that in many cases there were sufficient elements of consistency to allow for prediction) was formed from his early experience as a barrister and then later as a magistrate.[28]

Sawer responded to what he had learnt from the realists in a number of ways. When studying case law, Sawer looked beyond the way in which judges explained their application of a body of rules. Like the realists, he accepted that 'law is not a body of rules but a collection of facts (ie judicial decisions), and that jurisprudence is not a rational study but an empirical study of events'.[29] While Sawer argued that jurisprudence permitted some objective study, he also accepted the realists' claims that there were areas of subjectivity. One of his most substantial and significant

[23] ibid 21.
[24] ibid 19.
[25] ibid 18.
[26] Sawer (n 6); Sawer and Paton (n 3) 480–81; Sawer (n 9) 71–72.
[27] Sawer and Paton (n 3) 480–81.
[28] See Sawer (n 9) 71–72.
[29] Paton (n 22) 20–21 quoting H Kantorowicz, 'Some Rationalism about Realism' (1934) 43 *Yale Law Journal* 1240.

bodies of work – the very first project that he began at the RSSS – was, in essence, a historical factual study that provided the materials he believed were needed to understand the first 50 years of Australian constitutional law decision-making and federal politics.[30]

The impetus for this early and important contribution arose from studies he had conducted while still at the University of Melbourne. Sawer's interest in public law was made plain shortly after he joined Australia's infant legal academy.[31] In the late 1940s, he became enthralled by what he believed to be the most important Australian constitutional law case of the time: the *Bank Nationalisation Case*.[32] The case became the vehicle for Sawer's first strong attempt at contextualising constitutional law decision-making to better understand the relationship between judicial decision-making, politics and the personal values of judges.

Sawer also attributed his changing perspective on constitutional science (moving towards viewing the study of constitutional law as part of political science) to the opportunity he had been given by an editor at the Melbourne University Press to write a general introduction to Australian law and political science.[33] Sawer was approached on the strength of a number of lectures that he had delivered in political science (shortly before the outbreak of the war, when a politics lecturer took leave),[34] and of his various experiments with an approach to teaching constitutional law that located doctrine within its political and historical context.[35] The book, *Australian Government Today* (1948), would be his best-selling work.[36] It became a standard textbook in courses on government and constitutional law, and in final-year secondary school courses, and added to his reputation as both a legal scholar and political scientist. This reputation was consolidated in 1951, when Sawer became founding member of the Australian Political Studies Association.[37]

Bank Nationalisation

Sawer was employed as an adviser to the Labor government in the *Bank Nationalisation Case* and also studied and wrote about the case for scholarly publication.

[30] G Sawer, *Australian Federal Politics and Law 1901–29* (Melbourne, Melbourne University Press, 1956); G Sawer, *Australian Federal Politics and Law 1929–49* (Melbourne, Melbourne University Press, 1963).

[31] G Sawer, 'Autrefois Acquit and Decision Not "On the Merits"' (1941) 2 *Res Judicatae* 203; G Sawer, 'The Blackout Cases and their Relation to Administrative Law' (1941) *Australian Law Journal* 103.

[32] Considered later in this chapter. See also the vivid account of this case in D Marr, *Barwick* (Sydney, George Allen & Unwin, 1980) 52–74.

[33] M Pratt, Interview with Geoffrey Sawer (Oral History Interview, Canberra, 16 November 1971), https://nla.gov.au/nla.obj-214869908/listen.

[34] ibid.

[35] N Stephen, 'A Recollection of Geoffrey Sawer' (1980) 11 *Federal Law Review* 261, 261.

[36] G Sawer, *Australian Government Today* (Melbourne, Melbourne University Press, 1948).

[37] *History and Overview*, Australian Political Studies Association, http://www.auspsa.org.au/about/history.

Evatt, who was Attorney-General of Australia at that time, sought Sawer's advice on the case and arranged for him to travel with the legal team to London (Sawer's first overseas trip) when the case came before the Privy Council.[38] In both Australia and London, at the end of each trial day Sawer reviewed the transcript of court proceedings and provided legal advice to assist counsel. He said that he 'became completely absorbed in the litigation – even more so than the barristers'.[39] Sawer's subsequent writing about the case was therefore influenced by his vantage point as an expert adviser, as opposed to a disinterested observer. In a sense, his position and these first-hand insights into the government's reasoning and strategies in the matter gave him a degree of sociological insight.

For Sawer, the case brought the intersection between law and politics into sharp focus. In his writing about the case he signalled that, to study constitutional law, it was essential to consider both the political and judicial arms of government. The case involved the desire of the federal Labor government to further its collectivist – socialist – agenda through the introduction of a regulatory scheme for Australia's banking system. It made two attempts. First, the government took steps to centralise all government banking through the national Commonwealth Bank. State governments and private banks successfully challenged the scheme in the High Court.[40] Second, in response to the High Court decision, the government took the drastic step of implementing a scheme that effectively abolished all private banking in Australia. Pursuant to the scheme, the Commonwealth Bank was to be given a monopoly over Australian banking. A High Court challenge ensured that the matter made it all the way to the Privy Council.

Sawer argued that the *Bank Nationalisation Case* was one of the most important constitutional law cases ever to have arisen in Australia. He observed that 'an honours seminar at the National University's School of Advanced Studies could, without difficulty, spend a year in running down the hares which were started during the argument of the case, either by Counsel or by the Bench, but not pursued'.[41] The case was, he wrote, 'one of the most celebrated politico-legal disputes in Australia's history',[42] in which 'every major express proposition and unstated assumption of Australian Constitutional structure fell to be debated'.[43] Sawer was interested in the way that the judicial decisions frustrated the government's political agenda, as well as the implications of the High Court's reasoning for constitutional law. In particular, he commented on the 'willingness of Justice Owen

[38] Evatt did so on the strength of Sawer's writing on the government's first attempt to centralise all government banking: Pratt (n 33).

[39] Sawer (n 5), part 35, 2.

[40] *Melbourne v Commonwealth* (1947) 74 CLR 31 (*State Banking Case*); *Bank of New South Wales v Commonwealth* (1948) 76 CLR 1 (*Bank Nationalisation Case*).

[41] G Sawer, 'Bank of New South Wales and Others v Commonwealth – The Bank Nationalisation Case' (1948) 22 *Australian Law Journal* 213, 213.

[42] G Sawer, 'The Case of Bank Nationalisation – a Study in Australian Government' (1950) 32 *Journal of the Society of Comparative Legislation and International Law* 17, 18.

[43] ibid 18.

Dixon and most of his High Court colleagues to modify the pro-Commonwealth power reasoning of the 1920 *Engineers Case*'.[44] On several occasions, Sawer challenged attempts by Dixon (to whom he referred as the 'grey eminence of the High Court') to modify this reasoning.[45]

The case provoked the very busy Sawer to write and publish four articles.[46] The most important of these was published in the English *Journal of the Society of Comparative Legislation and International Law*.[47] In this article, Sawer moved beyond doctrine to provide an account of the 'complex interaction between political forces, judicial doctrines and the influence of strong personalities'.[48] It is appealingly written (with a clear and inviting introduction). Sawer provides a short explanation of the implied instrumentality doctrine, describes the Australian political context which gave rise to the challenge (including the socialist agenda of the Labor Party and its interest in strengthening the central regulation of Australia's banking system), and explains the High Court's decision in relation to the first challenge. Sawer then returns to politics and explains the Labor government's response (its attempt to abolish private banks), outlines how this move was received politically, and explains the High Court's decision with respect to the second challenge. An analysis of judicial decision-making is integrated with an account of the political events surrounding that decision-making in order to contextualise the High Court doctrine. This article represented a significant change in Sawer's approach to legal scholarship, which would endure throughout his career.

Australian Federal Politics and Law

Sawer's pieces on the *Bank Nationalisation Case* formed the template for his later, much larger two-volume work, entitled *Australian Federal Politics and Law* (1956).[49] This work is important for several reasons. First, it provided extensive and irrefutable evidence that politics was a part of Australian High Court judging, and that constitutional law cases in the first half of the twentieth century were often decided on the basis of factors sitting outside the rules themselves and processes of inductive and deductive logic. Sawer's extensive study made it very difficult for an informed practitioner or lawyer to deny that one of the realists' basic tenets – that judging was something more than mechanical jurisprudence – applied to Australian public law. As such, the work made a strong case against law's

[44] Sawer (n 5) part 35, 1.
[45] ibid part 33, 1.
[46] Sawer (n 41); Sawer (n 42); G Sawer, 'Implication and the Constitution – Part I' (1948) 4 *Res Judicatae* 15; G Sawer, 'Implication and the Constitution – Part II' (1949) 4 *Res Judicatae* 85.
[47] Sawer (n 42).
[48] ibid 18.
[49] Sawer (n 30).

autonomy at a critical stage in the development of the discipline and practice of law in Australia. Second, the work is important in that it demonstrated the importance of studying rules and principles in context and with an appreciation of the complex web of factors that influence High Court decision-making. It remains the only work of its kind on Australian constitutional law and politics.

Later in life, Sawer explained the object of this work, and why it was limited to the first half of the twentieth century, as follows:

> The main purpose of this work was to trace the inter-relation between the course of federal politics and legislation on the one hand the course of High Court decisions on constitutional questions affecting the work of the politicians. I began it with a tentative thesis that politics and judicial decisions tended to be out of step with each other – the judges giving decisions which invalidated legislation desired by the current government and party majority, or the judges giving decisions which might encourage parliamentary outcomes which the current legislative majority didn't want. I soon found that the actual situation over the years was quite complex, and could not be expressed in any simple way. However, the outcome was a narrative of events and personalities which no one else had attempted. Nor did I attempt to carry the story on beyond 1950, partly because of my confidential relations with both judges and members of parliament, and prominent executive officials such as departmental heads, and partly because my own interests had shifted to other aspects of the work … of lawyers and the structure of the law.[50]

Both volumes of *Australian Federal Politics and Law* follow the format of an almanac, divided into chapters that represent each term of Australia's federal government from 1901 to 1949. In each chapter, Sawer identifies all of the factors that bore upon Australian federal legislation, policy and judicial decision-making in the relevant period. He carefully documents the formation and agenda of federal political parties; the legislation proposed; the content of federal budgets and their effect on the states; and the constitutional issues arising in both the courts and the parliament. The decisions of the High Court are explained, together with an account of why judges were appointed and a description of their personalities and politics.[51] However, they are not the primary focus of the work; they share the spotlight with other political actors and events. Very early in the collection Sawer provides clear evidence of the political nature of High Court decision-making. He notes that, as early as 1906, it was evident that, in exercising the 'function of holding a balance between the units of the federation',

> the Court necessarily had to apply some general political theory of the system of governmental relations established by the constitution; the cases reaching it were almost of necessity incapable of being decided by a literal application of the words of the constitution, since the cases arose precisely because relevant sections of the document were general, vague or ambiguous. It soon became evident, and was hardly surprising, that the Court's political philosophy approximated that of the political centre in the federal

[50] Sawer (n 4) part 45, 4.
[51] Sawer, *Australian Federal Politics and Law 1929–49* (n 30) 33–34.

> parliament – say, between that of conservative Protectionists like Forrest and Quick, and liberal Protectionists like Deakin and Groom.[52]

Sawer believed that the early history of Australian Constitutional decision-making showed the need to give up the myth that judging in this field involved the making of logical deductions. Instead, scholars and judges should concentrate their efforts on value preferences that ought to underlie the development of constitutional law:

> The First Court took office expecting to be more concerned with the Constitution than with anything else, and its members had been through a political experience which enabled them to adopt a set of broad assumptions without any feeling that they were departing from the judicial tradition of the common law world. But as soon as Higgins and Isaacs began to oppose those assumptions with another set, equally strongly held and expressed with some vehemence, then the spectre of judicial politics was raised and subsequent Justices, horrified at the result, tried to get along without such 'general views.' Individual Justices can be shown to have had particular mental habits and value preferences, but in relation to the constitutional task of the Court these were not such as to ensure consistency nor facilitate prediction.[53]

By contextualising constitutional law decision-making, Sawer could assess whether the High Court's decisions helped or hampered a government's attempt to win popularity and thereby influenced elections. He also considered how the federal compact played to the interests of the political parties; for example, he spoke of the 'anti-socialist bias of the federal constitution'.[54] The work examines each budget proposed by the federal government and the role of taxes in facilitating the growth of the federal government.[55] It therefore provides a clear indication of the nature of Australia's federal compact and federal balance borne out by 50 years of history.

Sawer's two volumes demonstrated both the relevance of the broader political and social context to any understanding of constitutional law doctrine. They also showed that a legal scholar was capable of studying and writing about matters beyond court decision-making. Sawer did not, however, believe that it was a project that sat squarely within the discipline of law. In a letter to Kenneth Wheare (one of the founders of the RSSS), then based at Oxford, Sawer expressed his belief that the work he was doing sat outside the discipline. He said that he had

> been delving deep into the federal parliamentary history of 1901–50; strictly speaking it is work for historians and political scientists, but since none of them have embarked upon it, I do not mind combining a bit of political history with my constitutional studies.[56]

[52] Sawer, *Australian Federal Politics and Law 1901–29* (n 30) 58.
[53] ibid 329–30.
[54] ibid 329–30.
[55] See, eg, ibid 25–9.
[56] Sawer to Kenneth Wheare, 6 March 1952 and Sawer to Erwin Griswold, 8 April 1952, Professor G Sawer Correspondence, Australian National University Archives.

Regardless of Sawer's own view of his suitability for this project, his efforts proved that a lawyer was capable of a project that moved beyond court doctrine and statutory interpretation, and his work provided a critical perspective on the nature of constitutional law and decision-making.

The volumes have served as valuable reference tools for many legal scholars as well as political scientists,[57] yet initial reactions were mixed. Some legal scholars gave the books high praise, recognising their weight, usefulness and industry;[58] others seemed puzzled about their purpose.[59] Such confusion is perhaps a reflection of the state of the legal academy. As there were so few legal scholars and no full-time researchers in law, it might have been difficult for some to appreciate who would reap the benefit of these extensive volumes. Clifford Pannam, a senior lecturer at the University of Melbourne, observed that, 'Sawer often steps out of his guise as cataloguer to thrust a critical dagger through his subjects'.[60] He considered that Sawer provided insufficient reasons to support these types of evaluations.[61] Given the ambitious scale of the project, it would seem unreasonable to expect Sawer to attempt anything more than a catalogue; however, Pannam seems correct in his assertion that, where attempts are made to advance criticisms, they ought to be fully substantiated. These evaluative aspects of Sawer's work are lively and interesting, but have a journalistic, rather than strong scholarly, style.

Despite such criticism, it is clear that the volumes were a significant achievement and established Sawer as *the* expert on Australian constitutional law. De Smith commented that, '[w]hat Professor Geoffrey Sawer does not know about Australian constitutional law (or, for that matter, Australian politics: see his volumes on *Australian Federal Politics and Law*) is probably not worth knowing'.[62] They were – and remain – monumental works, which set a high standard for future constitutional law studies and sought to demonstrate the inadequacies of purely doctrinal studies. Their existence meant that the founding of modern constitutional law scholarship was grounded in an expansive view of law that made a strong case for contextualisation. The two volumes thus served as foundational works for studies in law and politics, including Sawer's own future work. His later popular work, *Australian Federalism in the Courts* (1967),[63] is in some ways a

[57] Macintyre refers to it as one of several 'fundamental points of reference for national scholarship' produced by the founding members of the RSSS: S Macintyre, *The Poor Relation – A History of Social Sciences in Australia* (Melbourne, Melbourne University, 2010) 104.

[58] G Marshall, 'Book Review: *Australian Federal Politics and Law* by Geoffrey Sawer and *The Constitutions of the Australian States* by RD Lumb' (1965) 28 *Modern Law Review* 239, 239.

[59] JQ Ewens, 'Book Review: *Australian Federal Politics and Law 1929–1949* by Geoffrey Sawer' (1964) 165 *Federal Law Review* 165, 166.

[60] CL Pannam, 'Book Review: *Australian Federal Politics and Law 1929–49* by Geoffrey Sawer' (1963) 4 *Melbourne University Law Review* 290, 292.

[61] ibid.

[62] SA De Smith, 'Book Review: Australian Federalism in the Courts by Geoffrey Sawer and Australian Federal Constitutional Law and Australian Federal Constitutional Law by Colin Howard' (1969) 32 *Modern Law Review* 460, 460.

[63] G Sawer, *Australian Federalism and the Courts* (Melbourne, Melbourne University Press, 1967).

direct successor to the earlier book, in that Sawer uses the insights gleaned from his factual study to form theories about Australia's federation from the vantage point of the High Court. While written for the general reader, this later work is also designed to instil in a beginner an understanding of the multi-layered nature of federalism, which derives as much from the political actors and context as it does from constitutional law itself. Sawer, therefore, persistently made the case for recognising the relationship between politics and law.[64]

Strengthening the Doctrine of Precedent

Treating constitutional law decision-making as a collection of facts to be studied alongside other facts (politics, the economy and so on) was one of the ways in which Sawer responded to realist thought. Another was to formulate prescriptions that would promote greater certainty and consistency in judicial decision-making. Even though judging was partly the product of an individual judge's personal characteristics – their values and politics – this did not, according to Sawer, mean that judging was 'entirely whimsical'.[65] In the context of Australian constitutional law, Sawer believed that effort should be concentrated on identifying and setting a limit on the number of permissible values and policies that a court could deploy.[66]

Prior to his appointment to the RSSS, Sawer had published an article that explained judicial reasoning in a manner and in terms that signalled his belief in the broader qualities of legal reasoning.[67] His analysis bears a loose resemblance to the types of classification and analysis advanced by Hart and Dworkin. Sawer never wrote a monograph devoted entirely to his concept of legal reasoning, but it is clear, as demonstrated in the following passage from an early article, that he had firm views which formed the basis of much of his other scholarship. He said:

> These cases [considered in the article], therefore, represent the familiar situation of courts driven towards a particular conclusion by considerations of value or policy and endeavouring to reconcile their decisions with an established system of concepts, the concepts themselves being so ill-defined that their re-definition is still possible. It is interesting to notice that in this example, the propositions on which the purely conceptual argument depends do not enter into the statement of the relevant operative rules of law; they are merely explanatory. The only operative rules of law involved were as follows; spouses shall not be permitted to sue each other for personal injury; masters

[64] N Raeburn, 'Book Review: Geoffrey Sawer, *Australian Federalism in the Courts*' (1968–70) 3 *University of Tasmania Law Review* 232, 234.

[65] Sawer and Paton (n 3) 481.

[66] This is explained below.

[67] G Sawer, 'Husband-and-Wife versus Master-and-Servant; A Collision of Concepts' (1953) 27 *Australian Law Journal* 323.

> shall pay for the torts of their servants. There is no compelling necessity for any explanation of these rules. They do not need to be derived from any supposedly more general rule of law, nor from any judicially recognised social value dressed up as 'public policy'; it is quite likely that in a codification of English civil law, each would appear as a dogmatic rule and anyone inquiring *why* such a rule exists could be met with the sovereign answer *stet pro ratione voluntas mea*. If the rules are considered in unexplained isolation, there is no propositional relation between them at all, and the problem of the instant cases would be simply solved by pointing out that to allow the spouse to sue the employer involves no disobedience to either rule. …
>
> There is no logical or semantic reason why statements as to the 'rationale' of legal rules should not be a part of the statement of the rules themselves. But it is quite exceptional for any legal system to pursue consistently a course of exposition plus explanation, whether the system be codified or unenacted; the British professional tradition particularly inclines us to treat only the minimum behaviourist expression of a legal obligation as constituting 'the law,' more general explanations or derivations of the rule being treated as a subsidiary logical structure which though within judicial behaviour has a lesser claim to validity. There is an analogy between this situation and that which obtains in the natural sciences, where observed behaviour is often distinguished from a hypothetical explanatory set of concepts. But the scientists tend to treat the explanatory system as *more* 'real' than the observed behaviour, whereas with the lawyers, the explanatory system is usually felt as *less* 'real.' Doubtless this is because the scientific concepts have a high predictive value, while the legal concepts have only a low one.[68]

By drawing attention to the rationale and explanatory system of concepts that underlie rules, Sawer clearly expressed his belief that judging involved much more than the formal application of rules and that often the determining factor was the values and policies sitting behind the rule.

For Sawer, the task faced by scholars following on from American Legal Realism was one of increasing the predictive value of the explanatory system by bringing the system into sharper focus. In the case of constitutional law, Sawer considered that when, in the early 1900s, High Court Justices Higgins and Isaacs introduced a new set of assumptions about the interpretation of the constitution, it caused alarm and other Justices responded by attempting to proceed in the absence of any general assumptions.[69] Despite their intention to rid the law of the uncertainty created by political assumptions, in Sawer's view by removing any recourse to enduring values or preferences, the approach of these judges simply created greater idiosyncrasies in constitutional law decision-making.[70] For Sawer, therefore, the challenge was to identify a set of circumscribed fundamental values that should guide the court.[71]

[68] ibid 326.
[69] Sawer, *Australian Federal Politics and Law 1901–29* (n 30) 329–30.
[70] ibid.
[71] ibid; Sawer (n 63) 197.

Even though Sawer acknowledged the role of values in decision-making, throughout his career he also remained of the view that logic was an important part of judicial decision-making: 'To give up all reliance on logical principles would be as wise as giving up the use of eyes because occasionally they see what is not there'.[72] In order to increase the predictability of law by strengthening the operation of the doctrine of precedent, Sawer, along with Paton, had tentatively suggested that reforms be introduced to mandate appellate courts to deliver unanimous judgments; they also recommended that each appellate case be heard by an odd number of justices to ensure a clear majority.[73] As Duxbury more recently noted, the article stands in contrast to the despair of some American Legal Realists, including Karl Lewellyn and Herman Oliphant, and constitutes a 'constructive' approach to one of the major realist challenges to traditional understandings of law.[74]

'We're All Socio-Legal Now' (and Always Have Been)[75]

Much has been made of HLA Hart's suggestion at the start of *The Concept of Law* that his work was an exercise in 'descriptive sociology'.[76] Some social scientists have argued that the work was really that of an analytical philosopher and that its failure to consider the broader context – 'historical and social facts'[77] – of law meant that it could not be considered either descriptive[78] or a work of sociology.[79] Hart's response was to suggest that he had used the description 'to signal his move away from the more rigidly conceptual theories of John Austin and Hans Kelsen in favour of an approach which helps us to look at the complex social phenomenon of law'.[80]

Given the controversy over Hart's categorisation of his own work, his praise for Sawer's sociological scholarship might be considered a weak endorsement. Sawer's scholarship was, however, different from Hart's. In the *Federal Politics and Law* volumes, Sawer attempted to gather together the historical and social facts from

[72] Sawer and Paton (n 3) 481.
[73] ibid.
[74] N Duxbury, *The Nature and Authority of Precedent* (Cambridge, Cambridge University Press, 2008) 79.
[75] The quote is a play on the title of a well-known article on legal education: R Collier, '"We're All Socio-Legal Now?" Legal Education, Scholarship and the "Global Knowledge Economy" – Reflections on the UK Experience' (2004) 26 *Sydney Law Review* 504.
[76] HLA Hart, *The Concept of Law* (Oxford, Clarendon Law Series, 1961) v.
[77] N Lacey, *A Life of HLA Hart – The Nightmare and the Noble Dream* (Oxford, Oxford University Press, 2004) 229.
[78] ibid 230.
[79] ibid 229.
[80] ibid 229.

which strong sociological studies of Australian law and politics could follow. Sawer did not engage in strong political theorising (hence Pannam's criticisms). Furthermore, he did not follow the two volumes with a work of sociological or analytical theory of a similar kind to HLA Hart, Ronald Dworkin, Talcott Parsons or Max Weber. In one sense, the work was empirical. However, Sawer was not wholly sold on empirical legal studies, observing that many existing works in the genre were 'flat and obvious'.[81] In correspondence with Hart about his book, Sawer wrote that he 'wished to avoid the title "Sociology of Law", partly because it is pretentious in a non-sociologist and partly because there are already two books of that name known to us – neither very good'.[82] This frank assessment suggests that he appreciated that both he and Hart shared the same cautious sentiment when it came to sociological jurisprudence.

While Sawer's work was different from Hart's, his views on the value of sociology to law were similar. Like Hart, Sawer adopted an expansive definition of sociology. He opened his book for the Clarendon Law Series – *Law in Society*[83] – with a defence of Hart's claim that *The Concept of Law* was a work of descriptive sociology. He argued that jurisprudential scholars have always been sociologically inclined because they have an awareness that the legal system is part of organised society.[84] To Sawer, sociology in law was both a broad church and nothing new. In his inaugural speech as Professor of Law in the RSSS ('The Role of a Lawyer in the Social Sciences'), Sawer provided the following example of one of his own studies:

> [I]n a recent article in the *Australian Law Journal* (27 *ALJ* 323), I considered some cases dealing with rights of suit between spouses and their respective employers, as affected by the old common law rule that husband and wife, being one, cannot sue each other. Besides giving the detailed rules applicable to this matter, the article considered some sociological factors governing the decisions, and also the logical character of certain types of explanatory concept which lawyers often put forward to support the chain of reasoning by which they arrive at a decision.[85]

Sawer believed that the inclusion of logical legal analysis did not mean that his work was not sociological. He took the expansive position that all judging and legal scholarship which recognised that legal reasoning involved something more than the mechanical application of rules and principles was, at least in part, sociological.[86] Further, he argued that where judges chose to take a strict legalist

[81] Sawer (n 9) 4.

[82] Sawer to HLA Hart, 8 July 1963, Professor G Sawer Correspondence, Australian National University Archives.

[83] Sawer (n 9).

[84] ibid 4–5.

[85] G Sawer, *The Place of a Lawyer in the Social Sciences* (Melbourne, Melbourne University Press, 1953) 14.

[86] ibid 10, 15–16.

approach, on the grounds that the approach would better serve society than its alternatives, then they, too, were taking a sociological position. Controversially, Sawer applied this reasoning to suggest that Sir Owen Dixon's judging had a sociological quality.[87] He argued that Dixon had reached his position on how to reason based on a sociological analysis of what society needed.[88] Sawer suggested that the idea of a sociological approach to viewing law was nothing new or threatening.[89] In this way, his book sought to build bridges between the analytical and sociological schools. He held Hart's mistrust for sociology,[90] but, unlike Hart, matched this with scepticism over the potential for philosophy and analytical jurisprudence to guide the discipline. Sawer did not attempt to bring the discipline closer to philosophy. Nonetheless, *Law in Society* played to Hart's interests in dampening enthusiasm for the grand sociological theorists.

In *Law in Society*, Sawer made it clear that he did not fully embrace any of the sociological schools, nor did he think that their insights for law were any better or worse than the traditional analytical schools. Each had its limitations. Sawer's purpose in writing the book was to introduce the novice to the major ideas on the sociology of law, provide a brief assessment of their merits, and relate them to traditional schools of thought. As Lindell noted, for Sawer, the various schools of thought were all 'grist for the mill' and he took nothing with 'special reverence'.[91] One of the central threads of the book is that, while there were some radical elements, the new sociological thinking largely did not challenge or better what was already known. Rather, it added depth and an incentive for further thought and reflection. As Cedric Jones, a lecturer at the University of Dublin, commented in his review of this work, '[i]t is not so ambitious a book but it introduces and reflects faithfully contemporary sociological jurisprudence: so many questions tentatively answered'.[92] He aptly described Sawer as the 'sensible evaluator'.[93] He suggested – I believe rightly – that Sawer's book would not 'inspire' its readers as much as the sociological theorists would, adding that '[o]ddly, it is the very distortions of the theorist that arouse such enthusiasm'.[94] Sawer's failure to prescribe or point to an inspiring programme for sociological jurisprudence – instead expressing general caution – no doubt appealed to Hart.

Several reviewers confirmed what appears to have been the underlying premise of the book: that the majority of the profession, as well as law teachers, were ignorant of the broader theories, and that this ignorance impaired their view of

[87] ibid 15–16.

[88] ibid.

[89] ibid 3–5, 15–16 and ch 1 of Sawer (n 9).

[90] D Sugarman, 'Hart Interviewed: HLA Hart in Conversation with David Sugarman' (2005) 32 *Journal of Law and Society* 267, 289.

[91] Lindell (n 10).

[92] TC Jones, 'Book Review: *Law in Society* by Geoffrey Sawer' (1966) 17 *Northern Ireland Legal Quarterly* 220, 221.

[93] ibid 222.

[94] ibid.

law and made them sceptical about thinking and argument that challenged law's autonomy.[95] Sawer's book was shorter and lacked the clarity of Paton's *A Textbook of Jurisprudence*. (Paton wrote beautifully.) Yet, the format and approach of *Law in Society* – instructing the beginner in the central schools without assuming any knowledge and providing some evaluation – made Sawer's book an excellent companion work to Paton's. Together, they provided a strong Australian contribution to strengthening theoretical reflections on law.

Before Sawer's book appeared, the Clarendon Law Series had been met with a degree of scepticism, with scholars believing that the works were largely 'lawyers' books',[96] liable to promote conservative understandings of law. Sawer's contribution signalled a change in direction that seems to have allayed some of these concerns. Sawer's attempt to move the discipline forward, by increments, was appreciated by one reviewer, Lyall, who said that the book 'is not a direct attack on the errors of uninformed positivism but rather weans one away from the linguistic preoccupations of that attitude. Positivism is good only if allied to social consciousness'.[97] Similarly, Peter Brett believed that Sawer had helped with efforts to inspire a cultural change, saying that 'lawyers will not be inattentive to the social relations of law or the part which natural science and systematised social knowledge can play in solving legal problems'.[98]

Generally speaking, Sawer avoided grand sociological theorising. He developed arguments that were closely intertwined with his analysis and evaluation of the facts on topics such as federalism and law reform. In the course of his career he did, however, employ some sociological concepts. For example, in his substantial comparative work on federal systems, *Modern Federalism* (1969), he used Weber's concept of 'ideal types' to explain different versions of federalism and the trajectory of countries operating under a federal system.[99] These ideal types helped Sawer to explain why the trajectory of federal systems was not always, or necessarily, a movement towards centralisation. The book received strong reviews, with one reviewer describing it as 'profound'.[100]

In '"Law as Socially Neutral" – Karl Renner', the chapter in *Studies in the Sociology of Law* that caught Hart's attention, Sawer explored the theories of Marxist philosopher Karl Renner, and considered how experiences in Australia conformed

[95] RB Jamieson, 'Book Review: *Law in Society* by Geoffrey Sawer' (1968) 54 *American Bar Association Journal* 67, 67; P Brett, 'Book Review: *Law in Society* by Geoffrey Sawer' (1966–67) 2 *Federal Law Review* 139, 140; E Kahn, 'Book Review: *Law in Society* by Geoffrey Sawer' (1966) 83 *South African Law Journal* 236, 237; FH Newark, 'Book Review: *Law in Society* by Geoffrey Sawer' (1966) *The Quarterly Review* 118, 121.

[96] Jones (n 92) 221.

[97] F Lyall, 'Book Review: *Law in Society* by Geoffrey Sawer' (1966) 9 *Journal of the Society of Public Teachers in Law* 275, 276.

[98] Brett (n 95) 140.

[99] G Sawer, *Modern Federalism* (London, Watts, 1969) 64–73.

[100] LA Sheridan, 'Book Review: GF Sawer, *Modern Federalism*' (1969) 20 *Northern Ireland Legal Quarterly* 225, 225.

to, or contradicted, his central philosophies.[101] Sawer argued that some Australian experiences demonstrated that 'law has an instrumental quality', and that it is 'capable of expression in such a way as to serve the interests of any social value'.[102] This bore out some of Renner's theories and suggested that they had relevance beyond the Soviet Union. The chapter appeared in a book which contained essays from a range of Sawer's colleagues within the RSSS, and arose from a seminar series Sawer had arranged on the topic of the sociology of law. In the preface, Sawer voiced caution about the sociological theorising covered by the various authors of the book:

> Sometimes these propositions are incorrigible generalisations – either because so general, or because they are so qualified with *exceptions and escape clauses that no observation can invalidate them.* Considered as natural-scientific propositions, they are at best *tentative hypotheses.* Their *predictive power is apt to be small.*[103]

Again, this demonstrates that Sawer was measured in his appraisal and promotion of the benefits of sociological theory to law. In Sawer's view, scholars ought to be aware of grand theories, but this did not mean they should embrace them uncritically.

Sawer's scholarship suggests that one reason Australian legal scholars did not advance their own brand of jurisprudence was because they believed that the existing and older schools did not do enough to advance the discipline. Sawer believed that the existing schools placed too much emphasis on the courts instead of examining other methods of law reform. In the later years of his career, Sawer became increasingly bold in this assessment. Writing on the ongoing debates between Hart and Devlin and many others over the relationship between law and morality, Sawer bluntly stated that he believed 'that most of this stuff is pretty worthless'.[104] He explained:

> It is dressed up as a dispute about legal and philosophical theory, but the key questions are really ones of social organisation and social psychology, and the better view may vary from society to society and at different stages of development of the same society. When there is general stability and prosperity, or at least contentment, and the system of government is open and flexible enough for legal change to be relatively easy, the better view may well be that existing law is law and ought normally to be obeyed; it may then be said that the path of good conscience is to accept existing law but work vigorously to change it or secure appropriate provisos and exceptions where it works unjustly. If, however, rapid social changes in value systems are under way and if in addition the system of government is resistant to change and frustrates principled efforts at reform, then it may well be that it is better to deny the title 'law' to rules which are felt to

[101] Sawer (n 13).
[102] ibid 137.
[103] G Sawer, 'Introduction' in G Sawer, *Studies in the Sociology of Law* (Canberra, Australian National University Press, 1961) viii (emphasis added).
[104] Sawer (n 7) 71.

be grossly unjust, and to obstruct the operations of the legal system by all means short of imitating the immorality of which the system is accused.[105]

Towards the end of his career, Sawer reached the same conclusion as Brett: that efforts were better spent considering the jurisprudence of law reform bodies other than the courts.[106] His writing on the Ombudsman, the first of its kind, was controversial in that it suggested that there were deficiencies in Australia's political and legal system.[107] Following his proposal, other scholars and lawyers wrote on the topic and moves were made to create a Commonwealth merits review tribunal of administrative decisions as well as an Ombudsman,[108] and, in July 1977 the first Commonwealth Ombudsman was appointed.

Sawer's career has substantial sociological threads that he wove into his scholarship in his own distinctive way. He believed that the sociological jurisprudential scholars had said something important, and his scholarship embodies his response to both aspects of the sociological school as well as the realists. He prompted lawyers and scholars to look beyond positivism. His efforts worked towards a significant cultural shift, both in Australia's legal academy and the profession.

A Middle Ground

It is clear that Sawer developed a strong view about the role of law and how it ought to be studied while he was at the ANU. To better contextualise his position within the larger realm of legal ideas, it is important to acknowledge that his career was flanked by two distinct and opposing attitudes towards law's autonomy. During the first two decades of his career, Sawer operated in an environment where full-time academics were in the minority in law schools; they were a small group who taught some but not all of the law curriculum. The most influential and prevalent ideas about the law often stemmed from judges, and for many the legitimacy of law was tied to its autonomy. Shortly after he moved to ANU, Sawer noted 'the unfriendly attitude which some Australian judges can be expected to take towards American-style legal research'.[109] He recalled an incident where a member of the judiciary had objected to an exam question set by Sawer which implied that a

[105] ibid.

[106] See, eg, Sawer (n 8); G Sawer, 'The Legal Theory of Law Reform' (1970) 20 *University of Toronto Law Journal* 183; G Sawer, *Ombudsmen* (Melbourne, Melbourne University Press, 1964). See also G Sawer, 'The Ombudsman and Related Institutions in Australia and New Zealand' (1968) (May) *Annals of the American Academy of Political and Social Science* 62; G Sawer, 'The Ombudsman Comes to Alberta' (1968) 6 *Alberta Law Review* 95; G Sawer, 'The Jurisprudence of Ombudsmen' (n 8).

[107] Lindell (n 10).

[108] This was through the efforts of the Kerr Committee: Sir Anthony Mason, Professor Harry Whitmore and Sir John Kerr.

[109] Sawer (n 85), 17–18. Lindell concurred with this attitude and said that it was a 'struggle' to get people interested in a contextual approach even in the 1960s': Lindell (n 10).

judge's personal characteristics affects the judge's decision-making.[110] In an article about his role in the RSSS, Sawer acknowledged that:

> The influence of political movements upon the lawyers … is a much more delicate and difficult field of inquiry, and a good many lawyers are disposed to argue that it should never be attempted at all, or else that it would be a useless study because there is no influence of politics on law.[111]

During the course of his career, from the 1930s to the 1970s, Australian judges continued to display suspicion towards probing inquiries into the factors beyond precedent that may have entered into their decision-making.[112] As a reviewer of one of Sawer's books remarked:

> He is not, of course, a conservative traditionalist in the mould of so much of the Australian legal profession and the verve with which he throws off his contentious ideas makes even some of the abler members of that profession feel somewhat uncomfortable.'[113]

Sawer's attempts to encourage sitting and former members of the court to expose their attitudes and methods of judicial reasoning were generally met with resistance.[114]

Sawer wrote and spoke to Dixon many times in response to his High Court decision-making, often offering critique; Dixon was courteous in his responses, sharing amusing anecdotes. In one telephone note of a conversation with Dixon, Sawer wrote:

> He discussed Isaacs – vain, over-elaborate in this thinking, but extremely learned. Isaacs knew Dixon's father and once claimed to have handled Dixon as a child. Sir Frank Gavan Duffy who heard this said 'No doubt, Isaacs, you are sorry now that you didn't drop him on his head.'[115]

Sawer's attitudes and views on judging accorded more strongly with the progressive English judge, Lord Denning, who sought out Sawer's company and views on English cases.[116] To friends, such as Victorian Supreme Court judge Vincent

[110] ibid 18.

[111] Sawer (n 85) 14–15.

[112] Sawer gave the example of former Australian judge, Sir Alan Taylor, who refused to reveal which school he attended because he believed it was no one's business and of no relevance to his later career: Pratt (n 33).

[113] LF Crisp, 'Book Review: Geoffrey Sawer, *Modern Federalism*' (1969) 3 *Federal Law Review* 302. Crisp cited the following review of Sawer's work by a judge of the New South Wales Court of Appeal as an example of such discomfort: JD Holmés, 'Book Review: Geoffrey Sawer, *Australian Federalism in the Courts*' (1968) 3 *Federal Law Review* 144, 144–45. Holmes described Sawer's work as 'provocative and worthy of consideration if not always of acceptance'.

[114] See, eg, Chief Justice Barwick's negative response to Sawer's request that he provide comment on the Court's current methods. Barwick to Sawer 16 November 1966, Papers of Geoffrey Sawer, National Library of Australia.

[115] Sawer telephone note, 27 February 1958, Papers of Geoffrey Sawer, National Library of Australia.

[116] Lord Denning to Sawer, 7 March 1972, Papers of Geoffrey Sawer, National Library of Australia.

Barry, Sawer advocated more robust critiques of Australian judges,[117] but in print he never issued a full-blown attack on Dixon's strict legalism. There appeared to be a line concerning criticism of Dixon which legal scholars in the 1950s and 1960s would not cross for fear of alienating the profession and damaging the reputation of the growing academy.

At the end of Sawer's career in the 1970s, the size and number of law schools had grown significantly. Some law schools and individual scholars were opposed to traditional conceptions of law and believed that law schools should distance themselves from the interests and traditions of the legal profession. As explained in the chapters of this book on Alice Erh-Soon Tay, various attitudes circulated, including the Marxist view that the law was the product of oppressive ideologies which served to subjugate and marginalise various groups, including women, the poor and racial minorities. While Sawer was never extremely cutting in his criticisms of them, his earlier position on Marxism meant that he was largely unsympathetic to the work of this new generation of critical scholars.

Throughout his career, Sawer's position and interests were therefore at odds with prevailing attitudes. To understand Sawer's contributions and motivations properly, it is worth considering how he responded to these opposing attitudes and whether he attempted to pitch his ideas and position in a way that made them more palatable to these very different audiences.

When Sawer moved to the RSSS, he was a promising academic with a solid but not yet remarkable scholarly reputation. He moved into a role that was entirely alien to existing notions of the legal scholar. At that time, the primary function of legal scholars – the reason they were entitled to draw full-time salaries from the government and why the government injected money into the expansion of universities – was to provide an education suitable for legal practitioners. Sawer's challenge, among other things, was to convince the legal profession and legal academy that a full-time legal scholar in a research school for social sciences – who did not teach undergraduates and therefore did not prepare future lawyers for practice – could perform a useful role. What is important to note here is that the message he conveyed to his Australian audience was consistent with the ideas he advanced in other aspects of his scholarly work.

When Sawer publicly explained his role, he presented the idea of a lawyer within the social sciences as a non-threatening prospect. He argued that previous Australian professors, as well as High Court justices, had been sociological in their approach.[118] Sawer's broad definition of the sociology of law, described earlier, indicates that these characterisations were sincere. Sawer genuinely believed that his placement within the RSSS represented an incremental, rather than radical, step towards formalising connections between law and the social sciences.[119]

[117] Judge Vincent Barry to Sawer, 3 July 1958, Papers of Geoffrey Sawer, National Library of Australia.
[118] Sawer (n 85) 10, 15–16.
[119] Sir Anthony Mason believed that, while Sawer was progressive and innovative, he was not a radical: A Mason, 'Geoffrey Sawer: The Priceless Professor', *Canberra Times* 21 December 1990, 7.

He sympathised with practitioners who believed that the question of law's autonomy was linked to its legitimacy.[120] Sawer, too, believed that maintaining the legitimacy of courts was paramount to the standing of law and the profession. It was therefore important for Sawer to convince both his audience and himself that nothing would be lost by acknowledging that values and politics play a part in judicial reasoning. His goal was to introduce the uninitiated to new ways of thinking about law without condemning their existing beliefs.

Given his location and role, it might have been tempting for Sawer to proclaim, or simply accept, that law was part of the social sciences. Not only was Sawer located in a social science school, he was also one of the early members of what later became the Academy of Social Sciences in Australia.[121] In 1972, he became its chairman.[122] And yet, despite his position, he never stated that law was a social science. Instead, he argued that it was a 'social technology, one of several available for the organisation of human society'.[123] Sawer did not fully explain what he meant by this expression, but he was presumably characterising law as a collection of technical and intellectual skills and knowledge that could be put to use in shaping a society. To understand society, one needs to have regard to the role of that technology; to understand the technology, one needs to appreciate its role and impact on society. Those engaged in law therefore needed recourse to the social sciences. But, according to Sawer, from this relationship it did not follow that law was a social science.

In some of Sawer's scholarship, he demarcated the technical skills and knowledge of law by employing Sir Courtenay Ilbert's phrase 'lawyers' law'.[124] Sawer's use of the phrase is controversial, as, contrary to his own convictions, it could imply that law is autonomous.[125] Instead, Sawer used the phrase to suggest only that there were aspects of law that were solely the province of lawyers. He believed that the phrase served as neat shorthand – like a sociological concept – that could be used to explain when and why lawyers were needed. Again, this points to Sawer's belief that embracing sociology did not involve abandoning traditional conceptions of law.

Towards the end of his career, Sawer extended the same thoughtful consideration he had shown to the 1950s legal profession to a new generation of legal

[120] Sawer's commitment to the integrity of the courts was made clear in the article he co-authored with Paton (Sawer and Paton (n 3)), in his inaugural speech as Chair of Law in the Department (Sawer (n 85) 18–19), and in chs 5 and 6 of *Law in Society*, Sawer (n 9).

[121] Macintyre (n 57), 82.

[122] ibid 189.

[123] G Sawer, 'Who Controls the Law in Australia?: Instigators of Change and Obstacles Confronting Them' in AD Hambly and JL Goldring (eds), *Australian Lawyers and Social Change* (Sydney, Lawbook, 1976) 181–82. Else-Mitchell also drew attention to this aspect of Sawer's characterisation of law's relationship with the social sciences: R Else-Mitchell, 'Introduction' in L Zines (ed), *Commentaries on the Australian Constitution: A Tribute to Geoffrey Sawer* (Sydney, Butterworths, 1977) xix, xxi.

[124] Sawer (n 123) 120; Sawer (n 9) 112, 116, 126–36, 172, 175, 183, 186, 190, 202–03, 208; Sawer (n 85) 11.

[125] This was an objection raised by (Sir) Anthony Mason. See, eg, AF Mason, 'Law Reform in Australia' (1970–71) 4 *Federal Law Review* 187, 215.

academics and students, the 'young Turks' of the 1970s. Of course, Sawer was not in favour of the Marxist sentiment that was again sweeping through universities in the 1970s, and did not believe that legal education or the law itself ought to be radicalised in the way that mainly younger scholars and students were suggesting at this time. However, he did not ignore or flatly reject the movement. Unlike Tay, he did not present as an elder statesman dismayed by the impatience and ignorance of youth. When asked to present a paper at a seminar arranged by a number of younger legal academics on the topic of lawyers and social change, he accepted and his paper was followed by open discussion and provoked a large amount of criticism. He thoughtfully considered and addressed the criticism in a paper that formed an epilogue to the book that was eventually published from the seminar. The 'broad aim of the seminar was to assess the responsiveness of Australian law and lawyers to social change, and to consider the extent to which the law and lawyers can, and should, be used as instruments for promoting change'.[126] It is clear from the book that the organisers and most of the contributors held the view that the law and lawyers served as obstacles to, rather than facilitators of, change. Sawer's paper was at odds with this view: he believed that there were sufficient lawyers servicing the poor and disadvantaged, and he maintained the view expressed in his previous works that the better instrument for social reform was parliament, not the courts. He said:

> If I thought that the courts did or could play a major role in social reform through legal reform I would go further. As things stand, however, it seems to me that judicial legislation is of such marginal importance so far as any large measures of social reform are concerned, and that judicial integrity is so important to the stabilisation of whatever measures of social reform are otherwise carried into law, that it would be best to interfere very sparingly with the present situation of the judiciary, including the law as to contempt. For believers in continuous revolution, whatever that may mean, the situation is obviously different.[127]

Sawer considered that, rather than abandoning traditional approaches to law and lawyering, 'lawyers' law' served a useful function. He believed that it should sit alongside more radical attempts at reform by the legislative and administrative arms of government. He added the caveat that this did not mean that law schools should teach law in a narrow technocratic way. Instead, he favoured a liberal curriculum in universities and separate schools, where the profession took responsibility for imparting 'legal craftsmanship'.[128]

Despite his measured response to the problems posed by the conference organisers, his paper drew little support. Some contributors misconstrued his message, believing that he was advocating for law's insularity, while others simply could

[126] AD Hambly and JL Goldring, 'Preface' in AD Hambly and JL Goldring (eds), *Australian Lawyers and Social Change* (Sydney, Lawbook, 1976) v.
[127] Sawer (n 123) 136.
[128] ibid 181–82.

not accept that lawyers were only bit-players in social change. For some, the time had come to radicalise the legal profession instead of working around it. The experience sheds further light on Sawer's character and manner. He was a man of strong convictions who believed that ideas were worth listening to and also worth defending. He promoted by example the respectful exchange of opposing ideas. These examples suggest that he did not temper his convictions based on his audience or prevailing trends and attitudes. He was a scholar of integrity and diplomacy.

Concluding Remarks

Many things could be said about Sawer's scholarship and its contribution to constitutional law. Here, however, the focus has been on Sawer's theoretical perspectives and what he did to change cultures and attitudes within Australia's legal academy and profession. In this chapter I recognise that Sawer was at heart a legal theorist – perhaps for the first time this has happened in the literature regarding Sawer. His appointment to the RSSS at a time when his ideas and scholarship were moving into a phase of maturity meant that he had time to carefully reflect on where his studies and interests were taking him and to contemplate the needs of the discipline. His decision to provide a solid, factual basis for future constitutional studies (including his own) and to provide the necessary guidance for other scholars and lawyers to learn about the major ideas that supported contextual and theoretical approaches to the study of law was both wise and responsible. It represents the two sides of Sawer – a man of high intellect, imagination and ambition, but tempered with a strong sense of responsibility. Unlike Tay, who devoted much of her energy to creating a particular academic environment within the Department of Law at the University of Sydney, and unlike Brett whose life was cut short, Sawer was able to take the time and opportunity to fully develop his scholarship, publishing a vast number of books and articles. Once he had laid what he believed to be the appropriate foundations for Australian constitutional law scholarship and Australian legal theory, he then used the insights gained to develop more sophisticated work that shone light on new areas of scholarship and contextualised Australia's constitutional law within an international sphere.

From the collection of the Australian National University Archives: Photographs of people at the Australian National University, ANUA 225-1101, Professor Geoffrey Sawer, 1953

Geoffrey and Mamie Sawer (approximately 1960) printed with permission of copyright owner, Elizabeth Penhallurick, image currently held by National Library of Australia, image 7755283, <https://nla.gov.au/nla.obj-642350534/view>

Geoffrey Sawer reading in chambers (approximately 1940)) printed with permission of copyright owner, Elizabeth Penhallurick, image currently held by National Library of Australia, image 7755305, <https://nla.gov.au/nla.obj-642349868/view>

14

Sawer and the Research School of Social Sciences

Introduction

Sawer's appointment as the first professor of the Research School of Social Sciences (RSSS), and the inclusion of the Department of Law within the School, were the initiative of the founders of the Australian National University (ANU). None of the founders had been members of Australia's legal academy and Sawer had no say over the inclusion of law in the RSSS. In fact, before receiving an invitation to join the Department, Sawer had reservations about the role of both ANU and the RSSS, believing it would be better to strengthen existing Australian universities than create a new national university.[1] As I explain in this chapter, the founders of the RSSS had very vague ideas about law's role within the School. Its inclusion was not the result of Sawer's strong intellectual conviction – nor that of anyone else – that law was a social science; it did not indicate that either some or the majority of members of Australia's legal academy believed that law should shed its technocratic associations and embrace learning from the social sciences. The mere fact of Sawer's appointment to the first chair in the RSSS constitutes an interesting quirk of history, rather than a momentous event in the context of Australian legal education.

What is, however, important about Sawer's position in the RSSS is that it allowed him more time than other Australian legal scholars to devote to laying down strong intellectual foundations for the discipline of law. As explained in the previous chapter, this included a strong basis for the further study of constitutional law and a legal theory that attempted to move both the profession and the legal academy away from the view that law was an autonomous discipline. With the benefit of hindsight, through his substantial work and novel contributions, Sawer demonstrated that a full-time legal researcher (as opposed to teacher and part-time researcher) represented a worthwhile occupation and a good use of public funds.

Despite his industry and stature, there are signs that Sawer held reservations about his role. Comments he made at various times suggest that he was never fully

[1] G Sawer, 'Outline Biography', Geoffrey Sawer Papers, National Library of Australia, Manuscript Collection 14; M Pratt, Interview with Geoffrey Sawer (Oral History Interview, Canberra, 16 November 1971), https://nla.gov.au/nla.obj-214869908/listen.

convinced of the utility of his position as a full-time researcher and was uneasy about the fact that he did not have undergraduate students to prepare for practice.[2] At times, he attempted detailed explanations of how his role was different from that of other Australian legal scholars, how the Department of Law had different aims and functions from other law schools, and how it was not designed to be a large independent institute devoted to the study of law.[3] However, these messages were not received as well as they might have been, and assessments of the Department of Law were often made on the assumption that the Department was destined to become a large research institution and/or a law school.

Of the three scholars who are the focus of this book, Sawer was the least divisive figure and has attracted the greatest admiration and praise. However, even some of his greatest admirers point to one major shortcoming: he did not create a large lively Department of Law within the RSSS.[4] As this could be construed as a very damning criticism of Sawer, and one which might weaken the earlier claim that he made a significant contribution to law's disciplinary identity in Australia, it is worth exploring further the way he ran the Department and viewed its role.

An assessment of Sawer and his Department must be made on its own terms and with an appreciation of the broader context. Such an assessment should not be coloured by an idealised vision of what a large research institute in law should look like today. These were different times that called for different measures. This does not, however, ignore the possibility that, had Sawer done more to build the Department of Law in the RSSS, Australia's discipline of law might have diversified and embraced interdisciplinary studies more rapidly. In the late 1960s and 1970s, the Department might have provided a forum for sociologically inclined legal scholars to join forces to create initiatives that widened law's intellectual credentials. The consequences of Sawer's failure to build the Department are considered further in chapter fifteen. In this chapter, my goal is to ascertain whether he had good reasons for not taking up what now seems to have been a golden opportunity.

Sawer's Appointment to a World-class Australian University

The idea for a national university in Australia originated in the 1940s with three Australian intellectuals: Professor of Medicine, Douglas (Panzee[5]) Wright, and

[2] Sawer wrote that, while there was enough work for the RSSS to be a pure research institution, 'We do not feel content with that role alone, at least not in the social sciences'. See, eg, G Sawer, 'Law at the Australian National University' (1959) 5 *Journal of the Society of Public Teachers of Law* 20, 21–22, 25.

[3] ibid.

[4] Such views are explained further below.

[5] 'Panzee' was the nickname given to Wright, as his long arms reminded others of a chimpanzee: G Sawer, 'Partly Unreliable Memoir', Geoffrey Sawer Papers, National Library of Australia, Manuscript Collection, part 19, 3.

two public servants, Alfred Conlon and Herbert Cole Coombs.[6] Each was heavily engaged with the war effort, and at the same time looked optimistically towards nation-building initiatives that could be implemented at the end of the Second World War.[7] The creation of the ANU was a product of that optimism. Coombs's vision was for a university devoted to research work at a postgraduate level, which could engage in joint research projects with government to solve the nation's social problems.[8] The need for more postgraduate work was highlighted when Sir Howard Florey visited Australia and described medical research in Australia as being in a 'parlous state'.[9] At the instigation of these three individuals, the federal government supported the establishment of the ANU.

To a modern Australian scholar, what is particularly fascinating about ANU is the extent to which the Commonwealth Parliament and, in particular, the Prime Minister, Joseph Benedict (Ben) Chifley, were involved in its creation. The government and founders placed great stock in gathering together a group of internationally renowned scholars who could head each of the new schools, looking primarily to expatriate Australians living in London. A pivotal moment in the establishment of the university occurred when Chifley travelled to London. During that trip Chifley met Mark Oliphant, a leader in experimental research in nuclear physics, then at the University of Birmingham.[10] So strong was the impression Oliphant made on Chifley, with his talk of the possibility of Australia moving to 'the forefront of nuclear research',[11] that the Prime Minister undertook to get Oliphant to Canberra no matter what the cost. This meeting with Oliphant set ANU along the path of a much grander and more ambitious academic enterprise than had initially been envisaged by the Australian government. The interim council then placed emphasis on recruiting the very best intellectuals to lay the foundations for each school.

Former Chief Justice of the High Court of Australia, Sir Anthony Mason, described with approval the way that the subsequent Liberal Prime Minister, Sir Robert Menzies, adopted Chifley's ambitions:

> I'm very strong on this … . The Menzies idea was to create one university which in terms of research, teaching and influence at the highest level could compete with the leading American and UK universities and therefore it was important to concentrate your greatest intellectual ability, the people who had the greatest intellectual ability, at a research postgraduate university.[12]

[6] Coombs was commonly referred to as 'Nugget' due to his stocky physique: SG Foster and MM Varghese, *The Making of the Australian National University* (St Leonards, NSW, Allen and Unwin, 1996) 3.

[7] ibid 3.

[8] ibid 15.

[9] ibid 12.

[10] ibid 21.

[11] ibid 21.

[12] Interview with Sir Anthony Mason (Sir Anthony Mason's Chambers, Sydney, 9 December 2014).

While the medical and science schools duly proceeded along these lines, the founding of the RSSS at ANU did not go as planned. William Keith Hancock, an eminent Australian historian based in England, originally took on the task of establishing the School and went so far as to outline a detailed manifesto.[13] According to Hancock's initial vision, the School would consist of chief researchers in 'economics, statistics, population and health studies, law, political science, social anthropology, psychology, history and philosophy, sociology, geography'.[14] He later revised his vision a number of times, until it eventually entailed 'a more coherent grouping of subjects', focusing on economics, politics and sociology, each of which would have a professorial head.[15] He also sought a basis for historical research by appointing a 'readership in the sources of Australian history'.[16] The revision made no mention of law. Hancock believed that 'history and philosophy were essential, to ensure that the School did not degenerate into "an aggregate of people myopically focused upon their own tiny segment of place and time and research material"'.[17] Despite his enthusiasm and efforts, Hancock gave up the opportunity to bring his vision to fruition. He resigned from the advisory committee when the Vice-Chancellor of ANU, Douglas Copland, rejected Hancock's proposal to integrate the social science and Pacific studies schools.[18] This meant that the School of Social Sciences effectively began both without a director and without a clear vision.

Although Hancock was replaced by another social scientist, Kenneth Wheare, it was clear that Wheare wanted only limited involvement with the RSSS and did not wish to become the full-time director of the School. Wheare held a position at the University of Oxford and intended to remain there.[19] The task of bringing the School to fruition largely fell to Copland and Sir Frederic Eggleston. Eggleston was a lawyer and graduate of the Law School at the University of Melbourne. He was appointed to various public offices (including Attorney-General, Solicitor-General and Minister of Railways in the Allan–Peacock Victorian state government) and wrote a number of political and historical works.[20] Eggleston, then in his 70s (he died in 1954 at the age of 79), was not in a position to become the new director.[21]

The idea behind the ANU was always to attract the best researchers who could compete on a world stage. However, attracting such eminent scholars, particularly to the RSSS, proved difficult. Before abandoning his post, Hancock had made

[13] Foster and Varghese (n 6) 39–40.
[14] ibid 39.
[15] ibid 39.
[16] ibid 39.
[17] ibid 39, quoting Hancock.
[18] ibid 45–47. Hancock eventually returned to become Director of the RSSS in 1957.
[19] Sawer (n 5) part 37, 1.
[20] W Osmond, 'Eggleston, Sir Frederic William (1875–1954) in *Australian Dictionary of Biography* (Melbourne, Melbourne University Press, 1981), http://adb.anu.edu.au/biography/eggleston-sir-frederic-william-344.
[21] ibid.

several attempts to recruit eminent social scientists from England.[22] These attempts failed, and the founders' ambition to populate the RSSS with expatriate Australians who had built their careers in England was largely abandoned.

With Hancock's departure, the RSSS was left without a director, and with an appointment committee comprising Copland (the Vice-Chancellor of ANU), Wheare (an 'old school friend' of Sawer's from Scotch and Melbourne University,[23] then the Gladstone Professor of Government at All Souls, Oxford), Bailey (Sawer's teacher and colleague from Melbourne), Eggleston, Coombs and LF Crisp. All had varying levels of familiarity with Sawer and all liked him. For example, Bailey had written a reference for Sawer for a position at Melbourne where he had said Sawer was the 'best of the applicants for the Chair',[24] while Eggleston, who, like Sawer, was a graduate from Melbourne Law School, had been in frequent correspondence with Sawer; for example, seeking his views on an essay on the United Nations.[25] The decision fell to Wheare, then living in England, who although a friend of Sawer's from school and university days[26] had less familiarity with Sawer's professional academic life. Copland wrote to him: 'I think in this matter you would be able to give us a more objective view than most of us who are too close to the scene'.[27] Wheare undertook the task of getting to know Sawer a little better, and his investigations led to a favourable impression. He reported back to the committee:

> I have seen more of Sawer since I returned to Melbourne. He took part in a seminar which I held here on Tuesday (16th August). I feel more and more satisfied about him. I think he is very good. Any doubts I had about him get less. I really think that we might put him in as Professor of Law. I think he is of that quality. Probably Eggleston is right when he says that the Chair of Political Science would not be right for him, but I think he is of professorial standing all right.[28]

Despite the ANU founders' initial ambitions of attracting eminent foreign scholars – or Australian scholars with considerable overseas experience – Wheare considered that:

> [I]t would be desirable to have an Australian in the Chair of Law, or at least someone who was well versed in the problems of constitutional law in Australia and their bearing upon economic and social policy.[29]

[22] Foster and Varghese (n 6), 44.

[23] Sawer said that Wheare encouraged him to believe that he could write literature, and he looked up to Wheare like a 'kind uncle or elder brother': Pratt (n 1).

[24] Kenneth Bailey to the Vice-Chancellor of the University of Melbourne, 23 May 1947, University of Melbourne Registrar's Correspondence, University of Melbourne Archives.

[25] See, eg, Frederic Eggleston to Sawer, 23 June 1947, and Eggleston to Sawer, 28 July 1947, Frederic Eggleston Papers, National Library of Australia, Manuscript Collection.

[26] Sawer (n 5), part 37, 2.

[27] Douglas Copland to Kenneth Wheare, 15 August 1949, Research School of Social Sciences – General, Australian National University Archives.

[28] Memorandum entitled, 'The Australian National University School of Social Sciences Chair of Law by Douglas Copland', 25 August 1949, Research School of Social Sciences – General, Australian National University Archives.

[29] ibid.

It seems that Wheare, Egglestone and Coper placed weight on the social cohesion of the new school and were reluctant to appoint academics who, while brilliant, might prove to be divisive. Foster and Varghese recount how Karl Popper, now regarded as one of the leading philosophers of science in the twentieth century, was considered for the Chair in Philosophy at ANU but ultimately rejected because 'he attracted disciples and violent detractors wherever he went'.[30] While Sawer was in favour of Popper's appointment, he is also quoted as saying that any new appointee to the School had to be 'clubbable'.[31] This approach of appointing 'agreeable' academics arguably limited the ambitions and potential of the new institution.

Although Sawer was a strong and popular candidate among the committee members, he was not, at that time, an eminent Australian scholar, and he was not the committee's first choice. The committee had earlier approached one of Sawer's colleagues at the University of Melbourne, Wolfgang Friedmann, who declined the position. They had also considered Frank Beasley, Professor of Law at the University of Western Australia.[32] A few years earlier, Sawer had missed out on gaining Chairs at both the University of Melbourne and the University of Sydney.[33] Friedmann had beaten him to the Chair at Melbourne.[34] During the Melbourne appointment round, Sawer's Australian undergraduate credentials and relatively meagre publication record meant that he was no match for the applicants short-listed for the position.[35] Sawer's heavy teaching load during the war,[36] as well as his engagement in a number of additional public activities, meant that he did not produce a large amount of scholarship in the 1940s.

Even Sawer himself recognised that he was not an obvious choice for the Chair of Law at the RSSS.

> I had no expectation of going there myself; I assumed that if they had a law department (which was not at all certain), it would attract Julius Stone or Paton, since they both had a well established reputation as theorists of law, particularly interested in the kind

[30] Foster and Varghese (n 6) 104.

[31] ibid 105.

[32] Minutes of the Interim Council – Committee on the Establishment of the Research School of Social Sciences, 8 September 1949, Research School of Social Sciences – General, Australian National University Archives. Sawer thought that this might have been the case, but never asked Beasley whether he had been approached (Sawer (n 5), part 33, 3).

[33] Resolution of Council of the University of Melbourne, 2 June 1947, University of Melbourne Registrar's Correspondence, University of Melbourne Archives; Kenneth Bailey to the Vice Chancellor of the University of Melbourne, 23 May 1947, University of Melbourne Registrar's Correspondence, University of Melbourne Archives.

[34] Interestingly, Friedmann also sought to promote contextual studies of law: W Twining, 'Wolfgang Friedmann' (1972–73) 12 *Journal of the Society of Public Teachers in Law* 311, 311.

[35] Table entitled, 'The University of Melbourne Summary of Applications for the Chair of Public Law', November 1946, University of Melbourne Registrar's Correspondence, University of Melbourne Archives. Sawer knew that he had no serious prospects of getting the position at that time: Pratt (n 1).

[36] G Sawer, 'An Australian National School of Law' (1951–1953) 2 *University of Western Australia Annual Law Review* 483, 483.

> of sociological aspects which would be appropriate to the Research Schools of Social Sciences and Pacific Studies.[37]

According to Foster and Varghese's history of the ANU, Sawer was considered a safe bet: 'Wheare thought well of him', Eggleston thought he was 'likely to take an interest in the scientific aspects of law', and the council believed that with 'a substantial work on Australian constitutional cases to his credit, as well as a popular paperback on Australian government, he was regarded as a solid investment'.[38]

Recruitment to the RSSS proved difficult in all fields of research. The experimental nature of the ANU and RSSS no doubt deterred some potential recruits, as did the University's location. At that time, Canberra was 'little more than a bush town of about 20,000 permanent residents'.[39] While the 'real community spirit'[40] – and the potential to play various roles in the community – enticed Sawer, this was not a widespread attitude.[41] The first recruits to the RSSS were generally young, ranging from 32 to 41, with varying publication records (some had not published anything), and several lacked postgraduate qualifications.[42] Sawer's credentials were among the strongest. He was initially joined by Trevor Swan, an economist; HP (Horrie) Brown, a statistician; WD (Mick) Borrie, a demographer; Laurie Fitzhardinge, a historian; and Leicester Webb, a political scientist. Apart from Webb, who was from New Zealand, they were all Australians. As Stuart Macintrye, in his history of social sciences in Australia, pointed out, the 'failure to attract any senior scholars from the other Australian universities was striking'.[43] The absence of a director to lead the School meant also that the experience of the RSSS was different from that of both the Medical School, which 'benefited from the supervision of Howard Florey', and the School of Physics, which 'had the immense prestige of Mark Oliphant'.[44] As a result, the social sciences seemed 'more makeshift, less distinguished'.[45]

The fact that law was even included at this early stage is attributable largely to Eggleston's thinking. According to Sawer, Eggleston was the member of the interim council who convinced the others of the desirability of law's inclusion, but even he only thought that it would be a kind of 'spare part' to deal with the

[37] Sawer (n 1), 15. Sawer also mentioned Frank Beasley, the Dean of the University of Western Australia, as a more likely appointee: Sawer (n 5), part 33, 3.

[38] Foster and Varghese (n 6), 54.

[39] G Eccles, 'It's a Different Australia', *Herald* 26 December 1975, 4. Several of the people interviewed for this project made similar comments.

[40] ibid.

[41] ibid. Sir Anthony Mason described Canberra in the 1960s as 'like a base construction camp': Mason (n 12).

[42] ibid 54–55.

[43] S Macintyre, *The Poor Relation – A History of Social Sciences in Australia* (Melbourne, Melbourne University, 2010) 62.

[44] ibid.

[45] ibid.

legal issues that might arise in particular projects.[46] He suggested that there be one reader in law.[47] As a lawyer, diplomat and politician it is unsurprising that his vision for the RSSS included studies of political institutions. He envisaged a school of political science that

> should concern itself with the nature and structure of political institutions and their methods of operation. It should cover a wide ambit from constitutions and federations to public administration.[48]

A scholar such as Sawer, with a strong interest in public law, could contribute productively to such studies.

Like Hancock and other members of Sawer's appointment committee, Eggleston believed that Australia needed scholars who took a constructive rather than 'abstract' approach to their studies. At this time both Australian legal scholars (including Sawer) and social scientists generally frowned upon 'abstract' scholarship.[49] According to many members of this generation, what was needed were studies that would more obviously, visibly and, perhaps, immediately, contribute to the 'practical' task of nation-building. In one memorandum about the School, Eggleston said:

> What usually goes under the name of social or political philosophy is really a history of political ideas. It takes a procession of thinkers, such as Plato, Aquinas, Hobbes, Locke and Rousseau, and traces the evolution of their ideas on political authority and obligation over a long period of time. In most cases, the ideas of these thinkers are abstractions. There is no inherent objection to this, but implied in teaching of this kind is the idea that their ideas were readily translatable into practice. That these ideas had an influence on political events cannot be denied. Most modern ideologies are traceable to them. But I do not think it can be suggested that their ideas were operative or that they played any serious part in ordering the affairs of communities or their members.[50]

Sawer's work for government and his constructive attitude therefore complemented Eggleston's and fitted with the mood of the time. It was imperative that the School should contribute constructively and obviously to the nation-building effort.

Sawer was therefore appointed to the Chair of Law at the RSSS because of Eggleston's vague idea that the School should conduct studies into Australia's system of government and on the strength of Sawer's public law studies and interest in politics. There are few signs that the committee, following Hancock's

[46] Pratt (n 1).
[47] ibid.
[48] Memorandum entitled, 'The Australian National University re the School of Social Sciences' by Sir Frederic Eggleston, undated, Research School of Social Sciences – General, Australian National University Archives.
[49] See S Bartie, 'A Full Day's Work – A Study of Australia's First Legal Scholarly Community' (2010) 29 *University of Queensland Law Journal* 67, 94–95.
[50] Eggleston (n 48).

departure, engaged in broader, in-depth thinking about the nature of law and its potential and contested status as a social science. The decision to appoint Sawer and include law in the RSSS was a constructive decision made by a temporary committee, not a philosophical decision made by scholars who wished to lead the School in accordance with a set of ambitious academic ideals or cohesive mission. It was clear that the founders believed that law would play a minor role in the Department. Sawer both respected and agreed with this vision and the founders' belief that political science, economics and history would eventually take centre stage.[51] For Sawer, the appointment was a promotion and gave him much-desired research time. Having spent the 1940s taking on a wide range of responsibilities and teaching tasks to keep Melbourne's Law School going and help with the war effort, this would give him the opportunity to make up for lost ground in his scholarship.

The Department of Law

Sawer believed that law could play a useful role in a school for social scientists. He did not, however, believe that law *was* a social science. He therefore had a strong intellectual basis for his position that law should play a subsidiary rather than primary role, both within the RSSS and in studies of society.[52] He argued that such projects should be created and run by his social science colleagues,[53] and the Department of Law would provide assistance only.[54] In Sawer's vision, he and his handful of colleagues in the Department would divide their time between providing information about the law to help the social scientists, and advancing their own projects, which would resemble the traditional types of doctrinal work and jurisprudential studies that their colleagues at the existing Australian law schools were performing.[55] Of course, as noted above, Sawer did undertake a series of large, ambitious projects that launched him into the role of a political scientist and historian. Indeed, he has been acknowledged as one of the early founders of Australian political science. However, he justified these projects on the basis of need.[56] There was no one else at that time – neither political scientists nor historians – in a position to carry them out. Sawer needed such studies to advance his own Australian constitutional law scholarship. The fact that the Department was a bit-player in the RSSS therefore appears to be consistent with Sawer's

[51] Pratt (n 1).

[52] G Sawer, *The Place of a Lawyer in the Social Sciences* (Melbourne, Melbourne University Press, 1953) 12–14.

[53] ibid.

[54] ibid.

[55] ibid.

[56] See, eg, Sawer to Kenneth Wheare, 6 March 1952, Professor G Sawer Correspondence, Australian National University Archives.

intellectual convictions. It is also consistent with his tendency to do things on the basis of practical necessity, rather than burning desire.[57]

Sawer believed that, in founding the university, the government intended to prioritise the sciences over the social sciences and he supported this prioritisation. This may have also influenced his approach to the Department. In his inaugural address at ANU, he characterised the inclusion of social sciences within the ANU as a generous measure:

> It was a tribute to the courage and foresight of those who founded the University that they managed to create any place at all for the social sciences, since even in the optimistic days of 1946, when the initial plans were being developed, it was obvious that the expense of the research in the natural sciences was going to be very heavy. Probably it is an exaggeration to say that the late John Curtin [Prime Minister of Australia 1941–45] wanted a new brand of penicillin, and the late Ben Chifley [Prime Minister of Australia 1945–49] an atom bomb, but the statement does give an indication of the emphasis which existed in the minds of many of those whose goodwill was essential to bringing the University into existence. It required pushing from the natural scientists concerned, as well as from the many men from our State university social science faculties who were consulted in the early days, to ensure that the nucleus of a complete university was provided, and in the blueprint so fashioned it was inevitable that the proportionate funds for social science research was smaller. Moreover, there was a sound pragmatic justification for giving the social sciences less money, since the State universities already provide excellent training, including post graduate research, in most (though not all) of the social science subjects contemplated for the Canberra school, whereas in the natural sciences the intention was as far as possible to concentrate on things for which there was no close parallel in any existing Australian university.[58]

These comments suggest that Sawer believed the social scientists should be grateful for having any role at all at ANU. Later in his career Sawer suggested that because research produced by the social scientists was less significant than the natural sciences, it was important that they maintain a postgraduate teaching role.[59] He therefore was not disposed to challenging the hierarchy that had emerged, and was sustained throughout the twentieth century, between the natural and social sciences.[60]

Sawer believed that it was important that the social sciences within the School came together as a coordinated and cohesive body. The RSSS had come under criticism several times in the 1950s. Oliphant and others criticised the departments within the RSSS for developing in isolation. They were criticised for having no common objective and therefore being an antithesis to the academy.[61] Oliphant

[57] See, eg, the reasons Sawer gave for studying Constitutional Law and Jurisprudence: Sawer to Registrar of the University of Melbourne, 20 February 1940, Faculty of Law Historical and Centenary Papers, University of Melbourne Archives.

[58] Sawer (n 36), 484.

[59] Sawer (n 2).

[60] For a detailed historical analysis of this subordination, see Macintyre (n 43).

[61] Foster and Varghese (n 6) 111.

also complained that, with so many academics drawn from the public services, it was being run like a government department.[62] These comments were no doubt known to Sawer and influenced how he conceived his role.

What is particularly interesting about Sawer's conception is that he believed that law could constitute an obstacle to the achievement of a coordinated science of society – one that would mark 'out a distinctive domain of knowledge that could be extended cumulatively and systematically'.[63] For this reason, he believed law should be auxiliary to the social sciences, not a core part of the school in its own right. He said:

> The object of the twin Schools of Social Sciences and Pacific Studies is to carry on basic research in the social sciences, regarding the latter as comprising in some sense a coherent body of doctrines or at least as a series of studies which ought to be brought into as close relationship with each other as possible. This is obviously quite foreign to the purpose of a law school organized as such, no matter how broad and liberal the education provided by the law school may be. There are respectable grounds for treating law as a possible focus of studies in the social sciences, but the method of study would need to be much more sociological than legal; the commoner, and probably the more useful, approach to a synthesis of the social sciences is to take general sociology and anthropology, or economics, politics, and history, pursued in close association with each other, as the main disciplines.[64]

According to Sawer, the study of law as part of the science of society was a matter for disciplines other than law to explore. Sawer's role, as he conceived of it, was primarily to help his social science colleagues in their studies of social problems that involved law and in their studies of law itself. As law was 'one of the most important kinds of social control', it was something that social scientists had to study.[65] In this, Sawer would be able to provide them with knowledge of the rules and principles at play. Law at the RSSS would principally be a 'service department'.[66]

Even if we accept Sawer's reasoning for keeping the Department to a modest size and his belief that it should play a subsidiary role, why was it so small and lacking in vibrancy? The answer lies in a number of different causal factors. Some provide sound justification for Sawer's decision to keep the Department small, while others suggest that he could – and should – have done more to strengthen and enliven it. These factors are detailed below.

Early Ambitions

What is clear from an investigation of the archives is that, after winning the post, Sawer was initially very enthusiastic about his position in the RSSS and believed

[62] ibid 111.
[63] Macintyre (n 43) 31.
[64] Sawer (n 36) 485.
[65] Sawer (n 52) 11.
[66] ibid 12.

that he and his colleagues could advance large collaborative projects. In 1949, immediately before he took up his appointment at ANU, Sawer spent a year visiting universities in America (primarily) and England (to a lesser extent). It was his first trip to America and second trip overseas. Paton had nominated Sawer for a Carnegie grant that financed most of the travel,[67] while Copland arranged for further funding to enable Sawer to visit England.[68] Copland considered that the trip would provide Sawer with an opportunity to investigate social science schools in America, seek out potential recruits for the RSSS, and visit England to speak with others involved in the establishment of the ANU. Copland and Eggleston drew on their contacts and organised many meetings for Sawer throughout the US.[69] Sawer was equipped with photographs of the ANU campus and did his best in conversations to present the new venture in the best possible light.[70]

Sawer visited a large number of law schools, political science schools and institutions that aimed to further collaborative work within the social sciences. He also spoke to many eminent scholars in America (for example, Hans Kelsen, Albert Einstein, Roscoe Pound, Learned Hand, Jerome Frank, Ralph Bunche, Max Radin, Felix Frankfurter and Huttington Cairns).[71] Sawer's travels left him sceptical about the potential for the RSSS to engage in large collaborations involving multiple members of the social sciences:

> While filled with admiration for the amount of social science research going on in the USA and for the results of its application in some fields, I was surprised at the relative lack of success of the Americans in bringing about large-scale cooperation between social scientists working in different fields. There has been a great deal of effort in this direction; many institutions have been established with the object of putting economists, sociologists, political scientists, psychologists, lawyers etc into teams of one kind or another, in the hope that together they would produce the balanced synthesis, the general theory. I investigated briefly nine such institutions, of which the most ambitious was the Institute of Human Relations at Yale. I also discussed the subject with [Charles] Dollard of Carnegie, who has had to investigate it because of the amount of money his organisation has been asked to spend on such experiments. It would take too much space to set out in detail the results of this enquiry but I can summarise my conclusions as follows: (a) Limited partnerships between two or at the most three men from closely related disciplines are possible and often very fruitful; eg the social

[67] Sawer (n 1) 13.

[68] Douglas Copland to Kenneth Wheare, 12 October 1949, Geoffrey Sawer Staff Files, Australian National University Archives; Report entitled, 'Tour of USA and Britain' by Geoffrey Sawer, May 1950, Geoffrey Sawer Staff Files, Australian National University Archives.

[69] See, eg, Huntington Cairns, of the Smithsonian Institute, to Frederic Eggleston, 24 October 1949, Frederic Eggleston Papers, National Library of Australia, Manuscript Collection; EF Penrose, at John Hopkins University, to Douglas Copland, 24 October 1949, Australian National University Archives.

[70] Sawer to Ross Hohnenn, the Registrar of ANU, 21 September 1949, Geoffrey Sawer Staff Files, Australian National University Archives.

[71] Sawer (n 68).

> anthropologist with the social psychologist. (b) It is often better for the man[72] in one field to undertake a thorough course in the methods and vocabulary of adjacent fields – for the criminal lawyer to study criminal psychology – than to seek a practitioner from those fields.[73]

Sawer therefore abandoned the idea that he would be working with all or most of his colleagues on large collaborative projects. Further, he did not believe that the head of the Department could do much more than encourage conversations between its members. His time in the US suggested to him that they could not direct large-scale collaborative projects. Sawer hoped that they would recruit Americans to the Department and that the Department would follow the American tradition of laying the necessary groundwork for studies of Australian society:

> My own taste, however, favours the American tendency to accumulation and measurement of facts in the social sciences rather than the European and British tendency towards personal memoir, aesthetic appreciation of character and a priori historicism; it seems to me that in this field we need a lot more Keplers before we can achieve a Newton. For the same reason I prefer the American vice of rushing into print to the British vice of devoting an age at least to every line. It is a difficult preference to maintain, since even in the USA itself one notices that Americans with considerable European experience, such as Pollock at Ann Arbor and Elliott at Harvard, or transplanted Europeans, such as Kelsen at Berkeley and Driver at Yale, have a kind of gusto and also a kind of fastidiousness which the purely American-trained man frequently lacks. Nevertheless, it seems to me that Australia in particular needs above all the rapid accumulation of relevant facts in the light of existing hypotheses, rather than the cultivation of imaginative genius, at this stage of its development, assuming that we have to put the emphasis on one or the other – I mean, of course, in this matter of social science; I am not referring to aesthetic genius in any form. … I strongly urge that the National University should do its best to obtain first-rate Americans, trained in such techniques as those used in the various public administration and sociology research institutes, for either the Political Science or the Sociology chairs or even both.[74]

Sawer must therefore have been disappointed by the inability of the Department to recruit any Americans.

Sawer's investigations in America inspired a vision for an initial research project. He pitched the idea to Copland as follows:

> Commonwealth administration is badly in need of an overhaul. Would it be feasible to launch your social science school with a sort of Australian Hoover commission,

[72] Given Sawer's earlier liberal attitudes and the fact that his wife held a law degree, it is curious that he speaks of 'men' rather than 'people'. It is, however, consistent with the later composition of the Department. While Sawer's Department had a small number of women as doctoral students (eg, Tay), they did not employ women academics and this arguably narrowed the potential breadth and vision of the Department and the RSSS: G Strachan, 'Still Working for the Man? Women's Employment Experiences in Australia since 1950' (2010) 45 *Australian Journal of Social Issues* 1.

[73] ibid.

[74] Sawer, Report on Tour of USA and Britain, May 1950, Geoffrey Sawer Staff Files, Australian National University Archives.

> investigation being carried out by your political science, economics, sociology etc blokes? The sort of thing I had in mind was to get one of the top American blokes at this sort of thing eg Gulick or a Brookings man, with a short-term chair while doing that job and teaching readers etc of Australian origin the American technique. Should be a popular notion with Menzies. If you do discuss this with any politicos keep my name right out; I am suspect to most of them. I would of course be happy to do legal work in such a set up but the less said about that the better for the Nat University. … Ah, well, perhaps it's just a pipe dream, but I would certainly like to see the social science school start off by getting its teeth into a real job like these American johnnies instead of considering its collective navel in the Oxford manner.[75]

This proposal demonstrates Sawer's commitment to a constructive project that would assist with the reform of government. Again, it shows signs of preferring the concrete to the abstract.

The note also suggests that Sawer did not feel confident that he could personally convince the government of the merits of such a project or drive negotiations. Sawer's lack of confidence was perhaps the product of one of his central experiences during the Second World War. He had begun his appointment at the University of Melbourne at the onset of the war and, although he never fought,[76] many of his activities during that decade were shaped by the events and aftermath of the war. He was involved in various war efforts; for example, as Officer in Charge of the short-wave broadcasts of the Australian Broadcasting Service from Australia to Japan and the Japanese-occupied territories.[77] This propaganda unit was set up by the political scientist William MacMahon Ball, and it was Ball who intervened when Sawer took steps to join his old militia battalion in 1941.[78] Sawer had never felt a strong urge to enlist, but did feel obliged to get involved when Japan became more threatening to Australia.[79]

Sawer's experience with the propaganda unit is important for various reasons, including that it gave him a direct line to Australian politics and government strategies. But its relevance here lies in the fact that it ultimately served to weaken – rather than strengthen – some of Sawer's key political connections and earned him the reputation of being a loose cannon. Towards the end of his service,

[75] Sawer to Douglas Copland, 13 December 1949, Geoffrey Sawer Staff Files, Australian National University Archives.

[76] Later in life Sawer said that he had 'never felt any urge to go to war' and believed that sending troops out of Australia when there was a Japanese threat was a dangerous strategy: Sawer (n 1) 6.

[77] 'Geoffrey Sawer 1910 –' (1980) 11 *Federal Law Review* 259, 259; J Farquharson, 'Starke, Joseph Gabriel (Joe) (1911–2006)' in Obituaries Australia (Australian National University) http://oa.anu.edu.au/obituary/starke-joseph-gabriel-joe-932/text933. Sawer was also engaged by Evatt to draft a peace treaty with Japan; however, the Australian draft was not used.

[78] Vice-Chancellor of the University of Melbourne to Mr Calwell, 29 June 1945, University of Melbourne Registrar's Correspondence, University of Melbourne Archives; J Waugh, *First Principles – The Melbourne Law School 1857–2007* (Melbourne, Miegunyah Press, 2007) 140–41.

[79] Sawer (n 1) 11–12.

Evatt, then Attorney General and Minister of Foreign Affairs, convinced Sawer to make a number of broadcasts making the case for Indonesian self-governance.[80] This was a position that Evatt – but not the rest of the Australian government – supported.[81] Part of Evatt's argument consisted of criticisms of both the Americans and the Dutch.[82] Sawer incorporated these criticisms into his planned broadcasts; however, not all of them went to air.[83] Sawer believed that a member of the Dutch camp, working in the building where Sawer made his broadcasts, leaked the transcripts he had prepared to a Melbourne newspaper (the *Sun*), which published them.[84] Embarrassed by the leaked broadcasts and newspaper headlines that suggested that Sawer, and by implication the Australian government, backed the Japanese leaders in Indonesia, the Prime Minister, Ben Chifley, summoned Sawer to Canberra (his first plane trip) and 'encouraged' Sawer's return to academia.[85]

When Sawer began planning for his position at the RSSS, the embarrassment he had caused Chifley through his radio broadcasts might have remained central to his thinking. At least in Sawer's mind, the experience potentially lessened his influence with the government and politicians. It also meant that he could not call on their support for his ambitious project involving the review of government. Sawer's affiliation with the Labor Party may have also been a factor that worked against him. His broadcasting work and role in the *Bank Nationalisation Case* derived from his friendship with Labor politicians. From 1949 to 1966, Australia was governed federally by the Liberal Party, with Robert Menzies as Prime Minister. It may be that the Liberals were suspicious of Sawer's loyalties and positions, although Sawer himself said that, while he did more work for Labor, he was always happy to work for either party.[86]

Sawer's doubts about how he was regarded by the government, coupled with law's status within the RSSS, explain why his more ambitious plans to review the operations of the government were never fully implemented. While he was the first professor appointed to the RSSS, he did not have a mandate to shape the School in any way that he wished.[87] Sawer was very much concerned with how the RSSS would operate and, through his travels, sought to draw lessons from the United States. He was not, however, the obvious person to lead the School.

[80] Sawer (n 5) part 31.
[81] ibid.
[82] ibid.
[83] ibid.
[84] ibid.
[85] ibid.
[86] Sawer (n 1) 13.
[87] Douglas Copland to Geoffrey Sawer, 22 December 1949, Geoffrey Sawer Staff Files, Australian National University Archives.

Dean of the RSSS

Notwithstanding his subordinate status, for six years Sawer took up a new temporary leadership position as Dean of the RSSS (as opposed to Director).[88] As Sawer explained:

> In early 1951 the five of us on the ground (Swann, Webb, Borrie, Fitzhardinge) foregathered with Copland and they elected me to the interim position of Dean of the School, with the general intention of still trying to get Hancock or some eminent expatriate as Director. In fact, I continued as Dean until 1956 when Hancock finally accepted appointment.[89]

Sawer said that the reason that the others expected him to fulfil the interim role of Dean was because the Department of Law was expected to be a small enterprise, whose work would be less demanding than the other departments. He explained:

> It was moved and carried that a Dean be appointed from those present, to chair Faculty meetings and liaise with Vice-Chancellor and Registrar. Whom to choose? I suddenly found all eyes turned on me. After all, *my appointment was a late afterthought, and I was only a sort of spare part* – there was no question of having a proper Law School. So it was moved and carried nem. con.[90]

Rather than signalling Sawer's and law's credentials to take a leading role in the RSSS, his appointment as Dean reinforced their subordination. The role also meant that Sawer spent more of his time contributing to the general management of the RSSS rather than concentrating on developing the Department of Law.

Sawer acknowledged that he did not at that time possess the qualities required to be a director of the RSSS. Later he described Hancock as 'a jolly good Director' and wrote that he was 'encouraging, accessible, an excellent chairman, and having something which I necessarily lacked = contacts and a scholarly reputation in England and the USA'.[91] These were qualities Sawer would, however, gain over the following two decades. He was appointed Director of the RSSS in 1973, the same year in which he suffered a heart attack. He survived.

The circumstances of Sawer's appointment as Dean and conversations with the founders therefore indicate that he had grand ambitions for the RSSS but that he considered himself a small player within the School. These factors shed further light on why the Department remained small. What they do not do, however, is explain why Sawer did not at least embed more modest initiatives within the Department.

[88] Pratt (n 1).
[89] Sawer (n 1) 16.
[90] Sawer (n 5) part 42, 3 (emphasis added).
[91] Sawer (n 5) part 42, 3.

Entrepreneurial Qualities

While each of the five lawyers and scholars interviewed for this project held Sawer in high esteem, all questioned why he did not do more to build the Department. Four of the five, each having worked at ANU in various capacities, issued the following general criticisms:

> I guess the downside to Geoff – who was, as I say, an absolutely wonderful man – is that he didn't really build the Department into anything of great substance. I've never been quite sure why. … He was very encouraging to me, and to one or two other people in the law school who had dealings with him, but he didn't go out, as it were, and sell the place as it happened with other departments.[92] [Emeritus Professor Dennis Pearce]
>
> I thought that Law was too small an operation. I don't know enough about how it was structured and what policies they were pursuing, but I think that there was too much emphasis on research and not enough emphasis on encouraging PhD students to work with leading figures there.[93] [Sir Anthony Mason]
>
> I don't think that the Department of Law was fated to be an empire and you have to lay some of that at the feet of Geoff Sawer.[94] [Professor Geoffrey Lindell]
>
> My impressions of Geoff were that he was highly respected around the school but that he didn't have a strategy or grand vision for the Department and that it was very much a department of individuals.[95] [Justice Ross Cranston]

The interview participants provided a number of possible explanations. The first was that Sawer was 'not an empire builder';[96] nor was he enthusiastic about the prospect of managing a large department. This explanation requires further consideration. Both Sir Anthony Mason and Professor Lindell were strong in their views that Sawer did not seem interested in creating and leading a large institution:

> I have an idea that Geoffrey Sawer was not an entrepreneur, not a person who was ambitious to build an empire. I don't think he was that sort of person. I think he saw himself more as a commentator, whether the commentary be a weekly column in a newspaper or in a learned article or a book of some kind, and I think that is how he saw himself.[97] [Sir Anthony Mason]
>
> He was not an empire builder. Look across the road and there is Jack Richardson building up the law school from practically nothing. He was not the first dean of the Law School when it was created in 1960, but he was in many ways much like Justice Marshall of the US Supreme Court, the first real Chief Justice and an empire builder. He puts it on the map, gets resources, fights for resources, knows quite a lot of people from his days

[92] Interview with Dennis Pearce (by telephone, 30 April 2015).
[93] Mason (n 12).
[94] Interview with Geoffrey Lindell (Woodbridge Community Centre, Tasmania, 23 March 2015).
[95] Interview with Justice Ross Cranston (by telephone, 30 October 2014).
[96] Lindell (n 94); Mason (n 12).
[97] Mason (n 12).

> in the public service. All the names you will see on the campus – people like Copeland. These were ex public servants who Jack would have known and made use of. That was not Geoff Sawer and it wasn't Leslie Zines[98] either – they were not empire builders.[99] [Professor Geoffrey Lindell]

These observations might suggest that Sawer lacked some of Alice Erh-Soon Tay's entrepreneurial spirit and maven qualities. And yet, in the formative stages of Sawer's career, we find that he did possess several of the qualities that made Tay such a successful academic entrepreneur. For example, he was able to develop a rich network of scholars, lawyers and politicians who each held him in very high regard. It was a network that outnumbered Tay's and, in Sawer's later life, extended around the globe. Like Tay, people sought out Sawer's company. Sir Anthony Mason recalled that 'he had great personality',[100] and that:

> He was very likeable and he had a great sense of humour. You always enjoyed talking to him. If there were a few people in a room and Geoff was there, you would walk over to Geoff and start talking to him.[101]

Similarly, Dennis Pearce observed:

> Oh, he was lovely. He was an absolutely lovely man. He was generous in attitude. I was very young doing this work and he treated me very kindly … He ran meetings in a gentle and kindly sort of fashion. He was just a super guy.[102]

Michael Coper, former Professor and Dean of Law at ANU and a friend and mentee of Sawer, described him as the 'kindest of men'.[103] Mason, Lindell and Pearce all said that one could talk to Sawer about almost any topic, that he had a wide range of interests.[104] Mason added that Sawer 'was interested in people, he enjoyed talking to people',[105] and that he was charming.[106] Cranston described him as outgoing and remembered that at work he would always say, 'G'day'.[107] In fact, Sawer was perhaps more successful in fostering and maintaining relationships than Tay, as he 'wasn't divisive … not at all'.[108]

It is also apparent that Sawer commanded respect and could lead. Lindell described Sawer as 'the great man',[109] Pearce referred to him as 'the big name',

[98] The late Professor Leslie Zines was a close friend of Sawer's and the closest thing to Sawer's successor in the field of constitutional law scholarship.

[99] Lindell (n 94).

[100] Mason (n 12).

[101] ibid.

[102] Pearce (n 92).

[103] M Coper, 'Geoffrey Sawer and the Art of Academic Commentator: A Preliminary Biographical Sketch' (2014) 42 *Federal Law Review* 389, 412.

[104] Mason (n 12); Lindell (n 94); Pearce (n 92).

[105] Mason (n 12).

[106] ibid.

[107] Cranston (n 95).

[108] Mason (n 12).

[109] Lindell (n 94).

and Taylor spoke of his 'remarkable reputation'.[110] At the same time, descriptions of Sawer suggest that he was unassuming. He did not brag about or promote his successes.[111] Unlike today, self-promotion was generally viewed as a sign of arrogance or insecurity and was frowned upon.[112] Sawer's apparent humility therefore also endeared him to many. Pearce said that, 'If someone like the Governor-General wanted to have a chat about something, it would be Geoff he would go to. Geoff was very discreet; he would never talk about it'.[113] Taylor noted that he was surprised at just how ordinary Sawer – a man of such high reputation – appeared to be:

> He was seen as one of the leading – if not *the* leading – academics, in constitutional law in Australia at that time. And, indeed, I remember when I was awarded the scholarship, the Commonwealth fellowship or whatever it was called when I was in the US, when we were talking about this – it was a real honour to be selected and to think that he would be supervising the research project. So I felt extremely privileged. I came to him with a young person's expectations of a giant, if you like, in the field and there is no question that, when meeting him, his breadth of knowledge and erudition in legal topics was palpable, it was very clear. As an individual, he didn't have the sense of presence that I had expected.[114]

While there are signs that Sawer did not wish to be a full-time manager or administrator, there was nothing within his personal make-up that would inhibit his ability to attract support for, and visitors, to the Department. This suggests that there were other reasons the Department remained a small, and in some ways inconsequential, enterprise.

Strengthening International Networks

Sawer took several steps to raise his intellectual profile and develop networks around the globe. Compared with other Australian universities, the ANU offered a very generous study leave arrangement, which meant that every three or four years he could spend between six and 12 months visiting overseas institutions. His first sabbatical was in 1955. He spent the bulk of his time at the Institute of Advanced Legal Studies at the University of London, using the Institute as a base for talks and travel within the United Kingdom and Europe. In 1956, he was invited to speak at a distinguished gathering in Paris, organised by the Committee

[110] Interview with John Taylor (by telephone, 26 November 2014).
[111] Lindell (n 94).
[112] eg, there were reservations about Copland's appointment as Vice-Chancellor at ANU, as in 'an academic world where the quality of one's mind was most esteemed when it was self-evident, he was seen as something of a self-promoter': Foster and Varghese (n 6), 31.
[113] Pearce (n 92).
[114] Taylor (n 110). Sir Ninian Stephen also spoke of Sawer's laidback style and self deprecating nature: N Stephen, 'A Recollection of Geoffrey Sawer' (1980) 11 *Federal Law Review* 261, 261.

on Science and Freedom.[115] In 1959, he spent his study leave first in London, and then in Germany at the Max Planck Institute.[116] In 1964, Sawer spent a whole year in America, devoting most of this time to the Institute of Public Administration, Vanderbilt Law Centre, where he was involved in a systematic and comparative study of court work, concentrating on courts in America and England.[117] From 1968 to 1969, he again spent study leave in the Max Planck Institute and then later at All Souls College at the University of Oxford. In Germany, he studied German public law, and in England he researched matters of law reform and spent time at the Law Reform Commission in London.[118] From mid-1972 to mid-1973, Sawer spent another year in England at All Souls and at the University of Cambridge.[119]

This travel was not always easy. On 9 April 1957, shortly before Hancock joined the RSSS and took over the leadership of the school, Sawer's wife, Mamie, suffered a stroke and then developed epilepsy.[120] On returning from work that day, Sawer found her unconscious, 'sprawled on the floor across the [bedroom] door'.[121] Mamie survived the ordeal but part of her body was paralysed, there was a risk of further brain haemorrhages, and she required substantial medical and other care. This took a considerable toll on Sawer. In his personal diary, he described the event as the 'most terrible experience since Mum came home dying of cancer', and noted his severe bouts of depression in the subsequent years.[122] Shortly after Mamie's stroke, he said that he contemplated 'mutual suicide'.[123] Despite her delicate condition, Mamie accompanied Sawer on his trips and on one occasion was able to seek treatment from specialist doctors in Germany.[124] Sadly, however, she died 12 years later from an unrelated and misdiagnosed illness during his 1968–69 sabbatical, while the pair were at All Souls in Oxford.[125] Sawer appears to have soldiered on, despite his grief and his new responsibilities, yet one imagines that this must have dampened some of his enthusiasm for building the Department of Law. Mamie's illness also meant that Sawer sought other opportunities to improve

[115] Sawer to the Vice-Chancellor of ANU, 15 May 1956, Geoffrey Sawer Staff Files, Australian National University Archives.

[116] Report on Study Leave by Geoffrey Sawer, 1960, Geoffrey Sawer Staff Files, Australian National University Archives.

[117] Report on Study Leave by Geoffrey Sawer, 5 February 1965, Geoffrey Sawer Staff Files, Australian National University Archives. The results were published as a book: D Karlen, EM Wise and G Sawer, *Anglo American Criminal Justice* (Oxford, Clarendon Press, 1967).

[118] Report on Study Leave by Geoffrey Sawer, July 1969, Geoffrey Sawer Staff Files, Australian National University Archives.

[119] Report on Study Leave by Geoffrey Sawer, 17 July 1973, Geoffrey Sawer Staff Files, Australian National University Archives.

[120] Diary entry, 9 April 1957, Geoffrey Sawer Papers, National Library of Australia, Manuscript Collection.

[121] Sawer (n 5) part 50, 1.

[122] ibid.

[123] ibid.

[124] Sawer (n 116).

[125] Sawer (n 118). Mamie was buried in Oxford.

their finances and provide his wife with the care she needed. For example, he took on journalism work to supplement his income.[126]

On 2 July 1971, Sawer married Nancy Parker, an artist, illustrator and teacher he had known for some time (she had been married to a fellow in Social Sciences at ANU).[127] They remained married until Sawer's death in 1996. The pair were married for just four years prior to Sawer's retirement from the Department in 1975.

In total, Sawer spent one-fifth of his tenure at the ANU (five out of 25 years) on sabbatical, undertaking activities at overseas institutions and universities which contributed vitally to his growing international reputation and comparative law studies. While this resulted in a strong network of scholarly contacts, it also meant that he had less time to spend at the RSSS building the Department of Law. Taken with his first wife's illness, this may provide another reason why Sawer did not build a large and lively Department of Law.

Recruitment

The Department never comprised more than a small number of legal scholars. This was due to a number of factors. First, it appears that Sawer set very high standards and was often dissatisfied with the candidates who applied for advertised positions. For example, in September 1953, Sawer drafted the first advertisement for a senior fellow in the Department.[128] Following the advertisement, he received only three applications.[129] Of the three, he deemed only one candidate to be of the requisite standard, and even then he still had reservations.[130] That candidate was, in fact, Peter Brett.[131] Sawer ultimately considered that Brett was unsuitable, as his interests were in criminology, which, in Sawer's view, 'should be carried on only at the state universities in close proximity to the major collections of criminals, gaols, etc'.[132] This comment points to a further reason the Department remained small. Sawer did not seek to compete with the state universities: he believed that they were better placed to conduct both research and postgraduate teaching in many areas.

[126] Sawer's journalistic work drew criticism from politician Eddie Ward, who thought it suggested that Sawer had too much time on his hands. When Sawer explained his predicament to Ward, the politician sent a note of apology. Diary entry, 9 April 1957, and EJ Ward to Geoffrey Sawer, 9 October 1958, Geoffrey Sawer Papers, National Library of Australia, Manuscript Collection.

[127] 'Quiet Office Marriage', *Canberra Times* 3 July 1971, 1.

[128] Sawer to the Registrar of ANU, 21 September 1953, Geoffrey Sawer Staff Files, Australian National University Archives.

[129] Sawer to the Registrar of ANU, 12 January 1954, Geoffrey Sawer Staff Files, Australian National University Archives.

[130] ibid.

[131] ibid.

[132] ibid.

In 1954, Sawer recruited a permanent research fellow, Sam Stoljar, who held the attributes sought in his advertisement of the previous year.[133] Stoljar became one of the early proponents of quasi-contract and unjust enrichment, and published several works which earned him an international reputation.[134] However, his scholarship sat uncomfortably with the social sciences, being more in the nature of analytical jurisprudence. Sawer said that, 'Stoljar was primarily an expert on the common law which Australia inherited from Britain, but he also had strong theory of law credentials'.[135] Stoljar's appointment was therefore in keeping with Sawer's notion that the legal academics could lead projects in traditional legal fields (jurisprudence and doctrinal fields) and would leave the direction of large social science projects to the social scientists, who might ask for guidance and assistance from the lawyers.

In the 1960s and 1970s, the Department grew marginally in vitality and size. In 1961, Joe Starke was appointed a Research Fellow in the Department. This Rhodes Scholar from Western Australia specialised in international law, and was later a member of the League of Nations secretariat.[136] Starke remained with the Department until 1976.[137] Sawer said that he 'proved an awkward colleague, unwilling to discuss his own subject and participate in our weekly discussions about the draft papers of scholars and staff; he seemed to fear that students in particular would pinch ideas from him'.[138] In 1971, Peter Sack (one of Sawer's PhD students from Germany) was made a Research Fellow in the Department.[139] His thesis was devoted to German law in the former colony of New Guinea. In the 1960s and 1970s, Sawer invited scholars to spend six months as visiting fellows in the Department (for example, DJ Whalen from the University of Auckland, and EI Sykes and Colin Howard from the University of Melbourne). However, overall the number of visiting scholars was small.

When the Faculty of Law was established at ANU in 1960 (now the ANU College of Law), which occurred when Canberra University College (previously a part of the University of Melbourne) was integrated into the ANU, both faculty members and teaching activities remained separate from Sawer's Department.[140] Members of the Faculty of Law and Sawer's Department did not collaborate. Both Lindell and Pearce said that the Faculty of Law and the Department within the RSSS were kept entirely separate and that it was rare for scholars from the Faculty to even visit the Department to attend seminars.[141] Similarly, Taylor said that

[133] R Cranston, 'Samuel Jacob Stoljar' (1991) 4 *Journal of Contract Law* 146, 146.
[134] ibid 148–49.
[135] Sawer (n 5), part 53, 1.
[136] Farquharson (n 77).
[137] ibid.
[138] Sawer (n 5) part 53, 1.
[139] Minutes of the Faculty Board of the RSSS, 26 March 1971, Australian National University Archives.
[140] Sawer (n 5) part 56, 3.
[141] Pearce (n 92); Lindell (n 94).

when he was a PhD student neither Sawer, nor anyone else from the Department, encouraged him to visit the Faculty, nor did they suggest that he should do some part-time teaching there.[142] Rather than facilitate an expansion of the activities of the Department, according to Sawer, the existence of the Faculty of Law made the situation of the Department even less tenable.[143] Reflecting on the small stature of the Department in 1982, Sawer said:

> I was always a bit reluctant to build up the Department of Law in the Research School of Social Sciences to any great extent, because I soon became aware of the fact that you either had to have a very large number of lawyers in one place, or you had to have the lawyers in some sense scattered among other disciplines. It was out of the question to spend the enormous amount of money that would have been required to have a research department of law, consisting say, of 20 or 25 people. But that's probably the minimum number that can successfully carry on a totally integrated complete, across the board, legal enterprise and that's plus the library facilities that that requires, which are present in the National Library for example, but certainly not present in the Australian National University library.[144]

Sawer went so far as to indicate that he fully supported moves to close the Department in the late 1970s and early 1980s.[145] He did not waver from his early view that the Department was only ever intended to be a 'spare part' within the RSSS.

Doctoral Students

Although the RSSS awarded very generous scholarships, there were very few postgraduate students in the Department. Up until 1957, Sawer had no PhD students in law. Part of Sawer's initial reservations about the creation of ANU and the RSSS was that, at that time, law schools in Australia simply did not offer PhDs.[146] The idea of a law department consisting purely of research and the teaching of postgraduate students was indeed an odd notion.[147] Before 1957, Sawer had been involved as a secondary supervisor to several students located in other departments whose theses touched on legal matters. His first PhD student who concentrated entirely on law was Rhodes Scholar and future Prime Minister, Bob Hawke. Hawke, however, never completed his thesis. His heavy involvement in trade union activities delayed progress of his thesis and he sought several extensions, the last of which Sawer refused.

Another notable PhD candidate of the Department was Israeli student Abraham Harari. Stoljar supervised Harari's thesis in the area of negligence. One of Harari's

[142] Taylor (n 110).
[143] I Hamilton, Interview with Geoffrey Sawer (Oral History Interview, Canberra, 16 July 1982).
[144] ibid.
[145] ibid.
[146] Pratt (n 1).
[147] ibid.

initial examiners was HLA Hart. The examiners said that the thesis would require substantial revision before it could be accepted as a doctoral thesis. Harari at first refused to carry out the revisions, suggesting that Hart had been unfair in his examination as the thesis criticised some of his and Tony Honoré's work on causation.[148] While Harari eventually resubmitted, the new examiners, Glanville Williams and Professor W Pedrick of Northwestern University, reached the same conclusion.[149] Nicola Lacey has detailed Harari's lingering bitterness towards Hart and the various ways that Harari then ran a personal campaign against him, writing letters to Hart containing strong personal attacks as well as a larger 'Open Letter' (of 96 pages) that contained heightened criticisms of Hart's work and integrity.[150] It was a saga filled with tragedy. Lacey notes that Harari's attacks caused Hart considerable anguish and that Harari died of a brain tumour shortly after writing the 'Open Letter'.[151] The fact that students had failed to complete their theses, and that – in the case of Harari at least – this was widely known, would not have encouraged others to take up a scholarship at ANU.

While it is difficult to ascertain the exact number, it appears from a review of the minutes of governance boards of RSSS that, within the Department, Sawer supervised fewer than 20 pure law PhD students during his tenure. Several of the students were from overseas. The absence of a lively student culture and lack of visitors led some students to abandon their studies.[152] Sawer provided the following explanation for the small number of doctoral students:

> Reverting to the matter of student-teaching at the ANU in my time, there was a substantial reason why my Law Department should have relatively few students reading for a law doctorate. This was the absence from the ACT in those days of any substantial body of important courts and of legal practitioners. The High Court didn't as yet sit in Canberra, and the greatest number and eminence of both barristers and solicitors was (and indeed still is) in the state capitals, in particular Sydney and Melbourne … and I fairly frequently had cause to advise budding law students to seek a place in state law schools.[153]

Sawer continued to favour growth in the state law schools rather than in the Department. In 1970, John Taylor commenced a PhD in law within the Department under Sawer's supervision. He had previously studied at the University of Adelaide, achieving first class honours in an illustrious class of students, and had then won a scholarship to study at Harvard Law School. Both experiences had

[148] Sawer to Sir Owen Dixon, 5 October 1961, Geoffrey Sawer Papers, National Library of Australia, Manuscript Collection.

[149] Minutes of the Meeting of Faculty of the RSSS, 21 September 1962, Australian National University Archives.

[150] N Lacey, *A Life of HLA Hart – The Nightmare and the Noble Dream* (Oxford, Oxford University Press, 2004) 274–77.

[151] ibid 276–77.

[152] Taylor (n 110); Mason (n 12).

[153] Sawer (n 5) part 56, 1–3.

drawn him towards a career within the legal academy. He enjoyed the vibrant activity of both Adelaide and Harvard and was inspired by dynamic teachers such as the international law scholar Daniel O'Connell. However, his experience at the RSSS prompted him to abandon such ambitions. He said:

> Harvard Law School blew my mind. It was totally exceptional. I had never experienced anything like it before and so I thought, 'Oh gosh, this is what academia is about'. When I came back to Australia and ANU, it was a fantastic environment if you wanted to shut yourself out from the real world and get down and do a thesis, do pure research. It couldn't have been better. The facilities that the Research School provided were as good as anywhere if not better than anywhere in the world, but it was like going from – I don't know, I guess it was like going from a major railway station, you know like Grand Central Station in New York or Paddington Station here in London, so busy, so active, so dynamic, to a little country railway station. You know, one train a day coming in.[154]

Taylor said that, apart from weekly or fortnightly meetings with Sawer, there was very little to do within the Department.[155] While he was committed to the topic of his thesis – a comparative constitutional law thesis on s 92 of the Australian Constitution – and believed that it would have made for a solid doctorate, after eight and a half months he decided to abandon his studies, as he simply was not enjoying the environment.[156] He went on to pursue a very successful professional career in international law and finance. For example, he devised initiatives for the World Bank and played a leading role in negotiations and as General Counsel in leading international financial institutions on four continents.

In interviews conducted for this book, both Professor Pearce and Sir Anthony Mason suggested that negative attitudes within Australia's legal profession might have discouraged Sawer from building a large, ambitious department with a lively postgraduate research culture.[157] Many members in the legal profession simply believed that it was unnecessary.

PhD students provided a teaching outlet that might have further demonstrated the utility of the Department. However, reservations about the role of pure research in law, Sawer's view that Australian law schools were better equipped to supervise doctorates, and a general lack of interest in doctoral studies, led to a small postgraduate culture in law.

Concluding Remarks

After Sawer retired from the RSSS, the ANU advertised a new Chair of Law. It is clear from the advertisement that what they wanted was another Sawer; however,

154 Taylor (n 110).
155 ibid.
156 ibid.
157 Pearce (n 92); Mason (n 12).

they were not able to find one. Sawer had done much to demonstrate that placing a full-time legal scholar within a social science school could prove very valuable, and the advertisement is proof that others at ANU believed he was an asset to the university. However, his failure to recruit and nurture similarly equipped legal scholars and students engendered the belief that Sawer was an individualistic legal scholar. Sawer's experience had caused others to believe that productive collaborations between the social sciences and law were made possible because Sawer was exceptional. Sawer did not build a case for making law a social science and it always remained a bit-player within the RSSS. The primary reason for this was Sawer's intellectual belief that the role of his Department was to assist the other departments that *were* social sciences. As such, he believed it should not take up too many resources.

Although Sawer had good reasons for choosing not to build an empire, at the end of these investigations I nonetheless consider that Sawer should have done a little more institutionally to secure law's interdisciplinary identity. In the following chapter I further examine the significance of Sawer's leadership of the Department in the context of summarising his overall contribution to the discipline of law in Australia.

15

Sawer and the Future of Australian Academic Law

The Path Not Taken

Imagine that, after having spent 10 years in a law school where most of your time was fully occupied with teaching, you are thrust into a research-only role in a school of social sciences. Your promotion comes at a time where Australian law schools around the country are tiny affairs; many have just two or three full-time members of staff, with the majority of teaching carried out by practising legal practitioners. Some of those full-time staff members wish to build larger schools where students study full-time; others do not. There are almost no textbooks to explain the body of doctrine that has emerged from Australia's courts and statute books, and local contributions to legal scholarship are modest. Much of the profession reveres Sir Owen Dixon, a judge of the High Court of Australia, who advances views which are interpreted to mean that the practice of law is craft-based and can be advanced chiefly by practitioners whose expertise lies in deductive and inductive reasoning and their ability to assimilate a mass of cases. You, on the other hand, believe that history, economics and politics can throw strong light on our understanding of the discipline and can enrich the practice of law. You also believe that there is a small sphere of knowledge and skills which remains the province of lawyers. The challenge, in your view, lies in expanding, not abandoning, the existing terrain.

Imagine, further, that you have practised as a barrister, so you know that lawyers can get by without deeper learning. Yet, you believe that their practice – and Australian society – would be so much richer if their thinking extended to other conceptions of law and to the investigation of other bodies of knowledge. You also know that members of the Australian legal profession – including its most senior judges – are suspicious of claims concerning the interdisciplinary and value-laden dimensions of law because of their potential to undermine the status of the profession. Such claims might imply that existing lawyers, who see and study the law in a different way, are inferior practitioners; they might also suggest that judging is entirely whimsical. You believe, like many judges, that certainty and predictability are important functions of the courts. At the same time, you are convinced that it is possible to reason in a way that permits the making of some value judgements. However, you also believe that judges are restricted in the scope of those value judgements. Your colleagues in the Research School of Social Sciences (RSSS), especially the political scientists, view you as a useful resource, but they do not consider that the Department of Law sits at the heart of the School. Its founders also took this view. What would you do?

One response to this hypothetical is to say that a person holding such views should not have been appointed to lead such a department. Instead, a person believing that the discipline of law *was* a member of the social sciences, rather than an entity that should work in close collaboration with the social sciences, ought to have held the reins. A person possessing such beliefs might have been driven to change the course of the discipline through advocacy and by building a new identity for law and cementing it into the institutional architecture. It seems obvious that had Julius Stone or Wolfgang Friedmann occupied Sawer's post, they would have sought to lead new law projects firmly grounded in the social sciences or sociology of law. Instead of Sawer's tempered and balanced explanation of the role of law in the Department, they would have issued visionary statements that placed law at the centre, rather than at the periphery, of the social sciences. Looking at Stone's track record in Sydney, it could be expected that he would have had much greater success than Sawer in bringing foreign legal scholars with sociological dispositions to Australia. Perhaps Sawer's agenda was limited by what he conceived was possible within the Australian environment. Unlike Sawer, Stone and Friedmann had spent their formative years outside Australia; they might, therefore, have felt that a more ambitious and creative agenda was both feasible and warranted. They might not have been so easily deterred by the mixed success of social science bodies in the US or the negative attitudes of Australia's legal profession. Instead, they might have carved out a vibrant research body that joined forces with, rather than sat apart from, the Australian National University's (ANU's) law school.

But would Stone's legacy have been so strong if he had been removed from the classroom and placed in a research-only institution? By teaching jurisprudence and international law to undergraduates, Stone had something in common with all other Australian law teachers. His approach might have seemed odd to some, but at least this teaching role gave him a clear purpose. Further, his reputation was made in Australia largely through his students, especially those who later became judges and academics and had been impressed by the way he taught. Had he been removed to a research-only institution, his supporters would have been limited in number.

Further, without student support, both Stone and Friedmann would have struggled to get members of the profession to support their more ambitious research agendas. Would this have mattered? After all, the new department was funded by the university not the profession, and the absence of undergraduate law students meant that it did not need to consider whether the profession would recognise its agenda for the purpose of professional entry requirements. Even if they failed to get the profession on board, the department would nonetheless have provided future generations of Australian legal scholars with a new identity that recognised the value of research in law.

This new identity could have envisaged law as a part of the social sciences, with learning about the role of law in society forming a central component of legal education and scholarship. It might have also have helped to make a better case for recognising legal research as an end in and of itself. Waugh has suggested that Sawer's appointment to the RSSS was confirmation of the status of law as a field of academic research and not just professional expertise.[1] On the surface, this appears to have been the case. But if we look to Sawer's explanation of his role, we find that he continued to believe that legal research was best carried out in the context of a school of law that prepared its students for practice. Stone or Friedmann might have stood a better chance of severing this connection between legal research and law teaching.

A second response is to say that Sawer's position was carefully considered and well-reasoned, and the best that could be done in the circumstances. Even if a scholar with a grander vision for law and social sciences had been appointed, it is doubtful that they would have been able to do more to move the discipline towards the social sciences. Both the academic and legal community were hostile to the notion of a research-only scholar. A scholar who advanced notions entirely alien to conventional norms would have been strongly condemned. With this in mind, one could argue that Sawer's measured response had greater potential to influence some members of the profession to concede that knowledge from disciplines beyond law might be worthy subjects for a lawyer's consideration, and that legal reasoning was something more than a logical inductive and deductive process. Michael Coper suggests that we 'should not underestimate' Sawer's impact in moving practitioners away from mechanical understandings of law.[2] Given Dixon's hold over the High Court and ongoing allegiances to legalism, it might have seemed foolhardy to adopt US notions which placed lawyers at the heart of social change. To suggest otherwise might be to ignore the context. Would a Stone or a Friedmann have had as much success as Sawer in bringing about this change within the profession? Further, would they have been moved towards directing more collaborative projects? Most legal scholars of this age, both in Australia and abroad, worked on their scholarship in isolation. It is perhaps unlikely that either Stone or Friedmann would have abandoned their own preference for individual projects.

What Might Have Been

Sawer's conception of law as a discipline that benefits from, but is not strictly part of, the social sciences endured for most of the second half of the twentieth century

[1] J Waugh, *First Principles – The Melbourne Law School 1857–2007* (Melbourne, Miegunyah Press, 2007) 127.

[2] M Coper, 'Geoffrey Sawer and the Art of Academic Commentator: A Preliminary Biographical Sketch' (2014) 42 *Federal Law Review* 389, 415–16.

in Australia. Similarly, his position that law was best taught and studied within the context of a law school endured throughout this time. Sawer was not the only, or perhaps even the principal, architect or proponent of these conceptions. However, his position at the RSSS meant that he was in a position to advance a stronger case for an identity for law that went well beyond the professional. Instead, he presented the case for an incremental step towards broadening thinking about law.

Sawer advanced this incremental step because it accorded with his intellectual beliefs and his assessment of the Australian terrain. He assumed that there would always be law schools in each of the Australian states, that law would be recognised as a profession of some importance and prestige, and that law professors would have a large degree of autonomy over the running of those law schools. Strong and rising student numbers in law in the 1950s and 1960s no doubt suggested to him that law would continue to be an important and valued part of universities well into the future. Linking legal research to teaching within law schools no doubt seemed a wise way to proceed, given that is the reason why law schools were able to grow from the middle of the twentieth century.

Despite his strong political connections and interests, it is unlikely that Sawer anticipated the extent to which the commodification of research would overrun the management of Australian universities by the end of the twentieth century. While he clearly knew of the government's early and continual emphasis on advancing the natural sciences, he probably did not foresee the extent to which that emphasis on the natural science model, and the monetary value attached to it, would eventually serve to demote the position of social sciences, humanities and law within all Australian universities.[3] He could not have anticipated the extent to which research funding would drive the priorities of universities, or that teaching would be given much less importance. With hindsight, aligning law largely with law school teaching and downplaying the purely research role of law was a poor strategy, given the priorities that emerged within Australian universities from the 1980s onwards, partly in response to global trends. Law's relatively meagre success in attracting research funding from Australia's chief research body, the Australian Research Council, has reduced the discipline's standing within Australian universities. Had Sawer made a case for recognising interdisciplinary research in law as sitting at the heart of the discipline and the curriculum, and demonstrated the value of legal research outside the context of law schools, legal academics might have been better prepared for the present age.

Sawer might, in fact, have had greater success in changing professional attitudes and promoting interdisciplinary work within law had he remained within a law school. Ninian Stephen, former High Court judge and a student of

[3] For a full historical explanation of this demotion, see S Macintyre, *The Poor Relation – A History of Social Sciences in Australia* (Melbourne, Melbourne University, 2010).

Sawer's at the University of Melbourne, provided an endearing image of Sawer's teaching at Melbourne in the 1940s:

> [Sawer] gave dry doctrine its context in the social and economic forces of the day. Names took on new significance. Menzies was no longer just the current leader of the Liberal Opposition but was seen turning the Court around in the *Engineers' Case*. Evatt was no longer the current Minister for External Affairs but instead the apostle of a section 92 which could accommodate nationalisation. We saw Dixon, Starke and Rich trailing personal legends across the pages, and Williams ever at his tax cases.[4]

Stephen's recollection suggests that Sawer encouraged his students to reject the idea that law should be given special reverence. Instead, he hoped that his students would see that it had its imperfections and was created by mere mortals who brought with them a range of interests and assumptions. Had more practitioners been exposed to these aspects of Sawer's teaching, this might have created a stronger band of lawyers and academics willing to challenge initiatives, such as the 'Priestley 11',[5] which have served to narrow the scope of the law curriculum and limit the number of interdisciplinary studies within that curriculum. It might also have led to a bolder critique of the courts. In short, it might have led to greater changes to professional and academic culture than Sawer was able to achieve through his scholarship alone.

What Occurred

Within the discipline of law in Australia, Sawer's importance springs from two central contributions. The first is the considerable start he gave to contextual studies of Australian public law and politics. He produced first-class public law scholarship which suggested that future scholars and lawyers would be unwise to ignore politics, economics and history. Unfortunately, future interdisciplinary collaborations did not reach their full potential. Mason, Lindell and Coper point to factors that frustrated Sawer's legacy (factors Sawer himself anticipated[6]); namely, that increased specialisation both in law and other disciplines would make it very difficult for future legal scholars to carry out Sawer's brand of contextual studies.[7] Lindell recalled that, at an interdisciplinary seminar in the 1980s, Sawer displayed considerable anguish over his perception that members of the various disciplines

[4] Quoted in Coper (n 2) 390.

[5] The 11 subjects (mainly common law categories such as Torts, Contract and Criminal Law) that must form part of any Australian Law degree: see D Barker, *A History of Australian Legal Education* (Sydney, Federation Press, 2017) 5–6.

[6] G Sawer, *Law in Society* (Oxford, Clarendon Press, 1965) 209.

[7] Interview with Sir Anthony Mason (Sir Anthony Mason's Chambers, Sydney, 9 December 2014); interview with Geoffrey Lindell (Woodbridge Community Centre, Tasmania, 23 March 2015); and Coper (n 2) 418.

'simply can't talk to each other anymore'.[8] Sawer arguably went further than most Australian legal scholars of the twentieth century in attempting to build bridges between law and other disciplines.

Sawer's second significant contribution was to help bring about a small, yet significant, cultural change within the legal profession. He wrote textbooks on public law, legal theory and political commentary for the novice. Rather than directly attacking existing ideas, he attempted to persuade through education. This is why he assumed the role of a public commentator. The object of this study has not been to measure the extent to which Sawer's efforts contributed to the cultural change that led Australian judges and lawyers, including certain members of the High Court during the Mason era, to embrace broader conceptions of law and legal reasoning. However, it is significant that, when asked about the similarities between Sawer's position on judging and his own, Sir Anthony Mason acknowledged that they held similar views.[9] Of course, Sawer had not taught Mason or, from the 1950s onwards, any other law graduate. However, his books – both the monographs and his textbooks for the beginner – were in wide circulation. Coper also speaks of the influence that Sawer had on High Court justice Ninian Stephen and argues, with considerable force, that Sawer ought to be recognised, alongside Stone, as an early Australian scholar who helped bring about a significant change in High Court decision-making.[10]

The 'Acknowledgements' sections of Sawer's books demonstrate his role in building a community of Australian legal scholars by inviting different members of the academy to contribute feedback and advice on his work.[11] His acknowledgements also demonstrate that Sawer was seeking opinions from a range of Australian political actors, including judges, politicians and parliamentary draftsmen.[12] He was attempting to understand the nuances of Australian political and legal life, and drew inspiration from Australia's unique political and social environment.

Much more could be said about Sawer. Fortunately, several short studies thoughtfully detail other aspects of Sawer's life and career, including his early life, his time as a magistrate, his advisory work, his journalistic outputs,[13] his part in

[8] Lindell (n 7).

[9] Mason (n 7).

[10] Coper (n 2) 416–17.

[11] See, eg, G Sawer, *Australian Government Today* (Melbourne, Melbourne University Press, 1948); G Sawer, *Cases on the Constitution of the Commonwealth of Australia* (Sydney, Law Book Company, 1948); G Sawer, 'The Record of Judicial Review' in G Sawer (ed), *Federalism: An Australian Jubilee Study* (Melbourne, Cheshire, 1952) 211.

[12] See, eg, G Sawer, *Australian Federal Politics and Law 1901–29* (Melbourne, Melbourne University Press, 1956); G Sawer, *Australian Federal Politics and Law 1929–49* (Melbourne, Melbourne University Press, 1963); and G Sawer, 'The Separation of Powers in Australian Federalism' (1961) 35 *Australian Law Journal* 177.

[13] As noted in the Introduction, a whole book could be devoted to Sawer's journalistic work, most notably his regular column in the *Canberra Times*, as well as other work for various television and news outlets. Throughout his life, he was friends with journalists and he established the first media law course for journalists, the materials for which were published as: G Sawer, *A Guide to Australian Law for Journalists, Authors, Printers and Publishers* (Melbourne, Melbourne University Press, 1949). From 1982 to 1984, Sawer was the Chairman of the Press Council of Australia.

(and commentary on) the Whitlam dismissal, his poetry, and his broader legacy.[14] None of what is set out in this examination of Sawer contradicts these other works. What is different about this study is its focus on examining comprehensively and in depth – based on a close reading of all archival material relating to Sawer and all of his scholarship – what Sawer did for Australian legal theory, how his contribution sits among other schools of thought, and what the minor status of the Department within the RSSS says about Sawer's approach and legacy. While many more lines of investigation could, and no doubt will, flow from Sawer's rich life and career, this study demonstrates Sawer's significance for Australia's legal academy.

[14] The most detailed work of this kind is by Professor Michael Coper: see Coper (n 2). Judge Ross Cranston's work on Sawer and the social sciences is the second most detailed work on Sawer: R Cranston, 'Lawyer in the Social Sciences – Geoffrey Sawer' (1980) 11 *Federal Law Review* 263. The remaining works consist of the obituaries and personal tributes that have been referenced throughout the previous three chapters.

16

Conclusion

Learning Lessons

> It is an important thing for any culture to know where the ideas in its past and present came from. It is an important thing for any culture to understand what those ideas meant in their time and place and how that meaning has changed, if it has, over time. It is important for any culture to have intellectual heroes (and goats), individuals who exemplify what it is to be a serious (or frivolous) intellectual.[1]

Quite a few years before I began this study, I read several books and articles by John Henry Schlegel and Neil Duxbury.[2] The power of their writing led me to other authors who have similarly sought to contextualise legal scholars in strong socio-legal and biographical works: William Twining, David Sugarman, Nicola Lacey, Laura Kalman, Fiona Cownie, David Rabban, W Wesley Pue and Susan Carle amongst others. The more I read such works, the more I began to study and think about the academy differently. There seemed to be so much that I did not know about the discipline that had launched first my professional, and then my academic, career. Wanting to understand my own environment a little better, I looked for Australian works within the genre, but, of those, I found none took that quite the same approach or asked the same kinds of questions as the American and English scholars who had made such an impression on me. This pointed to an obvious gap in the literature, and I wondered whether it would be possible to carry out a similar investigation into Australian scholars. This book – an intellectual experiment – is perhaps the natural conclusion of those musings. I hope that it, too, helps others to think about the discipline in new ways, and that it goes some way towards achieving the important objectives that Schlegel identified in the quotation that begins this concluding chapter. Returning to Schlegel's work today, I realise that he provided the internal mantra that has driven this study.

While I expected that the context of these influential scholars would provide some richer and deeper insights, I have been surprised by how, over the course

[1] JH Schlegel, *American Legal Realism and Empirical Social Science* (Chapel Hill, University of North Carolina Press, 1995) 259.

[2] Most notably Schlegel's work on American Legal Realism (n 1), N Duxbury, *Frederick Pollock and the English Juristic Tradition* (Oxford, Oxford University Press, 2004) and N Duxbury, *Patterns of American Jurisprudence* (Oxford, Clarendon Press, 1995).

of writing this book, chapters that were once overflowing with citations to their scholarly work have now evolved to give equal billing to archival material and interviews. These previously untapped primary sources allow this new work to speak to my three subjects' institutions and their opinions about universities and law schools, as well as their relationships with colleagues and the significant work each performed outside their university. While debate among historians and jurisprudential scholars continues about the value of history to understanding legal ideas,[3] I stand convinced that, at least in Australia, the shape of legal theory, education and the discipline itself has been contingent on circumstance. I am also convinced that this is an important history and that the scholars studied here are, in their different ways, admirable and worth remembering.

From Neil Duxbury's work on Frederick Pollock I learnt that transposing labels and experiences within the discipline of law from one country to another was ill-advised. I also learnt that it was vital to look beyond the scholars whose major monographs had been eulogised in order to find other scholars and other contributions that might prove just as important to shaping the discipline.[4] As my investigations were made on behalf of the whole of the discipline, rather than for the benefit only of those who claim to be legal philosophers or jurisprudential scholars, it was important to set aside my own assumptions about what might amount to an important or 'jurisprudential' contribution. The boundaries of jurisprudence have never been precisely defined, and – perhaps like Duxbury's study of Pollock – my scholars belong to a 'juristic as opposed to [a] jurisprudential tradition'.[5] To avoid unnecessary controversy, I group them under the label 'legal theorists'.

One of the central claims of this project is that the terrain of Australian legal theory is both diverse and a product of its context. In Australia, at least since the 1950s, legal theory has not been synonymous with legal philosophy. The social sciences had a considerable influence on each of the scholars studied here. Of the three, Peter Brett perhaps took the greatest interest in legal philosophy. And yet, his investigations into the philosophy and sociology of science led him to advocate for greater collaborations with the social sciences. Alice Erh-Soon Tay also read broadly but adopted sociological methods. Geoffrey Sawer was fascinated by politics, and became convinced that public law ought to be informed by political science along with economics and history. All three sought to integrate learning and methods from the social sciences into law. None was a positivist or subscribed to narrow views on Dixonian strict legalism. Their experiences suggest that the conventional portrayals and generalisations about this generation of legal

[3] For two recent manifestations of debate on this topic see: Symposium, 'Jurisprudence and (Its) History' (2015) 101 *Virginia Law Review* 849; Symposium, 'Legal Life Writing and Marginalised Subjects and Sources' (2015) 42 *Journal of Law and Society* 1. See also M Del Mar and M Lobban (eds), *Legal Theory and Legal History* (Farnham, Ashgate, 2014) vol 4.

[4] Duxbury, *Pollock* (n 2) 326.

[5] ibid 327.

academics overlook a great deal. Julius Stone was not the only early legal scholar in Australia who was adventurous and sought to draw from the social sciences.

It is intriguing that, in the 1960s and 1970s, at least two of the discipline's most prominent legal scholars (Brett and Sawer), who were, by then, elder statesmen, reached the same conclusion: traditional jurisprudential inquiry – that which occupied the minds of the leading English and American scholars – had run aground and greater efforts ought to be devoted to a new jurisprudence of law reform. This suggests that a progressive and reformist sentiment was an important part of the discipline before the critical legal studies movement, and that Australian legal theory has had distinctive features. Tay, too, wanted to reform Australia's legal academy, while at the same time believing, as a result of her Soviet studies, that stability was extremely important in any legal system.

Given the scant secondary literature about my subjects, most of my efforts have gone into establishing what their various contributions were, rather than providing a strong critique of those contributions. I have, however, examined and commented on several of their shortcomings. To understand my subjects' roles in the discipline, it was important to take each of them on their own terms and view them in a detached and impersonal way. Like Schlegel

> I have attempted to identify … where their ideas came from. I have tried to show how those ideas changed over time. I have even attempted … to explain why those ideas took the shape that they did and how they worked out in the practices that these thinkers believed that their ideas implied.[6]

I believe that, in doing so, I have deepened our understanding of the shape of the discipline of law in Australia. I have demonstrated that the reductionist tendencies of commentators on the discipline mean that they have missed much that matters, and I have made a case to move beyond them. At a time when many speak as if the future of the legal academy involves fulfilling externally imposed expectations – and has no room for pioneers – life histories can serve as an important motivating force for those scholars who wish to reclaim the discipline.[7]

Put simply, in this book I explain how leading Australian legal scholars responded to their times and the surrounding social and institutional conditions. My approach has been both to challenge and advance a range of views about the nature of law and the enterprise of the discipline.[8] By focusing on the careers of Brett, Tay and Sawer, I demonstrate that ideas about law and legal education in Australia have always been contingent. Significantly, I also illuminate the ways in which the ideas of this pioneering generation of Australian legal scholars were

[6] Schlegel (n 1) 259.

[7] Various arguments about the purpose of such works can be found in: S Bartie, 'Histories of Legal Scholars – The Power of Possibility' (2014) 34 *Legal Studies* 305.

[8] Like Cotterrell, I believe that legal theory 'can usefully be understood, to a large extent, as responses to particular political conditions': R Cotterrell, *The Politics of Jurisprudence: A Critical Introduction to Legal Philosophy* (Philadelphia, University of Pennsylvania Press, 1989) v.

shaped by their life and context.[9] Because of the contingent and contextual nature of their ideas, their contributions as legal theorists, teachers, managers, moral authorities and public intellectuals have been distinctive.

To understand the discipline of law, it is necessary to investigate the practical and intellectual strategies that have been deployed by its members in response to their environment. In the case of each of my subjects, by reading all of their scholarship, reviewing all available Australian, and some overseas,[10] archival material and conducting interviews, I was able to trace in detail some of the central aspects of their scholarly careers and demonstrate that all were, in their own ways and endeavours, trailblazing scholars.

Lives and Careers

Brett, Tay and Sawer were canny political operators whose backgrounds made them tough and resilient, which in turn fostered strong independent agendas. When their early lives, attributes and formative beliefs are considered, it is little wonder that they devised innovative strategies that departed from English orthodoxy and did not fully embrace any one tradition. Each had the capacity to survey the state of the discipline and legal practice in Australia and respond in ways that they believed would make a difference. Their remarkable rise to the top of the scholarly hierarchy no doubt added to the belief that they could effect real change.

None of these scholars was an obvious candidate for a professorship in legal theory. Brett was a Jewish man from a lower middle-class family in Britain, and could not afford to study law – or any other subject – at university on a full-time basis. Before joining the legal academy, Tay had spent very few years in formal education. As a child in Singapore, she had to work to support her family. Born in Burma, Sawer was a war orphan who grew up in a working-class family and did not have the means to study at an elite foreign institution. All three became members of Australia's legal elite thanks to the opportunities afforded to them in their adopted country.

All three scholars held ambitions that extended beyond merely securing an income and engaging in the type of work that suited them best. Their early experiences motivated them to act in ways that they believed might lead to real social change. Brett wanted to create a society where the type of culture and attitudes inherent in Nazi Germany could not prosper. He aimed to create practitioners who

[9] Sugarman argues that Nicola Lacey's work on HLA Hart achieves this objective: D Sugarman, 'From Legal Biography to Legal Life Writing: Broadening Conceptions of Legal History and Socio Legal Scholarship' (2015) 42 *Journal of Law and Society* 7, 20.

[10] Some attempt was made to locate international material, with documents sourced from Harvard University for Brett and from the UK for Tay and Sawer.

would appreciate that law was more than a blunt instrument of the state and who would play a role not only in interpreting the law, but also ensuring that it embodied principles that reflected morality. Tay wanted to put in place institutions that could counter the type of tyrannical regimes that had plagued her childhood and discriminated against her family. Her comparative law and human rights scholarship, as well as her move from the Department of Jurisprudence to the Human Rights and Equal Opportunity Commission, are obvious extensions of this early goal. Sawer wanted to ensure that the discipline and Australian law more generally were based on strong intellectual foundations, through careful study of law and its relationship with politics. He sought to bring about measured and incremental cultural and legal change, so that the courts would update principles to reflect societal attitudes while also acting as a safeguard against government overreach. He looked to other mechanisms beyond the courts – to Parliament, the Ombudsman, and new law reform bodies – to bring about change. He wanted law and political systems to achieve much-needed social reform that would lead to greater equality.

Collectively, their careers make a case for studying the outsider, and for the deeper insights that viewing the discipline and Australia's laws from an outsider's perspective can bring. Tay was, of course, the ultimate outsider. She was so different to those around her that she could not be placed in any one box and this worked to her advantage. Leading legal and political figures regarded her as both exotic and interesting. Tay, along with Brett and Sawer, support the notion that diversity can bring very different perspectives and act as a force for change within the discipline. Irrespective of whether one supports their various agendas and contributions, it cannot be denied that each sought to do something very different from prevailing practices: this allowed them to shape the discipline in ways that would break down some of its insularity. This has added to the distinctiveness of Australian academic law.

Local Conditions

Their particular institutional and social environments also provided Brett, Tay and Sawer with incentives and inspiration to shape their careers in particular ways. The law school at Melbourne and the leadership of Zelman Cowan gave Brett the opportunities and confidence to pursue an ambitious (at least for the time) theoretical path. It gave him the courage to assume a role akin to an acclaimed American law professor. He acted as moral authority, elder statesman, expert adviser and intellectual leader. He demonstrated that a legal scholar could perform a strong public role. His friends, Justice Barry and Norval Morris, gave him the support and encouragement he needed to relentlessly pursue his objective of ensuring the rights of the accused and criminals. He was a compassionate, focused and strategic intellectual leader. He had a strong dislike of elitism and snobbishness and his move from England to a smaller and more egalitarian society encouraged him to call out and condemn such practices in his adopted country. He was a persistent and forceful advocate for change to rid Australia's legal profession and universities of nepotism and complacent practices.

Tay, on the other hand, never bathed in a warm congenial atmosphere. At the law school at ANU she felt that she had little in common with her colleagues, while at Sydney some strongly opposed her position on maintaining the Department of Jurisprudence. Eugene Kamenka drew Tay's attention to certain notable scholars, including the fathers of the social sciences. He also introduced her to scholars who had risked much to maintain their independence and oppose oppressive dictatorships. In Australia, she found a strong legal system but (to her mind) some lazy and complacent academics who did not fully appreciate their important social role. Rather than deterring her, this predicament played to what seemed to be Tay's natural inclination to fight. While there are signs that the friction between the two Departments within the Faculty of Law at Sydney took a personal toll, it is also clear that many of her arguments worked best when there was an enemy to condemn and overthrow. Tay believed that it was necessary to create an environment where exceptional scholars were insulated, both from the broader fray and external agendas. Her position at the University of Sydney gave her the opportunity to do this. The politics of her environment were central to what she achieved.

Sawer, by contrast, was presented with a blank canvas. He was the first Australian full-time legal scholar with no undergraduate teaching responsibilities and the first Australian legal scholar to be situated within a school of social sciences. Freed from the responsibility of teaching, Sawer was able to advance scholarship of an unprecedented depth and scale. He was also able to carefully assess the intellectual terrain and consider ways in which he could move the legal profession and academy towards a stronger interdisciplinary path. He believed that the best prospects rested with advancing scholarship that would educate the profession and students about a range of views on law and open up debate and knowledge without threatening prior learning. Unlike Tay, he educated rather than criticised. He devoted his energies to producing scholarly tomes rather than a strong Department. His goal was to maintain and improve the standing of the discipline within the eyes of the profession and the University, while moving it to a broader terrain. This influenced how Sawer conceptualised his role and the work that he did. He made a case against the autonomy of law and in favour of legal academics addressing subjects and adopting methods drawn from other disciplines. He was inspired by the American Legal Realist view that the law ought to be treated as a bundle of facts, to sit alongside other social facts, rather than as a body of rules. And in the course of his studies of Australia's legal and political system, he appears to have proven this thesis. He took a middle road between the conservative attitudes of the profession and the radical ideas that had fascinated him as a university student.

Any appraisal of the legal academy and discipline should include larger questioning that transcends local concerns. As Tay explained, 'Our Australian reality is one we live in. But law schools need not only to serve it, but to help transform it'.[11] One of the central objectives of the three scholars studied here was to link Australia's legal academy with leading thought and scholars around the world. While all three took inspiration from international scholars, their experiences suggest that the environment within Australia was nonetheless important to fostering strong scholarly contributions. None blindly followed the Legal Process, Legal Realist or Sociological traditions that inspired them. Indeed, they believed that the insights gleaned from Australian conditions could enrich and provide critiques to the work performed within these intellectual schools.

Despite its short history and modest beginnings, there are few signs that Brett, Sawer and Tay believed that advancing their intellectual agendas within Australia's discipline of law put them at a disadvantage. Australia provided more opportunities than obstacles. Brett and Sawer felt most restricted by the profession's perception that judges remained the most authoritative legal knowers, which in turn elevated Dixon's legalism and writings on the role of courts and legal academics. But they did what they could to attempt to ensure that in time these attitudes would change.

The Heart of Australian Law Schools

Brett, Tay and Sawer's experiences suggest that they considered teaching to be at the heart of a law school. Brett and Tay devoted the bulk of their intellectual energies to teaching, while Sawer's failure to build his Department of Law at the RSSS was, in part, a product of his belief that a university law department devoted solely to research did not make sense. All three privileged teaching because they wished to bring about cultural change within the profession and believed that law school teaching was the most obvious way to achieve this aim. Brett and Tay believed they had a moral responsibility to educate their students in a way that would bring about cultural change, and that this would help lawyers – and in Tay's case, future legal academics – better serve society and challenge oppression.

None of them privileged teaching because they were poor scholars or because they did not enjoy scholarship and research. My first encounter with Brett came through a project that analysed the book reviews of the first community of Australian legal scholars. Of all the members of this community, he was the most prolific reviewer, devouring the law, philosophy and science books that later inspired his ambitious scholarship. Tay published hundreds of articles and papers

[11] A Tay, 'Aimless Perspectives – A Comment on Chapter One of the CTEC "Discipline Assessment" of the Australian Law Schools' (1987) 11 *Bulletin of the Australian Society of Legal Philosophy* 154, 156.

and was one of the first Australian legal scholars to attract significant research funding. Sawer spent 25 years at the RSSS, predominantly engaged in scholarship and research work. Despite their own heavy investment in scholarship and creating early research models, Brett, Tay and Sawer would have disagreed strongly with the notion that the discipline should prioritise research over teaching, or that this was a sign of its growing sophistication.

Brett, Tay and Sawer's experiences further disprove the allegations sometimes made by members of the current generation of legal scholars that previous generations were unreflective and uninventive teachers.[12] Frustrations about current practices should not be attributed to a 'tradition' of complacent law teachers. For many decades, Australian law school have had pioneering and thoughtful teachers, who have drawn on their substantial theoretical studies of law and other disciplines to inform their practices. The teaching and study of jurisprudence (or legal theory) promoted reflective practices. Should current generations emulate the particular approaches of those scholars? No. They are out of date and do not fit the times. Brett, Tay and Sawer did little to try to understand what their students had learnt from their classes through, for example, empirical study, and their focus was on encouraging students to learn and critique the current laws and systems to improve, rather than topple, them. The current malaise in Western democracies and the chequered success of Australia's legal profession suggest, perhaps, that their liberal ideas and models ought to be scrutinised rather than emulated. At the same time, current law teachers would do well to embody their pioneering spirit.

Law Schools and Society

No one gave Brett, Tay or Sawer a rulebook on how to be a legal scholar. And, even if they had been provided with a guide, they probably would not have followed it. They were driven by their own ambitions and their own appraisals of what the discipline and Australian society needed. They drew a clear connection between the two. Each believed that strengthening the intellectual credentials, culture and status of the legal academy was of significant benefit to society. They did not need additional reasons to do what they did: being a serious academic was enough. Their endeavours often did not conform to prevalent attitudes within the legal profession or even the universities in which they worked. They did not follow fads and fashions, but instead devised scholarly and teaching models and contributed to a subversive liberal culture that sought to challenge Sir Owen Dixon's command over Australian law and lawyers as well as the notion that law was

[12] A similar argument with respect to the first community of legal scholars more generally is made in S Bartie: 'Towards a History of Law as an Academic Discipline' (2014) 38 *Melbourne University Law Review* 444, 448–50.

an autonomous discipline. Sawer often voiced views that were unpopular at the time; Brett and Tay made significant enemies. All three were troubled by doubts: Brett was hesitant about moving away from doctrinal study at a time when so little Australian law had been catalogued; continuing the Department of Jurisprudence took a strong personal toll on Tay; while, for Sawer, the idea of being a research-only scholar in a nascent academy brought a feeling of unease. And yet, all three pursued agendas that meant that they had to proceed in spite of their doubts.

Among other things, Brett, Tay and Sawer's careers help make an argument for fashioning an academic agenda around a set of beliefs about the discipline and its relationship to the profession and society. This raises the question of whether current legal scholars advance their careers with the health of the discipline and a similar set of convictions in mind. My sense is that the rapid growth of the legal academy and its seemingly fixed place within the university landscape discourage this type of questioning, as does the extent of external direction from some university managers and professional bodies. While today's legal scholars might research and teach in ways that have the potential to reform the law and legal systems, it seems they do not perceive that their activities could fundamentally alter the future of the discipline – at least not in the way that Brett, Tay and Sawer did. This is regrettable and has very real consequences. Current and future generations of legal scholars may soon find that, for the first time in the history of Australian law schools, the models they create will be vital to the very survival of their institutions. The changes to the legal profession foreshadowed in the Introduction – with technology, diversity among practitioners and new practice models disrupting longstanding approaches to lawyering and reducing employment opportunities for graduates – will eventually lead the profession, government and potential law students to subject the content of law curriculums to greater scrutiny than in the past. The discipline is entering an age which will be in desperate need of pioneers who will take legal education, and student learning,[13] seriously.

I conclude with the words of Robert Stevens, who observed that his history of American law schools was important because law schools are 'a significant force in the American establishment', they play an important 'function in the social evolution of law, lawyers and higher education' and because 'the very concept' of law 'has shaped and been shaped by legal education'.[14] The more I learn about the three scholars studied here and thought about the history of Australia's legal academy, the more I come to believe that Australian law schools have, although not to the same extent, also performed an important function and exerted considerable

[13] William Twining makes a convincing and provocative case for the ongoing need for law teachers to shift their focus from what they teach to what students learn: W Twining, 'Rethinking Legal Education' (2018) 52 *The Law Teacher* 241, 250.

[14] R Stevens, *Law School: Legal Education in America from the 1850s to the 1980s* (Chapel Hill, University of North Carolina Press, 1983) xiii.

influence. They hold power. Even if Australian law schools have not reached the American heights, it is clear from this study that, over the generations, some leading legal scholars have wanted Australian law schools to play a role similar to their American counterparts. Whether this is a desirable goal – and, if so, how it might best be fulfilled – clearly warrants further contemplation. Such contemplation ought to be based on strong intellectual foundations, including more careful examination of the leading thought and activities of those who took responsibility for the development of Australia's legal academy. This study represents one attempt to achieve that aim.

Appendix A: List of Peter Brett's Publications

A. Articles/Book Chapters

Brett, P, 'The Dominant Lease' (1950) 14 *The Conveyancer and Property Lawyer* 264.

Brett, P, 'The Retrospective Lease' (1950) 14 *The Conveyancer and Property Lawyer* 367.

Brett, P, 'The Right to Take Flowing Water' (1950) 14 *The Conveyancer and Property Lawyer* 154.

Brett, P, 'Compulsory Purchase and Covenants Affecting Land' (1951) 15 *The Conveyancer and Property Lawyer* 8.

Brett, P, 'Civil and Criminal Defamation in Western Australia' (1951–53) 2 *University of Western Australia Annual Law Review* 43.

Brett, P, 'The Theory of Interpreting Statutes' (1952–55) 2 *University of Queensland Law Journal* 99.

Brett, P, 'Abnormal Propensity or Plain Bad Character' (1953) 6 *Res Judicatae* 471.

Brett, P, 'Manslaughter and the Motorist Part I' (1953) 27 *Australian Law Journal* 6.

Brett, P, 'Manslaughter and the Motorist Part II' (1953) 27 *Australian Law Journal* 89.

Brett, P, 'Consortium and Servitium: A History and Some Proposals Part I' (1955) 29 *Australian Law Journal* 321.

Brett, P, 'Consortium and Servitium: A History and Some Proposals Part II' (1955) 29 *Australian Law Journal* 389.

Brett, P, 'Consortium and Servitium: A History and Some Proposals Part III' (1955) 29 *Australian Law Journal* 428.

Brett, P, 'The Case of the Statutory Petard' (1956) 29 *Australian Law Journal* 635.

Brett, P, 'Conditional Pardons and the Commutation of Death Sentences' (1957) 20 *Modern Law Review* 131.

Brett, P, 'North Borneo: Redrafting the Land Legislation of Brunei' (1957) 6 *The American Journal of Comparative Law* 565.

Brett, P, 'A Limitation on Executive Power' (1960) 23 *Modern Law Review* 310.

Brett, P, 'Irresistible Impulse and the M'Naughten Rules' (1960) 23 *Modern Law Review* 545.

Brett, P, 'Overseas Influence on English Law: Australia' (1961) 105 *The Solicitors' Journal and Weekly Reporter* 754.

Brett, P, 'Compensation for the Victims of Crime: New Zealand's Pioneer Statute' (1964) 5 *The Australian Lawyer* 21.

Brett, P, 'The Rebirth of Natural Justice' (1964) 6 *Malaya Law Review* 100.

Brett, P, 'Mistake of Law as a Criminal Defence' (1965–67) 5 *Melbourne University Law Review* 179.

Brett, P, 'Free Speech, Supreme-Court Style: A View from Overseas' (1967–68) *Texas Law Review* 668.

Brett, P, 'The Beamish Case: A Rejoinder' (1967–68) 8 *University of Western Australia Annual Law Review* 115.
Brett, P, 'Reflections on the Canadian Bill of Rights' (1969) 7 *Alberta Law Review* 294.
Brett, P, 'The Physiology of Provocation' (1970) *Criminal Law Review* 634.
Brett, P, 'The Law and the Changing View of Man' (1971) 5 *Australian and New Zealand Journal of Psychiatry* 78.
Brett, P, 'Law in a Scientific Age' in N Morris and M Perlman (eds), *Law and Crime: Essays in Honor of Sir John Barry* (New York, Gordon and Breach, 1972) 80.
Brett, P, 'The Implications of Science for the Law' (1972) 18 *McGill Law Journal* 170.
Brett, P, 'Legal Decision-Making and Bias: A Critique of an "Experiment"' (1973) 45 *University of Colorado Law Review* 1.
Brett, P, 'A Rejoinder to the Researchers' (1973–74) 45 *University of Colorado Law Review* 24.
Brett, P, 'Strict Responsibility: Possible Solutions' (1974) 37 *Modern Law Review* 417.
Brett, P, 'The Blessings of Liberty' (1974) *Summons* 5.

B. Books

Brett, P and Waller, PL, *Cases and Materials in Criminal Law* (Sydney, Butterworths, 1962).
Brett, P, *Cases and Materials in Constitutional and Administrative Law* (Sydney, Butterworths, 1962).
Brett, P, *An Inquiry into Criminal Guilt* (Sydney, Lawbook, 1963).
Brett, P and Waller, PL, *Cases and Materials in Criminal Law*, 2nd edn (Sydney, Butterworths, 1965).
Brett, P, *The Beamish Case* (Melbourne, Melbourne University Press, 1966).
Brett, P and Hogg, PW, *Cases and Materials on Administrative Law* (Melbourne, Butterworths, 1967).
Brett, P and Waller, PL, *Criminal Law – Cases and Text*, 3rd edn (Sydney, Butterworths, 1971).
Brett, P, *An Essay on a Contemporary Jurisprudence* (Sydney, Butterworths, 1975).
Brett, P and Waller, PL, *Criminal Law – Text and Cases*, 4th edn (Sydney, Butterworths, 1978).

C. Book Reviews/Review Essays

Brett, P, 'Book Review: *An Introduction to Criminal Law* by Rupert Cross and Asterley Jones and *Cases on Criminal Law* by Rupert Cross and Asterley Jones' (1951–53) 2 *University of Western Australia Law Review* 665.
Brett, P, 'Book Review: *An Introduction to Evidence* by GD Nokes' (1951–53) 2 *University of Western Australia Law Review* 459.
Brett, P, 'Book Review: *International Review of Criminal Policy* by the United Nations Department of Social Affairs' (1951–53) 2 *University of Western Australia Law Review* 458.
Brett, P, 'Book Review: *Joint Torts and Contributory Negligence* by Glanville L Williams' (1951–53) 2 *University of Western Australia Law Review* 174.

Brett, P, 'Book Review: *Justice and Administrative Law* by William A Robson' (1951–53) 2 *University of Western Australia Law Review* 462.
Brett, P, 'Book Review: *Justice in Magistrates' Courts* by Frank J Powell' (1951–53) 2 *University of Western Australia Law Review* 668.
Brett, P, 'Book Review: *Police Offences of Queensland* by WKA Allen' (1951–53) 2 *University of Western Australia Law Review* 177.
Brett, P, 'Book Review: *The Construction of Deeds and Statutes* by Charles E Odgers' (1951–53) 2 *University of Western Australia Law Review* 667.
Brett, P, 'Book Review: *The Habitual Criminal* by Norval Morris' (1951–53) 2 *University of Western Australia Law Review* 465.
Brett, P, 'Book Review: *The Technique of Advocacy* by John H Munkman' (1951–53) 2 *University of Western Australia Law Review* 460.
Brett, P, 'Book Review: *The Contracts of Public Authorities: A Comparative Study* by JDB Mitchell' (1954–56) 3 *University of Western Australia Law Review* 183.
Brett, P, 'Book Review: *The Law of Homicide* by Roy Moreland' (1954–56) 3 *University of Western Australia Law Review* 181.
Brett, P, 'Book Review: *Theft, Law and Society* by Jerome Hall' (1954–56) 3 *University of Western Australia Law Review* 179.
Brett, P, 'Book Review: *Sexual Offences, A Report of the Cambridge Department of Criminal Science*' (1956) 2 *Sydney Law Review* 618.
Brett, P, 'Book Review: *Criminal Law: The General Part* by Glanville Williams' (1956–58) 2 *Sydney Law Review* 199.
Brett, P, 'Book Review: First United Nations Congress of the Prevention of Crime and the Treatment of Offenders' (1957) 1 *Melbourne University Law Review* 282.
Brett, P, 'Book Review: *Law and Orders* by Sir Carleton Kemp Allen' (1957) 1 *Melbourne University Law Review* 279.
Brett, P, 'Book Review: *The Sanctity of Life and the Criminal Law* by Glanville Williams' (1958) 1 *Melbourne University Law Review* 556.
Brett, P, 'Book Review: *Administrative Law Treatise* by Kenneth Culp Davis' (1960) 38 *Texas Law Review* 349.
Brett, P, 'Book Review: *Legal Education and Public Responsibility* by Julius Stone' (1960) 2 *Melbourne University Law Review* 568.
Brett, P, 'Book Review: *Causation in the Law* by HLA Hart' (1961) 4 *Melbourne University Law Review* 93.
Brett, P, 'Book Review: *Oxford Essays in Jurisprudence* by AG Guest (editor)' (1962) 3 *Melbourne University Law Review* 402.
Brett, P, 'Book Review: *The Citizen and the Administration: The Redress of Grievances*, a report by JUSTICE' (1962) 3 *Melbourne University Law Review* 555.
Brett, P, 'Book Review: *Appellate Courts in the United States and England* by Delmar Karlen' (1963) 4 *Melbourne University Law Review* 299.
Brett, P, 'Book Review: *Criminal Law: Problems for Decision in the Promulgation, Invocation and Administation of a Law of Crimes* by Richard C Donnelly, Joseph Goldstein and Richard D Schwartz' (1963) 4 *Melbourne University Law Review* 162.
Brett, P, 'Book Review: *The Constitutions of the Australian States* by RD Lumb' (1964) 4 *Melbourne University Law Review* 423.
Brett, P, 'Book Review: *Studies in Criminal Law* by Norval Morris and Colin Howard, *Strict Responsibility* by Colin Howard and *A Casebook on Criminal Law* by DW Elliott and JC Wood' (1965) 5 *Melbourne University Law Review* 106.

Brett, P, 'Book Review: *Law in Society* by Geoffrey Sawer' (1966–67) 2 *Federal Law Review* 139.
Brett, P, 'Book Review: *Human Law and Human Justice* by Julius Stone' (1967) 5 *Melbourne University Law Review* 510.
Brett, P, 'Book Review: *The Courts and Criminal Punishments* by Sir John Vincent William Barry' (1969–70) 7 *Melbourne University Law Review* 585.

D. Theses

Brett, P, *The Penal System of Western Australia, A Critical Study* (unpublished Masters Thesis, University of Western Australia, 1953).
Brett, P, *An Inquiry into Criminal Guilt* (unpublished PhD Thesis, Harvard University, 1960).

Appendix B: List of Alice Erh-Soon Tay's Publications

A. Articles/Book Chapters

Tay, A, '"Conditional Release" under the Preservation of Public Security Ordinance' (1959) 1 *Malayan Law Review* 341.

Tay, A and Heah, JMH, 'Some Notes on the Malayan Law of Negligence' (1960) 9 *Cleveland-Marshall Law Review* 490.

Tay, A and Kamenka, E, 'Karl Marx's Analysis of Law' (1959) 1 *Indian Journal of Philosophy* 19.

Tay, A and Kamenka, E, 'Karl Marx on the Law of Marriage and Divorce' (1960) 15 *Quadrant* 17.

Tay, A and Kamenka, E, 'Singapore-City State' (1960) 26 *Current Affairs Bulletin* 146.

Tay, A, 'Moral Guilt and Legal Liability' (1961) 59 *Hibbert Journal* 44.

Tay, A, 'The Chinese in South East Asia' (1962) 4 *Race* 34.

Tay, A, 'Bailment and the Deposit for Safe-Keeping' (1964) 6 *Malaya Law Review* 229.

Tay, A, '"Brides v Hawkesworth" and the Early History of Finding' (1964) 8 *American Journal of Legal History* 224.

Tay, A, 'Possession and the Modern Law of Finding' (1964) 4 *Sydney Law Review* 383.

Tay, A, 'Problems in the Law of Finding: The US Approach' (1964) 37 *Australian Law Journal* 350.

Tay, A, 'The Concept of Possession in the Common Law: Foundations for a New Approach' (1964) 4 *Melbourne University Law Review* 476.

Tay, A, 'Possession, Larceny and Servants: Toward Tidying Up an Historical Muddle' (1965) 16 *University of Toronto Law Journal* 145.

Tay, A, 'The Essence of a Bailment – Contract, Agreement or Possession?' (1965) 5 *Sydney Law Review* 239.

Tay, A, 'The Law of Inheritance in the New Russian Civil Code of 1964' (1968) 17 *International and Comparative Law Quarterly* 472.

Tay, A, 'Law in Communist China – Part 1' (1969) 6 *Sydney Law Review* 153.

Tay, A, 'The Foundation of Tort Liability in a Socialist Legal System: Fault Versus Social Insurance in Soviet Law' (1969) *University of Toronto Law Journal* 1.

Tay, A, 'The Principles of Liability and the "Source of Increased Danger" in the Soviet Law of Tort' (1969) 18 *International and Comparative Law Quarterly* 424.

Tay, A and Kamenka, E, 'The Life and Afterlife of a Bolshevik Jurist' (1970) 19 *Problems of Communism* 72.

Tay, A and Kamenka, E, 'Beyond the French Revolution: Communist Socialism and the Concept of Law' (1971) 21 *University of Toronto Law Journal* 109.

Tay, A, 'Civil Liberties in the Soviet Union' (1971) 2 *The Bridge* 37.

Tay, A, '*Gemeinschaft, Gesellschaft*, Mobilisation and Administration: The Future of Law in Communist China' (1971) 1 *Asia Quarterly* 257.

Tay, A, 'Law and Morality: Communist Theory and Communist Practice' (1971) 21 *Philosophy East and West* 395.

Tay, A, 'Law and Society in the People's Republic of China' (1971) 2 *Lawasia* 135.

Tay, A, 'Law in Communist China – Part II' (1971) 6 *Sydney Law Review* 335.

Tay, A, 'The Status of Women in the Soviet Union' (1972) 20 *American Journal of Comparative Law* 662.

Tay, A and Kamenka, E, 'Beyond Bourgeois Individualism: The Contemporary Crisis in Law and Legal Ideology' in E Kamenka and RS Neale (eds), *Feudalism, Capitalism and Beyond* (London, Edward Arnold, 1975) 126.

Tay, A, 'Property and Law in the Society of Mass Production, Mass Consumption and Mass Allocation' in G Dorsey (ed), *Property: Papers from the St Louis World Congress on Philosophy of Law and Social Philosophy* (Stuttgart, Franz Steiner Verlag, 1976) 87.

Tay, A, '"Smash all Permanent Rules": China as a Model for the Future' (1976) 7 *Sydney Law Review* 400.

Tay, A and Kamenka, E, 'Participation, "Authenticity", and the Contemporary Vision of Man, Law and Society' in R Cohen and others (eds), *Essays in Memory of Imre Lakatos* (Dordrecht, D Reidel, 1976) 335.

Tay, A and Kamenka, E, 'Socialism, Liberty and Law' in O Harries (ed), *Liberty and Politics: Studies in Social Theory* (London, Pergamon Press, 1976) 81.

Tay, A, 'Law, the Citizen and the State' in E Kamenka, R Brown and A Tay (eds), *Law and Society* (London, Edward Arnold, 1977) 1.

Tay, A and Kamenka, E, 'Socialism, Anarchism and Law' in E Kamenka, R Brown and A Tay (eds), *Law and Society* (London, Edward Arnold, 1977) 48.

Tay, A, 'Marxism. Socialism and Human Rights', in E Kamenka and A Tay (eds), *Human Rights* (London, Edward Arnold, 1978) 104.

Tay, A and Kamenka, E, 'Freedom, Law and the Bureaucratic State' in E Kamenka and M Krygier (eds), *Bureaucracy: The Career of a Concept* (London, Edward Arnold, 1979) 112.

Tay, A, 'Introduction' in E Kamenka and A Tay (eds), *Justice* (London, Edward Arnold, 1980) 1.

Tay, A, 'Legal Education, Legal Research and Legal Reform in Poland' (1980) 54 *Australian Law Journal* 142.

Tay, A, 'The Sense of Justice in the Common Law' in E Kamenka and A Tay (eds), *Justice* (London, Edward Arnold, 1980) 79.

Tay, A and Kamenka, E, 'Marxism and the Problem of Legal Continuity: Recent Trends in Communist Legal Theory' (1980) *Bulletin of the Australian Society of Legal Philosophy* 30.

Tay, A and Kamenka, E, 'Marxism-Leninism and the Heritability of Law' (1980) 6 *Review of Socialist Law* 261.

Tay, A and Kamenka, E, 'Editor's Introduction: Law, Lawyers and Law-Making in Australia' in A Tay and E Kamenka (eds), *Law-Making in Australia* (London, Edward Arnold, 1980) 20.

Tay, A and Kamenka, E, 'Human Rights in the Soviet Union' (1980) 19 *World Review* 47.

Tay, A and Kamenka, E, 'New Legal Areas, New Legal Attitudes' in A Tay and E Kamenka (eds), *Law-Making in Australia* (London, Edward Arnold, 1980) 247.

Tay, A and Kamenka, E, 'Social Traditions, Legal Traditions' in E Kamenka and A Tay (eds), *Law and Social Control* (London, Edward Arnold, 1980) 105.

Tay, A, 'Socialism and Human Rights' in A Tay (ed), *Teaching Human Rights: An Australian Symposium* (Canberra, Australian National Commission for UNESCO, 1981) 73.

Tay, A and Kamenka, E, 'Human Rights and "The" Australian Tradition' in A Tay (ed) *Teaching Human Rights: An Australian Symposium* (Canberra, Australian National Commission for UNESCO, 1981) 1.

Tay, A and Kamenka, E, 'Commune and Community in the USSR and China' in E Kamenka (ed), *Community* (London, Edward Arnold, 1982) 99.

Tay, A, 'Law and "Legal Culture"' (1983) 27 *Bulletin of Australian Society of Legal Philosophy* 15.

Tay, A and Kamenka, E, 'Marxism and the Problem of Continuity or Heritability of Law' in FJM Feldbrugge and WB Simons (eds), *Perspectives on Soviet Law of the 1980s* (Alphen aan den Rijn, Sithoff and Noordhoff, 1983) 1.

Tay, A and Kamenka, E, 'Public Law – Private Law' in SI Benn and GF Gaus (eds), *Public and Private in Social Life* (London, Croom Helm, 1983) 67.

Tay, A and Kamenka, E, 'The Sociology of Justice' in AR Blackshield (ed), *Legal Change: Essays in Honour of Julius Stone* (Sydney, Butterworths, 1983) 107.

Tay, A, 'China and Legal Pluralism' (1984) 8 *Bulletin of the Australian Society of Legal Philosophers* 23.

Tay, A, 'Law and the Cultural Heritage' in I McBryde (ed), *Who Owns the Past? 1983 Australian Academy of the Social Sciences Symposium* (Melbourne, Oxford University Press, 1984) 77.

Tay, A, 'Law and Legal Culture' in S Jorgenson and others (eds), *Tradition and Progress in Modern Legal Culture* (Stuttgart, Franz Steiner Verlag, 1985) 165.

Tay, A, 'The Traditions of Justice' (1985) 5 *Law and Philosophy* 281.

Tay, A and Kamenka, E, 'Elevating Law in the People's Republic of China' (1985) 9 *Bulletin of Australian Society of Legal Philosophy* 69.

Tay, A and Kamenka, E, 'Marxism, Socialism and the Theory of Law' (1985) 23 *Columbia Journal of Transnational Law* 217.

Tay, A and Kamenka, E, 'Kinaa Koskevan Liitteen Kirjoittaneet' in R David (ed), *Contemporary Legal Systems* (Helsinki, Suomen Lakimiesliiton Kustannus Oy, 1986) 299.

Tay, A and Kamenka, E, 'Law, Legal Theory and Legal Education in the People's Republic of China' (1986) 7 *New York Law School Journal of International and Comparative Law* 1.

Tay, A and Kamenka, E, 'Life under Communism: The Soviet Union and China' (1986) 30 *Quadrant* 66.

Tay, A and Kamenka, E, 'Socialist Legality or Administrative Justice in the USSR and China?' (1986) 10 *Bulletin of the Australian Society of Legal Philosophy* 225.

Tay, A, 'Aimless Perspectives – A Comment on Chapter One of the CTEC "Discipline Assessment" of the Australian Law Schools' (1987) 11 *Bulletin of the Australian Society of Legal Philosophy* 154.

Tay, A, 'The Struggle for Law in China' (1987) 21 *University of British Columbia Law Review* 561.

Tay, A, 'Women, Culture and the Quality of Life' in L Sandell and EE Schmidt (eds), *Women of the Year – A Collection of Speeches by Australia's Most Successful Women* (Boorowa, NSW, Watermark Press, 1987) 23.

Tay, A and Kamenka, E, 'Chinese Law from the Epoch of the Ancient Dynasties to the Cultural Revolution' (1987) 7 *Eripainos Lakimies-Lehdesta* (Helsinki) 761.

Tay, A and Kamenka, E, 'Marxism, Legal Theory and Criminal Justice' (1987) 10 *Criminal Justice Ethics* 1.

Tay, A and Kamenka, E, 'Marxist Ideology, Communist Reality, and the Concept of Criminal Justice' (1987) 6 *Criminal Justice Ethics* 3.

Tay, A and Kamenka, E, 'Zum soziologischen Verständnis der Gerechtigkeit' in W Krawietz and W Ott (eds), *Formalismus und Phänomenologie im Rechtsdenken der Gegenwart: Festgabe für Alois Troller* (Berlin, Duncker & Humblot, 1987) 443.

Tay, A, 'Law and the Soviet State: Some Thoughts about the Future' in A Shtromas and MA Kaplan (eds), *The Soviet Union and the Challenge of the Future* (New York, Paragon House, 1988) 453.

Tay, A and Kamenka, E, 'New Marxism for Old: Contemporary Radicalism and Legal Theories' (1988) 1 *University of California Davis Law Review* 605.

Tay, A and Kamenka, E, 'Some Theses on Property' (1989) 11 *University of New South Wales Law Journal* 1.

Tay, A, 'Communist Visions, Communist Realities and the Role of Law' (1990) 17 *Journal of Law and Society* 1.

Tay, A, 'Law and the Soviet State – Some Thoughts about the Future in the Soviet Union and the Challenge of the Future' in *Stasis and Change* (New York, Paragon Hand Publishers, 1990) 453.

Tay, A, 'One World? One Culture? One Law?' in Sack, Wellman and Yasaki (eds), *Monistic or Pluralistic Legal Culture? Anthropological and Ehthnological and Foundations of Traditional and Modern Legal Systems* (Berlin, Duncker & Humblot, 1990) 23.

Tay, A and Kamenka, E, 'Affirming the Rights of Man and the Citizen: French Revolutionary Zeal Versus Australian Pragmatism' in A Tay (ed), *Australian Law and Legal Thinking Between the Decades* (Sydney, University of Sydney, 1990) 287.

Tay, A and Kamenka, E, 'New Forms of Governance? Human Values and Post-Industrial Technologies in Law Policy and Administration' in GE Lasker and RR Hough (eds), *Advances in Supporting Systems Research: Transdisciplinary Methodologies to Analyse, Design, Implement and Evaluate Support Oriented Processes and Policies in Natural and Artificial Systems* (Ontario, The International Institute for Advanced Studies in Systems Research and Cybernetics, 1990) 105.

Tay, A and Kamenka, E, 'Property: Some Natural, Social and Legal Realities' in Korean Association of IVR (eds), *Festschrift in Honour of Suh Ton-Kaka* (Seoul, Bobmum Publishing Co, 1990) 19.

Tay, A, 'The Role of Law in the Twentieth Century: From Law to Laws to Social Science' (1991) 13 *Sydney Law Review* 247.

Tay, A, 'The Western Legal Tradition and Internationalisation of Law' (1991) 6 *Connecticut University Law School Journal* 529.

Tay, A and Kamenka, E, 'Communism, Civil Society and Freedom' in C Kukathas, D W Lovell and W Maley (eds), *The Transition from Socialism: State and Civil Society in the USSR* (Melbourne, Longman Cheshire, 1991) 59.

Tay, A, 'Introduction: The Juridical Person in Legal Theory, Law and Comparative Law' (1992) *Indian Socio-Legal Journal* 1.

Tay, A and Kamenka, E, 'Legal Entities, Property and the Collapse of Communism' (1992) *Indian Socio-Legal Journal* 156.

Tay, A and Kamenka, E, 'International Law, International Justice and the Autonomy of Tibet' (1993) *Australian Society for Legal Philosophy Bulletin* 36.

Tay, A and Kamenka, E, 'The Law as Reasonable: Applying Perelman's Dictum to Common Law and to Continental Civil Law' (1993) *Australian Society for Legal Philosophy Bulletin* 1.

Tay, A and Kamenka, E, 'The Aboriginal People of Australia: Past Injustice, Present Hopes and Uncertainties' (1994) *Australian Society of Legal Philosophy Bulletin* 59.

Tay, A, 'The Internationalisation of the Sydney Law School' in International Legal Services Advisory Council, *Australian International Legal Education and Training: Directions, Issues and Opportunities* (1995) 135.

Tay, A, 'Legal Culture and Legal Pluralism in Common Law, Customary Law and Chinese Law' (1996) 26 *Hong Kong Law Journal* 194.

Tay, A, 'A Policy for Human Rights in the Asia Pacific' in B Galligan and C Sampford (eds), *Rethinking Human Rights* (Sydney, Federation Press, 1997) 87.

Tay, A, 'Human Rights Problems - Moral, Political, Philosophical' in B Galligan and C Sampford (eds), *Rethinking Human Rights* (Federation Press, 1997) 23.

Tay, A and Tan, P, 'Legal Pluralism in East Asia: Diversity, Unity, Universality' in P Tan (ed), *Asian Legal Systems – Law Society and Pluralism in East Asia* (Sydney, Butterworths, 1997) 390.

Tay, A, 'People's Republic of China' in P Tan (ed), *Asian Legal Systems – Law, Society and Pluralism in East Asia* (Sydney, Butterworths, 1997) 14.

Tay, A, 'Human Rights and Wrongs' in M Friedman, L May, K Parsons and J Stiff (eds), *Essays in Honor of Carl Wellman* (Dordrecht, Kluwer Academic Publishers, 2000) 121.

Tay, A, 'The New Century, Globalisation and Human Rights' (2000) 8 *Asia Pacific Law Review* 139.

Tay, A, 'Recognising Rights' in C Sampford and T Round (eds), *Beyond the Republic: Meeting the Global Challenges to Constitutionalism* (Sydney, Federation Press, 2001) 184.

Tay, A and Redd, H, 'China: Trade, Law and Human Rights' (2002) 7 *International Trade and Business Law Annual* 303.

B. Edited Collections

Kamenka, E and Tay, A (eds), *Human Rights* (Edward Arnold, 1978).

Kamenka, E, Brown, R, and Tay, A (eds), *Law and Society: The Crisis in Legal Ideals* (Edward Arnold, 1978).

Kamenka, E and Tay, A (eds), *Justice* (London and Melbourne, Edward Arnold, 1979).

Kamenka, E and Tay, A (eds), *Law and Social Control* (London, Edward Arnold, 1980).

Tay, A and Kamenka, E (eds), *Law-Making in Australia* (London and Melbourne, Edward Arnold, 1980).

Tay, A (ed), *Teaching Human Rights: An Australian Symposium* (Canberra, Australian National Commission for UNESCO, 1981).

Tay, A (ed), *Australian Law and Legal Thinking between the Decades* (Sydney, University of Sydney, 1990).

Tay, A and Leung CSC (eds), *Australian Law and Legal Thinking in the 1990s* (Sydney, University of Sydney, 1994).

Tay, A and Leung, CSC, *Greater China: Law, Society and Trade* (Sydney, Lawbook, 1995).

C. Theses

Tay, A, *The Concept of Possession in the Common Law* (unpublished PhD Thesis, Australian National University, 1964).

Appendix C: List of Geoffrey Sawer's Publications

A. Articles/Book Chapters

Sawer, G, 'Accession in English Law' (1935) 9 *Australian Law Journal* 50.
Sawer, G, 'A Trustee May Not Set Off a Gain in One Transaction Against a Loss in Another' (1936) 1 *Res Judicatae* 106.
Sawer, G, 'Competitions Involving Chance and Skill' (1937) 11 *Australian Law Journal* 114.
Sawer, G, 'Non-feasance in Relation to "Artificial Structures" on a Highway' (1938) 12 *Australian Law Journal* 231.
Sawer, G, 'Proper Law of Contract – Intention of Parties – Moratorium Legislation' (1938) 11 *Australian Law Journal* 332.
Sawer, G, 'Bankruptcy Act, s 95 – Preference to Sureties' (1939) 13 *Australian Law Journal* 13.
Sawer, G, 'Legal Realism' (1939) 2 *Res Judicatae* 68.
Sawer, G, 'Bankruptcy Act, 1924–33 – Relation Back and Protection to Purchasers' (1940) 13 *Australian Law Journal* 438.
Sawer, G, 'Autrefois Acquit and Decision Not "On the Merits"' (1941) 2 *Res Judicatae* 203.
Sawer, G, 'The Blackout Cases and Their Relation to Administrative Law' (1941) *Australian Law Journal* 103.
Sawer, G, 'Two Notes on *Clements v Ellis*' (1942) 15 *Australian Law Journal* 341.
Sawer, G, 'Injunction, Parliamentary Process, and the Restriction of Parliamentary Competence' (1944) 60 *Law Quarterly Review* 83.
Sawer, G, 'Contract Between the Crown and Its Civil Servants' (1946) 62 *Law Quarterly Review* 22.
Sawer, G, 'The Defence Power of the Commonwealth in Time of War' (1946) 20 *Australian Law Journal* 295.
Sawer, G, 'The Privy Council, the High Court and Section 92' (1947) 3 *Res Judicatae* 155.
Sawer, G and Paton, G, 'Ratio Decidendi and Obiter Dictum in Appellate Courts' (1947) 63 *Law Quarterly Review* 461.
Sawer, G, '*Bank of New South Wales and Others v Commonwealth* – The Bank Nationalisation Case' (1948) 22 *Australian Law Journal* 213.
Sawer, G, 'Price Control and the Validity of Contracts' (1948) 22 *Australian Law Journal* 173.
Sawer, G, 'Legal Education in the United States' (1948–50) 1 *University of Western Australia Law Review* 398.
Sawer, G, 'Implication and the Constitution – Part I' (1948) 4 *Res Judicatae* 15.
Sawer, G, 'Implications and the Constitution – Part II' (1949) 4 *Res Judicatae* 85.
Sawer, G, 'Some Problems in the Law of Copyright' (1949) 4 *Res Judicatae* 155.

Sawer, G, 'The Transitional Defence Power of the Commonwealth' (1949) 23 *Australian Law Journal* 255.
Sawer, G, 'Legal Education in the United States' (1950) 1 *University of Western Australia Annual Law Review* 398.
Sawer, G, 'The Case of Bank Nationalisation – A Study in Australian Government' (1950) 4 *Journal of the Society of Comparative Legislation and International Law* 17.
Sawer, G, 'Crown Liability in Tort and the Exercise of Discretions' (1951) 5 *Res Judicatae* 14.
Sawer, G, 'Fifty Years of the Australian Constitution' (1951) 7 *Current Affairs Bulletin* 147.
Sawer, G, 'An Australian National School of Law' (1951–53) 2 *University of Western Australia Law Review* 483.
Sawer, G, 'A Uniform Limitation of Actions Law' (1952) 26 *Australian Law Journal* 375.
Sawer, G, 'Australian Legislative Practice' (1952) 38 *American Bar Association Journal* 413.
Sawer, G, 'Recent Decisions Affecting Public Administration' (1952) 11 *Public Administration* 1.
Sawer, G, 'The Record of Judicial Review' in G Sawer (ed), *Federalism: An Australian Jubilee Study* (Melbourne, Cheshire, 1952) 211.
Sawer, G, 'Australian Government' in WV Aughterson (ed), *Taking Stock – Aspects of Mid-Century Life in Australia* (Melbourne, Cheshire, 1953) 127.
Sawer, G, 'Copyright in Reports of Legal Proceedings' (1953) 27 *Australian Law Journal* 82.
Sawer, G, 'Husband-and-Wife versus Master-and-Servant: A Collision of Concepts' (1953) 27 *Australian Law Journal* 323.
Sawer, G and Street, H, 'Tactical Irritation of Tenants – and Tactless Irritation of Dominions' (1953) 16 *Modern Law Review* 522.
Sawer, G, 'The Crown and "Per Quod Servitium Amisit" – Are Policemen Servants?' (1953) 16 *Modern Law Review* 374.
Sawer, G, 'A Judicial Confession' (1954) 17 *Modern Law Review* 387.
Sawer, G, 'Constitutional Issues' in A Davies and G Serle (eds), *Policies for Progress* (Melbourne, Cheshire, 1954) 13.
Sawer, G, 'Error of Law on the Face of an Administrative Record' (1954) 3 *University of Western Australia Annual Law Review* 24.
Sawer, G, 'Guests and Lodgers at Inns' (1954) 17 *Modern Law Review* 272.
Sawer, G, 'Judicial Decisions Affecting Public Administration, October 1951 – October 1953' (1954) 13 *Public Administration* 25.
Sawer, G, 'Judicial Power of the Commonwealth – Decisions by Registrars in Bankruptcy' (1954) 28 *Australian Law Journal* 341.
Sawer, G, 'Master and Servant – Vicarious Liability – Right of Indemnity Against Servant' (1954) 28 *Australian Law Journal* 205.
Sawer, G, 'The Public Corporation in Australia' in WG Friedmann (ed), *The Public Corporation* (Toronto, Carswell, 1954) 3.
Sawer, G, 'Execution of Treaties by Legislation in the Commonwealth of Australia' (1955) 2 *University of Queensland Law Journal* 297.
Sawer, G, 'Non-Feasance Revisited' (1955) 18 *Modern Law Review* 341.
Sawer, G, 'The Crown and "Per Quod Servitium Amisit" – Are Policemen Servants? (No 2)' (1955) 18 *Modern Law Review* 488.
Sawer, G, 'Councils, Ministers and Cabinets in Australia' (1956) *Public Law* 110.
Sawer, G, 'Judicial Decisions Affecting Public Administration 1953–1956' (1956) 15 *Public Administration* 132.

Sawer, G, 'Per Quod Servitium Amisit and Crown Servants' (1956) 30 *Australian Law Journal* 387.

Sawer, G, 'Some Constitutional Case-Books' (1956) 30 *Australian Law Journal* 287.

Sawer, G, 'Problems of Australian Foreign Policy, June 1956 – June 1957' (1957) 3 *Australian Journal of Politics and History* 1.

Sawer, G, 'Shield of the Crown Revisited' (1957) 1 *Melbourne University Law Review* 137.

Sawer, G, 'Some Legal Assumptions of Constitutional Change' (1957) 4 *University of Western Australia Annual Law Review* 1.

Sawer, G, 'The Second Uniform Tax Case' (1957) 31 *Australian Law Journal* 347.

Sawer, G, 'The Supreme Court and the High Court of Australia' (1957) 6 *Journal of Public Law* 482.

Sawer, G, 'The United Nations' in G Greenwood and ND Harper (eds), *Australia in World Affairs 1950–55* (Melbourne, Cheshire, 1957) 92.

Sawer, G, 'Constructive Desertion of Children' (1958) 32 *Australian Law Journal* 42.

Sawer, G, 'Government as Personalised Legal Entity' in LC Webb (ed), *Legal Personality and Political Pluralism* (Melbourne, Melbourne University Press, 1958) 158.

Sawer, G, 'Judicial Decisions Affecting Public Administration, 1956–58' (1958) 17 *Public Administration* 97.

Sawer, G, 'Law at the Australian National University' (1959) 5 *Journal of the Society of Public Teachers of Law* 20.

Sawer, G, 'Per Quod Servitium Amisit – Menial Servants' (1959) 75 *Law Quarterly Review* 460.

Sawer, G, 'Retrospectivity of Decrees of Nullity in Marriage' (1959) 32 *Australian Law Journal* 394.

Sawer, G, 'Town Planning by Judges: The County of Cumberland Scheme in NSW' (1959) 45 *Journal of the Town Planning Institute* 109.

Sawer, G, 'Confirmation of Provisional Maintenance Orders: The British Commonwealth System' (1960) 34 *Australian Law Journal* 233.

Sawer, G, 'Federal Legal Persons and Dual Citizenship' (1960) 2 *University of Malaya Law Review* 1.

Sawer, G, 'Judicial Decisions Affecting Public Administration, 1958–60' (1960) 19 *Public Administration* 230.

Sawer, G (ed), 'Justice MC Kriewaldt's The Application of the Criminal Law to the Aborigines of the Northern Territory of Australia' (1960) 5 *University of Western Australia Law Review* 1.

Sawer, G, 'Politics and the Constitution in West Germany' (1960) 14 *Australian Outlook* 136.

Sawer, G, 'Reforming the Federal Constitution' (1960) 32 *Australian Quarterly* 29.

Sawer, G, 'State and Private Property in Australian Law' in H Strebel (ed), *Staat und Privateigentum* (Cologne, C Heymanns Verlag, 1960) 209.

Sawer, G, 'Federalism in West Germany' (1961) *Public Law* 26.

Sawer, G, 'Judge Martin Kriewaldt, Nine Years of Northern Territory Supreme Court' (1961) 1 *Adelaide Law Review* 148.

Sawer, G, 'Judicial Power under the Constitution' in R Else-Mitchell (ed), *Essays on the Australian Constitution* (Sydney, Lawbook, 1961) 71.

Sawer, G, 'Law as Socially Neutral – Karl Renner' in G Sawer (ed), *Studies in the Sociology of Law* (Canberra, Australian National University, 1961) 137.

Sawer, G, 'State Statutes and the Commonwealth' (1961) 1 *Tasmanian University Law Review* 580.

Sawer, G, 'The Separation of Powers in Australian Federalism' (1961) 35 *Australian Law Journal* 177.
Sawer, G, 'Estoppel in Worker's Compensation' (1962) 36 *Australian Law Journal* 91.
Sawer, G, and Doeker, G, 'The European Economic Community as a Constitutional System' (1962) 4 *Inter-American Law Review* 218.
Sawer, G, 'Federal-State Co-Operation in Law Reform: Lessons of the Australian Uniform Companies Act' (1963) 4 *Melbourne University Law Review* 238.
Sawer, G, 'Political Questions' (1963) 15 *University of Toronto Law Journal* 49.
Sawer, G, 'Substance and Form in the Relations between Federal and State Legislation in Australia' (1963) *Archiv für Rechts- und Sozialphilosophie* 61.
Sawer, G, 'Australia – Embarrassing Interlude' (1964) 11 *Bulletin of the Copyright Society of the USA* 313.
Sawer, G, 'Emergency Powers in Nigerian and Malayan Federalism' (1964) 6 *Malaya Law Review* 83.
Sawer, G, 'Australian Constitutional Law in Relation to International Relations and International Law' in DP O'Connell (ed), *International Law in Australia* (Sydney, Lawbook, 1965) 35.
Sawer, G, 'Judicial Administration: The Subject and Some Applications' (1965) 8 *Journal of the Society of Public Teachers of Law* 301.
Sawer, G, 'TPNG – The Problem of a Constitution' (1965) 5 *Australian Territories* 2.
Sawer, G, 'Division of a Fused Legal Profession – The Australian Experience' (1966) 16 *University of Toronto Law Journal* 245.
Sawer, G, 'Nonfeasance under Fire' (1966) 2 *New Zealand Universities Law Review* 115.
Sawer, G, 'The Australian Constitution and the Australian Aborigine' (1966) 2 *Federal Law Review* 17.
Sawer, G, 'The Constitution and its Politics' in H Mayer (ed), *Australian Politics – A Reader* (Melbourne, Cheshire, 1966) 86.
Sawer, G, 'Copyright in Letters Unpublished at Writer's Death' (1967) 3 *Archives and Manuscripts* 27.
Sawer, G, 'The High Court' (1967) 40 *Current Affairs Bulletin* 82.
Sawer, G, 'Redevelopment and the Law of Town Planning' in PN Troy (ed), *Urban Redevelopment in Australia* (Canberra, Australian National University Press, 1967) 136.
Sawer, G, 'Sabbatical Leave' (1967) 49 *Quadrant* 69.
Sawer, G, 'The Ombudsman and Related Institutions in Australia and New Zealand' (1968) May *Annals of the American Academy of Political and Social Science* 62.
Sawer, G, 'The Ombudsman Comes to Alberta' (1968) 6 *Alberta Law Review* 95.
Sawer, G, 'The United Nations' in G Greenwood and N Harper (eds), *Australia in World Affairs 1961–65* (Melbourne, Cheshire, 1968) 234.
Sawer, G, 'Australian Constitutional Development since 1954' in G Leibholz (ed), *Jahrbuch des Öffentlichen Rechts der Gegenwart* (Tübingen, Neue Folge, 1969) 681.
Sawer, G, 'The Commonwealth Copyright Act 1968' (1969) 43 *Australian Law Journal* 8.
Sawer, G, 'Nationalism in the Working of the Federal Constitution' (1969) 3 *Teaching History* 36.
Sawer, G, 'Administrative Control of Companies – The Life Insurance Example' (1970) 44 *Australian Law Journal* 303.
Sawer, G, 'Appeals to the Privy Council – Australia' (1970) 2 *Otago Law Review* 138.
Sawer, G, 'Getting Around the Constitution' (1970) 29 *Public Administration* 25.
Sawer, G, 'The Constitution Reconsidered' (1970) 10 *Australian External Territories* 2.

Sawer, G, 'The Control of Administrative Discretions' (1970) 29 *Public Administration* 145.
Sawer, G, 'The Legal Theory of Law Reform' (1970) 20 *University of Toronto Law Journal* 183.
Sawer, G, 'Conservation and the Law' in AB Costin and HJ Frith (eds), *Conservation* (Melbourne, Penguin, 1971) 262.
Sawer, G, 'Copyright and Letters Not Published at the Author's Death' (1971) 4 *Archives and Manuscripts* 1.
Sawer, G, 'Papua-New Guinea Government: Patterns of Devolution' in LK Young (ed), *Constitutional Development in Papua and New Guinea* (Sydney, International Commission of Jurists, 1971) 4.
Sawer, G, 'The Commonwealth and the States' (1971) 47 *Current Affairs Bulletin* 51.
Sawer, G, 'The Jurisprudence of the Ombudsmen' (1971) 30 *Public Administration* 221.
Sawer, G, 'The Privilege of Members of Parliament from Detention' (1971) 7 *University of Queensland Law Journal* 226.
Sawer, G, 'Conscience as Objection in the Law' in TP Grundy (ed), *Conscience in the '70s* (Canberra, Australian National University Centre for Continuing Education, 1972) 66.
Sawer, G, 'The Criminal Law Cannot Stand Still' (1972) 5 *Australia and New Zealand Journal of Criminology* 137.
Sawer, G, 'The Dynamics of Australian Federalism' (1972) 62 *Round Table* 441.
Sawer, G, 'The Judgments of Sir John Barry' in N Morris and M Perlman (eds), *Law and Crime: Essays in Honor of Sir John Barry* (New York, Gordon and Breach, 1972) 3.
Sawer, G, 'The British Connection' (1973) 47 *Australian Law Journal* 113.
Sawer, G, 'Conservation and the Law' in R Dempsey (ed), *The Politics of Finding Out: Environmental Problems in Australia* (Melbourne, Cheshire, 1974) 168.
Sawer, G, 'The Future of State Taxes: Constitutional Issues' in RL Mathes (ed), *Fiscal Federalism – Retrospect and Prospect* (Canberra, Centre for Research on Federal Financial Relations, ANU, 1974) 193.
Sawer, G, 'The States and Indirect Taxation' in RL Mathews (ed), *Intergovernmental Relations in Australia* (Melbourne, Angus and Robertson, 1974) 178.
Sawer, G, 'The Theory of Law' in P Biskup (ed), *Australian Law* (Sydney, McGraw-Hill, 1974) 99.
Sawer, G, 'Constitutional Change – Australian and Overseas Experience' in RL Mathews (ed), *Making Federalism Work* (Canberra, Centre for Research on Federal Financial Relations in association with the Centre for Continuing Education, ANU, 1976) 69.
Sawer, G, 'Singulars, Plurals and Section 57 of the Constitution' (1976) 8 *Federal Law Review* 45.
Sawer, G, 'The Governor-General of the Commonwealth of Australia' (1976) 52 *Current Affairs Bulletin* 20.
Sawer, G, 'The Whitlam Revolution in Australian Federalism – Promise Possibilities and Performance' (1976) 10 *Melbourne University Law Review* 315.
Sawer, G, 'Who Controls the Law in Australia? Instigators of Change and Obstacles Confronting Them' in AD Hambly and JL Goldring (eds), *Australian Lawyers and Social Change* (Sydney, Lawbook, 1976) 118.
Sawer, G, 'Federalism' in S Encel, D Horne and E Thompson (eds), *Change the Rules! Towards a Democratic Constitution* (Melbourne, Penguin, 1977) 54.
Sawer, G, 'Constitutional Issues in Australian Federalism' (1977) 7 *Publius* 21.
Sawer, G, 'Seventy-Five Years of Australian Federalism' (1977) 36 *Australian Journal of Public Administration* 1.

Sawer, G, 'Towards a New Federal Structure?' in G Evans (ed), *Labor and the Constitution 1972–1975* (Melbourne, Heinemann, 1977) 1.

Sawer, G, 'The External Affairs Powers of the Commonwealth and Kowarta's Case' (1982) 54 *Australian Quarterly* 428.

Sawer, G, 'Judicial' (1983) 1 *LAWASIA* 4.

Sawer, G, 'The External Affairs Power' (1984) 14 *Federal Law Review* 199.

B. Books

Barry JV, Paton, GW and Sawer, G, *An Introduction to the Criminal Law in Australia* (Melbourne, Melbourne University Press, 1948).

Sawer, G, *Australian Government Today* (Melbourne, Melbourne University Press, 1948). [In 1987 the thirteenth and final edition of this book was published.]

Sawer, G, *Cases on the Constitution of the Commonwealth of Australia* (Sydney, Law Book Company, 1948). [In 1964 the third edition of this book was published, authored by Sawer. Subsequent editions were updated by new authors.]

Sawer, G, *A Guide to Australian Law for Journalists, Authors, Printers and Publishers* (Melbourne, Melbourne University Press, 1949). [In 1983 the third and final edition of this book was published.]

Sawer, G (ed), *Federalism: An Australian Jubilee Study* (Melbourne, Cheshire, 1951).

Sawer, G, *The Place of a Lawyer in the Social Sciences* (Melbourne, Melbourne University Press, 1953).

Sawer, G, with Matthews, RE, and others (eds), *Labor Relations and the Law* (Boston, Little Brown, 1953).

Sawer, G, *Australian Federal Politics and Law 1901–29* (Melbourne, Melbourne University Press, 1956).

Sawer, G (ed), *Studies in the Sociology of Law* (Canberra, Australian National University Press, 1961).

Sawer, G, *Australian Federal Politics and Law 1929–49* (Melbourne, Melbourne University Press, 1963).

Sawer, G, *Ombudsmen* (Melbourne, Melbourne University Press, 1964). [In 1968 the second and final edition of this book was published.]

Sawer, G, *Law in Society* (Oxford, Clarendon Press, 1965).

Karlen, D, Wise, EM and Sawer, G, *Anglo-American Criminal Justice* (Oxford, Clarendon, 1967).

Sawer, G, *Australian Federalism in the Courts* (Melbourne, Melbourne University Press, 1967).

Sawer, G, *The Australian and the Law* (Melbourne, Penguin, 1968). [In 1972 the second and final edition of this book was published.]

Sawer, G, *Modern Federalism* (London, Watts, 1969). [In 1974 the second and final edition of this book was published.]

Sawer, G and Frith, HJ (eds), *The Murray Waters: Many, Nature and a River System* (Sydney, Angus and Robertson, 1974).

Sawer, G, *The Australian Constitution* (Australian Government Publishing Service, 1975). [In 1988 the second and final edition of this book was published.]

Sawer, G, *Federation under Strain: Australia 1972–75* (Melbourne, Melbourne University Press, 1977).

BIBLIOGRAPHY

Primary Sources

Archival Collections

National Library of Australia

Barry, Sir John Vincent Barry, Papers of, 1917–69, series 1, MS2505.
Brett, Peter, Papers of, 1950–75, MS5603.
Brett, Peter, Biographical Cuttings, 241234.
Eggleston, Sir Frederic William, Papers of, 1911-45, series 1, MS423.
Sawer, Geoffrey, Papers of, MS2688.
Sawer, Geoffrey, Biographical Cuttings, 2020722.
Tay, Alice and Kamenka, Eugene, Biographical Cuttings, 200146.

Harvard Law School Library, Historical and Special Collections

Henry Melvin Hart Papers, 1927–69, HOLLIS 601611.
Lon L Fuller Papers, 1926–77, HOLLIS 601606.
Sheldon Glueck Papers, 1916–72, HOLLIS 601626.

Oxford University Press

Law in Society, OP587/4137.

University Archives

Australian National University Archives (Noel Butlin Archives)

Law School Minutes, ANUA 53 Box 731.
Eugene Kamenka Staff Files, ANUA 19.
Minutes of the Research School of Social Sciences, ANUA 53 09.1.4.1.
Research School of Social Sciences – General, ANUA 53 9.1.1.0 (1-12).
Research School of Social Sciences – Publications, ANUA 168.
Sawer, Geoffrey, Collection of Correspondence, Writing and Diaries, ANUA7.
Sawer, Geoffrey, Staff Files, ANUA19.
Tay, Alice Erh-Soon, Staff Files, ANUA19.

University of Melbourne Archives

Brett, Peter, Papers of, 1975.0095.
Ford, Harold Arthur, Papers of, 1984.0033.0000.0014.
Faculty of Law, University of Melbourne, 1920–85, 1996.0065.
Faculty of Law, University of Melbourne, 1932–77, 1984.0033.
Faculty of Law, University of Melbourne, 1953–58, 1984.0033.0000.0007.
Faculty of Law, University of Melbourne, 1971–79, 2003.0058.
Law Dean's Correspondence 1953–1961, 1984.0033 84/33.
Law AULSA 1846–1962, 1984.0033.0000.0005.
Orr Case, Papers of, 1968.0024.
Registrar's Correspondence Series, University of Melbourne, UM 312, 2001.0030.

University of Sydney Archives

Academic Board Minutes, G51/1.
Faculty of Law Minutes, G3/2.
Professorial Board Minutes, G2/1.

Secondary Sources

A. Articles/Books/Book Chapters

Anthony, T, Crofts, P, Crofts, T, Gray, S, Loughnan, A and Naylor, B, *Waller and Williams Criminal Law – Text and Cases*, 12th edn (Sydney, LexisNexis, 2013).

Arendt, H, *Eichmann in Jerusalem: A Report on the Banality of Evil* (London, Faber and Faber, 1963).

Athaide, A, 'Alex Castles on the Recognition of Australian Legal History 1955–63' (2003) 7 *Australian Journal of Legal History* 107.

Auchmuty, R, 'Recovering Lost Lives – Researching Women in Legal History' (2015) 42 *Journal of Law and Society* 34.

Austin, RP, 'Academics, Practitioners and Judges' (2004) 26 *Sydney Law Review* 463.

Ayres, I, 'Discrediting the Free Market' (1999) 66 *University of Chicago Law Review* 273.

Ayres, P (ed), *David Derham: Talks on Universities, History, and the Law* (Melbourne, Oryx Publishing, 2009).

Baker, D, '"Colonial Cap, Gown and Wig" – The Origins of Australian Legal Education' (2012) 1 *Journal of Australasian Law Teachers Association* 1.

Baker, RW, 'Book Review: *Cases on Constitutional and Administrative Law* by Peter Brett' (1962) 1 *Tasmanian University Law Review* 760.

Ball, M, 'Legal Education and the "Idealistic Student": Using Foucault to Unpack the Critical Legal Narrative' (2010) 36 *Monash University Law Review* 80.

Barker, D, *A History of Australian Legal Education* (Sydney, Federation Press, 2017).

Barry, JV, 'Book Review: *An Inquiry into Criminal Guilt* by Peter Brett' (1963) 4 *Melbourne University Law Review* 293.

Barry, JV, Paton, GW and Sawer, G, *An Introduction to the Criminal Law in Australia* (London, Macmillan, 1948).

Bartie, S, 'A Full Day's Work – A Study of Australia's First Legal Scholarly Community' (2010) 29 *University of Queensland Law Journal* 67.

Bartie, S, 'The Lingering Core of Legal Scholarship' (2010) 30 *Legal Studies* 345.

Bartie, S, 'The Social Sciences in Australia and the Experience of Law' (2012) 34 *Sydney Law Review* 371.

Bartie, S, 'Histories of Legal Scholars – The Power of Possibility' (2014) 34 *Legal Studies* 305.

Bartie, S, 'Towards a History of Law as an Academic Discipline' (2014) 38 *Melbourne University Law Review* 444.

Bartie, S, 'Studying Women Legal Scholars: The Challenges of Life History' (2018) 25 *International Journal of the Legal Profession* 279.

Barzun, CL, 'Common Sense and Legal Science' (2004) 90 *Virginia Law Review* 1051.

Barzun, CL, 'The Forgotten Foundations of Hart and Sacks' (2013) 99 *Virginia Law Review* 1.

Barzun, C and Priel, D, 'Jurisprudence and (its) History' (2015) 10 *Virginia Law Review* 849.

Bates, AP, Buddin, TL and Meure, DJ, *The System of Criminal Law: Cases and Materials: New South Wales, Victoria, South Australia* (Sydney, Butterworths, 1979).

Bavin, T, *The Jubilee Book of the Law School of the University of Sydney 1890–1940* (Sydney, University of Sydney, 1940).

Bennett, JM, 'Out of Nothing – Professor Pitt Cobbett 1890–1909' in J Mackinolty and J Mackinolty (eds), *A Century Down Town – Sydney University Law School's First Hundred Years* (Sydney, Sydney University Law School, 1991) 57.

Bilinsky, B, 'Shatwell, Kenneth Owen (1909–88)' in *Australian Dictionary of Biography*, vol 18 (Melbourne, Melbourne University Press, 2012).

Bingham, EM, 'Book Review: Cases and Materials in Criminal Law by P Brett and Peter L. Waller' (1962) 1 *Tasmanian University Law Review* 761.

Blackburn, E, *Broken Lives* (Melbourne, Hardie Grant, 2001).

Blackshield, A, 'The Legacy of Julius Stone' (1997) 20 *University of New South Wales Law Journal* 215.

Blainey, G, *A Centenary History of the University of Melbourne* (Melbourne, Melbourne University Press, 1957).

Bradley, CM, 'Legal Education in Australia: An American Perspective' (1989) 14 *Journal of the Legal Profession* 27.

Braun, A, 'Professors and Judges in Italy: It Takes Two to Tango' (2006) 26 *Oxford Journal of Legal Studies* 665.

Braun, A, 'Burying the Living? The Citation of Legal Writings in English Courts' (2010) 58 *American Journal of Comparative Law* 27.

Brown, AJ, *Michael Kirby – Paradoxes and Principles* (Sydney, Federation Press, 2011).

Brown, J, 'The American Law School' (1905) 21 *Law Quarterly Review* 69.

Brown, W Jethro, 'The Purpose and Method of a Law School: Part I' (1902) 18 *Law Quarterly Review* 78.

Brown, W Jethro, 'The Purpose and Method of a Law School: Part II' (1902) 18 *Law Quarterly Review* 192.

Brown, W Jethro, 'Law Schools and the Legal Profession' (1908) 6 *Commonwealth Law Review* 3.

Burns, C, *The Tait Case* (Melbourne, Melbourne University Press, 1962).

Buti, A, 'Book Review: *A Matter of Conscience* – Sir Ronald Wilson' (2009) 31 Sydney Law Review 331.

Caine, B, *Biography and History* (London, Palgrave MacMillan, 2010).

Campbell, E, 'Occasional Address, Law Graduation Ceremony, University of Tasmania' (1993) 12 *University of Tasmania Law Review* 1.

Campbell, R, *A History of the Melbourne Law School 1857–1973* (Melbourne,Melbourne University Press, 1977).

Carrigan, F, 'They Make a Desert and Call It Peace' (2014) 23 *Legal Education Review* 313.

Castles, AC, 'Working with our Legal History – A Revolution Just Beginning' (2003) 7 *Australian Journal of Legal History* 5.

Castles, A, Ligertwood, A and Kelly, P, *Law on North Terrace – 1883–1983* (Adelaide, University of Adelaide, 1983).

Chase, WC, *The American Law School and the Rise of Administrative Government* (Madison, University of Wisconsin Press, 1982).

Chesterman, M and Weisbrot, D, 'Legal Scholarship in Australia' (1987) 50 *Modern Law Review* 709.

Christian, B, *Presumed Guilty: When Cops Get it Wrong and Courts Seal the Deal* (Melbourne, Hardie Grant, 2013).

Clarsen, G, *Eat My Dust: Early Women Motorists* (Baltimore, John Hopkins University Press, 2008).

Cole, CM, 'John Anderson' in EN Zalta (ed), *The Stanford Encyclopedia of Philosophy* (Winter 2012 edn).

Collier, R, '"We're All Socio-Legal Now?" Legal Education, Scholarship and the "Global Knowledge Economy" – Reflections on the UK Experience' (2004) 26 *Sydney Law Review* 504.

Collini, S, 'What is Intellectual History?' (1985) 35 *History Today* 46.

Connell, WF, Sherington, GE, Fletcher, BH, Turney, C and Bygott, U, *Australia's First – A History of the University of Sydney*, vols 1–2 (Sydney, University of Sydney, 1995).

Coper, M, 'Geoffrey Sawer and the Art of Academic Commentator: A Preliminary Biographical Sketch' (2014) 42 *Federal Law Review* 389.

Cosgrove, RA, *Scholars of the Law: English Jurisprudence from Blackstone to Hart* (New York, New York University Press, 1996).

Cosgrove, RA, 'The Culture of Academic Legal History – Lawyer's History and Historian's Law 1870–1930' (2002) 33 *Cambrian Law Review* 23.

Cotterrell, R, *The Politics of Jurisprudence – A Critical Introduction to Legal Philosophy* (London, Butterworths, 1989).

Coutts, JA, 'Book Review: *Law, Liberty and Morality* by HLA Hart and *An Inquiry into Criminal Guilt* by Peter Brett' (1964) 80 *Law Quarterly Review* 279.

Cowen, Z, *A Public Life – The Memoirs of Zelman Cowen* (Melbourne, Miegunyah Press, 2006).

Cownie, F, 'Women in the Law School – Shoals of Fish, Starfish or Fish Out of Water?' in P Thomas (ed), *Discriminating Lawyers* (London, Cavendish, 2000) 63–86.

Cownie, F, *Legal Academics – Culture and Identities* (Oxford, Hart Publishing, 2004).

Cownie, F, 'The United Kingdom's First Woman Law Professor: An Archerian Analysis' (2015) 42 *Journal of Law and Society* 127.

Crabb, A, *The Wife Drought* (Sydney, Ebury Press, 2014).

Cranston, R, '"Lawyer in the Social Sciences" – Geoffrey Sawer' (1980) 11 *Federal Law Review* 263.

Cranston, R, 'Samuel Jacob Stoljar' (1991) 4 *Journal of Contract Law* 146.

Creyke, R, Hamer, D, O'Mara, P, Smith, B and Taylor, T, *Laying Down the Law* (Sydney, LexisNexis Butterworths, 2017).

Crisp, LF, 'Book Review: *Modern Federalism* by Geoffrey Sawer' (1969) 3 *Federal Law Review* 305.

Crisp, LF, 'Book Review: *Modern Federalism*, 2nd ed, by Geoffrey Sawer' (1976–77) 8 *Federal Law Review* 107.

Cross, R and Jones, PA, *An Introduction to Criminal Law*, 3rd edn (London, Butterworth & Co, 1953).

Cross, R and Jones, PA, *Cases on Criminal Law*, 2nd edn (London, Butterworth & Co, 1953).

Cross, R, 'Book Review: *Cases and Materials in Criminal Law* by Peter Brett and Peter L Waller' (1962) 3 *Melbourne University Law Review* 546.

Cutt, J, 'Book Review: *Australian Lawyers and Social Change* by David Hambly and John Goldring (eds)' (1976) 7 *Federal Law Review* 253.

Daunton-Fear, MW, 'Book Review: *An Inquiry into Criminal Guilt* by Peter Brett' (1963) 1 *Tasmanian University Law Review* 883.

Davis, R, *100 Years – A Centenary History of the Faculty of Law, University of Tasmania 1893–1993* (Hobart, University of Tasmania Law School, 1993).

De Smith, SA, 'Book Review: *Cases on Constitutional and Administrative Law* by Peter Brett' (1961–2) 3 *Melbourne University Law Review* 544.

De Smith, SA, 'Book Review: *Australian Federalism in the Courts* by Geoffrey Sawer and *Australian Federal Constitutional Law* by Colin Howard' (1969) 32 *Modern Law Review* 460.

Deflem, M, 'Ferdinand Tönnies (1855–1936)', *Routledge Encyclopaedia of Philosophy* (online), (Taylor and Francis, 2001).

Del Mar, M and Lobban, M (eds), *Legal Theory and Legal History* (Farnham, Ashgate, 2014).

Denzin, NK and Lincoln, YS (eds), *Handbook of Qualitative Research*, 2nd edn (Thousand Oaks, SAGE Publications, 2000).
Derham, D, *George Paton's A Textbook of Jurisprudence*, 3rd edn (Oxford, Oxford University Press, 1964).
Derham, D, 'Legal Education – A Challenge to the Profession' (1969) 43 *Australian Law Journal* 530.
Devlin, P, *The Enforcement of Morals* (Oxford, Oxford University Press, 1965).
Dixon, M, *Thirty Up – The Story of the UNSW Law School 1971–2001* (Sydney, UNSW Law School, 2001).
Dixon, O, 'Concerning Judicial Method' in SHZ Woinarski (ed), *Jesting Pilate* (Melbourne, Law Book Co, 1965) 155.
Doeker-Mach, G and Ziegert, KA (eds), *Alice Erh-Soon Tay – Lawyer, Scholar, Civil Servant* (Stuttgart, Franz Steiner Verlag, 2004).
Doeker-Mach, G and Ziegert, KA, *Law, Legal Culture and Politics in the Twentieth Century, Essays in Honour of Alice Erh-Soon Tay* (Stuttgart, Steiner, 2004).
Duxbury, N, 'In the Twilight of Legal Realism – Fred Rodell and the Limits of Legal Critique' (1991) 11 *Oxford Journal of Legal Studies* 354.
Duxbury, N, 'The Narrowing of English Jurisprudence' (1991) 95 *Michigan Law Review* 1990.
Duxbury, N, 'Struggling with Legal Theory' (1993) 43 *University of Toronto Law Journal* 889.
Duxbury, N, 'History as Hyperbole' (1995) 15 *Oxford Journal of Legal Studies* 477.
Duxbury, N, *Patterns of American Jurisprudence* (Oxford, Clarendon Press, 1995).
Duxbury, N, 'When Trying is Failing: Holmes's "Englishness"' (1997) 63 *Brooklyn Law Review* 145.
Duxbury, N, 'When We Were Young – Notes in the *Law Quarterly Review* 1885–1925' (2000) 116 *Law Quarterly Review* 474.
Duxbury, N, *Jurists and Judges* (Oxford, Hart Publishing, 2001).
Duxbury, N, *Frederick Pollock and the English Juristic Tradition* (Oxford, Oxford University Press, 2004).
Duxbury, N, *The Nature and Authority of Precedent* (Cambridge, Cambridge University Press, 2008).
Eddy, WHC, *Orr* (Brisbane, Jacaranda, 1961).
Edgeloe, VA, 'The Adelaide Law School – 1883–1983' (1983–85) 9 *Adelaide Law Review* 1.
Elkington, GB, 'Book Review: *The System of Criminal Law: Cases and Materials* by AP Bates, TL Buddin and DJ Meure' (1981) 9 *Sydney Law Review* 497.
Elliott, ID, 'Book Review: *Modern Federalism* by Geoffrey Sawer' (1969) 7 *Melbourne University Law Review* 310.
Else-Mitchell, R, 'Introduction' in L Zines (ed), *Commentaries on the Australian Constitution – A Tribute to Geoffrey Sawer* (Sydney, Butterworths, 1977) xix.
Ely, M, Vinz, R, Anzul, M and Downing, M, *On Writing Qualitative Research – Living by Words* (London/Washington DC, Falmer Press, 1997).
Eskridge, WN and Frickey, PP (eds), *Henry M Hart Jr and Albert M Sacks, The Legal Process: Basic Problems in the Making and Application of Law* (Westbury, Foundation Press, 1994).
Eskridge, WN and Frickey, PP, 'The Making of the Legal Process' (1994) 107 *Harvard Law Review* 2031.
Ewens, JQ, 'Book Review: *Australian Federal Politics and Law 1929–49* by Geoffrey Sawer' (1964) 165 *Federal Law Review* 165.
Farrar, J, 'Professor Mary Hiscock' (2003) 15 *Bond Law Review* 7.
Fernandez, A and Dubber, MD (eds), *Law Books in Action – Essays on the Anglo-American Legal Treatise* (Oxford, Hart Publishing, 2012).
Ferzan, KK, 'Commentary' (2015) 101 *Virginia Law Review* 947.
Ferzan, KK, 'Of Weevils and Witches: What Can We Learn From the Ghost of Responsibility Past?' (2015) 10 *Virginia Law Review* 947.
Fifoot, CHS and Zutshi PNR (eds), *The Letters of Frederic William Maitland*, 2 vols (Cambridge and London, Selden Society, 1965–95).
Fikentscher, W, 'Book Review: *Law, Legal Culture and Politics in the Twenty First Century – Essays in Honour of Alice Erh-Soon Tay* by Guenther Doeker-Mach and Klaus A Ziegert (eds)' (2007) 56 *Journal of Legal Pluralism* 113.

Finn, J, *Educating for the Profession – Law at Canterbury 1873–1973* (Christchurch, Canterbury University Press, 2010).
Finnane, M, *JV Barry – A Life* (Sydney, UNSW Press, 2007).
Finnane, M, 'The Origins of Criminology in Australia' (2012) 45 *Australian and New Zealand Journal of Criminology* 157.
Finnane, M, 'Law as an Intellectual Vocation' (2015) 38 *Melbourne University Law Review* 1060.
Fiss, O, *Pillars of Justice – Lawyers and the Liberal Tradition* (Cambridge, Harvard University Press, 2017).
Fisher, WW, 'Texts and Contexts: The Application to American Legal History of the Methodologies of Intellectual History' (1997) 49 *Stanford Law Review* 1065.
Forsyth, H, *A History of the Modern Australian University* (Sydney, NewSouth, 2014).
Fox, R, 'Book Review: *Cases and Materials on Criminal Law and Procedure* edited by ML Friedland' (1969) 7 *Melbourne University Law Review* 146.
Fletcher, GP, 'The Fall and Rise of Criminal Theory' (1998) 1 *Buffalo Criminal Law Review* 275.
Foster, SG and Varghese, MM, *The Making of the Australian National University* (Sydney, Allen & Unwin, 1996).
Franklin, J, *Corrupting the Youth* (Sydney, Macleay Press, 2003).
Fridman, GHL, 'Book Review: *An Essay on a Contemporary Jurisprudence* by Peter Brett' (1976) 74 *Canadian Bar Review* 220.
Fried, BH, *The Progresssive Assault on Laissez Faire – Robert Hale and the First Law and Economics Movement* (Cambridge, Harvard University Press, 1998).
Friedman, W, 'Book Review: *Cases on the Constitution of the Commonwealth of Australia* by Geoffrey Sawer' (1957) 57 *Columbia Law Review* 1195.
Fuller, LL, 'Positivism and Fidelity to Law: A Reply to Professor Hart' (1958) 7 *Harvard Law Review* 630.
Fuller, LL, 'Mediation – Its Forms and Functions' (1971) 44 *Southern California Law Review* 305.
Fuller, L, 'The Case of the Speluncean Explorers' (1949) 62 *Harvard Law Review* 616.
Galligan, DJ, 'Judicial Review and the Textbook Writers' (1982) 2 *Oxford Journal of Legal Studies* 257.
Gava, J, 'Introductory Essay' (1988–89) 5 *Australian Journal of Law and Society* 1.
Geertz, C, 'Thick Description: Toward an Interpretive Theory of Culture' in C Geertz, *The Interpretation of Cultures* (New York, Basic Books, 1973) 3.
'Geoffrey Sawer 1910–' (1980) 11 *Federal Law Review* 259.
Gilbert, F, 'Intellectual History: Its Aims and Methods' (1971) 100 *Daedalus* 80.
Girard, P, 'Judging Lives – Judicial Biography from Hale to Holmes' (2003) 7 *Australian Journal of Legal History* 87.
Goldring, J, 'Legitimacy, the High Court and Australian Politics' (1987) 10 *University of New South Wales Law Journal* 189.
Goodson, IF (ed), *Studying Teachers' Lives* (London, Routledge, 1992).
Gordon, RW, 'The Past as Authority and as Social Critic: Stabilizing and Destabilizing Functions of History in Legal Argument' in TJ McDonald (ed), *The Historic Turn in the Human Sciences* (Ann Arbor, University of Michigan Press, 1996) 359.
Grbich, C, *New Approaches in Social Research* (London, SAGE Publications, 2004).
Griffin, SM, 'Legal Liberalism at Yale' (1997) 14 *Constitutional Commentary* 535.
Griswold, EN, 'Observations on Legal Education in Australia' (1953) 2 *University of Western Australia Law Review* 197.
Hall, J, *Studies in Jurisprudence and Criminal Theory* (New York, Oceana Publications, 1958).
Hambly, AD and Goldring, JL, 'Preface' in AD Hambly and JL Goldring (eds), *Australian Lawyers and Social Change* (Sydney, Lawbook, 1976) v.
Harding, D, 'Professor Harry Whitmore' (1982) 5 *University of New South Wales Law Journal* 189.
Hardy, H and Pottle, M (eds), *Affirming – Letters 1975-97 by Isaiah Berlin* (London, Chatto and Windus, 2015).
Harris, DR, 'Comment' (1963–64) 4 *Melbourne University Law Review* 498.

Harrison Moore, W, 'Legal Education in the United States' (1913) 13 *Journal of the Society of Comparative Legislation* 207.
Hart, HLA, 'The Ascription of Responsibility and Rights' (1949) 49 *Proceedings of the Aristotelian Society* 171.
Hart, HLA, 'Positivism and the Separation of Law and Morals' (1958) 71 *Harvard Law Review* 593.
Hart, HLA, *The Concept of Law* (Oxford, Clarendon Law Series, 1961).
Hart, HLA, *Law Liberty and Morality* (Oxford, Oxford University Press, 1963).
Hart, HLA, *Punishment and Responsibility: Essays in the Philosophy of Law* (Oxford, Oxford University Press, 1968).
Hart, HLA, *Essays on Bentham: Studies in Jurisprudence and Political Theory* (Oxford, Clarendon Press, 1982).
Hart, HM and Sacks, AM, *The Legal Process: Basic Problems in the Making and Application of Law* (Cambridge, Tentative Edition, 1958).
Head, B and Walter, J (eds), *Intellectual Movements and Australian Society* (Oxford, Oxford University Press, 1988).
Heydon, JD, 'Judicial Activism and the Death of the Rule of Law' (2003) 2 *Australian Bar Review*.
Hocking, J, *Gough Whitlam – His Time*, vol 2 (Melbourne, Miegunyah Press, 2012).
Hofri-Winogradow, A, 'Comments on David Rabban's *Law's History*' (2010) 1 *Jerusalem Review of Legal Studies* 72.
Holborn, G, *Sources of Biographical Information on Past Lawyers* (Warwick, British and Irish Association of Law Librarians, 1999).
Holmes, JD, 'Book Review: Geoffrey Sawer, *Australian Federalism in the Courts*' (1968) 3 *Federal Law Review* 144.
Holmes, OW, 'The Path of Law' (1897) 10 *Harvard Law Review* 457.
Horne, J, 'Alice Erh-Soon Tay, The Making of an Intellectual' in G Doeker-Mach and K Ziegert (eds), *Alice Erh-Soon Tay – Lawyer, Scholar, Civil Servant* (Stuttgart, Franz Steiner Verlag, 2004) 13.
Horne, J, 'The Cosmopolitan Life of Alice Erh-Soon Tay' (2010) 21 *Journal of World History* 419.
Horne, J and Sherington, G, *Sydney – The Making of a Public University* (Melbourne, Miegunyah Press, 2012).
Horwitz, MJ, 'The Conservative Tradition in the Writing of American Legal History' (1973) 17 *American Journal of Legal History* 275.
Horwitz, MJ, *The Transformation of American Law 1870–1960* (Oxford, Oxford University Press, 1992).
Howard, C, 'Book Review: *An Inquiry into Criminal Guilt* by Peter Brett' (1963–66) 2 *Adelaide Law Review* 139.
Hughes, G, 'Criminal Responsibility' (1964) 16 *Stanford Law Review* 470.
Hupper, G, 'The Rise of an Academic Doctorate in Law: Origins Through World War II' (2007) *American Journal of Law and History* 1.
Hupper, G, 'The Academic Doctorate in Law: A Vehicle for Legal Transplants?' (2008) 58 *Journal of Legal Education* 413.
Hupper, G, 'Educational Ambivalence: The Rise of a Foreign Student Doctorate in Law' (2015) 49 *New England Law Review* 319.
Hutley, FC, 'Cobbett, William Pitt (1853–1919)' in *Australian Dictionary of Biography*, vol 8 (Melbourne, Melbourne University Press, 2012).
Ibbetson, D, 'Historical Research in Law' in P Cane and M Tushnet (eds), *The Oxford Handbook of Legal Studies* (Oxford, Oxford University Press, 2005) 863.
Irving, H, Mowbray, J and Walton, K, *Julius Stone – A Study of Influence* (Sydney, Federation Press, 2010).
James, N, 'A Brief History of Critique in Australian Legal Education' (2000) 24 *Melbourne University Law Review* 965.
James, N, 'Power-Knowledge in Australian Legal Education: Corporatism's Reign' (2004) 26 *Sydney Law Review* 587.
Jamieson, RB, 'Book Review: *Law in Society* by Geoffrey Sawer' (1968) 54 *American Bar Association Journal* 67.

Jarvis, R, 'Law School Histories – A Panel Discussion' (2010) 32 *Campbell Law Review* 311.
Jones, TC, 'Book Review: *Law in Society* by Geoffrey Sawer' (1966) 17 *Northern Ireland Legal Quarterly* 220.
Josev, T, *The Campaign Against the Courts – A History of the Judicial Activism Debate* (Sydney, Federation Press, 2017).
Kadish, SH, 'Fifty Years of Criminal Law: An Opinionated Review' (1999) 87 *California Law Review* 943.
Kahn, E, 'Book Review: *Law in Society* by Geoffrey Sawer' (1966) 83 *South African Law Journal* 236.
Kalman, L, *Legal Realism at Yale 1927–1960* (Chapel Hill, University of North Carolina Press, 1986).
Kalman, L, *The Strange Career of Legal Liberalism* (New Haven, Yale University Press, 1996).
Kalman, L, 'The Power of Biography' (1998) 23 *Law and Social Inquiry* 479.
Kalman, L, *Yale Law School and the Sixties – Revolt and Reverberations* (Chapel Hill, University of North Carolina Press, 2005).
Kalman, L, 'Morton Horwitz and the General Historian' in DW Hamilton and AL Brophy (eds), *Law, Ideology and Methods – Essays in Honor of Morton J Horwitz* (Cambridge, Harvard University Press, 2011) 64.
Kamenka, E, 'Introduction' in E Kamenka, R Brown and A Tay (eds), *Ideas and Ideology, Law and Society, The Crisis in Legal Ideals* (London, Edward Arnold, 1978) vii.
Kamenka, E, 'A Childhood in the 1930s and 1940s: The Making of a Russian-German-Jewish Australian' (1985) 21 *Australian Journal of Politics and History* 1.
Kamenka, E, 'The ANU and Moscow State University' (1994) 30 *Australian Journal of Politics and History* 104.
Kamenka, E and Krygier, M, *Bureaucracy – The Career of a Concept* (London, Edward Arnold, 1979).
Keenan, P, 'Finders, Occupiers and Possession' (1983) 10 *Sydney Law Review* 180.
Kelley, D, 'What is Happening to the History of Ideas?' (1990) 51 *University of Pennsylvania Press* 3.
Kelley, D, *The Descent of Ideas: The History of Intellectual History* (Aldershot, Ashgate, 2002).
Kelly, D St L, 'Book Review: *Law in Society* by Geoffrey Sawer' (1963–66) 2 *Adelaide Law Review* 426.
Kennedy, D, 'Form and Substance in Private Law Adjudication' (1976) 89 *Harvard Law Review* 1685.
Kercher, B, *An Unruly Child – A History of Law in Australia* (Sydney, Allen & Unwin, 1995).
Kerwin, H and Rubenstein, K, 'Law' in *Australian Encyclopedia of Women and Leadership in Twentieth Century Australia* (Australian Women's Archive Project, 2014).
Kim, SHo, 'Max Weber' in EN Zalta (ed), *The Stanford Encyclopedia of Philosophy* (Fall 2012 edn).
Kimball, BA, *The Inception of Modern Professional Education – CC Langdell, 1826–1906* (Chapel Hill, University of North Carolina Press, 2009).
Kirby, M, '*Festschrift* for Professor Alice Erh-Soon Tay – The Future of Human Rights – Does it Have One?', www.michaelkirby.com.au.
Kirby, M, 'People in Criminal Law: Louis Waller AO' (2001) 25 *Criminal Law Journal* 215.
Kirby, M, 'Review Essay: HLA Hart, Julius Stone and the Struggle for the Soul of the Law' (2005) 27 *Sydney Law Review* 323.
Kirby, M, 'Is Legal History Now Ancient History?' (2009) 83 *Australian Law Journal* 31.
Kirby, M, 'The Graduating Class of Sydney Law School 1962: Talented, Lucky, Unquestioning' (2012) 36 *Australian Bar Review* 189.
Kirby, M, 'AR Blackshield and Realism in Australian Constitutional Law' (2013) 11 *Macquarie Law Journal* 7.
Kirby, M, 'Three Law Deans – and What They Teach of Deanship' (2014) 42 *Federal Law Review* 589.
Kirby, M, 'The Decline and Fall of Australia's Law Reform Institutions – and the Prospects for Revival' (2017) 91 *Australian Law Journal* 841.
Konefsky, AS and Schlegel, JH, 'Mirror, Mirror on the Wall – Histories of American Law Schools' (1982) 95 *Harvard Law Review* 833.
Kowalski, M, *Avoiding Extinction: Reimagining Legal Services for the 21st Century* (Bloomington, Iuniverse, 2012).
Krygier, M, 'Four Visions of Post-Communist Law' (1994) 30 *Australian Journal of Politics and History* 104.

Krygier, M, *Philip Selznick: Ideals in the World* (Stanford, Stanford Law Books, 2012).
Kuhn, T S, *The Structure of Scientific Revolutions*, 3rd edn (Chicago, University of Chicago Press, 1996).
Lacey, N, *A Life of HLA Hart – The Nightmare and the Noble Dream* (Oxford, Oxford University Press, 2004).
Lacey, N, 'Analytical Jurisprudence versus Descriptive Sociology Revisited' (2006) 84 *Texas Law Review* 945.
Lacey, N, 'HLA Hart's Rule of Law: The Limits of Philosophy in Historical Perspective' (2007) 36 *Quaderni Fiorentini* 1203.
Lacey, N, 'Jurisprudence, History and the Institutional Quality of Law' (2015) 101 *Virginia Law Review* 919.
Lahav, P, 'American Moment[s]: When, How, and Why Did Israeli Law Faculties Come to Resemble Elite U.S. Law Schools?' (2009) 10 *Theoretical Inquiries in Law* 653.
Lancaster, J, *The Modernisation of Legal Education: A Critique of the Martin, Bowen and Pearce Reports* (Sydney, Centre for Legal Education, 1993).
Larson, MS, *The Rise of Professionalism – A Sociological Analysis* (Berkeley, University of California Press, 1977).
Lawson, FH, *The Oxford Law School 1850–1965* (Oxford, Clarendon Press, 1968).
Le Brun, M and R Johnstone, R, *The Quiet (R)evolution – Improving Student Learning in Law* (Sydney, Lawbook, 1994).
Leavitt, J, 'Book Review: *An Inquiry into Criminal Guilt* by Peter Brett' (1963) 51 *California Law Review* 1031.
Leiter, B, 'Is There an "American" Jurisprudence?' (1997) 17 *Oxford Journal of Legal Studies* 367.
Lesses, K, '*PGA v The Queen* – Marital Rape in Australia: The Role of Repetition, Reputation and Fiction in the Common Law' (2014) 37 *Melbourne University Law Review* 786.
Liebmann, GW, *The Common Law Tradition – A Collective Portrait of Five Legal Scholars* (New Brunswick, Transaction, 2005).
Likhovski, A, 'Comments on David Rabban's *Law's History*' (2010) 1 *Jerusalem Review of Legal Studies* 72.
Lindsay, G and O'Connor, R (eds), 'Emeritus Professor Geoffrey Sawer' (1992) 66 *Australian Law Journal* 473.
Ling, C, 'Martin Krygier's Contribution to the Rule of Law' (2013) 4 *Western Australian Jurist* 211.
Lloyd of Hampstead, 'Book Review: *An Essay on a Contemporary Jurisprudence* by Peter Brett' (1976) 39 *Modern Law Review* 742.
Lücke, H, 'Legal History in Australia: The Development of Australian Legal/Historical Scholarship' (2010) 34 *Australian Bar Review* 109.
Lunney, M, 'Federation and Beyond: What the History of Australian Tort Law Can Tell Us' (2010) 33 *Australian Bar Review* 20.
Lunney, M, 'Legal Émigrés and the Development of Australian Tort Law' (2012) 36 *Melbourne University Law Review* 494.
Lunney, M, 'Fleming's *Law of Tort* – Australian-made or Foreign Import? Australia's Role in Making the "King" of Torts' (2013) 36 *Australian Bar Review* 211.
Lunney, M, A History of Australian Tort Law 1901–1945: England's Obedient Servant? (Cambridge, Cambridge University Press, 2018).
Lyall, F, 'Book Review: *Law in Society* by Geoffrey Sawer' (1966) 9 *Journal of the Society of Public Teachers in Law* 275.
Mackinolty, J and Mackinolty, J (eds), *A Century Down Town – Sydney University Law School's First Hundred Years* (Sydney, Sydney University Law School, 1991).
Mackinolty, J, 'Learned Practitioners – Professor John Peden 1910–41' in J Mackinolty and J Mackinolty (eds), *A Century Down Town – Sydney University Law School's First Hundred Years* (Sydney, Sydney University Law School, 1991) 57.
Macintyre, S, 'Universities' in C Hamilton and S Maddison (eds), *Silencing Dissent: How the Australian Government is Controlling Public Opinion and Stifling Debate* (Sydney, Allen & Unwin, 2007) 41.

Macintyre, S, *The Poor Relation – A History of Social Sciences in Australia* (Melbourne, Melbourne University Press, 2010).
Macintyre, S, 'What Makes a Good Biography?' (2011) 32 *Adelaide Law Review* 7.
Macintyre, S, and Selleck, RJW, *A Short History of the University of Melbourne* (Melbourne, Melbourne University Press, 2003).
MacMillan, C, 'Judah Benjamin – Marginalised Outsider or Admitted Insider?' (2015) 42 *Journal of Law and Society* 150.
MacMillan, M, *History's People* (London, Profile Books Ltd, 2017).
Maher, FKH, Waller, L and Derham, DP, *Cases and Materials on the Legal Process* (Sydney, Lawbook, 1966).
Maher, F, 'Ivory Towers and Concrete Castles: A Hundred Years War' (1986) 15 *Melbourne University Law Review* 637.
Malcolm, J, *The Silent Woman – Sylvia Plath and Ted Hughes*, 2nd edn (London, Granta Books, 2005).
Manne, R, *The Petrov Affair* (Melbourne, Text Publishing, 2004).
Marr, D, *Barwick* (Sydney, George Allen & Unwin, 1980).
Marshall, G, 'Book Review: *Australian Federal Politics and Law* by Geoffrey Sawer and *The Constitutions of the Australian States* by RD Lumb' (1965) 28 *Modern Law Review* 239.
Martin, L, 'From Apprenticeship to Law School: A Social History of Legal Education in Nineteenth Century New South Wales' (1986) 9 *University of New South Wales Law Journal* 111.
Mason, A, 'Law Reform in Australia' (1970–71) 4 *Federal Law Review* 187.
Mason, A, 'The Tort Law Review' (1993) 1 *Tort Law Review* 5.
Mason, J, *Qualitative Researching*, 2nd edn (London, SAGE Publications, 2010).
McInerney, M and Marsh, D, (eds), 'Lecturers' Quotes', *De Minimis* (Law Students' Society of Victoria), 6 May 1969.
McInnes, C and Marginson, S, *Australian Law Schools after the 1987 Pearce Report* (Canberra, Australian Government Publishing Service, 1994).
McInnes, G, *Humping my Bluey* (London, Hamish Hamilton, 1966).
McPaul, B, 'A Woman Pioneer' (1948) 20 *Australian Law Journal* 1.
McQueen, R, 'Together We Fall, Divided We Stand: The Victorian Legal Profession in Crisis 1890–1940' in WW Pue and D Sugarman (eds), *Lawyers and Vampires: Cultural Histories of the Legal Profession* (Oxford, Hart Publishing, 2003) 293.
Measor, L and Sikes, P, 'Visiting Lives – Ethics and Methodology in Life History' in IF Goodson (ed), *Studying Teachers' Lives* (London, Routledge, 1992) 209.
Mendelsohn, O and Lipman, M, 'The Emergence of the Corporate Law Firm in Australia' (1980) 3 *University of New South Wales Law Journal* 78.
Minichiello, V, Aroni, R, Timewell, E and Alexander, L, *In-Depth Interviewing – Principles, Techniques, Analysis*, 2nd edn (Melbourne, Longman, 1995) 2.
Molomby, T, *Ratten: The Web of Circumstance* (Melbourne, Outback Press, 1978).
Molomby, T, *Is There a Moderate on the Roof?* (Melbourne, William Heinemann, 1991).
Monk, R, *Ludwig Wittgenstein – The Duty of Genius* (London, Penguin Books, 1991).
Moore, WH, 'Legal Education in the United States' (1913) 13 *Journal of the Society of Comparative Legislation* 207.
Morison, W, 'Book review: *Cases on Private International Law* by Morris' (1954) 85 *Sydney Law Review* 285.
Morison, WL, 'Frames of Reference for Legal Ideals' in E Kamenka, R Brown and A Tay, *Law and Society* (London, Edward Arnold, 1978).
Morison, WL 'Professor K O Shatwell 1947–73' in J Mackinolty and J Mackinolty (eds), *A Century Down Town – Sydney University Law School's First Hundred Years* (Sydney, Sydney University Law School, 1991) 105.
Morris, N, *The Habitual Criminal* (Cambridge, Harvard University Press, 1951).
Morrissey, CT, 'On Oral History Interviewing' in R Perks and A Thomson (eds), *The Oral History Reader* (London, Routledge, 1998).

Moses, JA, 'Eugene Kamenka 1928–94 – The Great Cosmopolitan Australian' (1994) 40 *Australian Journal of Politics and History* 295.

Mulcahy, L and Sugarman, D, 'Introduction – Legal Life Writing and Marginalised Subjects and Sources' (2015) 42 *Journal of Law and Society* 1.

Naffine, N, 'Windows on the Legal Mind: The Evocation of Rape in Legal Writings' (1992) 18 *Melbourne University Law Review* 741.

Nelken, D, 'Is There a Crisis in Law and Legal Ideology?' (1982) 9 *Journal of Law and Society* 177.

Newark, FH, 'Book Review: *Law in Society* by Geoffrey Sawer' (1966) *The Quarterly Review* 118.

Novick, P, *That Noble Dream – The 'Objectivity Question' and the American Historical Profession* (Cambridge, Cambridge University Press, 1998).

O'Donoghue, F, 'Book Review: *Law in Society* by Geoffrey Sawer' (1966) 29 *Modern Law Review* 216.

Ondaatje, ML, *Black Conservative Intellctuals in Modern America* (Philadelphia, University of Pennsylvania Press, 2010).

Osmond, W, 'Eggleston, Sir Frederic William (1875–1954) in *Australian Dictionary of Biography*, vol 8 (Melbourne, Melbourne University Press, 1981).

Pannam, CL, 'Book Review: *Australian Federal Politics and Law 1929–49* by Geoffrey Sawer' (1963) 4 *Melbourne University Law Review* 290.

Parker, C and Goldsmith, A, '"Failed Sociologists" in the Market Place – Law Schools in Australia' (1998) 25 *Journal of Law and Society* 33.

Parry, RG, 'Is Legal Biography Really Legal Scholarship?' (2010) 30 *Legal Studies* 208.

Patapan, H, *Judging Democracy: The New Politics of the High Court of Australia* (Cambridge, Cambridge University Press, 2000).

Paton, GW, *A Textbook of Jurisprudence* (Oxford, Clarendon Press, 1946).

Paton, GW, *A Textbook of Jurisprudence*, 2nd edn (Oxford, Clarendon Press, 1951).

Patterson, D (ed), *A Companion to Philosophy of Law and Legal Theory* (Malden, Wiley-Blackwell, 2010).

Paulsen, MG and Kadish, SH, *Criminal Law and its Processes: Cases and Materials* (Boston, Little Brown, 1962).

Payne, D, 'Book Review: *The Beamish Case* by Peter Brett' (1965–66) 7 *University of Western Australia Annual Law Review* 576.

Payne, D, 'A Comment on Professor Brett's Rejoinder' (1967–68) 8 *University of Western Australia Annual Law Review* 132.

Pietsch, T, Empire of Scholars – Universities, Networks and the British Academic World 1850–1939 (Manchester, Manchester University Press, 2015).

Postema, GJ, 'Jurisprudence, The Sociable Science' (2015) 10 *Virginia Law Review* 869.

Prest, W, 'Antipodean Blackstone: The *Commentaries* "Down Under"' (2003) 6 *Flinders Journal of Law Reform* 151.

Pue, WW, 'Common Law Legal Education in the Dominion of Canada's Moral Project' in WW Pue, *Lawyers' Empire: Legal Professions and Cultural Authority, 1780–1950* (Vancouver, UBC Press, 2017) 148.

Pue, WW, 'British Empire Perspectives on the Case Method of Legal Education' in WW Pue, *Lawyers' Empire: Legal Professions and Cultural Authority, 1780–1950* (Vancouver, UBC Press, 2017) 149.

Pybus, C, *Gross Moral Turpitude: The Orr Case Reconsidered* (Melbourne, William Heinemann, 1993).

Rabban, DM, 'Reconsidering *Law's History* – A Response to the Symposium Comments' (2010) 1 *Jerusalem Review of Legal Studies* 106.

Rabban, DM, *Law's History* (Cambridge, Cambridge University Press, 2013).

Rackley, E and Auchmuty, R, 'Introduction' in *Women's Legal Landmarks* (Oxford, Hart Publishing, 2018) 1.

Ramsay, I, 'Professor Harold Ford and the Development of Australian Corporate Law' (2011) 29 *Companies and Securities Law Journal* 30.

Reaburn, N, 'Book Review: Geoffrey Sawer, *Australian Federalism in the Courts*' (1968–70) 3 *University of Tasmania Law Review* 232.

Reich, N, 'Sad Stories, Success Stories, and Untold Stories about American Legal Education – A Comment on John Henry Schlegel' (2011) 12 *German Law Journal* 96.

Robertson, B, *Oral History Handbook*, 5th edn (Unley, Oral History Association South Australian Branch, 2006).

Rodell, F, 'Goodbye to Law Reviews' (1936) 23 *Vanderbilt Law Review* 38.

Roe, OM, 'Jethro Brown – The First Teacher of Law and History in the University of Tasmania' (1977) *University of Tasmania Law Review* 210.

Roe, M, *Nine Australian Progressives: Vitalism in Bourgeois Social Thought 1890–1960* (St Lucia, University of Queensland Press, 1984).

Rubin, E, 'Passing Through the Door – Social Movement Literature and Legal Scholarship' (2001) 150 *University of Pennsylvania Law Review* 1.

Rundle, K, *Forms Liberate – Reclaiming the Jurisprudence of Lon L Fuller* (Oxford, Hart Publishing, 2012).

Rupke, NA and Lovell, DW, 'Introduction' (1994) 40 *Australian Journal of Politics and History* 1.

Ryle, G, *The Concept of Mind* (London, Hutchinson University Library, 1949).

Sadurski, W, 'Research in Australian Law Schools – Some Comments on Chapter 9 of the CTEC "Disicipline Assessment" of Australian Law Schools' (1987) 11 *Bulletin of the Australian Society of Legal Philosophy* 144.

Sands, P, *East West Street: On the Origins of Genocide and Crimes Against Humanity* (London, Weidenfeld and Nicolson, 2016.

Schick, A, 'Bibliography of Works by Geoffrey Sawer 1935–80' (1980) 11 *Federal Law Review* 271.

Schlegel, JH, 'Langdell's Legacy Or, The Case of the Empty Envelope' (1984) 36 *Stanford Law Review* 1518.

Schlegel, JH, 'The Line Between History and Case Note' (1988) 22 *Law and Society Review* 969.

Schlegel, JH, 'Legal Education – More Theory, More Practice' (1988) 13 *Legal Service Bulletin* 71.

Schlegel, JH, 'The Ten Thousand Dollar Question' (1989) 41 *Stanford Law Review* 435.

Schlegel, JH, 'A Certain Narcissism; A Slight Unseemliness' (1992) 63 *University of Colorado Law Review* 595.

Schlegel, JH, *American Legal Realism and Empirical Social Science* (Chapel Hill, University of North Carolina Press, 1995).

Schlegel, JH, 'Does Duncan Kennedy Wear Briefs or Boxers? Does Richard Posner Ever Sleep? Writing About Jurisprudence, High Culture and the History of Intellectuals' (1997) 45 *Buffalo Law Review* 277.

Schlegel, JH, 'Talkin' Dirty: Twining's Tower and Kalman's Strange Career' (1997) *Law and Social Inquiry* 981.

Schlegel, JH, 'A Life of HLA Hart' (2006) 24 *Law and History Review* 679.

Schlegel, JH, 'American Legal Theory and American Legal Education – A Snake Swallowing Its Tail?' (2011) 12 *German Law Journal* 67.

Schultz, U and Shaw, G, *Women in the World's Legal Professions* (Oxford, Hart Publishing, 2003).

Shaw, GC, 'HLA Hart's Lost Essay: *Discretion* and the Legal Process School' (2013) 127 *Harvard Law Review* 666.

Shelly, R, 'Book Review: Leonie Starr, *Julius Stone an Intellectual Life*' (1993) 16 *University of New South Wales Law Journal* 601.

Sheridan, LA, 'Book Review: GF Sawer, *Modern Federalism*' (1969) 20 *Northern Ireland Legal Quarterly* 225.

Siems, MM, 'A World without Law Professors' in M Van Hoecke (ed), *Which Kind of Method for What Kind of Discipline?* (Oxford, Hart Publishing, 2011) 71.

Silvey, C, *Jasper Jones* (Sydney, Allen & Unwin, 2009).

Simpson, AWB, *Biographical Dictionary of the Common Law* (London, Butterworths, 1984).

Simpson, BAW, 'The Elusive Truth about Holmes' (1997) 95 *Michigan Law Review* 2027.

Skinner, Q, 'Meaning and Understanding in the History of Ideas' (1969) 8 *History and Theory* 3.

Smith, M, 'Comparative Law and Legal Culture – A Tribute to David Allan and Mary Hiscock' (2003) 15 *Bond Law Review* 20.

Starke, JG, 'Charteris, Archibald Hamilton' (1874–1940) in *Australian Dictionary of Biography*, vol 7 (Melbourne, Melbourne University Press, 1979).
Starr, L, *Julius Stone – An Intellectual Life* (Oxford, Oxford University Press, 1992).
Strachan, G, 'Still Working for the Man? Women's Employment Experiences in Australia since 1950' (2010) 45 *Australian Journal of Social Issues* 1.
Stein, PG, 'Maine and Legal Education' in A Diamond (ed), *The Victorian Achievement of Sir Henry Maine: A Centennial Reappraisal* (Cambridge, Cambridge University Press, 1991) 195.
Stephen, N, 'A Recollection of Geoffrey Sawer' (1980) 11 *Federal Law Review* 261.
Stevens, R, *Law School – Legal Education in America from the 1850s to the 1980s* (Chapel Hill, University of North Carolina, 1983).
Stone, J, 'The Role of Universities: Views of a Scholar of the Last Century' in H Irving, J Mowbray and K Walton (eds), *Julius Stone, A Study in Influence* (Sydney, Federation Press, 2010) 38.
Stone, J, 'Commentary to Sawer, G, 'The Record of Judicial Review'' in G Sawer (ed), *Federalism: An Australian Jubilee Study* (Melbourne, Cheshire, 1952) 211.
Stone, J, *Legal System and Lawyers' Reasoning* (Stanford, Stanford University Press, 1964).
Sugarman, D, 'Is the Reform of Legal Education Hopeless? Or Seeing the Hole Instead of the Doughnut' (1985) 48 *Modern Law Review* 728.
Sugarman, D, 'Legal Theory, the Common Law Mind and the Making of the Textbook Tradition' in W Twining (ed), *Legal Theory and Common Law* (Oxford, Basil Blackwell, 1986) 26.
Sugarman, D, '"A Hatred of Disorder": Legal Science, Liberalism and Imperialism' in P Fitzpatrick (ed), *Dangerous Supplements – Resistance and Renewal in Jurisprudence* (London, Pluto Press, 1991) 34.
Sugarman, D (ed), *Law in History – Histories of Law and Society*, 2 vols (Aldershot, Dartmouth, 1996).
Sugarman, D, 'Reassessing Hurst – A Transatlantic Perspective' (2000) 18 *Law and History Review* 215.
Sugarman, D, 'Hart Interviewed: HLA Hart in Conversation with David Sugarman' (2005) 32 *Journal of Law and Society* 267.
Sugarman, D, 'Beyond Ignorance and Complacency – Robert Stevens' Journey through *Lawyers and the Courts*' (2009) 16 *International Journal of the Legal Profession* 7.
Sugarman, D, 'A Special Relationship? American Influences on English Legal Education, c 1870–1965' (2011) 18 *International Journal of the Legal Profession* 7.
Sugarman, D, '"Great Beyond his Knowing" – Morton Horwitz's Influence on Legal Education and Scholarship in England, Canada and Australia' in DW Hamilton and AL Brophy (eds), *Law, Ideology and Methods – Essays in Honor of Morton J Horwitz* (Cambridge, Harvard University Press, 2011) 504.
Sugarman, D, 'From Legal Biography to Legal Life Writing: Broadening Conceptions of Legal History and Socio-legal Scholarship' (2015) 42 *Journal of Law and Society* 7.
Sugarman, D, 'Robert W Gordon in Conversation with David Sugarman' (2018) 1 *Law and History Review: The Docket* (website).
Summers, RS, *Lon L Fuller* (Stanford, Stanford University Press, 1984).
Susskind, R and Susskind, D, *How Technology will Transform the Work of the Professions* (Oxford, Oxford University Press, 2015).
Susskind, R, *Tomorrow's Lawyers: An Introduction to Your Future*, 2nd edn (Oxford, Oxford University Press, 2017).
Swift, J, *Gulliver's Travels into Several Remote Nations of the World* (London, George Bell and Sons, 1892).
Symposium, 'Jurisprudence and (Its) History' (2015) 101 *Virginia Law Review* 849.
Symposium, 'Legal Life Writing and Marginalised Subjects and Sources' (2015) 42 *Journal of Law and Society* 1.
Taggart, M, 'Gardens or Graveyards of Scholarship? *Festchriften* in the Literature of the Common Law' (2002) 22 *Oxford Journal of Legal Studies* 227.
Taggart, M, 'Prolegomenon to an Intellectual History of Administrative Law in the Twentieth Century: The Case of John Willis and Canadian Administrative Law' (2005) 43 *Osgoode Hall Law Journal* 223.
Tamanaha, BZ, *Failing Law Schools* (Chicago, University of Chicago Press, 2012).

Teles, SM, *The Battle for Control of the Law* (Princeton, Princeton University Press, 2008).

Theobald, M, 'Teachers, Memory and Oral History' in K Weiler and S Middleton (eds), *Telling Women's Lives–Narrative Inquiries in the History of Women's Education* (Philadelphia, Open University Press, 1999) 9.

Thibaut, J, Walker, L and Lind, A, 'Adversary Presentation and Bias in Legal Decision-making' (1972) 86 *Harvard Law Review* 386.

Thibaut, J, Walker, L and Lind, A, 'In Response to Professor Brett' (1974) 45 *University of Colorado Law Review* 23.

Thomas, JC, 'Book Review: *The Australian and the Law* by Geoffrey Sawer' (1968–70) 5 *Victoria University Wellington Law Review* 402.

Thompson, EP, *Whigs and Hunters – The Origins of the Black Act* (New York, Pantheon Books, 1975).

Thompson, EP, *The Poverty of Theory and Other Essays* (New York, Monthly Review Press, 1978).

Thompson, EP, *The Making of the English Working Class* (London, Penguin Books, 1991).

Thompson, P, *The Voice of the Past – Oral History*, 3rd edn (Oxford, Oxford University Press, 2000).

Thornton, M, 'Portia Lost in the Groves of Academe Wondering What to Do About Legal Education' (1991) 34 *Australian Universities' Review* 26.

Thornton, M, 'The Dissolution of the Social in the Legal Academy' (2006) 25 *Australian Feminist Law Journal* 3.

Thornton, M, *Privatising the Public University: The Case of Law* (Abingdon, Routledge, 2012).

Tilbury, M, 'Book Review: *Thirty Up: The Story of the UNSW Law School 1971–2001* by Marion Dixon' (2002) 25 *University of New South Wales Law Journal* 255.

Tosh, J, *Why History Matters* (Basingstoke, Palgrave MacMillan, 2008).

Tosh, J and Lang, S, *The Pursuit of History*, 4th edn (Cambridge, Pearson Education, 2006).

Tracey, RRS and Sykes, EI, *Brett and Hogg Cases and Materials on Administrative Law* (Sydney, Butterworths, 1975).

Tushnet, M, 'Interdisciplinary Legal Scholarship – The Case of History-In-Law' (1996) 71 *Chicago-Kent Law Review* 909.

Tushnet, M, 'What Consequences Do Ideas Have?' (2008) 87 *Texas Law Review* 447.

Twining, W, 'Wolfgang Friedmann' (1972–73) 12 *Journal of the Society of Public Teachers in Law* 311.

Twining, W, *Karl Llewellyn and the Realist Movement* (London, Weidenfeld and Nicolson, 1973).

Twining, W, *Blackstone's Tower – The English Law School* (London, Sweet and Maxwell, 1994).

Twining, W, *Karl Llewellyn and the Realist Movement*, 2nd edn (Cambridge, Cambridge University Press, 2012).

Twining, W, 'Rethinking Legal Education' (2018) 52 *The Law Teacher* 241.

Vick, DW, 'Interdisciplinarity and the Discipline of Law' (2004) 31 *Journal of Law and Society* 163.

Walker, A, 'The Anti-Case Method: Herbert Wechsler and the Political History of the Criminal Law Course' (2009) 7 *Ohio State Journal of Criminal Law* 217.

Walker, L, Thibaut, J and Andreoli, V, 'Order of Presentation at Trial' (1972) 82 *Yale Law Journal* 216.

Waller, L, 'Book Review: *General Principles of the Criminal Law* by Jerome Hall' (1961) 3 *Melbourne University Law Review* 86.

Waller, L, 'Peter Brett Remembered' (1975) *Summons* 100.

Waller, L, 'Brett, Peter (1918–1975)', *Australian Dictionary of Biography*, vol 13 (Melbourne, Melbourne University Press, 1993).

Waller, L and Williams, CR, *Criminal Law – Text and Cases*, 11th edn (Sydney, LexisNexis Butterworths, 2009).

Walt, S, 'What Can the History of Jurisprudence do for Jurisprudence?' (2015) 10 *Virginia Law Review* 977.

Walter, M (ed), *Social Research Methods*, 2nd edn (Oxford, Oxford University Press, 2010).

Ward, JM, 'Peden, Sir John Beverley' (1871–1946) in *Australian Dictionary of Biography*, vol 11 (Melbourne, Melbourne University Press, 1998).

Waugh, J, *First Principles – The Melbourne Law School 1857–2007* (Melbourne, Miegunyah Press, 2007).

Waye, V, Verreynne, M, and J Knowler, J, 'Innovation in the Australian Legal Profession' (2018) 25 *International Journal of the Legal Profession* 213.
Weber, M, *Economy and Society*, revised edn (Berkeley, University of California Press, 1978).
Weblin, M (ed), *A Perilous and Fighting Life: From Communist to Conservative – The Political Writings of Professor John Anderson* (Melbourne, Pluto Press, 2003).
Weinberg, M, 'Moral Blameworthiness – The "Objective Test" Dilemma' (2003) 24 *Australian Bar Review* 31.
Weinberg, M, 'The Criminal Law – A "Mildly Vituperative" Critique' (2011) 35 *Melbourne University Law Review* 1177.
Weinberg, M, 'Evidence-Based Law: Its Place in the Criminal Justice System' (2014) 1 *Judicial College of Victoria* 23.
Weisbrot, D, 'Legal Scholarship in Australia' (1987) 50 *Modern Law Review* 709.
Weisbrot, D, *Australian Lawyers* (Melbourne, Longman Cheshire, 1989).
Weisbrot, D, 'Recent Statistical Trends in Australian Legal Education' (1990–91) 2 *Legal Education Review* 219.
Wells, C, 'The Remains of the Day – The Women Law Professors' Project' in U Schultz and G Shaw (eds), *Women in the World's Legal Professions* (Oxford, Hart Publishing, 2003) 225.
Wertheim, RP, 'Book Review: *An Inquiry into Criminal Guilt* by Peter Brett and *Law, Liberty and Psychiatry* by Thomas S Szasz' (1964) 64 *Columbia Law Review* 977.
White, GE, *Tort Law in America: An Intellectual History* (Oxford, Oxford University Press, 1980).
White, GE, 'The Origins of Modern American Legal History' in DW Hamilton and AL Brophy (eds), *Law, Ideology and Methods – Essays in Honor of Morton J Horwitz* (Cambridge, Harvard University Press, 2011) 48.
White, JB, 'Book Review: *The Habitual Criminal* by Norval Morris' (1952) 52 *Columbia Law Review* 435.
White, M, 'History of the Garrick Chair at the TC Beirne School of Law' (2010) 29 *University of Queensland Law Journal* 335.
Whitmore, H, 'Book Review: *Cases on Constituional and Administrative Law* by Peter Brett and *Principles of Australian Administrative Law* by Wolfgang Friedmann' (1963) 4 *Sydney Law Review* 313.
Williams, CR, 'Unlawful Act Manslaughter' (1975) 1 *Monash University Law Review* 234.
Williams, CR, 'Burdens and Standards in Civil Litigation' (2003) 25 *Sydney Law Review* 165.
Williams, GL (ed), *Salmond – Jurisprudence*, 10th edn (London, Sweet and Maxwell 1947).
Winton, T, *Cloudstreet* (Melbourne, Penguin, 2007).
Wolitz, D, 'Herbert Wechsler, Legal Process, and the Jurisprudential Roots of the Model Penal Code' (2016) 51 *Tulsa Law Review* 633.
Yule, P and Woodhouse, F, *Pericleans, Plumbers and Practitioners: The First Fifty Years of the Monash University Law School* (Melbourne, Monash University, 2015).
Ziegert, KA, 'AEST – An Attempt at Explaining the Phenomenon' in G Doeker-Mach and KA Ziegert (eds), *Alice Erh-Soon Tay – Lawyer Scholar, Civil Servant* (Stuttgart, Franz Steiner Verlag, 2004) 7.
Zines, L and Lindell, GJ, *Sawer's Australian Constitutional Cases* (Sydney, Lawbook Co, 1982).

B. Cases

Bank of New South Wales v Commonwealth (1948) 76 CLR 1.
Brown v Board of Education 347 US 483 (1954).
Director of Public Prosecutions v Smith [1960] 3 All ER 161.
Melbourne v Commonwealth (1947) 74 CLR 31.
Parker v R (1963) 111 CLR 610.
R v Dudley and Stephens (1884) 14 QBD 273.

C. Newspapers

‘A Man who Learnt a Hell of a Lot’, *The Canberra Times* (Canberra), 27 February 1975, 3.
‘Academics Identify Some of the Problems Facing Universities’, *The University of Sydney News* (Sydney), 12 March 1985, 37.
‘Brains-and-beauty Alice Has Her Life All Mapped Out’, *The Daily Mirror* (Sydney), 28 April 1975, 12.
‘Eugene Kamenka’ *The National Times* (Canberra), 25–31 May 1984, 12.
‘Ex Gratia Payment for Wrongly Jailed Man’, *The Sydney Morning Herald* (online), 2 June 2011, <http://www.smh.com.au//breaking-news-national/ex-gratia-payment-for-wrongly-jailed-man-20110602-1fhq6.html>.
‘Honorary ANU Degree for Professor Sawer’ *The Canberra Times* (Canberra) 2 October 1982, 3.
‘Obituaries: Geoffrey Sawer 1910–1996’, *Sydney Morning Herald* 12 August 1996, 34.
‘Public Lectures Popular’, *The Canberra Times* (Canberra), 6 July 1972.
‘Quiet Office Marriage’, *Canberra Times* 3 July 1971, 1.
‘Sawer book sales top 150,000’, Canberra Times 29 September 1977, 9.
Cowen Z, ‘Academic Shaped Legal Scholarship’, *Australian* 12 August 1996, 13.
Eccles, G, ‘It’s a Different Australia’, *Herald* 26 December 1975, 4.
Else-Mitchell, R, ‘Scholar’s Life on Public Record’, *Age* 30 August 1996, B2.
Humphrey, S, ‘Alice Tay’s Top Brain in Law’s Wonderland’, *The Australian* (Sydney) 15 March 1984, 10.
Leech, G, ‘Tay a Law unto Herself’, *The Australian* (Sydney) 31 July–1 August 1993, 6.
Mason, A, ‘Geoffrey Sawer: The Priceless Professor’, *Canberra Times* 21 December 1990, 7.
Nethercote J, ‘Lawyer Offered an Authoritative Insight into Federalism’, *Australian* 12 August 1996, 13.
Passmore, J, ‘Citizen of the World Whose Gift was Liberty’, *The Australian* (Sydney) 21 January 1994, 11.
Robatham, J, ‘Obituary for WL Morison’, *Sydney Morning Herald* (Sydney), 14 April 2000, 32.
Sheehan, P, ‘No Credit in Devalued Degree’, *Sydney Morning Herald* (online) 8 January 2003, http://www.smh.com.au/articles/2003/01/07/1041566407260.html.
Stephen, N, ‘Constitutional Lawyer and Gardener’, *Canberra Times* 10 August 1996.
Tonry, M, ‘Norval Morris’, *Guardian* (online), 9 April 2004, www.theguardian.com/news/2004/apr/09/guardianobituaries.prisonsandprobation.
Wild, D, ‘The Law is No Fossil, says a New Professor’, *The Australian* (Sydney) 21 January 1975, 3.

D. Other

Birch, C, ‘Professor Alice Tay’, Speech at Retirement Dinner for Professor Alice Tay (Sydney, 9 December 2002).
Campbell, R, Interview with Harold Luntz (University of Melbourne, 19 February 2003).
Committee on Australian Universities, Commonwealth of Australia, *Report* (1957) (Murray Report).
Curriculum Vitae of William Loutit Morison, Professor WL Morison Memorial (website).
Farquharson, J, ‘Starke, Joseph Gabriel (Joe) (1911–2006)’ in *Obituaries Australia* (Canberra, Australian National University).
Hamilton, I, Interview with Geoffrey Sawer (Interview, Canberra, 16 July 1982).
Kamenka, E, ‘Australia Made Me – But Which Australia is Mine?’, John Curtin Memorial Lecture, Australian National University (Canberra, 16 July 1993).
Legal Education in NSW – Report of Committee of Inquiry, *Report* (1979).
Pearce, D, Campbell, E and Harding, D, *Australian Law Schools: A Discipline Assessment for the Commonwealth Tertiary Education Commission* (Canberra, Australian Government Publishing Service, 1987) (The Pearce Report).
Percy, T, ‘John Button and Darryl Beamish Cleared of Murder four Decades after Serial Killer’s Execution’, *Justice Denied* (online) 6 June 2011.

Pratt, M, Inteview with Geoffrey Sawer (Interview, Canberra, 16 November 1971).
Roe, M, 'William Jethro Brown', Occasional Paper, University of Tasmania (Hobart, 27 April 1977).
Sappideen, C, 'Eulogy for WL Morison', Professor WL Morison Memorial (website).
Sawer, G, 'The Constitutional Crisis' (Interview, Canberra, 1975).
Stephen, N, 'War Crimes Trials and the Future', Speech delivered at the Inaugural Geoffrey Sawer Lecture, Centre for International and Public Law, Australian National University (Canberra, 21 May 1998).
The Australian Universities Commission's Committee on the Future of Tertiary Education in Australia, Commonwealth of Australia, *Report* (1964) (Martin Report).
Webber, J, 'In Memoriam – William L Morison', Professor WL Morison Memorial (website).
Wills, S, *The Politics of Sexual Liberation* (unpublished PhD Thesis, The University of Sydney, 1981).

INDEX